A Practitioner's Guide to Probate

First published in 1980 (under the title Probate Practice and Procedure)

Other titles in this series:

A Practitioner's Guide to Probate

by
Keith Biggs
District Probate Registrar for Winchester

Jonathan Golding ATT, TEP
Senior Tax Writer, LexisNexis UK

Seventh edition

LexisNexis™ UK

Members of the LexisNexis Group worldwide

United Kingdom	LexisNexis UK, a Division of Reed Elsevier (UK) Ltd, Halsbury House, 35 Chancery Lane, LONDON, WC2A 1EL, and 4 Hill Street, EDINBURGH EH2 3JZ
Argentina	LexisNexis Argentina, BUENOS AIRES
Australia	LexisNexis Butterworths, CHATSWOOD, New South Wales
Austria	LexisNexis Verlag ARD Orac GmbH & Co KG, VIENNA
Canada	LexisNexis Butterworths, MARKHAM, Ontario
Chile	LexisNexis Chile Ltda, SANTIAGO DE CHILE
Czech Republic	Nakladatelství Orac sro, PRAGUE
France	Editions du Juris-Classeur SA, PARIS
Germany	LexisNexis Deutschland GmbH, FRANKFURT, MUNSTER
Hong Kong	LexisNexis Butterworths, HONG KONG
Hungary	HVG-Orac, BUDAPEST
India	LexisNexis Butterworths, NEW DELHI
Ireland	Butterworths (Ireland) Ltd, DUBLIN
Italy	Giuffrè Editore, MILAN
Malaysia	Malayan Law Journal Sdn Bhd, KUALA LUMPUR
New Zealand	LexisNexis Butterworths, WELLINGTON
Poland	Wydawnictwo Prawnicze LexisNexis, WARSAW
Singapore	LexisNexis Butterworths, SINGAPORE
South Africa	LexisNexis Butterworths, DURBAN
Switzerland	Stämpfli Verlag AG, BERNE
USA	LexisNexis, DAYTON, Ohio

© Reed Elsevier (UK) Ltd 2003

A CIP Catalogue record for this book is available from the British Library.

First published in 1980

ISBN 0 75451 893 0

Typeset by Action Publishing Technology Ltd, Gloucester, GL1 5SR
Printed and bound in Great Britain by Hobbs the Printers Ltd, Totton, Hampshire

Visit LexisNexis UK at www.lexisnexis.co.uk

Preface

The first edition of this book, under the title *Probate Practice and Procedure*, was published in 1980 by Fourmat Publishing.

The intervening editions have all sought to provide easily accessible information and guidance on probate practice and procedure. This, the seventh edition – albeit under a new title – follows the tradition of previous editions.

The Review of the Delivery of Probate Services has now passed through its consultancy period. The effect that this will have is yet to be determined but may not be for some time to come.

Finance Acts are fully covered. The effect of the Inheritance Tax (Delivery of Accounts) Regulations 2002 are also dealt with.

References in the text to Rules are to the Non-Contentious Probate Rules 1987. References to statutes are set out in full except in Chapter 12, where abbreviations are used; for example 'FA' refers to a Finance Act and inheritance tax is shortened to 'IHT'.

Generally, the jurisdiction of District Judges and Registrars in both the Principal and the District Probate Registries is the same; where, however, their powers vary and, for instance, an application may be made to the Principal Registry only, this is explained in the text.

Precedents for all forms required for the procedures set out in the text are contained in Appendix 1. This edition contains several new precedent forms. The fees payable in non-contentious matters, extracted from the Non-Contentious Probate Fees Order 1999, are set out in Appendix 2. The District Registries and Sub-Registries, and their telephone numbers, are given in Appendix 3. A pre-grant application checklist is included as Appendix 4.

The authors again thank practitioners and colleagues who have made helpful suggestions for the improvement of the book. Their considered advice has, where appropriate, been incorporated into the text. The authors also wish to thank the publishers and especially the editor Alan Radford for his considerable effort in producing this edition.

AKB/JG
April 2003

Contents

Contents

Contents

Contents

Table of Cases

Table of Cases

Table of Statutes

Table of Statutes

Table of Statutory Instruments

Chapter 1

Jurisdiction

Historical jurisdiction

1.1   The Court of Probate Act 1857 provided that there should be a Court of Probate which would exercise all the jurisdiction for probate matters formerly exercised by a variety of ecclesiastical and secular courts.

The Act established a Principal Probate Registry in London and District Probate Registries throughout England and Wales. Each District Registry's jurisdiction was limited to a specified geographical area. The territorial limitation was removed by the Supreme Court of Judicature (Consolidation) Act 1925 with effect from 1 January 1926. A District Probate Registry may deal with any application for a grant of representation, providing the rules allow, irrespective of where the deceased lived.

By the Supreme Court of Judicature Act 1873 the jurisdiction of the Court of Probate was assigned to the High Court, and specifically to the Probate, Divorce and Admiralty Division.

The Probate, Divorce and Admiralty Division (euphemistically the 'Wills, Wives and Wrecks Division') was re-named the Family Division by the Administration of Justice Act 1970, which also re-named the Principal Probate Registry the Principal Registry of the Family Division. The jurisdiction in probate matters was divided into non-contentious probate ('common form') which remained assigned to what is now the Family Division, and contentious probate, which was assigned to the Chancery Division. The issue of a Part 57 CPR claim or other application in the Chancery Division provides the determining line. Once a claim is made, all proceedings take place in this Division. These applications may now be made in the Central Office, Royal Courts of Justice or in the provincial registries to which chancery matters may be commenced at Birmingham, Bristol, Cardiff, Leeds, Liverpool, Manchester, Newcastle-upon-Tyne and Preston. Only when the matter is finally determined does it return to the Family Division for the issue or revocation of the relevant grant of representation. These provisions of the 1970 Act were subsequently repealed and re-enacted by the Supreme Court Act 1981.

Statutory jurisdiction

Probate jurisdiction of the High Court

1.2   By the Supreme Court of Judicature (Consolidation) Act 1925 s 20 the probate jurisdiction of the High Court was defined as:

'(i)   all such voluntary and contentious jurisdiction and authority in relation to the granting or revoking of probate and administration of the effects of deceased persons as was at the commencement of the Court of Probate Act 1857, vested in or exercisable by any court or person in England, together with full authority to hear and determine all questions relating to testamentary causes or matters;

(ii)   all such powers throughout England in relation to the personal estate in England of deceased persons as the Prerogative Court of Canterbury had immediately before the commencement of the Court of Probate Act 1857, in the province of Canterbury or in the parts thereof within its jurisdiction in relation to those testamentary causes and matters and those effects of deceased persons which were at that date within the jurisdiction of that court;

(iii)   such like jurisdiction and powers with respect to the real estate of persons as are hereinbefore conferred with respect to the personal estate of deceased persons;

(iv)   all probate jurisdiction which, under or by virtue of any enactment which came into force after the commencement of the Supreme Court of Judicature Act 1873 and is not repealed by this Act [i.e. the Supreme Court of Judicature Act 1925], was immediately before the commencement of the Act of 1925, vested in or capable of being exercised by the High Court constituted by the Act of 1873.'

The jurisdiction was extended by the Administration of Justice Act 1932 to enable the High Court to make a grant of probate or administration in respect of a deceased person, notwithstanding that the deceased died leaving no estate.

The jurisdiction has been re-defined by the Supreme Court Act 1981 s 25 so as to include 'all such jurisdiction in relation to probates and letters of administration as it had before the commencement of this Act and in particular all such contentious and non-contentious jurisdiction as it then had in relation to:

(i)   testamentary causes or matters;

(ii)   the grant, amendment or revocation of probates and letters of administration; and

(iii)   the real and personal estate of deceased persons.'

In effect this means that, with one exception, the High Court exercises jurisdiction in all probate matters assigned to the respective Divisions mentioned above. The exception is that a judge of a county court may exercise the jurisdiction of the High Court in respect of a contentious probate matter concerning the granting or revocation of probate or administration, provided the deceased had, prior to his death, lived or had a place of abode within the jurisdiction of that county court; and provided the deceased's estate, after deducting funeral expenses, debts and incumbrances, does not exceed the monetary limit of jurisdiction of a county court. The Administration of Justice Act 1977 increased this jurisdiction to £15,000. The County Courts Jurisdiction Order 1981 further increased this jurisdiction to the current limit of £30,000 with effect from 1 October 1981. The limit has not been increased since that date. The county court may transfer any matter to the High Court at any of the Registries listed in paragraph 1.1.

Non-contentious probate business

1.3   Non-contentious or common form probate, as exercised by the Family Division, is defined by the Supreme Court Act 1981 s 128 as:

'the business of obtaining probate and administration where there is no contention as to the right thereto, including: (a) the passing of probates and administrations through the High Court in contentious cases where the contest has been terminated; (b) all business of a non-contentious nature in matters of testacy and intestacy not being proceedings in any action, and (c) the business of lodging caveats against the grant of probate or administration.'

Where a contested case has been decided by the Chancery court, or, where appropriate, the county court, these courts have no jurisdiction to issue a grant. The Chancery court notifies the Registry in which the grant application is pending, or in a revocation action the Registry from which the grant issued, of the outcome of the claim. Application for a grant in accordance with the judgment is made to that Registry. Where the claim concerned the validity of a will, and the court pronounces for the will, then it is said to be proved in 'solemn form', i.e. it has been pronounced for in court as opposed to being proved unopposed in 'common form'. Should a will be pronounced against, application on the basis of an intestacy (unless there is another valid will) is made to a Probate Registry in the usual way (see CHAPTER 9).

Contentious probate business

1.4   Contentious probate business is conducted in the Chancery Division of the High Court. This includes applications in respect of wills where there is a dispute over validity, testamentary capacity, duress etc. whether before submission to a Probate Registry for proof in common form or after proof.

3

Applications for revocation of grants (which are contested) or for rectification of a will (again contested) are assigned to the Chancery Division.

Application to remove and/or replace a personal representative, because of alleged maladministration or failure to administer, under s 50 of the Administration of Justice Act 1985 is made to a Registry exercising Chancery jurisdiction by using the procedure in Part 7 of the Civil Procedure Rules 1998 in accordance with Rule 57.13 of these rules.

Jurisdiction to construe testamentary documents

1.5   The Family Division's jurisdiction to construe testamentary documents is limited solely to the purpose of determining title to apply for the grant of representation, for example to determine whether the wording of a gift constitutes a gift of residue to enable the named beneficiary to take a grant of letters of administration (with will annexed) as the residuary legatee or devisee. It may also be necessary to determine whether a contingent gift has effect to enable the original or contingent beneficiary to take the grant. Statutory guidance on the interpretation of wills and the evidence required to assist in interpretation is prescribed by s 21 of the Administration of Justice Act 1982 in respect of deaths on or after 1 January 1983 (the commencement date of the Act). Any dispute about the meaning or construction of words or phrases used in a will, including a dispute which will affect title to the grant, falls to be determined on application to the Chancery Division. It follows, therefore, that the Family Division's jurisdiction to construe or interpret testamentary documents is limited to those cases where there is no active dispute. The probate court may grant temporary representation under the court's discretionary powers to enable any necessary administration to be effected while the dispute remains unresolved (see paragraphs 5.27–5.38 below).

Effect of grant

1.6   A grant of probate or letters of administration obtained in common form is acceptable to all courts in England and Wales as conclusive evidence of the executor's or administrator's title to administer the estate of the deceased. Where the grant is of probate or letters of administration with will annexed it is also acceptable as proof of the formal validity and contents of the will.

Any grant remains effective as authority to collect in estate and make payments or dispositions therefrom during the lifetime of the personal representative or until it is revoked.

The production of a grant of representation to any person or body holding funds in the deceased's name is sufficient authority for the release by that person or body of those funds to the person(s) named as the executor(s) or administrator(s) in the grant.

Section 27(1) of the Administration of Estates Act 1925 indemnifies and protects any person making or permitting any payment to be made notwithstanding any defect or circumstance affecting validity of the grant of representation. Section 27(2) of the Act affords protection to the personal representatives for all administration performed in good faith during the currency of a grant which is subsequently revoked. Indeed, it also provides for the grantee to retain and reimburse himself in respect of payments and dispositions made which the subsequent grantee might have properly made. This section also protects the asset holder for payments made to the personal representative under the grant before revocation and for any receipt given to be sufficient discharge.

The leading authority on the protection afforded by s 27(2) is *Hewson v Shelley [1914] 2 Ch 13*, which describes the circumstances in which a personal representative may claim protection for his acts done in good faith. As to revocation by the Probate Registries, see CHAPTER 18.

Section 204 of the Law of Property Act 1925 provides that an order of the court shall not be invalidated by want of, *inter alia*, jurisdiction. A grant of representation is considered to be an order of the court. It follows, therefore, that any conveyance or transfer of property effected pursuant to a grant is not invalidated if that grant is subsequently revoked, provided that the personal representative acted in good faith: see s 37 of the Administration of Estates Act 1925 which provides for a conveyance to be valid even if the grant under the authority of which it was executed is subsequently revoked.

A grant of representation is not *prima facie* evidence of the death or the date of death.

Estate covered by grant

1.7   An English grant of representation to the estate of a person dying before 1 January 1898 covered only the *personal* estate of the deceased. There was no jurisdiction to deal with *real* estate. Unless there was personal estate in England no grant could be issued.

The Land Transfer Act 1897, which was repealed and replaced by s 1 of the Administration of Estates Act 1925, empowered the court to issue a grant in respect of real estate. Since 1 January 1898 the grant, unless otherwise limited, covers all the estate which by law devolves upon and vests in the personal representative of the deceased.

The Administration of Justice Act 1932 empowered the court to issue a grant where there was no estate. That part of the Act, s 2(1), which gave the power was repealed and replaced by s 25 of the Supreme Court Act 1981 with effect from 1 January 1982. This power is usually invoked where a grant is required solely to vest title to property which does not form part of the deceased's estate, to pursue or defend legal proceedings, or to establish entitlement for the court in a foreign jurisdiction.

The Administration of Estates Act 1971 (ss 2 and 3) extended the authority of a grant issued in England and Wales in respect of a person dying domiciled in England and Wales, to estate in Scotland or Northern Ireland. Similarly a confirmation or grant issued in Scotland or Northern Ireland empowers the personal representative to deal with estate in England and Wales and Northern Ireland or Scotland, provided the deceased died domiciled in the country which issued the confirmation or grant and that the grant or confirmation bears a note of the domicile. (See also paragraphs 4.5–4.6 and 4.18 as to the vesting of estate prior to issue of the grant.)

Generally, property held by the deceased as a beneficial joint tenant passes to the remaining joint tenant(s) by survivorship and no grant is required in respect of such property. Similarly, no grant is required in respect of nominated assets which pass by virtue of the nomination to the nominee(s).

A grant may be resealed under the Colonial Probates Acts 1892 and 1927 in a reciprocating country to effect the administration of estate in that country. See CHAPTER 15 as to resealing grants of representation.

As to other payments which may be made without production of a grant of representation see CHAPTER 4.

A grant issued in England and Wales in respect of the estate of a person dying domiciled outside England and Wales is only acceptable as proof of title to estate in England and Wales. The values of the estate appearing in the grant relate only to the value of the estate in England and Wales passing under the grant.

Chapter 2

Wills

General definition

Form of will

2.1   In order for a document to constitute a will, it must:

(i)   dispose of property, either real or personal, situate in England and Wales; or

(ii)   appoint an executor or executors.

It must be in writing as required by, and be executed in accordance with, s 9 of the Wills Act 1837, as substituted by s 17 of the Administration of Justice Act 1982 (see paragraph 2.18 below).

The only exception to the foregoing would be in a case where the will was a 'privileged will', that is an informal will, the privilege of making which is allowed to soldiers, sailors and airmen on actual military service or seamen at sea (see paragraph 2.49 below).

Valid will must be proved even if in effect inoperative

2.2   Although a will does not contain an effective appointment of executors or a clause revoking another testamentary document, or revive a previous testamentary document, or may be inoperative (that is, the testamentary dispositions cannot be carried into effect), provided it fulfils either of the conditions in (i) or (ii) in paragraph 2.1 above the will must be proved if an application for a grant of representation is made. This is because the deceased died 'testate' and it cannot properly be sworn in the oath to lead the grant that he died 'intestate'.

A will, again provided it fulfils either of the conditions in (i) or (ii) in 2.1 above, must be proved even if there is no estate in England and Wales disposed of by the will. However, where there is indeed no such estate the District Judge or Registrar will not allow a grant to issue until satisfied that there is good reason for proving the will, for example to pass title to real property, to constitute a personal representative to take legal proceedings in another court, or to establish title for the benefit of estate in a foreign country. The usual procedure to satisfy the requirement is to recite the reason in the oath to lead the grant.

A will may be made which deals with, and is expressed to be only in respect of, property in a foreign country. It would not be admissible to proof in England and Wales (see *Re Coode's Goods (1867) LR 1 P & D 449*). However, if that will contains a general revocation clause, it would not operate to revoke another will made earlier in respect of estate in England and Wales (see *Re Wayland's Estate [1951] 2 All ER 1041*).

Connection with foreign law

2.3   Where a testator has any connection with a foreign system of law, the definition of a will has been clarified and extended under the Wills Act 1963 s 6, so as to include any testamentary instrument or act if validly made under the internal law of another country (see paragraph 2.11 below).

Therefore, if any testamentary intention made by the deceased is not valid according to the requirements of the law in England and Wales, it must then be considered whether it is valid by virtue of the provisions in respect of foreign law referred to in the 1963 Act.

Wills Act 1963

Extended definition

2.4   The Wills Act 1963 came into force on 1 January 1964 and applies to the wills of persons dying on or after that date. It extends the definition of a will to include any testamentary instrument or act if validly executed according to the internal law of another country, and its provisions apply to testators of any domicile or nationality. The Act extends to Scotland and Northern Ireland.

Section 1 of the Act provides that a will shall be treated as properly executed if:

> 'its execution conformed to the internal law in force in the territory where it was executed, or in the territory where, at the time of its execution or of the testator's death, he was domiciled or had his habitual residence, or in a state of which, at either of those times, he was a national.'

If the will has been accepted as valid by the court of the place of domicile, then clearly its validity is established. If the will has not been so accepted, then evidence to establish its validity by affidavit or law or natural statement in accordance with Rule 19 will be necessary.

Execution on board a vessel or aircraft

2.5   Section 2(1)(a) provides that, without prejudice to s 1, a will executed on board a vessel or aircraft of any description shall be treated as properly executed if:

'the execution of the will conformed to the internal law in force in the territory with which, having regard to its registration (if any) and other relevant circumstances, the vessel or aircraft may be taken to have been most closely connected.'

The definition of vessel here includes a hovercraft. These provisions are intended to assist in instances of doubt as to the actual place of execution of a will made on a vessel at sea, or an aircraft in flight.

Will in respect of immovable property

2.6   Under s 2(1)(b) of the Act, a will is again to be treated as validly executed if, so far as it disposes of immovable property, its execution conformed to the internal law in force in the territory where the property was situated. This provision is also without prejudice to s 1, but would allow a will to be proved, even if it met with none of the conditions in s 1, as long as it was executed in accordance with the internal law of the place where the property is situated. It is possible that this provision may allow a will, which otherwise would be invalid, to be proved in England and Wales so far as it disposes of immovable estate in this country, and in such a case it may be necessary for part only of the will to be admitted to proof.

Where such a circumstance arises, the will and an explanation of all the surrounding circumstances should be put before the District Judge or Registrar in the form of a 'pre-lodgment enquiry', that is, an application made for the court's consideration before an application for a grant is made. The District Judge or Registrar, if satisfied, will direct whether all, or which part or parts, of the will should be proved.

Similarly, as in paragraph 2.4 above, if the will has been accepted by the court of the country of domicile, validity is established, but, if not, evidence of the law of the country concerned will be necessary under Rule 19.

Revocation only

2.7   Section 2(1)(c) allows for a will to be treated as validly executed if:

'it revokes a will which under this Act would be treated as properly executed or revokes a provision which under this Act would be treated as comprised in a properly executed will, if the execution of the later will conformed to any law by reference to which the revoked will or provision would be so treated.'

Therefore, even if the revocatory document is neither executed in accordance with the internal law of England and Wales nor in such a way as to entitle it to proof under the Act, nonetheless it is effective as a revoking instrument as long as it was executed in accordance with any system of law which could be applied in order to establish the validity of the will that it was intended to revoke. In such a circumstance, however, the revocatory instrument or act would only be effective in so far as it revokes the earlier will, and if provisions intended to stand in place of those revoked did not conform with the requirements in s 1 of the Act, they would not be admissible to proof. In such a case the doctrine of 'dependent relative revocation' (see paragraph 2.75 below at (b)(iv)) may apply.

Power of appointment

2.8   Sections 2(1)(d) and 2(2) deal with wills made in exercise of a power of appointment. Under s 2(1)(d) a will is treated as validly executed in 'so far as it exercises a power of appointment, if the execution of the will conformed to the law governing the essential validity of the power'; and s 2(2) provides that 'a will so far as it exercises a power of appointment shall not be treated as improperly executed by reason only that its execution was not in accordance with any formal requirements contained in the instrument creating the power'. Therefore a will which exercises a power of appointment and is validly executed according to the provisions of s 1 or s 2(1)(d) of the Act, is admissible to proof even if it does not comply with any additional formal requirements stipulated in the settlement itself.

Foreign law requirements treated as formal requirements only

2.9   Section 3 of the Act provides that:

'where (whether in pursuance of this Act or not) a law in force outside the United Kingdom falls to be applied in relation to a will, any requirement of that law whereby special formalities are to be observed by testators answering a particular description, or witnesses to the execution of a will are to possess certain qualifications, shall be treated, notwithstanding any rule of that law to the contrary, as a formal requirement only'.

Change of domicile

2.10   Section 4 of the Act states that the construction of a will shall not be altered by reason of any change in the testator's domicile after the execution of the will.

Definition of 'internal law'

2.11   Section 6(1) defines, *inter alia,* 'internal law' as used in the Act. It states that 'internal law' used in relation to any territory or state 'means the law which would apply in a case where no question of the law in force in any other territory or state arose.'

Application of different systems of law

2.12   Section 6(2) provides that, where under the Act the internal law in force in any territory or state is to be applied in the case of a will, but there are in force in that territory or state two or more systems of internal law relating to the formal validity of wills, the system to be applied should be ascertained as follows:

'(a)   if there is in force throughout the territory or state a rule indicating which of those systems can properly be applied in the case in question, that rule shall be followed; or

(b)   if there is no such rule, the system shall be that with which the testator was most closely connected at the relevant time, and for this purpose the relevant time is the time of the testator's death where the matter is to be determined by reference to circumstances prevailing at his death, and the time of execution of the will in any other case.'

This subsection provides for a case where, for instance, reference needs to be made to the law of nationality of a testator who was a citizen of the United Kingdom and Colonies, where more than one system of law may apply. It would also apply in relation to a territory or state which applied different systems of law to different testators, for instance according to their religion or caste.

If there is no rule in force throughout the territory or state indicating which system can properly be applied to the case in question, then it will be necessary to establish with which system of law the testator was most closely connected at the relevant time, and then to apply that system.

Where it is necessary to rely on this provision in proving a will, then affidavit evidence must be supplied with the application for a grant, giving the facts which are relied upon to show that a testator's closest connection, at the time of execution of the will or at the time of death, was with a particular system of law (see *Re O'Keefe, Poingdestre v Sherman [1940] Ch 124, [1940] 1 All ER 216*).

Effective date at which law applied

2.13   Section 6(3) provides that:

'in determining for the purposes of this Act whether or not the execution of a will conformed to a particular law, regard shall be had to the formal requirements of that law at the time of the execution, but this shall not prevent account being taken of an alteration of law affecting wills executed at that time if the alteration enables the will to be treated as properly executed.'

Repeal of Wills Act 1861

2.14   The Act substantially extends the effect of the Wills Act 1861 which was repealed as from 1 January 1964, but any will executed in accordance with the provisions of the 1861 Act before its repeal is not invalidated. A will made before 1 January 1964 may still be established as validly executed by virtue of the Wills Act 1861, whatever the date of death of the testator, but because of the limitations of the Act (for instance, the limitation to wills dealing with personal estate), it is preferable, when possible, to establish the formal validity of the will of a testator dying on or after 1 January 1964 under the Wills Act 1963, rather than under the earlier Act.

Effect for English domiciliary

2.15   If the testator died domiciled in England and Wales, the Act is of assistance in cases where there are apparently unexecuted alterations and additions to an otherwise valid will, since these may be included for proof if it can be shown that they are valid by some other applicable system of law. Similarly, where a will made by a testator who was domiciled in England and Wales at the date of his death was not executed in accordance with s 9 of the Wills Act 1837, the will may be proved if it satisfies any of the conditions in the 1963 Act.

The will may not be proved in England and Wales if its execution does not comply with the internal law (see s 6(1) of the Act, referred to above) of the place where it was executed, for example under Swiss law a will may be valid if it is written entirely in the handwriting of the testator and mentions the place, year, month and day when made and signed. A will will fail if these internal law requirements are not met (see *Re Kanani; Engledow v Davidson (1978) 122 Sol Jo 611*: in this will the place of execution was printed on the paper, and not in the testator's handwriting).

Where a testator dies domiciled outside England and Wales, but his will has been executed in accordance with s 9 of the Wills Act 1837, recourse may again be made to the 1963 Act and affidavit evidence of foreign law will be rendered unnecessary where it can be shown that compliance with the internal law of England and Wales is sufficient to entitle the will to proof. Affidavit evidence of foreign law would not be required where one of the following conditions was met:

(i)   the will was executed in England or Wales;

(ii) the testator's habitual residence either at the date of execution of the will or at the date of death was in England and Wales;

(iii) the testator's domicile at the date of execution of the will was in England and Wales; or

(iv) the testator was a British national whose closest connection either at the time of execution of his will or at the date of his death, was with England and Wales and the English system of internal law as to the formal validity of wills.

Will in English form valid if executed in certain countries

2.16   The District Judge or Registrar may require evidence, on affidavit or by statement in the oath, to establish whichever of the facts mentioned above is claimed to establish validity of the will.

In addition, a will in English form is normally accepted as valid if:

(i)   the will was made in; or

(ii) the testator's habitual residence either at the date of execution or at the time of his death was in; or

(iii) the testator was at the date of his death or at the date of the will a national of; or

(iv) the testator was at the date of his death or the date of the will domiciled in –

Northern Ireland, the Republic of Ireland, Australia, Canada or New Zealand (Registrar's Direction dated 20 November 1972).

When affidavit evidence necessary

2.17   The practice when seeking to establish the validity of a will under the Wills Act 1963 is as follows. Where the law of any country other than England and Wales, Northern Ireland, the Republic of Ireland, Australia, Canada and New Zealand applies, then, unless the will has been proved or accepted as valid by the court of that country, an affidavit of foreign law deposed to by someone qualified in that law or certificate by, or act before, a notary practising in the country or territory concerned, showing that the execution of the will complied with the internal law of that country or territory (see paragraph 2.11 above), must be obtained.

Affidavit evidence of the facts appertaining to the case should be lodged either with the application for the grant of representation or, if preferred, as a preliminary application for the consideration of the District Judge or Registrar.

Affidavit evidence of law would not normally be required where it can be shown that the will was executed before a notary practising out of England and Wales and recorded by him. In such a case it may be assumed that the will was valid as to form according to the internal law of the place where it was made.

When a will has been proved, but not in the place where the deceased died domiciled, evidence of law may still be required notwithstanding that evidence of its acceptance to proof is available, since the court in which the will has been proved may have applied a system of law other than its own internal law to establish the formal validity of the will.

To fulfil the requirements of s 6(2) of the Act, the affidavit of law, or notarial statement, which should deal only with the internal law of the appropriate territory or state, should show whether a single system of law appertaining to the formal validity of wills is in force throughout the territory or state and, if not, whether there exists a rule indicating which system should be applied to that particular case. If such a rule is in force, the evidence in the affidavit should be founded on the application of that rule, and if there is no such rule, it should be shown upon which system the conclusions in the evidence are based and the grounds upon which it is claimed that the deceased was most closely connected with that particular system of law at the date of execution of the will or at the date of his death. See Form A1.62, page 430 for the form of affidavit.

Validity of a will under English law

Execution

2.18   To establish that a will is valid where the deceased died domiciled in England and Wales, it must have been executed in accordance with the Wills Act 1837 s 9 (as amended by the Administration of Justice Act 1982 s 17 in respect of deaths occurring on or after 1 January 1983). That section now provides that a will is duly executed if:

'(a) it is in writing, and signed by the testator, or by some other person in his presence and by his direction; and

(b) it appears that the testator intended by his signature to give effect to the will; and

(c) the signature is made or acknowledged by the testator in the presence of two or more witnesses present at the same time; and

(d) each witness either –

(i) attests and signs the will; or

(ii) acknowledges his signature,

in the presence of the testator (but not necessarily in the presence of any other witness),

but no form of attestation shall be necessary.'

Notwithstanding the provisions of s 9 of the Wills Act 1837 as set out above, a will may be valid if:

(a) it has been executed on behalf of a mental patient by some other person appointed by the direction of the court under s 96(1)(e) of the Mental Health Act 1983 (see paragraph 2.57 below); or

(b) it can be set up as a privileged will (see paragraph 2.49 below); or

(c) in respect of a death which occurred on or after 1 January 1964, it is comprised in a declaration of testamentary intentions which can be set up as valid under the provisions of a foreign law, although those intentions were not necessarily expressed in writing (Wills Act 1963).

Will to be in writing

2.19   The term 'writing' in the Wills Act 1837, as re-defined by the Interpretation Act 1978, includes typing, printing, lithography or photography or any other method of producing words in a visible form.

It follows therefore that a will written in shorthand, in braille or in code may be accepted to proof provided it is accompanied by a transcription into normal words and the transcription is verified on affidavit made by a person competent to transcribe the document. The verifying affidavit should also state the transcriber's qualifications to make the transcription.

Affidavit evidence

2.20   In all cases in this section where evidence is required, it must be in the form of an affidavit, and the relevant testamentary documents must be exhibited to the affidavit. The original of such documents is usually exhibited but, with leave, a copy may be substituted as the exhibit, and the affidavit should then refer to the document as being a copy.

The attestation clause

2.21   No form of attestation is necessary, but where the will contains an attestation clause showing that the will was signed by the testator in the presence of the witnesses and that each witness signed it in the presence of the testator, no other evidence as to execution will be required. To be effective the attestation clause must state that the witnesses signed, or acknowledged their signatures to the will, in the presence of the testator. It is not essential for the witnesses to have signed in the presence of each other.

The simplest form of attestation which is recommended is 'signed by the testator in our presence and by us in his'. This is the least number of words which can be used and therefore the less likely to cause an error in engrossing the will.

The witnesses should attest the will by signing with their full normal signatures. Where there is any doubt about a witness's signature (for example where the witness's name appears in capital letters or by initial only, giving a presumption that they were put in as a guide to where a signature should appear) the District Judge or Registrar may require evidence stating that the way the witness(es) subscribed the will was intended to be their signature to effect execution.

There is no requirement of the Wills Act 1837 for the witnesses to state their addresses.

Where there is no attestation clause or there is a defect in the clause, or where it appears to the District Judge or Registrar that there is doubt about the execution of the will, evidence of due execution will be necessary (but see *(i)* below). The affidavit in support of due execution should be made by one or more of the attesting witnesses. However, if there is no attesting witness conveniently available, the affidavit may be made by any other person present when the will was executed who can give evidence as to execution (see Forms A1.49 and A1.50, page 416 for forms of affidavit of due execution and affidavit of handwriting).

Signature of the testator and witnesses

Position of testator's signature

2.22   The signature of the testator may now appear anywhere on a will provided it is clear that the testator intended by his signature to give effect to the will. However where the signature of the testator is not in its customary place immediately following the end of the text of the will, an affidavit of due execution may be required. Where a testator made a signature in the heading of the will or otherwise at the beginning, intending to give effect to his will before he made any dispositive provisions, this has now been held by the Court of Appeal to constitute a valid execution sufficient to satisfy s 9 of the Act, provided that the signing and the making of the subsequent dispositive provisions all formed part of one transaction (see *Wood v Smith [1993] Ch 90, [1992] 3 All ER 556*).

Where the testator wrote his name in the attestation clause and the evidence indicated that the testator had intended to give effect to the document as his will, the handwritten name was a sufficient signature for the purposes of s 9 (see *Weatherhill v Pearce [1995] 2 All ER 492*). It appears therefore that a signature other than immediately after the dispositions, may be sufficient under paragraph (b) of s 9 to validate the will. That paragraph should effectively be read as including a provision for the *making or acknowledging* of the signature giving effect to the will. Evidence, on affidavit, will be required describing the circumstances of execution and stating specifically that the testator intended by the making or acknowledging of his signature (wherever it appears) to give effect to his will (see below as to execution by acknowledgment). Any will sought to be proved where the signature is not in the normal position should be referred to the District Judge or Registrar for directions.

Acknowledgment of testator's signature

2.23   Where the will has been signed in the usual place by the testator before it is presented to the witnesses, the testator may acknowledge the signature to be his. This may be by statement or otherwise, provided that it is clear that the witnesses could see the signature which the testator was acknowledging. The attestation clause should state that the signature was acknowledged in the presence of the witnesses and that they signed in the testator's presence.

Frail or unusual signature

2.24   If the testator's signature is weak or feeble, or is printed in lower case or written in capital letters indicating a doubt of the testator's ability to comprehend his actions, or there is some other reason to doubt its authenticity, or that the testator was aware of the act he was performing, or otherwise that he lacked the necessary capacity, affidavit evidence as to due execution may be necessary. A will may be accepted to proof where it is signed not with a signature but with some other recognisable and identifiable subscription, such as 'Dad', or by a mark. Affidavit evidence of the handwriting of the will and its subscription, whatever the manner of it, will be necessary. Similarly, a signature in foreign letters will require evidence to establish not only due execution but also that the testator had knowledge of the content of his will and the nature of the document he was signing.

Witnesses' signature

2.25   The witnesses must see or be able to see the testator sign or see his signature already made if it is acknowledged in execution. The signatures of the witnesses should follow immediately after the testator's. If the signature of a witness appears above that of the testator, there is a presumption that it was signed in this order, and evidence will be necessary to rebut the presumption.

A witness may acknowledge his already made signature in the presence of the testator (who also acknowledges his signature) and the other witness to give effect to due execution in accordance with s 9 of the Wills Act 1837 (see *Couser v Couser [1996] 3 All ER 256*).

A beneficiary or creditor may be a competent witness but the former may lose his benefit under s 15 of the Wills Act 1837. A minor may qualify as a competent witness, there being no statutory bar. A blind person does not so qualify (see *Re Gibson [1949] 2 All ER 90*) as witnessing means 'actual visual presence'.

Where there is doubt as to the competency of a witness or whether that witness was present, if the will bears the signature of a third witness this may be accepted as being that of one of the competent witnesses to give effect to due execution. Any signature which is not that of a testator is presumed to be that of a witness in attestation.

Affidavit evidence of due execution may also be required when a witness has printed his name in capital letters or by writing his initials only (but see paragraph 2.29 below).

A witness may 'sign' by his initials or mark provided that either the will bears a legend to the effect that this is the normal signature of the witness or the witness, in support of the application to prove, makes an affidavit establishing that the manner of his subscription is his normal signature or was intended as his signature in attestation.

Execution of wrong will

2.26 Where a testator, in making his will, wrongly signs another person's will, then both wills are invalid. It is essential therefore that when two persons (often husband and wife) execute their wills at the same time, care is taken to ensure each signs the correct will (see *Re Meyer's Estate [1908] P 353*). However, if the testator subsequently executes a codicil which confirms his will and refers to it by date, the will may be accepted to proof by incorporation in the codicil.

Doubt as to due execution

2.27 Rule 12 provides that where there is doubt as to the valid execution of a will it should be submitted to a District Judge or Registrar for a decision. The evidence to support the claim for validity is given on affidavit by, if possible, one or both of the attesting witnesses. If both witnesses are unable to give evidence, with the leave of the District Judge or Registrar, affidavit evidence may be obtained from another person present at the time of execution.

If the attesting witnesses have died, or cannot be found, or, as is frequently the case, cannot remember the circumstances, evidence as to the deceased's handwriting and signature, on affidavit by some person having knowledge thereof, may be filed together with any other evidence which may raise a presumption in favour of due execution.

Where all the evidence filed is inconclusive to determine due execution, the will may be admitted to probate provided all persons who would be prejudiced by the will's being proved in its present form are given notice of the application and do not object to its being proved. The affidavit in support of due execution, if inconclusive, should contain details of the events surrounding execution. Case law generally inclines towards a presumption in favour of due execution, with the probate courts usually adhering to the principle of *omnia praesumuntur rite esse acta* (see *Re Webb, Smith v Johnston [1964] 2 All ER 91*). Details of those prejudiced by proof of the will and any other relevant circumstances may be set out in separate affidavit evidence by the person seeking to prove the will. These details may, with the permission of the District Judge or Registrar, be contained in the oath to lead the grant. The District Judge or Registrar may require the consent in writing to the will's admission to proof from those prejudiced by its proof.

See Form A1.50, page 416 and Form A1.67, page 434 for the wording to be included in the affidavit and the form of consent.

Where, however, a witness to a will is known but refuses to provide evidence of execution on affidavit, application may be made by summons to a District Judge or Registrar under s 122 of the Supreme Court Act 1981 for an order compelling the witness to attend to give evidence (see Rule 50). Section 122 is not restricted to witnesses but allows the court to order 'any person' it reasonably believes has knowledge of a will to attend to give evidence.

Where the evidence clearly shows that the will was not properly executed, the affidavit should be filed with a request that the will be marked 'Probate refused' (see paragraph 2.29 below).

Execution by testator who is blind, illiterate, deaf or dumb: signature by other person

2.28   Rule 13 provides that where the validity of a will is sought to be established under s 9 of the Wills Act 1837 and the will was made by a blind or illiterate person, the District Judge or Registrar must be satisfied that the testator had knowledge of the contents of the will at the time of its execution. The same applies if the will was signed by some person on the direction of the testator, or if the testator was deaf and/or dumb. If the attestation clause does not sufficiently set out that the will was read to the testator or communicated to him by sign or other language and that he appeared to understand and approve the contents at the time of execution, affidavit evidence by an attesting witness if possible, or any other person present at the time of execution, will be required (see *In the Goods of Geale (1864) 3 SW & Tr 431*).

Where a will is signed by another person at the testator's direction, the will may be signed in the testator's name or in the name of the person signing. The 'other person' may be a witness to the will. In either instance, if it is not made clear in the attestation clause that the will was so signed, evidence as above of execution will be required. Where no such evidence is available affidavit evidence by the draftsman of the will or a solicitor who took the testator's instructions, stating that the contents of the will had been explained to the testator, who appeared to understand and approve them, may be sufficient.

If the will is signed by another person on behalf of the testator then, unless the attestation clause clearly shows that the will was signed 'by .... at the direction of and in the presence of the testator' and that the testator was aware of the content of his will, evidence to establish the above facts from a witness will be necessary before the will may be admitted to proof.

District Judge or Registrar's directions

2.29   The District Judge or Registrar may, after considering the evidence:

(a)   if he is satisfied as to proper execution, allow the application for the grant to proceed;

(b)   if after considering the evidence, he has doubts as to proper execution, call for further evidence or refer the matter to a judge on summons;

(c)   where he is satisfied that the will is invalid mark the will 'Probate refused'.

Where the evidence is lodged before application for a grant, the will will be marked 'Probate refused'. If, however, the evidence has been obtained before any reference to the court, the will need not be submitted for marking. Any will probate of which has been refused will be retained in the Registry. Application may then be made to prove an earlier will, or for letters of administration on the basis of an intestacy. The evidence and original will may, however, be lodged with the grant application for endorsement of the District Judge or Registrar's order.

Rule 12(3) provides that a District Judge or Registrar may accept for proof any will without evidence of execution provided he is satisfied that the distribution of the estate is not thereby affected (for example where a will leaves the entire estate to a surviving spouse who would be entitled to all the estate under an earlier will or if the deceased had died intestate). Where there is obvious doubt as to proper execution but the District Judge or Registrar is to be asked to exercise his discretion, it should be confirmed on application for the grant, that the distribution of the estate is not affected by proof of the will and that Rule 12(3) applies. This may be done by adding a statement to this effect in the oath to lead the grant.

Section 15 of the Wills Act 1837 provides that a beneficial gift to an attesting witness, or to the spouse of an attesting witness, is void. However, this does not affect the validity of the will itself, as long as the witness was competent. Any person appointed as an executor by a will is a competent witness to the will, but if the executor is also a beneficiary, he will lose his benefit by being an attesting witness (see also paragraph 8.30 below).

Confirmation of will by codicil

2.30   Where a will has not been properly executed or there is doubt as to proper execution, such a will may be accepted to proof without supporting evidence if it is confirmed by a properly executed codicil which expressly refers to and confirms the will. However, where there is doubtful reference and no confirmation, evidence in respect of the will's execution may be required. It may also be necessary in the affidavit evidence to deal with the doubtful reference in the codicil, to ensure that the codicil does not refer to, and attempt to revive, an earlier will. The directions of the court should be sought as to necessity of, and, if required, the form and content of, the evidence.

Date of the will

Introduction

2.31   As well as establishing that the will has been duly executed in accordance with s 9 of the Wills Act 1837, it is also necessary to establish the date of the will sufficiently clearly to be certain of proving the last will of the deceased. By virtue of Rule 14(4), an affidavit of due execution (see Form A1.50, page 416 for the form of affidavit) or such other evidence as is thought necessary will be required by the District Judge or Registrar where:

(a)   the date has been omitted from any testamentary document, or only partially completed; or

(b)   the will bears two different dates, one at the beginning and one later, and the later date appears in the attestation clause or is not in close connection with the signature, or there is a conflict with a date on any endorsement (but see below); or

(c)   there are two dates and the applicant's entitlement to the grant depends on the later date being the true date; or

(d)   the date in the will is not the date of execution of that will.

Will containing two dates

2.32   If the will bears two dates and the later one is at the foot or end of the will, or the date of the endorsement is earlier than that in the will and there is no reason to suppose that the later date is not the true one, the later date is accepted and no evidence as to the date of execution will be required. If, however, the date on the endorsement is later than the date shown in the will, evidence to confirm the date of execution is required. Where the difference in the dates is small, for example, the day before or day after, or even within a month, or the year is altered and execution took place early in a new year, the District Judge or Registrar may exercise his discretion to accept the will without evidence as to the true date of execution. There are no strict guidelines, the acceptance being a matter for discretion exercised in the light of all the circumstances. It is suggested that a request for the exercise of the District Judge or Registrar's discretion be made as a pre-lodgment enquiry.

Misrecital of date of will in codicil

2.33   Where a codicil misrecites the date of the will, or of an earlier codicil, to which it purports to refer, an explanatory affidavit must be filed with the Registry. If it can be shown that the incorrect date is merely an error in the drafting or engrossing of the codicil, and that the testamentary document to which it appears to refer does not exist, then the will and codicil (or codicils) will be admitted to proof with a notation made by the Registry on the codicil, the probate copy and the record copy to show that an affidavit of misrecital of date has been filed. If the error was not simply in drafting, then an affidavit of search may be required together with the affidavit of facts.

Misrecital of number of codicil

2.34   Where a codicil is wrongly entitled, for example, the third codicil is headed 'second codicil', perhaps, as is often the case, because the draftsman was unaware that a second codicil had already been made, affidavit evidence as to the facts must be lodged. Similarly, if a codicil appears to be missing, there being a first and third or subsequent codicil, evidence as to the existence, possible revocation and effect of the missing codicil, or the wrong heading of the missing codicil, in affidavit form, should be obtained from a person with knowledge of the facts. (See Form A1.48, page 415 for a form of affidavit of search.)

Where there are other testamentary documents in existence to which the codicil may refer, then the District Judge or Registrar will also consider the effects of republication and revival of revoked wills or codicils or omitting words from probate (see paragraphs 2.59 and 2.60 below).

Insufficient evidence of specific date

2.35   If it is impossible for evidence to be given to prove execution of the will on a specific date, evidence as to execution between specific dates (for example, 'between the 1st and 31st March 1994' where the month and year of execution only can be deposed to) will be accepted; where this is impossible, an affidavit of search (see Form A1.48, page 415 for the form of affidavit) will be required to show that a search for a later will has been made without success. In these circumstances, evidence as to how and why the approximation is arrived at must be included in the affidavit. The will is endorsed by the Probate Registry as to the filing of evidence concerning the date of execution. The copy will incorporated in the grant and the record copy will bear an appropriate notation of the date of, or approximate date of, execution.

Deponent to be one of the witnesses

2.36   The affidavit of due execution should, where possible, be by one of the attesting witnesses to the will. Where it is not possible for one of the attesting witnesses to give evidence, an affidavit by some other person present at execution or with knowledge as to when the will was executed may be accepted (see Rule 12(1)).

Condition of the will

Introduction

2.37   If a will appears to have been tampered with, for example where it has been torn or burnt indicating a possible attempt to revoke it; or where there is an addition to it in a different handwriting, typewriting or ink; or where it would appear that another document had at some stage been attached to it indicating that the will is incomplete, the District Judge or Registrar may require affidavit evidence as to the condition of the will.

The affidavit should deal with the condition of the will when it was executed and when it was found after the testator's death and where it had been kept after execution, to show that the will is complete and that the testator did not intend to revoke it. Where a will shows signs of attempted revocation there is a presumption that revocation was in the testator's mind; this must be rebutted by conclusive evidence to show the contrary (see Rule 15).

Where the evidence shows that the will was never retained by the testator, then clearly any of the points made in the first paragraph above cannot be attributable to the testator in an attempt to revoke.

Other document attached

2.38   In cases where it appears that another document may have been attached to the will and the document cannot be produced, the District Judge or Registrar may require evidence by way of an affidavit of search for other testamentary documents by the applicant for the grant (see Form A1.48, page 415 for the form of affidavit). Where possible, the deponent should depose to all the facts in a single affidavit. Where the pin or clip mark was caused by the attachment of a non-testamentary document which was found attached to the will, a certificate by the solicitor acting, accounting for the mark, is usually acceptable without formal affidavit evidence. Where the other document remains attached, it is preferable to leave it attached to the will, submitting it to the Registry so that it is obvious how the marks were caused.

Referral for directions

2.39   Where there is any doubt the directions of the District Judge or Registrar should be sought before application for the grant is made. The District Judge or Registrar has absolute discretion as to the evidence (if any) and the form in which such evidence shall be produced. Similarly the District Judge or Registrar may direct the form in which the will may be proved (for example, that an engrossment restoring the will to its original form and content is required). The District Judge or Registrar has a duty to ensure that all enquiries are answered to his satisfaction before he allows a grant to issue (see Rule 6(1)).

Deponent

2.40   Normally, evidence as to the condition of a will at the time of execution is given by (one of) the attesting witnesses. Where no such evidence is available, an affidavit by some other person with knowledge of the condition of the will when executed should be obtained together with evidence of the condition of the will at the time it was found after the death of the testator. It is frequently the case that evidence as to the will's condition at the time of execution cannot be obtained. Evidence as to the current condition and an explanation of the likely cause of the disfigurement should be obtained, the deponent to the affidavit should be the person best able to speak to the facts. (See Form A1.47, page 414 for the form of affidavit.)

Nuncupative wills and copy wills

2.41   Rule 54(1) provides for an application for an order admitting to proof a nuncupative will (that is, a will contained in an oral statement), or a will contained in a copy or reconstruction where the original is not available, to be made to a District Judge or Registrar. Application is made *ex parte* on affidavit prior to any application for the grant. The affidavit is usually made by the proposed applicant for the grant but may be made by the solicitor acting or another person able to speak to the relevant facts in support of the application (see below), and must contain such evidence as can be deposed to of:

(a)   the existence of the will after the testator's death, or where there is no such evidence, the facts on which the applicant relies to rebut the presumption that the testator revoked his will by destruction;

(b)   in respect of a nuncupative will, the contents of that will; and

(c)   in respect of a reconstruction of a will, the accuracy of the reconstruction. (see Rule 54(3)).

(See paragraph 5.9 below).

Where the original will was in the testator's possession before his death but cannot thereafter be found, there is a presumption that the will was revoked by destruction. This presumption may be rebutted by evidence indicating that the testator had referred to his will as existing without mentioning revocation; had not consulted solicitors or other professional advisers with a view to changing or revoking his will; or whatever the facts are to show that the testator did not, or is unlikely to have, revoked his will. The District Judge or Registrar will require strong evidence to rebut the presumption of revocation. Where it can be shown that the original will was never in the testator's possession after execution, no evidence will be necessary to rebut the presumption.

Where the original will has been mislaid in a solicitor's office or will drafting company's office or in the post from or to an executor or to the Probate Registry, after the testator's death the affidavit deposing to the facts of the will's disappearance may, with the District Judge's or Registrar's leave, be given by the solicitor or clerk dealing with the matter. It is preferable for such evidence to be given by someone with first hand knowledge of the facts.

Where the will is not available because it has been retained by a foreign court or official, a copy of the will duly authenticated by the court or official may be admitted to proof without the necessity of any order (see Rule 54(2)).

Damaged wills

2.42   Where a will or other testamentary document is found but has been damaged (for instance by fading caused by exposure to sunlight or through age), and there is doubt as to whether it can be proved, application may be made to admit a copy.

The procedure is the same as explained above under 'Condition of the will'. It will be necessary to show in the affidavit evidence that the damage was accidental and not caused by the testator's attempting to revoke the will. Where the original is so damaged as to be unsuitable for photocopying the District Judge or Registrar may direct a copy be admitted to proof (see paragraph 2.41 above) or that an engrossment be prepared (see CHAPTER 19). The engrossment should follow the original, line for line and word for word as far as possible, with the testator's and witnesses' names typed in followed by '(signed)'. A space of approximately 5 cm at the top of the first page should be left clear to allow for the endorsement of the District Judge's or Registrar's fiat. The original will should be marked by the deponent(s) and commissioner(s) and lodged with the engrossment. The engrossment will form the probate copy (the copy included in the grant) and record copy (the copy from which future copies will be made).

Alterations to the will

2.43   There is a presumption that any alteration made to a will was made after it had been executed. Unless, therefore, an alteration has been executed as though it were a will (see s 21 of the Wills Act 1837), or one of the following applies, the alteration is invalid:

(a)   the alterations are initialled or signed by the testator and attesting witnesses at the time of execution; or

(b)   they are mentioned in the attestation clause or in a separate note at the end of the will; or

(c)   the will is re-published, or re-executed and re-published including the alterations, in a codicil; and, where appropriate,

(d)   those persons who would be prejudiced if the will were to be proved in its altered form consent to the will being admitted (see Form A1.67, page 434 for form of consent).

Where the above conditions are not met the court may accept evidence from an attesting witness that the alterations were made before execution.

Where evidence from the witnesses cannot be obtained or is inconclusive, evidence on affidavit may be taken from any other person present at the time of execution, or from the person who drafted the will. If the alterations are non-testamentary in nature, such as a change from a request for burial to cremation or an alteration to a beneficiary's address, or are to contingent bequests which are inoperative, or are of no practical importance (such as a change to the appointment of substituted executors which substitution does not operate), the court may allow the will to proof containing the alterations without calling for evidence (see Rule 14(2)).

However, where evidence cannot be obtained to satisfy the court as to the inclusion of an alteration or addition to the will, the District Judge's or Registrar's directions should be sought as to the proving of a fiat copy, that is an engrossment (a made-up copy) of the will excluding the words added after execution and, where possible, substituting the words deleted. Where an alteration completely obliterates the original wording, the engrossment should leave a blank for the indecipherable words.

Where a will contains alterations clearly made after execution, perhaps because they are noted with a date, even if such alterations have been initialled by witnesses the will in its altered form cannot be admitted to proof unless the testator himself re-executes it (see *Re White, Barker v Gribble [1990] 3 All ER 1*).

Where title to apply for the grant turns on the validity of any alteration or there is serious doubt as to the form in which the will should be proved the court may allow the will to be examined by experts to determine the matters in question. However, the court is reluctant to allow forensic investigation on an original will for fear of damaging or destroying it. Practitioners' attention is drawn to the case of *Re Itter [1950] P 130, [1950] 1 All ER 68* where infra-red photography was allowed to discover words over-written in the will.

Where the unauthenticated alteration only partly obliterates words so that the original can still be read, the court will direct proof of the will in its original form. Where it is necessary for a fiat copy to be admitted to proof the engrossment is prepared by the applicant's solicitors and will be endorsed by the Probate Registry 'Let probate of the will of the within-named ...... be granted in accordance with this copy' and signed by the District Judge or Registrar. The probate copy will be prepared from the fiat copy and future requests for copies will be supplied with copies of that copy (see s 21 of the Wills Act 1837 and Rule 14(1)).

Incorporation of other documents in a will

Rule 14(3)

2.44   Rule 14(3) provides that where it appears that some other document has been attached to a will or codicil or there is reference in the will to another document, and that document, though not capable of being admitted to proof on its own, disposes of some part of the testator's estate, consideration must be given to the incorporation of that document in the will when it is proved. Any such document shall be produced to the District Judge or Registrar, who may direct incorporation, refuse incorporation or require evidence to be filed in regard to the incorporation of that document.

Reference and identification

2.45   The document sought to be incorporated must have been in existence, as the document referred to in the will, at the time the will was executed, and must be capable of precise identification from the reference to it in the will. The evidence referred to above may be in support of identification. If there is doubt whether a document should be incorporated the case should be referred to a District Judge or Registrar for directions before the will is sought to be proved. It follows therefore that an *expressed intention* in a will to compile a list or memorandum distributing specific assets excludes such list or memorandum from proof. However, if such list or memorandum is in existence before the execution of a codicil which re-publishes the will including the relevant reference to the other document, it should be incorporated. An improperly executed will re-published by a properly executed codicil may be admitted to proof by incorporation and provided there is express reference to the will in the codicil.

Testamentary instruction not to incorporate

2.46   To be considered for incorporation the document must contain a disposition or affect a disposition made in the will or any codicil. A statement only of the reasons for a bequest or the reasons why some person is not to receive a benefit will not be incorporated.

Where a will contains a specific instruction not to incorporate another document as part of the will, or the will contains a clause or statement to the effect that the document is not to create any trust or be binding on the executors, the other document will be excluded from proof. Similarly a statement in a will that the testator has given oral instructions as to the disposal of his estate precludes any incorporation of a written version of the statement. Generally, references to deeds, maps or plans will not require such documents to be incorporated unless a disposition is materially affected by the document.

Reference to another will

2.47   If a will refers to another will, either a former will of his or of another person, incorporating a provision of that other will in this will, then the other will or an extract from it will need to be incorporated.

Where a testator makes two or more wills, each disposing of estate in other countries but referring to the other will(s), the other wills are not incorporated by reference. The proviso to this is that each will must be expressed to have separate effect.

Wording of oath

2.48   Where there is incorporation of another document the oath to lead the grant should refer to the last will and testament of the deceased 'as contained in the paper writings marked "A" and "B" or "A" and "B" with a codicil or "A", "B" and "C" and so on depending upon the number of separate documents being proved. The will and list or memorandum must be marked accordingly and both marked by the deponents and commissioner in accordance with Rule 10.

Statutory will forms which are prescribed by the Lord Chancellor under s 179 of the Law of Property Act 1925 may be incorporated by reference to their number only. There is no provision for the incorporation by reference only of other 'standard' forms of will or 'standard' clauses unless the form of the will or clauses has been lodged with the Senior District Judge of the Family Division who has accepted it as sufficient lodgment as a published document.

It follows therefore that any reference to a standard form or clauses, such as the 'STEP' provisions, unless lodged with and approved by the Senior District Judge, must be incorporated with the will and proved with it, and will be included in the probate and record copies (see the Senior District Judge's Direction, 10 April 1995). The 'STEP' Standard Provisions, First Edition, have been lodged with and approved by the Senior District Judge, and may now be incorporated by reference only.

Privileged wills

Definitions

2.49   Section 11 of the Wills Act 1837, as extended by the Wills (Soldiers and Sailors) Act 1918, provides that any soldier or member of the Air Force being in actual military service, or any seaman or mariner being at sea, may direct the disposition of his estate without the formalities regarding execution of a will required by s 9 of the 1837 Act.

The words 'actual military service' equate with 'active service'. Both phrases are limited in definition to such military service as is in connection with operations which were or had been taking place, or were believed to be imminent (see *Re Wingham [1949] P 187, [1948] 2 All ER 908*). The definition has been extended to include a soldier on patrol in Northern Ireland (*Re Jones [1981] Fam 7, [1981] 1 All ER 1, [1981] 2 WLR 106*).

The words 'at sea' have been held to cover a variety of different situations, and apply to persons serving on vessels permanently in harbour or on a riverboat or even on shore leave before starting a voyage (see *Re*

Patterson's Goods (1898) 79 LT 123; Re M'Murdo's Goods (1868) LR 1 P & D 540; Re Newland's Goods [1952] P 71, [1952] 1 All ER 841).

The privilege cannot be claimed of a document intended to be a draft or where the document was intentionally not completed by the testator.

Whether the testator knew his oral statement would have testamentary effect does affect the statement being admitted.

Domicile

2.50   The privilege to establish validity of the will may only be claimed for persons domiciled in England and Wales at the time the will was made. Where the domicile was elsewhere it may be possible to establish the validity of the will by reference to a foreign law relating to the place of domicile, execution or nationality.

Testator under 18

2.51   The privilege may be claimed by any serviceman notwithstanding that he has not attained his majority.

Form of will

2.52   A privileged will may be in the form of a document or letter, written or prepared by the deceased, or in the form of a statement given orally by the testator to some other person. The will does not need to be signed by the testator, nor does it have to be witnessed. Where the 'will' is contained in a letter which contains other non-testamentary writings, application should be made to a District Judge or Registrar for directions as to the form of the will to be proved. The District Judge or Registrar may direct that an engrossment be prepared containing only the parts which are testamentary for the endorsement of the District Judge or Registrar's fiat. The District Judge or Registrar must be satisfied as to the terms of the will (see Rule 17).

Procedure for proof

2.53   Rule 54, which deals with applications to admit a copy or reconstruction of a will, applies to nuncupative or oral wills, that is an oral declaration of the deceased's wishes as to the disposition of his estate. Application for a District Judge or Registrar's order giving leave to admit the privileged will to proof is a prerequisite of the application for the grant.

Evidence required

2.54   The application should be supported by the consent of all the persons prejudiced by proof of the will, and by affidavit evidence of the facts, including how the privilege is claimed (see Rule 54(3)).

A will contained in an oral statement must be set down in writing and exhibited to the affidavit to lead the order. The statement must be headed 'Oral statement of .... (*name of deceased*) made on .... (*date*) before .... (*name of person who heard the statement*)'. When the District Judge or Registrar's order has been made, the written statement must be lodged with the other papers on application for the grant of representation, having been marked as the will by the person or persons applying for the grant and by the Commissioner before whom the oath was sworn.

Where the will is in writing but was not attested, affidavit evidence as to the testator's handwriting and signature must be lodged.

Alterations

2.55   If the will has been altered or amended affidavit evidence of the handwriting of the testator dealing with the alteration will be necessary (see Rule 18). There is a presumption that any alteration made by the testator to his will was effected during the same period of active service as that during which he wrote the original.

Revocation

2.56   The testator is able to revoke a privileged will without adhering to any of the formalities normally required by law. It would appear that the marriage of a testator after making a privileged will would be effective in revoking the privileged will just as in revoking one made without the privilege (see *Re Wardrop's Estate [1917] P 54*).

Will made on behalf of a mentally disordered person

2.57   Where a Judge having jurisdiction under the Mental Health Act 1983 is satisfied that a person is incapable, by reason of mental disorder, of managing and administering his property and affairs, s 96(1)(e) of the Act provides that the court may order:

'the execution for the patient of a will making any provision (whether by way of disposing of property or exercising a power or otherwise) which could be made by a will executed by the patient if he were not mentally disordered.'

This power may only be exercised if the person suffering from the mental disorder has achieved his majority (s 96(4)(a) of the Act).

The court may also direct, on application for an order to execute a will (or at any time on proper application being made), that *inter vivos* gifts may be effected (see *Re C (a patient) [1991] 3 All ER 866*).

Section 94(1) of the Act provides that the functions conferred by the Act on a Judge:

'shall also be exercisable by the Lord Chancellor or any nominated judge, by the Master of the Court of Protection, by the Public Trustee or by any nominated officer, but:

(a)   in the case of the Master, the Public Trustee or any nominated officer, subject to any express provision to the contrary in this part of this Act or any rules made under this part of this Act;

(b)   in the case of the Public Trustee, subject to any directions of the Master and so far only as may be provided by any rules made under this part of this Act or (subject to any such rules) by direction of the Master;

(c)   in the case of any nominated officer, subject to any directions of the Master and so far only as may be provided by the instrument by which he is nominated;

and references in this part of this Act to the judge shall be construed accordingly.'

Section 97(1) of the Act prescribes the manner in which a will must be executed when made on behalf of a mentally disordered person. It states that any will executed in pursuance of an order under s 96(1) must be expressed to be signed by the patient acting by the authorised person, and shall be:

'(a)   signed by the authorised person with the name of the patient, and with his own name, in the presence of two or more witnesses present at the same time, and

(b)   attested and subscribed by those witnesses in the presence of the authorised person, and

(c)   sealed with the official seal of the Court of Protection.'

The seal of the Court of Protection will not be affixed until after the execution and attestation in accordance with s 97(1) has taken place. It has been held that the sealing of the will may take place after the death of the testator, the crucial criterion to validate the will being the making of the order and its execution (see *Re Hughes (1999) Times, 8 January*).

The Act also provides, in s 97(2), that the Wills Act 1837 shall have effect in relation to any will executed in this manner as if it were signed by the patient by his own hand, except that in relation to any such will:

(a) s 9 of that Act (which makes provision as to the signing and attestation of wills) shall not apply; and

(b) in the subsequent provisions of that Act any reference to execution in the manner required by the previous provisions of that Act shall be construed as a reference to execution in the manner required by s 97(1).

Under ss 97(3) and 97(4) of the Act, where a person is domiciled in England and Wales at the time of execution of a will made on his behalf under s 97(1) of the Act, such a will (other than one relating to immovable property situate outside England and Wales) shall have the same effect for all purposes as if the patient were capable of making a valid will and the will had been executed by him in the manner required by the Wills Act 1837.

Where a patient is domiciled in Scotland or Northern Ireland or any country or territory outside the United Kingdom at the time of execution of a will on his behalf in this fashion, the will is to have effect only in so far as it relates to any property or matter in relation to which, by the law of his domicile, any question of his testamentary capacity would be determined in accordance with the law of England and Wales.

The court, when drafting the will, intends to make a will which the patient himself would have made, were he of testamentary capacity and aided by the advice of a competent solicitor.

The only persons who are entitled to apply under s 96(1)(e) of the Act for an order to execute a will on behalf of a mentally disordered person are listed in the Court of Protection Rules 2001, which came into effect on 1 April 2001. They are:

(a) the receiver for the patient; or

(b) any person who has made an application for the appointment of a receiver which has not yet been determined; or

(c) any person who, under any known will of the patient or under his intestacy, may become entitled to any property of the patient or any interest therein; or

(d) any person for whom the patient might be expected to provide if he were not mentally disordered; or

(e) any other person whom the court may authorise to make it.

When an application is made, in order to determine whether the patient is capable of making a valid will for himself, the court will require recent evidence of lack of testamentary capacity. The evidence to support the application should also include a statement of the patient's domicile, and should give details of the patient's capital and income, of his property, showing whether any immovable property would be affected by the proposed will, and, if it is affected, where any such property belonging to the patient is situated, of the patient's needs and circumstances, of his family and of the financial circumstances of the person or persons who seek to benefit under the will.

It is usual for the Official Solicitor to represent the interests of the patient. Generally all persons with interests under the will or otherwise will be given notice (subject to the directions of the Master) of the application.

Conditional wills

2.58   Where a will is expressed as being conditional upon some event occurring (for example 'In the event of my wife predeceasing me ....' or 'In the event of us both dying together ....'), the will may not be admitted to probate unless the expressed condition is fulfilled. In the second example given above, the deaths would have to have been contemporaneous for the will to have effect (see *Re Govier [1950] P 237*).

The oath to lead the grant should contain a statement that the condition imposed by the will has been met. If the District Judge or Registrar is not satisfied with the statement in the oath a further affidavit by the applicant, setting out the details of the condition and how it has been fulfilled, will be required.

Where the conditional event has not occurred or it is decided the condition is inoperative, the District Judge or Registrar may refuse probate of the will and may retain the oath and any affidavit in the Registry for consideration on any further application for a grant. However, consideration should be given to the decision in the case of *Corbett v Newey [1995] 1 All ER 570* where a will had been executed on the basis that it was subject to a condition which was not expressed in the will. The will was accepted to proof on evidence that the condition had later been fulfilled.

Any earlier will made by the deceased may now be effective. Such a will should be referred to the District Judge or Registrar for his directions. If there is no earlier will, the estate will pass under an intestacy.

Offensive or libellous words in a will

2.59   Where a testator includes in his will words which are offensive, libellous or blasphemous, application may be made to a District Judge or Registrar for these words to be excluded from probate. Although words may be of the above nature they will not be excluded if they make an effective disposition of the estate. They may be varied to give effect to the disposition but remove the offence. The court may refuse to grant probate if it considers the will contains offensive words until application is made to remove them. The court does not omit words lightly: the testator has a right to explain why he has disposed of his estate in the way he has. The offence need not be directed against any particular person (see *Re Bowker's Goods [1932] P 93*).

Application is made on affidavit by the applicant, exhibiting the will and the consent in writing of any persons who might be prejudiced by the exclusion of the words. Application must be made before application for a grant. If satisfied, the District Judge or Registrar will direct that an engrossment of the will be produced excluding the offensive words. The original will remains as executed, i.e. it is not altered. For the procedure on engrossments, see paragraph 19.1 below.

Should there be a dispute about the exclusion of words, application to exclude is made on summons to a District Judge of the Principal Registry. The District Judge may refer the matter to a Judge on summons. Any order directing the omission of words will be attached to the original will and remain with it. The engrossed copy of the will endorsed with the District Judge's or Registrar's fiat will be photocopied to form the probate and record copies. Any subsequent copies requested will be of the engrossment. No copy of the original will will be supplied.

Words included or excluded in error: rectification

2.60 Where the testator's death occurred before 1 January 1983 the court's power to rectify his will was limited to directing the exclusion of words. Generally, the court endeavours to admit to proof the true intentions of the testator and words included in his will in error may be omitted. This extends to the omission of a revocation clause where it is clear the testator did not intend to revoke a previous testamentary document (see *Re Phelan [1972] Fam 33, [1971] 3 All ER 1256, [1971] 3 WLR 888*).

Section 20 of the Administration of Justice Act 1982 enables the court, if satisfied that a will is so expressed that it fails to carry out the testator's intentions because of a clerical error or a failure to understand his instructions, to direct the will be rectified so as to carry out the testator's intentions. In effect this means the court may, where the testator's death occurred after 1 January 1983, rectify his will by the inclusion as well as the exclusion of words.

Section 21 of the 1982 Act, which also applies to deaths after 1 January 1983 and irrespective of the date of the will, empowers the court to accept extrinsic evidence, including evidence of the testator's intention to assist in the interpretation of a will. This section applies to a will in so far as any part of it is meaningless, the language used in any part of it is ambiguous on the face of it or there is evidence which shows that the language used in any part of it is ambiguous in the light of surrounding circumstances.

Although it is usual to apply for rectification before representation is granted, application to rectify may be made within six months of the issue of the grant, or after that time with the court's leave. See also *In the Estate of Ronald Chittock [2000] 1 WTLR 643.*

For the procedure on applications to rectify or interpret see paragraph 5.20 *et seq.* below.

Mutual and joint wills

Mutual wills

2.61   Mutual wills are usually separate documents executed by two persons in which they mutually agree to the disposition of their property, for example a husband and wife may each execute separate wills in which they each give the other their estate and agree that after the death of the survivor it passes to others. There does not, however, have to be a disposition in favour of the other testator for the doctrine of mutual wills to apply; see *Re Dale, Proctor v Dale [1993] 4 All ER 129.* To constitute mutual wills there must be a clear contractual agreement between the testators that their wills are binding on each other; see *Re Goodchild [1997] 3 All ER 63.* Even though the wills of two testators had the same effect, there must be an agreement between them or they are not mutual wills; see *Re Cleaver, Cleaver v Insley [1981] 2 All ER 1018.* There may be an agreement between testators as to how their property is to be disposed of but this is insufficient for the doctrine of mutual wills to apply unless there is also an agreement not to revoke their wills; see *Birch v Curtis [2002] EWHC 1158 (Ch), [2002] WTLR 965.*

It should be noted that a mutual will is revocable by either testator but if revoked by one after the death of the other the personal representatives of the last to die will hold the mutually disposed of estate on trust for the mutual beneficiaries. The survivor may therefore make another will after the death of the first to die, which may be admitted to proof, but any disposition of the mutually disposed of estate in the later will will be ineffective; see *Re Dale, Proctor v Dale* referred to above. The will will be proved in common form by the Probate Registry leaving any dispute over the disposition to be decided by claim to the Chancery Division.

Where there was a clear agreement as to the disposition of their estates *and* an agreement not to revoke, any property passing by survivorship is caught by the trust imposed by the mutual wills; see *Healey v Brown [2002] WTLR 849.*

If the first testator to die has made a minor but not insignificant alteration to his will, the second testator is not bound by the agreement but could leave the entire estate uninhibited by the terms of the mutual wills; see *Re Hobley (1997) Times, 16 June*, where the first testator had executed a codicil changing a legacy without the knowledge of the second testator.

Mutual wills are usually proved on the death of each testator, but the will of the first to die need not be proved on his death unless there is a need to obtain representation to effect the collection of any asset or make any disposition.

Joint wills

2.62 Where a will is executed by two persons and contains the dispositions of both, it is a joint will. A joint will is proved on the death of each testator, except where:

(i) property is jointly owned; or

(ii) the terms of the will are expressed so as to take effect when both persons have died.

In either of the above two circumstances, the will is proved on the death of the survivor. Otherwise, after being proved on the death of the first testator, the will is retained by the Probate Registry; when application for a grant is made in respect of the estate of the second testator, that application should be made to the Registry which issued the first grant. Unless the applicant can attend the Registry to swear the oath and mark the original will, an office copy will may be marked. If an office copy is marked the oath must recite this fact.

The first application to prove a joint will should contain the date of birth of the survivor or the date of death if the other testator has already died. After proof on the death of the first testator, it will be recorded in the index of grant applications maintained by the Senior District Judge in accordance with Rule 57; the index will be checked on any application in respect of the other testator's estate. This index is now maintained on the 'Probateman' computer system. After probate is granted of the first testator's estate the will remains in force for the survivor unless it is revoked by a later will. A joint will may be revoked by either testator but if revoked by one during the lifetime of the other the testator revoking should inform the other testator accordingly. In the event that a codicil is made by one of the testators, that codicil will be admitted to proof only on the death of that testator.

Any evidence required to validate a joint will on the death of the first testator should where possible be sufficient to establish due execution by the second testator to enable proof of the will to be obtained on the second testator's death.

Two or more wills

Will contained in two or more documents

2.63   Where there are in existence at the date of his death two or more validly executed wills of a testator, it is possible that more than one will may be proved.

If two or more wills have been validly executed by a testator and the dispositions in the wills are consistent with each other and in effect would constitute one will, they may be admitted to proof as together constituting the last will.

Similarly, where two wills exist and the later will is only partly inconsistent with the earlier, the earlier instrument is only revoked as to those parts which are inconsistent and both of the documents may be admitted for probate as together constituting the will and not as a will and codicil. Consideration must be given, based on the terminology of the later document, as to whether that document was intended to be a codicil although not expressed as such.

Possible revocation

2.64   Where there are two wills which are apparently inconsistent although neither of them contains a revocatory clause, and it is not possible to determine which will was the last to be executed, the court will endeavour to construe the wills so that together they express the entire testamentary wishes of the testator, and both wills will be entitled to proof.

On the other hand, where a testator had executed on the same day two wills which were not consistent, both containing statements revoking all previous wills, and no evidence could be provided to determine the order of their execution, neither will was admitted to proof, but it was held that the revocatory clauses were effective to revoke an earlier will; see *Re Howard, Howard v Treasury Solicitor [1944] P 39.*

When a will is revoked except in so far as it exercises a power of appointment and there is another valid will which is to be proved by the persons entitled to administer the estate of the testator, the portion of the revoked will which relates to the power of appointment may be proved by the appointees (or by one with the consent of the others) and the grant is limited to the property governed by the power.

Intention to have separate effect

2.65   Where there is a clear intention that two or more wills should take effect separately, as in a case where a testator has made one will dealing only with his estate in England and Wales, and one (or more) dealing only with his estate in other countries, only the will dealing with English estate will be proved. Where necessary, a court or notarially certified copy of the will (or wills) relating to property in other countries should be filed with the application to establish that the will to be proved is not affected by another will. The District Judge or Registrar may accept a plain copy of the will where the testamentary effect is clear.

Where the will relating to estate outside England and Wales (or the United Kingdom, as the case may be) is in a foreign language, an authentic translation should be lodged. Subject to the discretion of the District Judge or Registrar, an 'informal' translation, i.e. a translation not verified by the translator on affidavit, may be accepted. This is, of course, subject to the proviso that the will(s) dealing with estate outside England and Wales, if executed after that dealing with the English estate, do not contain a clause revoking *all* other wills and testamentary documents. Where an English will confirms the effect of a 'foreign will', the foreign will may be admitted by incorporation. Where a foreign will confirms an earlier English will, both should be admitted to proof.

It has been held that a will in English form dealing with estate in England and Wales and containing a revocation clause does not revoke an earlier will made in a foreign country (and valid there) dealing only with estate there. Both wills were admitted to proof; see *Re Wayland [1951] 2 All ER 1041*.

Practice

2.66   Where there may be doubt as to whether one or more testamentary documents should be submitted for proof, the directions of a District Judge or Registrar should be sought. As a general rule the Probate Registries will admit a will to proof rather than reject it, or admit all testamentary documents to proof so that all the relevant documents would be available to the Chancery Division if a question of construction were to arise.

Where two or more wills are proved together so as to constitute in their entirety the last will of a testator, they should be marked 'A' and 'B' (or as appropriate) and described in the oath to lead the grant as 'the true and original last will and testament, as contained in the paper writings marked "A" and "B"'.

Duplicate will

2.67   If a will has been executed in duplicate, only one part will be proved. Even so, if a will lodged in an application for probate contains a statement referring to execution in duplicate, the other part of the will must be produced, so that the two can be collated.

If the duplicate will cannot be produced, affidavit evidence will be required to explain its whereabouts, since, if one part of the will made in duplicate is destroyed by the testator, the will is revoked and therefore the other part cannot be proved. Even if there is no direct evidence of revocation by destruction by the testator, there is a presumption that any will which was in his possession, but cannot be found after his death, has been revoked. This presumption may only be rebutted by affidavit evidence to show that the will, or any part of it, was not revoked.

Codicils

Reference in rules

2.68   The rules which apply to wills apply also to codicils. A codicil must be executed in the same manner as a will. The term 'will' in all statutes and rules includes codicils.

When proved

2.69   Usually a codicil is proved with the will to which it refers. Where, however, there is a dispute as to a codicil and it is necessary for the estate to be administered without delay, the will alone may be proved provided the codicil does not alter the appointment of the executor(s) named in the will. The executor(s) to whom the grant is made in these circumstances is/are precluded from distributing the estate affected by the codicil until the dispute over the codicil is resolved. It may be preferable in these circumstances to apply for a grant *ad colligenda bona* limited to the administration of that part of the estate which requires urgent administration. See paragraph 5.34 *et seq.* below.

Where a codicil is discovered after a grant of probate has issued in respect of the will to which it referred, application may be made for probate of the codicil alone, provided it does not revoke or alter the appointment of the executor(s) in the will. Where a codicil is discovered after a grant of letters of administration (with will annexed) has been issued, that grant will have to be revoked and a fresh grant of letters of administration (with will and codicil annexed) applied for.

Application for probate of a codicil alone should be made to the same Registry which proved the will.

Re-publication of will

2.70   Unless a contrary intention is apparent, a properly executed codicil confirming a will is deemed to re-publish that will. Thus a codicil re-dates the will to the date of the codicil. Any document referred to in a will in the future tense which is dispositive may be incorporated if made before a codicil is executed confirming the will (see also paragraph 2.44 above).

Will validated by codicil

2.71   If a will has been improperly executed it is validated by a properly executed codicil which refers to it and confirms it. Provided the will is sufficiently identified in the codicil, it is incorporated by reference.

Revocation of codicil by further codicil

2.72   Where a codicil which revokes or amends the terms of the will to which it refers is subsequently revoked by another codicil, such revocation does not revive those parts of the will which were revoked or amended, unless the further revoking codicil specifically revives them. The revoked codicil should be submitted for proof with the other testamentary documents. If it has been destroyed, it may be admitted to proof as contained in a copy or reconstruction. The Registry will notate the will and codicil as to (partial) revocation and that the codicil is only a copy. If the earlier revoked codicil is destroyed and no copy exists and no reconstruction can be made, the Registry will also notate the will and codicil, that no copy exists.

Revival of earlier will

2.73   Where a codicil refers to a will executed earlier than the will now sought to be proved, there must be a clearly expressed intention to revive that earlier will. If the codicil does not itself express the intention then clear evidence of the intention to revive must be obtained before the earlier will and codicil may be accepted to proof. If the intention to revive is made out the earlier will and codicil will be proved, the codicil re-dating and re-publishing that will. If the earlier will contains a revocation clause then the later will is revoked by virtue of the codicil re-publishing and re-dating the earlier will.

Misrecital of date of will

2.74   Where a codicil misrecites the date of the will or of an earlier codicil to which it refers or is described as a second or later codicil when it is in fact the first or an earlier codicil, affidavit evidence by the person who drafted the relevant codicil or some other person who can explain the discrepancy must be filed with the application. If the misrecited date is the date of a former will, then the evidence must show that there was no intention to revive that will (see above). In the event of a doubt arising as to what constitutes the testamentary documents to be proved the matter should be referred to a District Judge or Registrar for directions.

Where the error is simply a clerical error the evidence may, with the leave of the District Judge or Registrar, be included in the oath to prove the will and codicil.

Revocation of a will

2.75   Sections 18 and 20 of the Wills Act 1837 provide three ways in which a will may be revoked:

(a)   *By another will*

By another will or codicil, or by any writing, provided that document expressly states that all previous testamentary documents are revoked, and is executed in the same way that a testamentary document must be executed. It is insufficient for the purposes of revocation of an earlier will for a later will to state that 'This is the last will and testament of ......' unless the later will expressly revokes the earlier will. Consideration must be given to a later testamentary document, which although not expressly revoking an earlier one, effectively revokes it by disposing of all the estate. If the two documents are inconsistent the latter revokes the earlier, but if the documents when read together appear to form the testator's wishes both may be proved either fully or in part; where there is doubt the directions of a District Judge or Registrar should be sought.

(b)   *By destruction*

By the testator, or some other person on the direction of the testator and in the testator's presence, burning, tearing or otherwise destroying the will.

(i)   Partial destruction

Where the will has only been partially destroyed it will be considered to have been revoked if evidence can be produced to the District Judge or Registrar that it was the testator's intention wholly to revoke the will. It was held in *Re Adams [1990] Ch 601* that the complete obliteration of his signature by the testator so that it could not be read was sufficient evidence of an intention to revoke. Where it appears that there has been or may have been an attempt at destruction, the District Judge or Registrar will require to be satisfied on the evidence as to the testator's intentions when it is sought to prove the will or to have it marked 'Probate refused'.

The mere tearing of a will may not be sufficient to show an intent to revoke. Consideration must be given to the degree of tearing which might be accounted for by other factors, for example the age of the will and where it has been kept. Where parts of the will have been removed, obliterated or erased, the question of partial revocation arises. Where partial revocation can, on evidence, be substantiated, the remainder of the will may be admitted to proof.

(ii) Presumption of revocation

There is a general assumption that a will which was known to exist and be in the testator's custody, but which cannot be found after the testator's death, has been revoked. It is for those seeking to prove the will to rebut this presumption.

(iii) Privileged will

A privileged will (see paragraph 2.49 above) may be revoked without the usual formalities required in the revoking of a non-privileged will, that is an oral will may be revoked by an oral statement provided there is evidence to this effect.

(iv) Dependent relative revocation

The doctrine of 'dependent relative revocation' (see s 20 of the Act) may allow a will to proof notwithstanding there is *prima facie* a valid revocation. Where a valid revocation was conditional upon the happening of an event or some circumstance which does not in fact occur, the revocation may be ineffective. To establish a will invoking this doctrine requires evidence, sufficient to satisfy the court, that the intended revocation was contingent upon an event or a mistaken belief of the testator. A testator had in two previous wills devised his house but that gift in his third will was inoperative as the intended beneficiary was a witness. It was held that there was an intention in the previous wills not revoked by the revocation clause in the third will; see *Re Finnemore [1992] 1 All ER 800*. This doctrine may be applied to the reinstatement of alterations or obliterations where such were performed by the testator subject to an event which does not occur (see *Re Botting's Estate [1951] 2 All ER 997* and *Re Itter [1950] P 130, [1950] 1 All ER 68* and s 19 of the Act).

(c) *By marriage*

— under s 18 of the Act, where the will was executed before 1 January 1983, by the testator marrying after he had made his will, except:

● where the will was made in contemplation of his marriage to a particular person and that marriage has in fact taken place; or

● where the will was made in exercise of a power of appointment, when the estate so appointed would not in default of appointment pass to the testator's heir, executor or administrator, or to the persons entitled to the estate if the deceased had died intestate;

—   where the will was executed on or after 1 January 1983, s 18 of the Act is amended so as to provide that a will is revoked on the testator's marriage, save where it appears from the will that at the time of execution the testator expected to be married to a particular person and it was his intention that the will should not be revoked by the marriage. Similarly, where it appears from the will that at the time it was executed the testator expected to be married to a particular person and that any disposition in the will should not be revoked by the marriage to that person, such disposition shall take effect notwithstanding the marriage, and any other dispositions in the will will remain effective unless it would appear the testator intended otherwise.

Section 18, as amended, also provides for a disposition in a will in the exercise of a power of appointment to be effective notwithstanding the testator's subsequent marriage, unless the property so appointed would, in default of appointment, pass to his personal representatives.

Generally, a will must contain a specific clause or direction that the will should survive the intended marriage so as to avoid any doubt arising. However, phrases such as 'to my fiancée' or 'to my future wife' followed by gifts have been held to be sufficient to establish an intention of marriage which the will was to survive.

Where it is sought to prove a will made before the testator's marriage and either of the exceptions in paragraph (c) applies, it will be necessary to recite in the oath to lead the grant details of the circumstances of the particular exception, for example by reciting 'that the marriage of the deceased and the said ..... took place on the .... day of ...... 19...'

Effect on a will of decree of dissolution or annulment

2.76   Section 18(2) of the Administration of Justice Act 1982 added s 18A to the Wills Act 1837. Section 18A, which applied to deaths on or after 1 January 1983, provided that where, after the testator has made his will, a civil court in England and Wales granted a decree dissolving or annulling his marriage, or declared it void; or the marriage was dissolved or annulled by a decree or order of a foreign court and the divorce or annulment was entitled to recognition in England and Wales by virtue of Part II of the Family Law Act 1986:

(a)   his will took effect as if the appointment of the former spouse as executor or executor and trustee of the will was omitted; and

(b)   any devise or bequest to the former spouse lapsed unless it appeared from the will that the testator had a contrary intention.

Although any bequest or devise lapsed, the surviving former spouse's entitlement to apply for relief under the Inheritance (Provision for Family and Dependants) Act 1975 was not affected. Section 18A also provided that where by the terms of a will an interest in remainder was subject to a life interest and that life interest lapsed by virtue of paragraph (b) above, such interest in remainder was to be treated as if it had not been subject to the life interest and, if it was contingent upon the termination of the life interest, as if it had not been so contingent.

It was held that the consequences of the lapse of a bequest or devise equated with those of a former spouse predeceasing the testator (see *Re Cherrington [1984] 2 All ER 285, [1984] 1 WLR 772*). However, the decision in *Re Cherrington* was further considered in the case of *Re Sinclair [1985] Ch 446, [1985] 1 All ER 1066, [1985] 2 WLR 795*, and it was held that the word 'lapse' should be given its ordinary meaning of 'failure', and that divorce should not be equated with death.

Section 18A was amended by s 3(1) of the Law Reform (Succession) Act 1995 in respect of deaths occurring on or after 1 January 1996. New paras (a) and (b) were substituted as follows:

'(a) provisions of the will appointing executors or trustees or conferring a power of appointment, if they appoint or confer the power on the former spouse, shall take effect as if the former spouse had died on the date on which the marriage is dissolved or annulled, and

(b) any property which, or an interest in which, is devised or bequeathed to the former spouse shall pass as if the former spouse had died on that date'.

It is the date of death from which the amendment has effect; the date of the will is immaterial.

The effect of *Re Sinclair* referred to above is nullified by the new s 18A. Provided that the will makes contingent dispositions to have effect on the spouse's death, then these dispositions will operate. The same provision for the effectiveness of the decree, made by a court in England and Wales or recognisable under Part II of the Family Law Act 1986, remains.

If the will contains no substitutional disposition in the event of the spouse predeceasing, then a (partial) intestacy will arise as to the distribution of the undisposed of estate.

Scottish wills

2.77 A will made in 'Scottish form' is acceptable to proof without supporting evidence provided it meets the following three requirements:

(a)   it must be subscribed by the granter (the testator), on the last page if it consists of one sheet of paper, or on each of the sheets or separate pages if it consists of more than one sheet;

(b)   it must be attested by two witnesses subscribing at the end of the deed;

(c)   the occupations and addresses of the witnesses must be specified, either in the body of the deed, in the testing (i.e. attestation) clause, or after their signatures. The occupations and addresses may be added at any time, even after the death, before the will is recorded in any register or founded on in any court, and they need not be written by the witnesses themselves.

It is not essential that the date or place of signing be specified. If all the particulars required in (c) above are added after the signature the testing clause is unnecessary.

The Requirements of Writing (Scotland) Act 1995 vary the above provisions so that in respect of wills made in Scotland on or after 1 August 1995 there need only be one witness. The other criteria remain the same. Where, however, a will – whether holograph or otherwise – is subscribed by the testator but not witnessed, it may still be accepted as valid if there is evidence to prove that the will was subscribed by the testator. This is done, on application for confirmation, by lodging affidavit evidence by someone familiar with the testator's signature.

Any will made in the manner prescribed above (depending on the form applicable at its date of execution) may be accepted as valid where the deceased died domiciled in England and Wales, the will being valid by virtue of the other criteria in s 1 of the Wills Act 1963 (see paragraph 2.4 above).

Where the deceased died domiciled in Scotland it is advisable to obtain a confirmation from the court in Scotland; such confirmation is effective to administer estate throughout the United Kingdom, whereas a grant issued in England and Wales is only effective to administer estate in England and Wales (see paragraph 4.5 below).

International wills

2.78   Sections 27 and 28 of the Administration of Justice Act 1982 provide for the form of and procedure relating to international wills. It should be noted that these sections have not, as yet, been brought into force. When in force they will allow to proof any will notwithstanding it does not comply with the Wills Act 1963 provided it complies with Sch 2 to the 1982 Act and the rules relating thereto.

Article 1 of Sch 2 to the Act of 1982 provides that a will shall be valid as to form, irrespective of the place of execution, the location of the assets disposed of, the nationality, domicile or residence of the testator if it complies with the following requirements:

(a)   the will must be in writing, but not necessarily written by the testator himself, and may be written in any language, by hand or by any other means;

(b)   the testator must have declared in the presence of two witnesses and a person authorised to act in connection with international wills (that is a notary public, a solicitor or a person authorised under s 6(1) of the Commissioners for Oaths Act 1889 to do notarial acts in a foreign country or place and authorised to act there in connection with international wills) that the document is his will and that he knows the contents thereof;

(c)   the testator must have signed the will in the presence of the witnesses and the authorised person, or if the will was previously signed, have acknowledged his signature in their presence, and the witnesses and authorised person must have attested the will by signing in the presence of the testator. Where, however, the testator was unable to sign the will, it will be valid if the reason therefor was indicated to the authorised person who noted the fact on the will. The will will also be valid if the testator had authorised another person to sign on his behalf in accordance with the law under which the authorised person was designated (Arts 3 to 5).

An international will cannot be valid if it disposes of the estate of two persons contained in one document (Art 2).

Articles 6 and 7 provide for the signatures to be made at the end of the will and, if the will consists of several sheets, each sheet must be numbered and signed at the foot. The authorised person must date the will and the date thereof must be the date that person appends his signature thereto.

Article 9 provides for the authorised person to complete a certificate in the form of, or in substantially the same form as, the certificate prescribed by Art 10 (see Form A1.82, page 449 for the form of certificate).

An international will may be deposited for safe-keeping in the Principal Registry of the Family Division (see CHAPTER 20 for the procedure for the deposit of wills of living persons).

Chapter 3

Proof of death and presumption of death

Proof of death

Statement on oath

3.1   Every oath to lead a grant of representation contains a statement that the deceased died on a certain date. In the absence of any special circumstance relating to the death, this statement is accepted (in applications other than personal applications) as proof of death without the necessity of producing a death certificate. The date of death (and the date of birth) as they appear in the death certificate must be recited in the oath (Practice Direction 12 January 1999). This applies only to UK registered deaths. There is no requirement to state the place of death.

Solicitor or probate practitioner applications

3.2   Where a solicitor or probate practitioner is instructed, it is his duty to satisfy himself as to the deceased's death and the date thereof before applying for a grant. In the light of the Practice Direction referred to above, a copy death certificate should be obtained from the client.

Personal applications

3.3   Where application is made as a personal application under Rule 5 the personal applicant must lodge with the application the death certificate supplied by the Register Office or a copy of it.

Uncertainty as to date

3.4   Where the exact date of death is unknown (for example where the deceased's body was not found until some time after the death and the precise date cannot be determined), the oath should contain a statement that the deceased 'was last seen alive on the ..... day of .... 20..' or 'was last known to be alive on the ..... day of .... 20 ..' 'and that his dead body was found on the ..... day of .... 20..'. It is commonplace for death certificates, where the date cannot be precisely given, to state 'died on or about ...'. This is, at present, not a form acceptable to the Probate Registries as the 'Probateman' computer system fails to recognise the statement. The information contained in the death certificate must be recited because of the Practice Direction referred to above leaving the Registries to input the date under the 'last seen/last known ....' reference. It may be necessary to obtain a more accurate date if the disposition of the estate is affected, for example where the dates given span the date to which the spouse must survive to attain a beneficial interest under an intestacy: 28 days from the date of death (see s 1 of the Law Reform (Succession) Act 1995), or the date an increase in inheritance tax was effected.

The date of death recorded in the grant of representation is not sufficient evidence of proof of death for purposes other than the application for that grant.

Death of member of armed forces

3.5   Where a member of the armed forces dies, a notification of that death, or of the presumption of that death, is issued to the next of kin by the Ministry of Defence. Where the notification specifies an exact date of death the recital of the date in the oath to lead the grant is acceptable without further evidence. However, where the notification does not specify an exact date but states the deceased was 'missing presumed dead' or 'died or was killed on or since ......', the notification, in the form issued by the Ministry, must be lodged with the papers to lead the grant.

Death of a merchant seaman

3.6   Evidence of death is provided by the Registrar General of Shipping and Seamen, and death certificates are issued in the following instances:

(a)   known deaths or losses in UK ships;

(b)   known deaths or losses of citizens of the UK and Colonies in other ships which call at UK ports;

(c)   known deaths abroad of seamen employed in UK ships.

In respect of deaths which occurred before 1 January 1980, Regulations 3 or 4 and 5 of the Merchant Shipping (Returns of Births and Deaths) Regulations 1972 applied and a certificate in Form RBD6 was issued. In respect of deaths occurring on or after 1 January 1980, Regulations 3 or 4 and 5 of the Merchant Shipping (Returns of Births and Deaths) Regulations 1979 apply and in those cases a certificate in Form RBD6 or RBD6a is issued.

3.6 Proof of death and presumption of death

Any of these certificates will be accepted as proof of death. All such details are recorded in the Marine Register of Deaths at the General Register Office in London, Edinburgh or Belfast as appropriate.

In cases of presumed death the Registrar General of Shipping and Seamen will issue on request a certified extract from the list of crew on Form RBD7 for merchant ships and Form RBD8 for fishing vessels. This is a certificate that the person named was recorded on the copy of the List of Crew required to be maintained ashore by Regulation 16 of the Merchant Shipping (Crew Agreements, Lists of Crew and Discharge of Seamen) Regulations 1972 and by Regulation 15 of the Merchant Shipping (Crew Agreements, Lists of Crew and Discharge of Seamen) (Fishing Vessels) Regulations 1972 and required to be delivered into official custody by Regulations 17 and 16 respectively of these Regulations.

In respect of deaths *presumed* to have occurred before 1 January 1980, Forms RBD7 and RBD8 also contained a certificate that the Registrar General of Shipping and Seamen had no information that the person named survived the loss. This certificate was only given after information had been obtained from the owners and, if appropriate, from the Consul or other official at or near the place where the ship was reported lost. If a body had been landed ashore and a post-mortem examination made by the authorities in a foreign country, the certificate was endorsed as to that fact on the reverse in red ink, and imprinted with the office stamp of the General Register Office of Shipping and Seamen.

Only certificates so endorsed were accepted as proof of death. If they were not so endorsed they were referred to the Registrar General of Shipping and Seamen for confirmation by the Registry. If confirmed, they were accepted as proof of death.

In certain other cases where there may be a supposition of death, although it may not be possible to issue one of the certificates described above, an inquiry into death can sometimes be held under s 61 of the Merchant Shipping Act 1970 as amended. Copies of the report of such an inquiry may be obtained by the next of kin from the Registry of Shipping and Seamen. If such a copy report is presented when the District Judge or Registrar is asked whether death has been sufficiently established or whether an order for leave to swear death is necessary, the District Judge or Registrar will consider whether the Registrar General of Shipping and Seamen should be asked if he has any further information. However, in some cases the Registrar General may have no information other than that contained in the Report. The Registrar will, on request, give directions as to an application for leave to swear death.

In respect of deaths *presumed* to have occurred on or after 1 January 1980, certified extracts from the Crew Lists will rarely be requested. If there was sufficient evidence available to enable a coroner or statutory inquiry to conclude that death had occurred upon the loss of a ship, then death will be registered and will be included in the class of case mentioned in (a)–(c) above. A certified extract on Form RBD7 or Form RBD8 in respect of a death on or after 1 January 1980 will, therefore, be no more than evidence that the person named was on board the ship at the time of its loss. It will not itself be evidence that death occurred as a result of the loss of the ship. Application will have to be made for leave to swear death (see paragraph 5.2 below).

Death on an offshore installation

3.7   When a person dies or is lost in circumstances such that it is reasonable to believe that person has died on or from an offshore installation, on a lifeboat or life-raft belonging to such an installation, or in the neighbourhood of such an installation, while engaged in any operation connected therewith, and there is no requirement to register the death under the Merchant Shipping Acts, such death or loss must be notified to the Registrar General of Shipping and Seamen. Such notification is registered by the appropriate Registrar of Births and Deaths, according to the ordinary residence of the deceased, in the Marine Register. A certified copy of entry may be obtained on request and such certificate is accepted as proof of death.

Other acceptable certificates of death

3.8   Certain Government Departments other than the Ministry of Defence issue certificates of death. The Secretary of State for Trade and Industry may issue such a certificate pursuant to the Civil Aviation Act 1949. Certificates of presumed death issued by the Commonwealth Relations Office (or the Colonial Office) are acceptable.

Presumption of death

Certificate of presumption of death

3.9   Where a person dies, or there are such circumstances for it to be presumed that a person has died, it may be possible to obtain a certificate of presumption of death if the person was in the employ of certain Government Departments. Any certificate of presumed death other than those usually issued may be accepted at the discretion of the Senior District Judge of the Family Division. Where there is doubt as to the acceptability of a certificate of death or presumption of death, it should be referred to the Senior District Judge of the Family Division at First Avenue House, High Holborn, for a decision.

A decree of presumption of death and dissolution of marriage granted under s 19 of the Matrimonial Causes Act 1973 is effective only in matrimonial proceedings and is unacceptable as proof of death for the purpose of issuing a grant of representation. Where such a decree has been pronounced, it – and the evidence leading to its being made – may be used in the evidence seeking an order for leave to swear death.

A certificate of death or presumed death issued from the register maintained under the Civil Aviation Act is acceptable as proof of death for the purpose of issuing a grant of representation.

Leave to swear death

3.10   In the absence of any certificate or where there is doubt whether the certificate is sufficient; or where there is no direct evidence of death but there is circumstantial evidence leading to a presumption of death, for example where the alleged deceased was known to have been on board a ship or aircraft which has disappeared or there is a presumption that the ship or aircraft has been lost; or the alleged deceased has not been heard of for a period of several years, application may be made for leave to swear death. See paragraph 5.2 below.

Where death is presumed, uncertainty as to entitlement to benefit may also arise. A beneficiary under a will or person entitled under an intestacy may also have died and there may be doubt as to who survived whom. Where such doubt arises application may be made under s 116 of the Supreme Court Act 1981 (see paragraph 5.27 below) or the practice in *commorientes* cases may apply (see paragraphs 3.12 and 3.14 below). Where the evidence is sufficient, an order will be made giving leave to swear death. The order entitles the applicant to apply for a grant of representation to administer the presumed deceased's estate. The order is not, and will not be accepted as, conclusive proof of the death. Where, for any legal purpose, it is necessary to obtain an order of conclusive presumption of death, application must be made by originating summons to the Chancery Division. Where a point of law or principle of evidence arises, the District Judge or Registrar may refer the matter to a Judge of the Family Division on summons.

Where the presumed deceased was domiciled outside England and Wales, any orders or declarations made by the court of the place of domicile should be obtained and lodged with the affidavit. An order made by such a court presuming death is insufficiently conclusive in itself and application must still be made for an order under Rule 53. Where possible, details, or, preferably, copies, of the evidence used before the foreign court should be obtained and exhibited to the affidavit. If, however, the foreign court has declared the presumed deceased dead, and a certificate of death has been issued, then evidence on affidavit as to the conclusive-

ness and acceptability of such an order under the law of the place of domicile, together with the certificate, may be accepted and obviate the need
to apply for an order under Rule 53. The order and any evidence available should be referred to the District Judge or Registrar for his
directions.

Where a grant issues following an order for leave to swear death and it is
subsequently discovered that the presumed deceased is still alive, application must be made to the Registry which made the order and issued the
grant for revocation of the order and grant (see CHAPTER 18).

Deaths in disasters

3.11   Where a person dies in any disaster (such as an aircraft crash) in
which there occurred two or more deaths, the Principal Registry records
details of the evidence which was accepted for an order for leave to swear
death in the first application made. Where an application for leave to
swear death is to be made in respect of a person presumed to have died
in such a disaster, application should be made to the Secretary of the
Principal Registry for a search to be made for any previous application.
If a previous application has been made, details of the evidence found
acceptable on that occasion will be supplied.

Where there were multiple deaths in a disaster such as the aircraft crash
at Lockerbie, the Principal Registry obtains evidence of the deaths and
passenger lists, and if satisfied, the Senior District Judge issues a circular listing the names of those who died and stating that it is inconclusive
as to who survived whom. When such a circular issues no further proof
of death is necessary, nor is there any need to apply for leave to swear
death; nor, where relevant, will evidence relating to *commorientes* (see
below) be required in respect of any person whose name appears in the
circular.

Commorientes

Evidence of survival

3.12   Section 184 of the Law of Property Act 1925 provides that where
two persons have died in circumstances rendering it uncertain which of
them survived the other, for all purposes affecting the title to property,
the younger shall be deemed to have survived the elder. The section
applies only where there is doubt as to survivorship. If medical evidence
is available which states that one person survived the other, albeit for only
a few minutes, the section does not apply. The deaths need not have been
the result of a common disaster; see *Hickman v Peacey [1945] 2 All ER
215.*

3.13   *Proof of death and presumption of death*

Husband and wife

3.13   Notwithstanding this section, in respect of deaths occurring after 1 January 1953 but before 1 January 1996, if the two persons were husband and wife and either or both died intestate, the normal provisions for the distribution of estate and entitlement to the grant in the event of intestacy, as provided by s 46 of the Administration of Estates Act 1925 (as amended) shall apply, irrespective of which spouse would, by the usual presumption, have survived the other (see paragraph 3.15 below).

Effect of will

3.14   The presumption, provided by s 184 (see paragraph 3.12 above), of the younger surviving the elder may also be overridden by the terms of the will of either of the deceased. A clause inserted in a will making provision for the disposition of the estate in the event of a husband and wife dying simultaneously will generally be effective, as where the will is worded 'provided that ...... survives me for a period of twenty-eight days'. Where no such provision is made in the will which effectively disposes of the whole estate the normal distribution is in accordance therewith, the presumption provided by s 184 applying to the testator. If there is a partial intestacy the estate undisposed of by the will is distributed in accordance with s 46. The general effect in cases of *commorientes* spouses where either died intestate *was* for the estate to pass as though neither survived the other: they died as widow and widower.

Law Reform (Succession) Act 1995

3.15   By s 1 of the Act a spouse must survive the other by 28 days before acquiring a beneficial interest. The Act came into force on 1 January 1996. It follows therefore that in respect of deaths on or after that date of intestate spouses where there is doubt as to survivorship (unless there is the remote possibility of survival by 28 days), each estate passes as though the other had predeceased. The oath to lead the grant should recite that there is no evidence of survivorship (*commorientes*) or that the survivor survived and died on ...... (survivorship less than 28 days).

Evidence required

3.16   Where there is doubt over survivorship, it is usual for the evidence of the circumstances of death to be deposed to in an affidavit, supported by medical evidence either in separate affidavit form or by statement exhibited thereto, to be lodged prior to the papers to lead the grant for the District Judge's or Registrar's directions. The result of any coroner's enquiry and evidence lodged in that court should also be exhibited, but it is unnecessary to wait until a coroner has made a decision before application may be made to a Probate Registry. Details of the distribution of the estate dependent upon these directions should also be set out.

The fact that the application is made under s 184 must be included in the oath to lead the grant and details of the survivorship or otherwise by virtue of seniority must be recited. If there is any doubt as to survivorship, the matter should be referred for directions to a District Judge or Registrar, who may, where there is a dispute or uncertainty, refer the matter to a Judge on summons.

Section 184 does not apply to cases of uncertainty about survivorship of persons dying domiciled outside England and Wales. Where the deceased persons were domiciled outside England and Wales, evidence of the law of survivorship of the place of domicile may be necessary. This evidence, to establish beneficial entitlement in support of an application for an order under Rule 30(1)(b), will not be necessary when the court of the place of domicile has entrusted someone with the administration of the estate, the person so entrusted being entitled to take a grant under Rule 30(1)(a), it being clear the foreign court was satisfied on the point of survivorship before granting representation. See also CHAPTER 14.

Chapter 4

Necessity for grant

Right to administer an estate

Rules 20 and 22

4.1   The right to administer (that is to recover and receive the assets, realise property, pay debts and encumbrances and distribute the residue) a deceased's estate is conferred by a grant of representation issued by the court:

(a)   where the deceased died testate, to the person(s) entitled in priority in accordance with Rule 20 (see paragraph 8.2 below where the order of priority is set out). A grant of probate will issue only to an executor. A grant made to those other classes referred to in the rule, or to the attorney of an executor, will be of letters of administration (with will annexed); or

(b)   where the deceased died intestate, to the persons having a beneficial interest in the estate in priority in accordance with Rule 22 (see paragraph 9.28 below where the order of priority is set out). The grant will be of letters of administration.

Nil estate grant

4.2   A grant may be required although there is no estate to be administered – a 'nil estate' grant, to constitute a personal representative so that legal proceedings can be taken or defended or to establish title or to perfect title to property held by the deceased as a trustee and not beneficially, or to deal with property held outside the United Kingdom. The person entitled to apply for such a grant is the same person as in the order of priority referred to above.

Second grants

4.3   A second or subsequent grant to the first grant may be necessary when the first grant ceases to be operative, for example where the grantee dies, and there remains unadministered estate. The orders of priority set out in Rules 20 and 22 mentioned above apply to second or subsequent grants. See paragraphs 10.8–10.21 below.

Preferences: Rules 27(5) and 35(1)

4.4   Rule 27(5) provides that unless otherwise directed by a District Judge or Registrar a grant of letters of administration (with or without will annexed) shall be made:

(a)   to a person of full age entitled thereto in preference to the guardian of a minor; and

(b)   to a living person in preference to the personal representative of a deceased person who, if living, would be entitled in the same degree in the order of priority prescribed by Rule 20 or 22.

This means, for example, that where two persons are equally entitled to apply but one of them is a minor, the person of full age will be preferred; a living child of full age takes preference over the personal representatives of a child of full age who survived the deceased but has since died.

Rule 35(1) provides that a capable person entitled to a grant shall be preferred to any person(s) entitled, under the provisions of Rule 35(2) or (4) (see paragraph 10.60 below), to apply for the use and benefit of a mentally incapable person. The preference in the Rule requires those equally entitled to be 'cleared off' by renunciation or citation before the remainder of the Rule operates.

Section 116 of the Supreme Court Act 1981 empowers the court, in circumstances where the court considers it appropriate, to make an order passing over persons entitled in priority under Rules 20 and 22 mentioned above and to give a grant to a person of lower, or indeed of no, entitlement (see paragraph 5.27 below).

Administration of Estates Act 1971

Grant effective to administer estate elsewhere in the United Kingdom

4.5   It is usually necessary to produce a grant to recover and/or receive any part of the deceased's estate.

Sections 2 and 3 of the Act provide that a grant of representation issued by a court in England and Wales either before or after the Act came into force (1 January 1972) is recognised and may be used to administer estate in Scotland and Northern Ireland, provided the deceased died domiciled in England and Wales.

Section 1 of the Act provides that confirmations and certificates of confirmation issued by a court in Scotland in respect of all or a part of the deceased's estate, or grants of representation issued by a court in Northern Ireland, are recognised and may be used to administer estate in England

and Wales provided the deceased died domiciled in the country from which the confirmation, certificate or grant was issued.

By section 4 of the Act the confirmation, certificate of confirmation or grant will be effective to administer estate throughout the United Kingdom provided it contains a statement that the deceased died domiciled in the country from which it issued.

Grant in England and Wales: domicile in Scotland or Northern Ireland

4.6   Where application for a grant is made to a Probate Registry in England and Wales in respect of the estate of a person who died domiciled in Scotland or Northern Ireland, the grant which issues will be limited until representation is granted by the court of the place of domicile and will entitle the grantee to administer only the estate in England and Wales. This is to avoid duplication of representation to the estate. A limitation will similarly apply to grants or confirmations issued in Scotland or Northern Ireland to the estates of persons dying domiciled in England and Wales.

It follows therefore that where the deceased had assets in more than one part of the United Kingdom it is administratively more convenient for representation to be obtained from the court of the place of domicile, one document being sufficient to administer all the deceased's estate wherever situate.

Confirmation in Scotland: trust property in England and Wales or Northern Ireland

4.7   Section 5 of the Act enables the Scottish courts when granting a confirmation to include in the confirmation reference to property held in trust by the deceased in England and Wales or Northern Ireland. A confirmation containing such reference will be accepted as sufficient to deal with the trust property.

Payment of assets without probate or letters of administration

Nominated assets

4.8   The rules of many Industrial and Provident Societies allow the depositor to nominate a person to whom funds held in his name may be paid on the depositor's death without the production of a grant of representation. Similarly, many company pension schemes provide for lump sum payments and pensions due on death to be paid to a nominee without requiring a grant to be produced.

Various statutory rules and regulations in respect of the individual schemes fixed a limit for payments without a grant of £500 in respect of deaths occurring on or after 5 September 1965. This limit was increased by amending rules and regulations to £1,500 in respect of deaths occurring or nominations effected on or after 10 August 1975; and further increased to £5,000 in respect of deaths occurring or nominations effected on or after 11 May 1984.

Small estates

4.9   Where the estate left by the deceased is small, it is sometimes possible for the assets comprising the estate to be obtained without making application for a grant of probate or letters of administration.

Statutory provisions

4.10   The Administration of Estates (Small Payments) Act 1965 provides a limit to the various public and local statutes which allow for payment without obtaining representation. It applies to assets held by various bodies such as the National Savings Bank (including premium bonds), Trustee Savings Banks, and assets comprising Government stock, but only if the amount held does not exceed £5,000 (£100 where the death was prior to 5 September 1965; £500 where the death was prior to 10 August 1975; £1,500 where the death was prior to 11 May 1984). The limit has not been increased since 11 May 1984.

None of these asset holders, or any other asset holders, are bound to pay any amount up to these limits without seeing a grant of probate or letters of administration. The provisions of the Act are permissive, not mandatory. If there is any complication it is likely that they will require production of a grant, and they are entitled to do so in any case if they see fit. Instances of such complications are where there is doubt about the validity of a will; where there are numerous persons sharing in the estate; where any beneficiary is under age or mentally incapable; or where there is doubt as to the competency of the person seeking to recover the asset to dispose properly of the estate, or, as is more frequently the case, his title to make the claim.

These provisions do not apply to moneys held by banks, building societies or insurance companies, but if there are no other assets and the matter is entirely straightforward, that is, there is no dispute about the entitlement to receive the benefit, such bodies will sometimes, in their discretion, pay over very small amounts without insisting on the obtaining of a grant. The figures provided by the statute are often quoted as guidelines.

Grants for other purposes

4.11   If a grant is necessary for other purposes, such as the transfer of real property or in connection with legal proceedings, it should of course be obtained. A grant is always required to deal with stocks or shares, however small the holding.

Discretionary payments

4.12 Although the Acts prescribe financial limits, there appears to be a discretion vested in some deposit-taking institutions to pay out sums in excess of those limits, where they are satisfied as to entitlement. Similarly, if the asset holder is not satisfied on title to benefit, a grant may be required even though the estate falls within the prescribed amounts.

It should be noted that many deposit-taking institutions require an indemnity to be signed, and make a charge for preparing this or any statements/declarations required by them as a prerequisite to releasing the money held. It is not infrequent for such an administration charge to exceed the fee payable to the Probate Registry for a grant (Note: there is *no* fee payable for a grant to an estate where the net value does not exceed £5,000, and estates over £5,000 now attract a fee of only £50). It may therefore be less expensive to the estate to apply for a grant notwithstanding it is not strictly required to facilitate collection of the assets.

Public servants

4.13 Payments may also be made to the person who would appear to be entitled to the deceased's estate, without production of a grant, of salary, wages or other benefit due to a public servant employed by a Government Department, Local Government Department, members of HM forces, merchant seamen and Members of Parliament. Similarly, funds held in court for the benefit of the deceased and money payable to him under the Social Security Acts may be paid out to the person entitled without first obtaining a grant to prove entitlement. Generally, all such payments are discretionary and subject to the limitations mentioned above.

The Probate Registries are unable to give any ruling as to whether it will be possible to realise an estate without obtaining a grant; this is a matter for decision by the body holding the assets. It is for the applicant to decide whether he will try to obtain the estate without a grant. Enquiry should be made of the asset holder before application for a grant is made.

Death grant

4.14 Any grant or discretionary payment under the Social Security Act 1975 payable to the person who is or intends to be responsible for the deceased's funeral expenses or any other discretionary payments to defray funeral expenses from the Department of Work and Pensions do not form part of the estate for inheritance tax or any other purpose.

Tax liability: small payments provisions

4.15 Although payment may be made without a grant, this does not exempt the estate from the payment of inheritance tax. Usually, before payment is made, the payer will require production of a certificate from the Inland Revenue showing that there is no tax liability or that any tax due has been paid. The burden of responsibility for payment of tax in cases where no grant or representation is applied for remains with the person who takes on the position of 'personal representative'. This person would usually be the person entitled in priority to take a grant of representation if one was applied for, but may be any person (an 'executor de son tort') who intermeddles in the estate.

Joint property

4.16 Where there is property owned by the deceased and another person on a beneficial joint tenancy, such property passes to the joint tenant by survivorship; it does not devolve upon the deceased's personal representative and will not form part of the value of the estate passing under a grant. If the estate consists solely of joint property held by beneficial joint tenants a grant of representation is not usually necessary, although a grant may be required to constitute a personal representative for purposes other than dealing with the disposition of the deceased's estate.

Where the property was held as tenants in common, a grant will be necessary to administer the deceased's share in the property.

Court of Protection: funds in court

4.17 Where a person who had been mentally incapable of managing his affairs during his lifetime dies with assets being administered by the Public Guardianship Office (Protection Division) those assets may be paid to the person entitled to them by that court, provided they do not exceed £5,000. Such payment is in the discretion of the court (Court of Protection Rules 2001, Rule 74(3)). Similarly, where there is a fund in court on the death intestate of the person entitled thereto, such fund, provided again it does not exceed £5,000, may be paid to the person entitled at the discretion of the court (Civil Procedure Rules 1998 Part 36 (para 8.5 of the Practice Direction)).

Vesting of property prior to grant issuing

4.18 In the absence of any special features (for example there being no executor appointed in the will, or the executor being a minor at the date

61

of the testator's death), all the testator's estate vests on his death in the executor named in the will. Where necessary an executor may commence proceedings before obtaining probate of the will but judgment cannot be obtained in his favour until he has proved the will and been constituted personal representative.

If the deceased died intestate, or there was no executor named or properly constituted in the will, and the will did not dispose of the whole estate, his estate formerly vested in the President of the Family Division until such time as a grant issued (s 9 Administration of Estates Act 1925).

Section 14 of the Law of Property (Miscellaneous Provisions) Act 1994 substituted a new s 9 to the 1925 Act. The new section, in force from 1 July 1995, provides for the estate of a person dying intestate to vest in the Public Trustee until the grant of letters of administration. It should be noted that s 9 now applies not only to cases of intestacy (as the previous legislation did), but also to where the deceased dies testate and (i) at the time of his death there is no executor with power to obtain probate of his will, or (ii) at any time before probate of the will is granted there ceases to be an executor with power to obtain probate. In these circumstances the real and personal estate disposed of in the testator's will vests in the Public Trustee until the grant of representation issues. Section 9, as substituted, applies to estates of persons dying before and after 1 July 1995. Subsection (3) provides that any estate vested in the President before 1 July 1995 now vests in the Public Trustee.

Until the grant issues, any notice, such as a notice to quit, which would normally be served on the personal representative of the deceased, should be served on the Public Trustee, Public Trustee's Office, 81 Chancery Lane, London WC2A 1DD (see also the Practice Direction of 12 June 1995 [1995] 3 All ER 192).

Who may extract grants of representation

4.19   Section 23(1) of the Solicitors Act 1974 as presently in force (i.e. as not amended by s 54 Courts and Legal Services Act 1990) allows a solicitor, barrister or certified notary public to prepare papers to lead the extraction of grants of representation.

Rule 4 of the 1987 Rules was amended with effect from 14 September 1998 to bring the rules in line with the statute and allow barristers and notaries to act in the extraction of grants.

Rule 5, which deals with personal applications, was also amended with effect from 14 September 1998; see paragraph 13.3 below.

Chapter 5

Pre-grant applications for discretionary orders

Introduction

5.1   This chapter deals with applications for discretionary orders required before application may be made for a grant.

All applications for discretionary orders under the Non-Contentious Probate Rules 1987 are made to a District Judge of the Principal Registry or Registrar *ex parte* on affidavit. There is no difference in the courts' jurisdiction. The Civil Procedure Rules 1998 do *not* apply to proceedings governed by the 1987 Rules: the Rules of the Supreme Court 1965 as in force on 26 April 1999 continue to apply.

The application should be made at the Registry from which it is intended the grant will issue.

The affidavit is usually made by the proposed grantee(s) but may, subject to the court's discretion, be made by the solicitor or probate practitioner instructed or other person able to speak to the facts relied on in support of the application. In each case the affidavit concludes with a request for the order in the terms applied for.

Rule 61 permits the District Judge or Registrar to require any matter to be brought before the court on summons (see CHAPTER 17).

Rule 62 permits the District Judge or Registrar to transfer any application to another District Judge or Registrar. Applications for directions in the course of an application – for example, whether a will can be considered privileged, whether a document is testamentary or whether a particular person has title to a grant – are usually made by letter and referred to the District Judge or Registrar informally.

Rule 65 provides for an appeal against any decision or requirement of a District Judge or Registrar to be made by summons to a Judge of the Family Division.

Leave to swear death

No proof of death

5.2   In the absence of a certificate or other document establishing death, or where there is no direct evidence of death but there are circumstances leading to a presumption of death, application may be made for an order giving leave to swear that death has occurred on or since a particular date.

Divorce decree: presumption of death

5.3   Even if there has been a decree, made under s 19 of the Matrimonial Causes Act 1973 (presumption of death), dissolving the marriage, application must be made for leave to swear death. However, the evidence to lead the pronouncement of the decree may be prayed in aid of the application for leave to swear death.

Application and evidence

5.4   The application is made *ex parte* on affidavit, usually by the applicant for the grant. In most cases the court will require the applicant to depose to the facts, he being the only person able to speak first hand to these facts. However, where there are special circumstances the affidavit to lead the order may be made by someone other than the applicant for the grant. Those points of evidence which can be deposed to only by a person or persons with personal knowledge of the facts (such as a member of the deceased's family) should be embodied in a corroborative affidavit.

Rule 53 provides for the affidavit to contain the grounds of the application, details of all insurance policies effected on the presumed deceased's life, and any other information required by the District Judge or Registrar.

In addition to the information required by the Rule the affidavit should contain details of:

(a)   the name of the insurance company or companies who insured the life of the presumed deceased, whether they are aware of the application and their views thereon;

(b)   the date the presumed deceased was last heard of, his age and the details of the applicant's belief of the death;

(c)   advertisements placed in newspapers for the deceased or for anyone having knowledge of his last known whereabouts;

(d)   any correspondence received from the deceased since he was last known to have been alive;

(e)   any will of the presumed deceased or, if he died intestate, the persons entitled to his estate;

(f)   the value of the estate and what comprises the estate;

(g)   any bank or savings accounts held in the name of the presumed deceased and whether such accounts or any credit card facilities have been operated since he was last known to be alive.

All correspondence relating to the above details, advertisements and replies, should be exhibited to the affidavit. The will, if any, should also be lodged. A precedent form of affidavit is set out at Form A1.53, page 419.

If supporting evidence to assist the presumption of death (for example evidence from any rescue service or the police – and, especially in the case of presumed death at sea, the coastguards – including those of foreign countries if the presumed death occurred abroad, and where necessary authenticated translations) is available, it should be obtained in affidavit form, or any reports made may be exhibited to and lodged with the main affidavit.

Order of another court

5.5   If another court of competent jurisdiction has made an order to the same or like effect as the order sought, an affidavit of facts in general terms may be lodged, exhibiting the order. Before such affidavit is prepared the view of the District Judge or Registrar as to his requirements should be sought. Where the presumed deceased was domiciled outside England and Wales, any orders or declarations made by the court of the place of domicile should be obtained and lodged with the affidavit. An order made by such a court presuming death is insufficiently conclusive in itself and application must still be made for an order under Rule 53. Where possible, details, or, preferably, copies, of the evidence used before the foreign court should be obtained and exhibited to the affidavit. If, however, the foreign court has declared the presumed deceased dead, and a certificate of death has issued, then evidence on affidavit as to the conclusiveness and acceptability of such an order under the law of the place of domicile, together with the certificate, may be accepted and obviate the need to apply for an order under Rule 53. The order and any evidence available should be referred to the District Judge or Registrar for his directions.

It is to be emphasised that orders for leave to swear death require strong evidence in support and such an order will be refused if any doubt arises as to the presumed deceased's death.

It is preferable for all the affidavit evidence to be submitted in draft, with the proposed exhibits, for the court's consideration.

Effect of order

5.6   The District Judge or Registrar may refer the matter to a Judge on summons, but where he is satisfied, an order will be made giving leave to swear death.

Where death is presumed, uncertainty as to entitlement to benefit may also arise. A beneficiary under a will or person entitled under an intestacy may also have died and there may be doubt as to who survived whom. Where such doubt arises application may be made under s 116 of the Supreme Court Act 1981 (see paragraph 5.27 below) or the practice in *commorientes* cases may apply (see paragraph 3.12 above).

The order entitles the applicant to apply for a grant of representation to administer the presumed deceased's estate. The order is not, and will not be accepted as, conclusive proof of the death. Where, for any legal purpose, it is necessary to obtain an order of conclusive presumption of death, application must be made to the Chancery Division.

Where a grant issues following an order for leave to swear death and it is subsequently discovered that the presumed deceased is still alive, application must be made to the Registry which made the order and issued the grant for revocation of the order and grant (see CHAPTER 18).

Abolition of guarantees: protection of grantee

5.7   The 1987 Rules abolished the requirement for an administration guarantee as a prerequisite of granting administration. However, the District Judge or Registrar may require the applicant to obtain or undertake to obtain a missing persons indemnity from an insurance company as a condition of making the order. Some insurance companies will insure such a risk on payment of a single fee, the size of which obviously depends on the size of the estate and the risk involved. This is as much to protect the grantee as to protect the value of the estate should the presumed deceased reappear.

Death in common disasters

5.8   The procedure, when many deaths occur in a common disaster (*commorientes*), and no death certificates are issued, is set out at paragraph 3.11 above.

Lost wills: copy wills: nuncupative wills

5.9   Where the original will (or any codicil) cannot be found after the testator's death, application may be made for leave to prove a copy, completed draft or reconstruction. This is, of course, on the basis that the original has not been destroyed with the intention of revocation.

Where the will is a nuncupative will application must be made to determine the form and content of the will to be proved.

Content of will unknown

5.10   Where there is evidence or a strong belief that the deceased had made a will, which remained unrevoked, but:

(a)   the original cannot be found after his death;

(b)   no copy of the will exists; and

(c)   there is no evidence of the content sufficient to make a reconstruction,

then application may be made for an order for letters of administration to issue 'limited until the original will or a copy be proved'.

Application is made on affidavit setting out the facts for the belief that there was an unrevoked will and that the content cannot now be ascertained. Application will be made by the person entitled under an intestacy to the grant; however, the oath will *not* recite that the deceased died intestate nor will the grant.

For a form of oath see Form A1.45, page 410.

Content of affidavit to lead order under Rule 54

5.11   Where the original document has been lost or mistakenly destroyed, the application, in accordance with Rule 54, is made *ex parte* on affidavit. The affidavit is usually made by the proposed grantee and must contain details of:

(a)   the existence of the will after the testator's death or, where there is no such evidence, the facts on which the applicant relies to rebut the presumption that the testator revoked his will by destruction (see below);

(b)   in respect of a nuncupative will, the contents of that will; and

(c)   in respect of a reconstruction of a will, the accuracy of the reconstruction (see Rule 54(3)).

In applications to prove a copy will, the affidavit must also establish the provenance of the copy sought to be proved, the efforts made to find the original, the details of when it was last known to exist and where it was retained, the circumstances of its loss and details of persons prejudiced by proof of the copy (that is, those persons who receive benefit or greater benefit under an earlier will or intestacy and who do not benefit in the same degree under the copy will sought to be proved). The copy or reconstruction sought to be proved must be exhibited to the affidavit as should (copies of) the correspondence seeking the original.

Presumption of revocation

5.12 Where the original will was in the testator's possession before his death but cannot thereafter be found, there is a presumption that the will was revoked by destruction. This presumption may be rebutted by evidence indicating that the testator had referred to his will as existing without mentioning revocation; had not consulted his solicitors or other professional advisers with a view to changing or revoking his will; or whatever the facts are to show that the testator did not, or is unlikely to have, revoked his will. The District Judge or Registrar will require strong evidence to rebut the presumption of revocation.

Will lost after testator's death

5.13 Where the original will has been mislaid in a solicitor's office or by the bank in whose custody it was deposited or in the post or document exchange from or to an executor or to the Probate Registry, after the testator's death the affidavit deposing to the facts of the will's disappearance should be given by the solicitor or clerk having the carriage of the application. It is preferable for such evidence to be given by someone with first hand knowledge of the facts.

Further evidence: consents

5.14 The District Judge or Registrar may direct that further evidence as to the due execution of the will be filed where the particular circumstances of the case so require (e.g. where the copy has no details of execution but is a copy made up after execution or a draft). He may also direct that notice be given to the person(s) who may be prejudiced if the will is proved and admitted. He may also direct, if appropriate, that their consent to the admission of the will be obtained and filed. Such consents are usually exhibited to the affidavit of facts (see Rule 54(4)).

Order to admit copy

5.15 The District Judge or Registrar, when satisfied, will order the admission of the copy or reconstruction and direct that the grant will be limited 'until the original or a more authentic copy of the will be proved'. Details of the order and the limitation must be recited in the oath to lead the grant. It follows, therefore, that application must be made as a pre-grant application and *not* at the time of application for the grant.

Where an original will is lost but an original codicil exists, the order will be for the admittance of the copy will. If an original will exists but a codicil is missing, the order will be for the admittance of the copy codicil limited until the original of it be proved.

The limitation may be varied by the District Judge or Registrar to fit the particular circumstances of the case.

Will retained by foreign court or official

5.16   Where the will is not available because it has been retained by a foreign court or official, a copy of the will duly authenticated by the court or official may be admitted to proof without the necessity of any order (see Rule 54(2)).

Order made by foreign court

5.17   When the deceased died domiciled abroad and a foreign court has given leave to prove a copy, application must still be made under Rule 54 for a copy to be proved. The order and certified copies of the evidence submitted to the foreign court should be exhibited to the affidavit. The affidavit must contain all the information relevant to an application notwithstanding the order of the other court.

Will retained by another person

5.18   Where the will is retained by another person abroad then, on sufficient evidence as to why the original cannot be produced, leave may be given to admit a copy.

If the will is retained by another person in the United Kingdom who refuses to release it for proof, application may be made under s 122 of the Supreme Court Act 1981 (Rule 50) for an order for that person to attend to give evidence regarding the will or for the issue of a subpoena requiring the will to be lodged in court (see paragraph 5.65 below).

Application to dispense with giving notice to non-proving executor

5.19   Rule 27(1) requires the proving executor(s) to give notice of the application for probate to all other executors appointed in the will (and codicil(s)) to whom power to take a like grant is to be reserved.

Rule 27(3) allows a District Judge or Registrar to dispense with the giving of notice under Rule 27(1) where he is satisfied that to do so is impracticable or would cause unnecessary delay or expense, for example where:

- one of the named executors' whereabouts are totally unknown;

- one of the executors is ill or mentally incapable of managing his affairs;

- one of the executors is on an extended holiday and his current whereabouts are unknown;

- one of the executors is a serving member of the armed forces currently serving overseas.

Strictly, applications to dispense should be made on affidavit but usually a letter from the extracting solicitor or probate practitioner setting out the facts will be accepted.

The oath to lead the grant should recite that 'the giving of notice to .... the executor to whom power is reserved was dispensed with by direction of the District Judge/Registrar .... dated ....'

The fact that notice had been dispensed with does not affect the non-proving executor's right to a grant of double probate (see paragraph 10.19 below). For the form of notice see Form A1.80, page 448.

Application to rectify will

Application to omit words

5.20   Where a will contains words which may be offensive, libellous or blasphemous, application should be made for their omission from the probate and record copies. The original will will not be altered but an engrossment in the form decided by the court will be lodged to be copied to form the probate and record copies.

If no application to omit words is made on application for the grant, the District Judge or Registrar will refuse to issue the grant until such application is made. Only words falling within the above three categories may be omitted. Unless the words come within these categories, they will stand – as will words which are in any way dispositive. In the event the offending words contain a proper disposition, the District Judge or Registrar will direct the form of wording to appear in the engrossment: to avoid the offence but retain the gift.

Uncontested applications are made to the District Judge or Registrar of the Registry from which it is intended to extract the grant *ex parte* on affidavit. The affidavit should recite the facts relating to the will and to the words sought to be excluded. The deponent may be the proposed grantee or solicitor able to speak to the relevant facts. If any person may be prejudiced by the omission of the offending words, the court may require their consents. If satisfied, the court will make an order to omit the offending words.

If the application is contested, it must be brought before a District Judge of the Principal Registry on summons.

Rectification: s 20 Administration of Justice Act 1982

5.21   Section 20 of the Administration of Justice Act 1982 enables the court, if satisfied that a will is so expressed that it fails to carry out the testator's intentions because of a clerical error or a failure to understand his instructions, to direct the will be rectified so as to carry out the testator's intentions. In effect this means the court may, where the testator's death occurred after 1 January 1983, rectify his will by the inclusion as well as the exclusion of words.

Uncontested applications

5.22   Application for rectification, where the matter is uncontested and unless a probate claim has been commenced, is made *ex parte* on affidavit, exhibiting the will in its original form together with, if appropriate, an engrossment showing the will in its proposed rectified form. The affidavit should be made, where possible, by the person who drafted the will or who took the instructions. If evidence from these sources is unavailable, the affidavit should be made by someone with personal knowledge of the facts and of how the error or misunderstanding arose. Where the application is to include words mistakenly omitted from a draft or from written instructions the draft or instructions should also be exhibited (see *Re Segalman [1995] 3 All ER 676*). The affidavit must set out the nature of any alleged clerical error or in what respect the testator's intentions were not understood. The affidavit should conclude with a request for the order sought.

The District Judge or Registrar may direct that notice of the application to rectify be given to any person interested under the will or whose interest may be prejudiced by the rectification applied for. Where the rectification affects the residuary estate, and especially in those cases where the residue is not wholly disposed of because of the error, then notice must be given to those who have an interest under any partial intestacy created by the failure to dispose properly of the residue. The comments (if any) of any person so notified must be exhibited to the affidavit in support. Where the rectification sought does not affect the interest of any person benefiting under the will or otherwise the District Judge or Registrar may make the order sought without notice being given (see Rule 55(3) as amended with effect from 14 September 1998).

On making an order the District Judge or Registrar will direct that an engrossed copy, including or excluding the relevant words, be lodged for his fiat to be endorsed (see Rule 11); for this purpose, a space approximately 5 cm deep should be left at the head of the engrossment.

5.23   *Pre-grant applications for discretionary orders*

Contested applications

5.23   In the event of a dispute, application is made by summons to a District Judge of the Principal Registry who may direct the application be made by summons to a Judge (see Rule 61 and paragraph 17.1 below). Where the rectification raises questions of construction, application is made to the Chancery Division, even if the application is unopposed. Generally, all opposed applications to rectify should be made to the Chancery Division direct.

Post-grant applications

5.24   Although it is usual to apply for rectification before representation is granted, application to rectify may be made within six months of the issue of the grant, or after that time with the court's leave.

The same procedure will apply as for a pre-grant application.

A memorandum of the order will be notated on the original grant and a copy of the will as rectified will be annexed to that grant. Any copy wills issued thereafter will be of the engrossed rectified copy.

Interpretation: s 21 Administration of Justice Act 1982

5.25   Section 21 of the 1982 Act, which also applies to deaths after 1 January 1983 and irrespective of the date of the will, empowers the court to accept extrinsic evidence, including evidence of the testator's intention to assist in the interpretation of a will. This section applies to a will in so far as any part of it is meaningless, the language used in any part of it is ambiguous on the face of it or there is evidence which shows that the language used in any part of it is ambiguous in the light of surrounding circumstances.

Application is made *ex parte* on affidavit in the same manner as an application to rectify.

If satisfied, the District Judge or Registrar will interpret the will accordingly. No engrossment of the will will be required. No order is drawn, the court simply interpreting the will in the manner requested.

The Probate Registries are not courts of construction. The construction of a will or part of it falls to the Chancery Division. It follows therefore that the Probate Registries' jurisdiction to interpret any clause or term is limited to establishing title to apply for the grant sought. This invariably relates to the clause appointing executors. If this clause fails to carry out the testator's intention then, on satisfactory evidence, it may be appropriately interpreted. Where title to the grant falls on the interpretation of a gift, then the application is more properly directed to the Chancery Division.

Application to join a co-administrator

5.26 Where a life or minority interest arises, whether under a will or intestacy, a grant of letters of administration must be made to a minimum of two grantees or a trust corporation (s 114(2) Supreme Court Act 1981). This does not apply to grants of probate where an executor may act alone even if such interest arises under the will.

Rule 25(1) provides that a person entitled in priority may apply with a person entitled in a lower capacity provided that there is no person with a higher capacity to the person joined or such persons renounce. For example, a life interest arises under a will: one of two residuary legatees may apply with a specific legatee on the renunciation of the other residuary legatee.

Rule 25(2) provides that where there is only one person entitled, application may be made *ex parte* on affidavit to the District Judge or Registrar for leave to join a person having no immediate right to apply or no right to apply.

The affidavit must set out the facts and exhibit the consent of the person sought to be joined as co-administrator.

No application under Rule 25(2) will be necessary if the person sought to be joined is nominated under Rule 32 (minor entitled: see paragraph 5.57 below) or Rule 35 (person entitled is mentally incapable: see paragraph 5.62 below) or is a trust corporation.

Subparagraph (2) of s 114 also allows the District Judge or Registrar to grant letters of administration to a sole grantee where it is considered expedient in all the circumstances of the case to do so. Consideration should be given to asking the District Judge or Registrar to exercise his discretion in favour of a sole grantee rather than adding a co-administrator.

Application under s 116 Supreme Court Act 1981

5.27 Rule 52 provides the procedure for applications under s 116 of the 1981 Act (discretionary grant to person with no statutory title).

Circumstances in which application may be made

5.28 Section 116 enables the court to exercise its discretion, in special circumstances, to pass over any or all persons with a prior entitlement to representation, including executors, and make a grant of letters of administration with or without will annexed to such person as it thinks fit. The court's discretion to grant representation to such a person is absolute and unfettered. The grant may be general, or limited in any way considered appropriate by the court. The circumstances where application may be made for an order under s 116 are, *inter alia*:

(i)   where the person entitled is considered unfit to administer by reason of his bankruptcy; or is considered to be of bad character and unsuitable to act as an administrator; or there is thought to be a risk to the estate being properly administered;

(ii)   where the person entitled has been convicted of the murder or manslaughter of, or some other offence within the provisions of the Forfeiture Act 1982 against, the deceased and refuses to renounce his title to the grant;

(iii)   where all the persons entitled are missing and their whereabouts are unknown;

(iv)   where there is or may be a dispute between persons equally entitled to the grant (including executors), to pass over their title (such application may require the consent of – or that notice be given to – those entitled, or application is made under Rule 27(6) (see paragraph 17.1 below) for the court to determine who shall take the grant);

(v)

(a)   where a person wishes to make an application for financial provision under the Inheritance (Provision for Family and Dependants) Act 1975, and no person is entitled or willing to apply for a grant, or the person entitled to the grant is also the person wishing to apply for relief under the Act. Where no person can be found who will take a grant of representation, the Official Solicitor has agreed (subject to his consenting) to apply for a grant under this section, so that he may be the defendant in the proceedings, but see now the notes to Part 57 CPR 1998 in *Civil Procedure*. It is now considered that there is no bar on a claimant under the Act also being the personal representative. An application does not impugn the validity of the grant (or any will). The personal representative is not required to defend the estate, the application being for redistribution of the estate and not an attack on it;

(b)   where the grant is required to enable proceedings under the Law Reform (Miscellaneous Provisions) Act 1934 to be brought. It should be noted that Part 19.8A CPR 1998 (which replaced RSC Order 15 r 15) which enables the court to nominate a person to represent the deceased's interest in an action or to proceed without a representative where no legal personal representative has been constituted, does not apply where the subject matter of the action is the deceased's estate;

(vi)   where a beneficiary's trustee in bankruptcy requires a grant to enable the benefit to pass to the beneficiary's estate in bankruptcy, or to any creditor where the executor or person with prior entitlement refuses or neglects to take the grant;

(vii) where a grant is required urgently to prevent a loss to the estate; or to preserve the estate (see *ad colligenda bona* grants, below);

(viii) where a person is solely entitled to the deceased's estate, but by reason of age or infirmity or other circumstances, is in residential accommodation provided by a local authority, that local authority may apply as custodian trustee (see paragraph 11.2 below), although this provision may not now be so widely used, as the provisions of Rule 31 allow any lawfully constituted attorney to apply;

(ix) where the deceased was a tenant for life, to enable title to estate to pass, or to vest or transfer property, so as to avoid the need for one or more 'leading grants' (see paragraph 9.6 below) to intermediate estates to establish title;

(x) where the person entitled to the estate survived the deceased but has since died without taking a grant and leaving estate for which no grant of representation was required, to avoid the need for a 'leading grant'.

The affidavit to lead the order

5.29   Application is made *ex parte* on affidavit to a District Judge or Registrar of the Registry to which it is intended to apply for the grant. A draft of the proposed affidavit may be submitted to the District Judge or Registrar for approval before swearing: the court may then give directions as to the evidence required to be given in the affidavit.

The affidavit (see Form A1.55, page 422 for the form of affidavit) is usually made by the proposed applicant for the grant, or one of them, setting out the details of the deceased and any will; the person(s) entitled to the grant in the normal order of priority; the reasons why this interest should be passed over; who is next or otherwise entitled to the grant; and conclude with a request for the order. The court may allow the evidence to be given by the solicitor acting for the proposed grantee if he is better able to speak to the facts or in cases of urgency.

Where the District Judge or Registrar has directed that notice be given to the person(s) whose interest is to be passed over, the letters giving such notice and any response should be exhibited.

Discretionary powers

5.30   The court's discretionary power to make an order is unlimited but is restricted to cases where the deceased died domiciled in England and Wales. Where the deceased had a foreign domicile, application for an order under Rule 30(1)(c) should be made (see paragraph 5.55 below). The court may order the passing over of an executor who has intermeddled in the estate (see *Re Biggs' Estate [1966] P 118, [1966] 1 All ER 358, [1966] 2 WLR 536*).

Life or minority interest

5.31   Where, however, a life or minority interest arises in the estate the grant must issue to at least two grantees or to a trust corporation with or without an individual applicant, unless application is also made under s 114(2) of the Supreme Court Act 1981 for an additional discretionary order to enable the grant to issue to an individual. This application and the evidence to support it may be contained in the same affidavit.

The order

5.32   Where the District Judge or Registrar is not satisfied on the affidavit of the applicant, he may require further evidence to be filed or direct that the application be brought before a District Judge or Registrar or Judge on summons. If notice has been given and the application is opposed, it may be brought before the District Judge or Registrar on summons. If an order is made under this section, the form of order is drawn up by the court and a copy sent to the applicant (or his solicitors).

Application for the grant

5.33   Application for the grant is made in the normal way, the oath to lead the grant reciting the details of the order giving the applicant his title to apply. The grant is a full grant to the estate and, unless there are other unusual circumstances, will issue without limitation. For the form of affidavit to lead the order, see Form A1.55, page 422, and for the form of oath following an order under s 116, see Form A1.39, page 400.

Application for order to lead *ad colligenda bona* grant

5.34   Application may be made in accordance with Rule 52(b) for an order for a limited grant *ad colligenda bona*.

Such a grant is always of letters of administration: no will is proved and the oath and grant are silent as to the deceased dying testate or intestate.

The grant will be limited to that part of the estate which now needs administration (but see paragraph 5.38 below).

Circumstances for application

5.35   Such a grant may be required because the deceased's estate needs the protection afforded by a grant of representation, but a full grant cannot now be applied for – where the circumstances are, *inter alia*:

- where the person entitled to the grant is unable at present to apply through illness or absence;

- where there is doubt as to who should be the personal representative;

- where the full value of the estate cannot be ascertained;

- where the deceased's will is or may be disputed;

- where the deceased's business will suffer unless dealt with;

- where a house must be sold without delay;

- where contracts to sell are about to be exchanged or have been exchanged and completion will take place before a full grant can be taken;

- to renew or renegotiate a lease on the deceased's business premises;

- where, for any other reason, the estate needs representation to preserve or protect it;

- where a grant is required to deal with stocks and/or shares; or

- where there is undue delay in applying for a grant (see *IRC v Stype Investments (Jersey) Ltd* and *Re Clore [1982] Ch 456, [1982] 3 All ER 419*).

Who may apply

5.36   Application may be made by the person(s) entitled to a full grant but who cannot, for good reason, immediately apply for that grant, or by any person who can show a need to protect the estate. A creditor may apply if he can show that there is a need for him to recover his debt and those entitled cannot or will not apply. The applicant does not have to be a person with a right to a grant or interest in the estate but someone (often the solicitor instructed) who is best able to act immediately to preserve the estate.

The affidavit to lead the order

5.37   The affidavit may be made by the proposed grantee or by a solicitor or probate practitioner able to speak to the facts. The affidavit must set out why the full grant cannot now be taken and the reasons for the temporary grant. The affidavit should conclude with a request for the order and the form of limitation required to be included in the grant. The actual limitation will be determined by the court. It is usually preferable for a draft affidavit to be approved by the District Judge or Registrar or at least to have the evidence required agreed by the court.

The order and the grant

5.38   If satisfied, the court will order the issue of the grant, which will always be a grant of letters of administration even if the deceased died testate. Unless there are special requirements the usual limitation imposed is 'limited for the purpose only of collecting and getting in and receiving the estate and doing such acts as may be necessary for the preservation of the same but no further or otherwise'. Where the grant is required to deal with more specific estate, the limitation will be varied accordingly.

The grant will also be limited until further representation be granted. No distribution may be effected under the grant. The grant ceases when the purpose for which it was issued has been achieved, or on the issue of a full grant to the estate. The court may also order the grant to issue to a sole grantee, notwithstanding that a life or minority interest arises, provided that good reason is given in the affidavit. Where the grant is required for urgent conveyancing, it is often preferable for the grant to issue to the solicitor instructed. This avoids further risks of delay and minimises the costs to the estate.

If the grant already taken is found to be insufficient to protect the estate or further events create a need, a further grant *ad colligenda bona* may be applied for. The same procedure described at paragraph 5.37 above applies to the second application save that the affidavit to lead the order must establish the need for the further grant and show that the original is insufficient.

If the grant is insufficient and further powers of administration are required, application may be made under s 116 of the Supreme Court Act 1981 (see above) for a full grant to the whole estate. Any will must be proved. It follows, therefore, that if the will is in dispute the only application available would be for an *ad colligenda bona* grant with as wide a limitation as the court considers appropriate.

Application under s 114 Supreme Court Act 1981

5.39   Where a life or minority interest arises under a will or intestacy, any grant of administration must be made to at least two persons or to a trust corporation. It should be noted that this applies only to grants of administration. A sole executor may take probate alone notwithstanding a life or minority interest arises in the estate.

Application to add co-administrator pre-grant under Rule 25

5.40   Where a life interest exists and only one person entitled to benefit is willing or able to take administration, application may be made to add as the additional proposed co-administrator a person with no interest in the estate. The proposed co-administrator may be the solicitor instructed or any other person thought fit and proper to act. Application to join a co-administrator is made on affidavit by the person entitled and with the consent of the person proposed to be added.

Application to add co-administrator post-grant under Rule 26

5.41　If at any time during the minority of a beneficiary or the subsistence of a life interest there is only one personal representative (not being a trust corporation), application may be made to add a personal representative. The personal representative may act while the minority or life interest remains and until the estate is fully administered.

Application is made *ex parte* on affidavit by the existing grantee and with the consent of the person proposed to be added.

The original grant must be lodged to enable the additional personal representative's name and address to be added.

Discretion to permit sole grantee

5.42　The court may on application allow a grant to a sole grantee where good reason exists for there to be only one administrator. Although it is proper for application to be made on affidavit, the District Judge or Registrar may accept, at his discretion, less formal application by letter (see s 114(2)).

Application under s 113 Supreme Court Act 1981

Introduction

5.43　Section 113 provides that the High Court may grant probate or letters of administration in respect of any part of the estate limited in any way the court thinks fit.

Where, however, the estate is known to be insolvent, the grant of representation to the estate may only be severed in respect of trust estate in which the deceased was a tenant for life but held no beneficial interest.

The affidavit

5.44　The affidavit to lead the order for a grant under s 113 must set out the grounds of the application; whether the estate is known to be insolvent; and showing how the person entitled to a grant in respect of the whole estate in priority to the applicant has been cleared off, for example by renunciation (see Rule 51).

If the person entitled to a grant in respect of the whole estate is not cleared off, his title may be passed over by application under s 116 of the 1981 Act (see paragraph 5.27 above). Application for this order may be embodied in the same affidavit.

The affidavit must also set out the part of the estate for which the grant is required and any other limitation considered appropriate.

Applications for an order under Rule 30 (deceased domiciled outside England and Wales)

Rule 30

5.45   Where the deceased died domiciled outside England and Wales, the normal order contained in Rules 20 and 22 (see paragraphs 8.2 and 9.28 below) as to priority of right to a grant of representation does not apply. The practice is governed by Rule 30 which provides:

'(1)   Subject to paragraph (3) below where the deceased died domiciled outside England and Wales a district judge or registrar may order that a grant, limited in such way as the district judge or registrar may direct, do issue to any of the following persons:

(a)   to the person entrusted with the administration of the estate by the court having jurisdiction at the place where the deceased died domiciled; or

(b)   where there is no person so entrusted, to the person beneficially entitled to the estate by the law of the place where the deceased died domiciled or, if there is more than one person so entitled, to such of them as the district judge or registrar may direct; or

(c)   if in the opinion of the district judge or registrar the circumstances so require, to such person as the district judge or registrar may direct.

(2)   A grant made under paragraph (1)(a) or (b) above may be issued jointly with such person as the district judge or registrar may direct if the grant is required to be made to not less than two administrators.

(3)   Without any order made under paragraph (1) above—

(a)   probate of any will which is admissible to proof may be granted—

(i)   if the will is in the English or Welsh language, to the executor named therein; or

(ii)   if the will describes the duties of a named person in

terms sufficient to constitute him executor according
to the tenor of the will, to that person, and

(b)   where the whole or substantially the whole of the estate in
England and Wales consists of immovable property, a grant
in respect of the whole estate may be made in accordance
with the law which would have been applicable if the
deceased had died domiciled in England and Wales.'

It is not for the Probate Registry to determine the deceased's domicile:
that is a matter for the applicant for the grant who will swear to it in the
oath to lead the grant. Any dispute over domicile may be resolved by
application to the High Court or a divorce county court under the
Domicile and Matrimonial Proceedings Act 1973.

Rule 30(1)(a): application by person entrusted with the administration

5.46   Where the law of the country of domicile requires a grant to issue
to enable administration of the deceased's estate in that country, and such
grant has issued, an order under Rule 30(1)(a) may be obtained and application for a grant of letters of administration in England and Wales made
by the person entrusted with the administration of the estate by the court
of the foreign country. The grant will always be of letters of administration. The entrusting document may be in the form of a grant recognisable
as such by comparison with an English grant, or may be a decree or order
of the foreign court. Whatever the document issued by that court, it must
give the person named therein the same, or substantially the same, authority as a full English grant.

Person entrusted not executor

5.47   Application may be made under Rule 30(1)(a) for an order allowing a grant to be made to the person entrusted with the administration of
the estate of the deceased by the court whose jurisdiction covers the place
where the deceased died domiciled. Such a person may apply for a grant
in England and Wales, notwithstanding that the will appointed an executor (who is a person other than the person entrusted) who has not applied
for a grant in England and Wales or renounced his right, without having
to obtain such a renunciation.

However, under Rule 30(3)(a)(i), an executor who is not the person
entrusted with the administration of the estate, may apply for a grant of
probate. Where there is doubt about the sufficiency of the grant, decree
or order of the foreign court, it should be referred to a District Judge
or Registrar for adjudication. Generally, no affidavit of law will be
necessary – nor will it be necessary to establish validity of the will,
the will having been accepted and proved by the court of the place of
domicile.

5.48 *Pre-grant applications for discretionary orders*

Orders to administer

5.48   Orders to administer and/or elections to administer taken by the Public Trustee of New Zealand or the Public Trustee of the relevant state in Australia are sufficient to constitute entrusting documents. In some circumstances the order or election, depending on its terms, may be suitable for resealing (see CHAPTER 15, and in particular paragraph 15.3 below).

Application through attorney

5.49   A person entrusted who is resident abroad, and similarly a foreign corporation appointed as executor, may appoint an attorney to obtain a grant of administration (with will annexed) for the use and benefit of that person or corporation and until further representation be granted (see paragraph 10.32 below for attorney grants).

Sufficiency of document

5.50   Subject to the comments made above, it is immaterial whether the deceased died testate or intestate – the criteria to be applied to the sufficiency of an entrusting document are the same, the person entrusted being accepted under the authority of the grant, decree or order notwithstanding that such person would not be entitled to a grant under English law.

If a limitation as to time is imposed on the powers of the person entrusted by the foreign court, a similar limitation will, if the District Judge or Registrar is satisfied that the limitation is proper for administering the estate in England and Wales, be imposed in the English grant.

Applying for the order

5.51   Application may be made by lodging any affidavit required; the original grant, order or other official document issued by the foreign court, or an officially certified copy or exemplified copy, together with a translation, if necessary (the translation may be court or notarially certified). If the foreign grant does not contain a copy of the will, a court certified copy or notarised copy of it; and any other relevant documents, as a preliminary application for the District Judge's or Registrar's order before application is made for the grant. However, it is not essential for an order under Rule 30(1)(a) to be made *before* application for the grant and therefore application for the order may be made by lodging the appropriate documents at the same time as the oath to lead the grant (the request for the order being contained in the oath). Usually, application for an order under Rule 30(1)(a) is made this way.

Rule 30(1)(b): grant to the person beneficially entitled to the estate

5.52   Application under Rule 30(1)(b) may be made for an order for a grant, where there is no person entrusted by the court of the place where the deceased died domiciled, to be issued to the person beneficially entitled to the estate of the deceased by the law of the place in which the deceased died domiciled. If there is more than one person beneficially entitled to share the estate the grant may issue to such one or more of them as a District Judge or Registrar may direct.

Application through attorney

5.53   A person entitled may appoint an attorney to obtain a grant for his use and benefit (see paragraph 10.32 below for attorney grants).

Application under Rule 30(1)(b) will always be necessary where there is no executor, no person entrusted (in countries where a grant is normally required to administer the estate), or the deceased died domiciled in a 'non grant issuing' country, or the grant, decree or order issued by the foreign court is insufficient to constitute an entrusting document.

Evidence required

5.54   There may be no document entrusting but there may be, and often is, a court pronouncement establishing entitlement. A certified copy of a Certificate of Inheritance or other document which states who benefits will be accepted.

An affidavit of foreign law (see Form A1.61, page 428) or a certificate by, or an act before, a notary practising in the country or territory concerned will be required by the District Judge or Registrar. The evidence must clearly show who is beneficially entitled to the deceased's estate by the law of the place of domicile. Where the person applying is one of several persons entitled, the evidence must set out their order of priority of entitlement to benefit if there is one. There is a discretion vested in the District Judge or Registrar to direct who may apply for the grant when there is more than one person beneficially entitled.

An affidavit of foreign law, provided it clearly defines the beneficial entitlement to the deceased's estate and provided the deponent by his knowledge, experience and qualifications shows he is entitled to make the affidavit, will be accepted by the District Judge or Registrar without further enquiry or evidence as to that law. Similarly, a notarial certificate will be accepted without further enquiry (see Rule 19). Where evidence is necessary to validate the will and to establish beneficial entitlement, it may be contained in the same affidavit or notarial statement.

The procedure for making the application is as for an order under Rule

30(1)(a), that is application may be made either before application for the grant or with the application for the grant (being contained in the oath to lead the grant), and Rule 30(2) as to the requirement for more than one administrator applies (see paragraph 5.45 above).

Rule 30(1)(c): court's discretionary power

5.55   Application is made under this provision where, in the opinion of the District Judge or Registrar, the circumstances require the grant should issue to such person as he may direct.

Even if application could be made under Rule 30(1)(a) or (b), the District Judge or Registrar may make an order for a grant to such other person as is thought fit under Rule 30(1)(c). Similarly, an order under Rule 30(1)(c) will be necessary where the person entitled to apply under paragraphs (1)(a) or (b) cannot or will not apply, or in the unlikely circumstance that there is no such person.

Where it is difficult to obtain evidence from the foreign country, or to obtain such evidence could cause problems for family or beneficiaries of the deceased still living in the deceased's country of domicile, or the costs of obtaining such evidence may be prohibitive in relation to the value of the estate, then application under Rule 30(1)(c) is appropriate.

Rule 30(1)(c) has the same effect for a foreign domiciled deceased as has s 116 of the Supreme Court Act 1981 for an English domicile – the court has discretionary power to grant representation to whomsoever it considers an appropriate person, overriding other persons' entitlements as executors, persons entrusted or beneficiaries. The solicitor with the carriage of the application may be considered an appropriate applicant.

Application for an order under this paragraph *must* be made as a preliminary to the application for the grant, as the oath to lead the grant must recite details of the District Judge's or Registrar's order. As well as, or, depending on the circumstances, instead of an affidavit of law or notarial certificate dealing, *inter alia*, with beneficial entitlement, evidence may be required of the facts of the case and the particular circumstances making it necessary to pass over the person(s) entitled to apply under paragraphs (1)(a) or (b) of Rule 30 or stating that there is no such person. The District Judge or Registrar may direct application be made by two persons under Rule 30(2) where two administrators are required, i.e. where the evidence shows that a life or minority interest arises.

When order not required

5.56   Rule 30(3)(b) (see paragraph 5.45 above) provides that where the deceased died domiciled outside England and Wales but the whole or substantially the whole estate in England and Wales is real estate, application may be made by the person entitled under English law under Rule 20 or 22 without order under Rule 30. Validity of any will must still be established.

Applications under Rule 32 (minor entitled)

Rule 32(1)

5.57 Where the only person entitled to a grant of administration, whether under a will or intestacy, is a minor, application may be made for the grant by the person having, or deemed to have, parental responsibility for him for his use and benefit. Parental responsibility is acquired by a parent under s 2(1) and (2) or 4 of the Children Act 1989; para 4 or 6 of Sch 14 to the Act; under an adoption order within the meaning of s 12(1) of the Act; by a guardian under s 5 or paras 12, 13 or 14 of Sch 14 to the Act; by any person who has obtained a residence order under s 8 of the Act; or by a local authority where a care order has been made under s 31(1)(a) of the Act.

The procedure where there is a person with parental responsibility able and willing to act is set out in CHAPTER 10 at paragraph 10.48.

Rule 32(2)

5.58 When the person or body having, or deemed to have, parental responsibility is unable or unwilling to act or there is no person or body with such responsibility, application must be made under Rule 32(2) for the appointment of two or more persons to apply for the use and benefit of the minor. Although para (3) of the Rule allows the person appointed to nominate a co-administrator, it is the usual practice to apply for the appointment of two persons.

Application to constitute personal representative for proceedings under the Inheritance (Provision for Family and Dependants) Act 1975

5.59 It can occur that a personal representative needs to be created by application under this rule to enable proceedings under s 1 of the Inheritance (Provision for Family and Dependants) Act 1975 to be commenced – where, for example, the person with parental responsibility for a minor seeks relief under the Act.

It is now regarded no longer to be a bar to the claimant for relief under the Act also being the personal representative, such an application not being one that requires the estate to be defended but being rather an application for the redistribution of the estate. See Notes to Part 57 CPR 1998 in *Civil Procedure*.

The affidavit

5.60   The affidavit is made by the proposed grantees, or one of them. The affidavit must recite details of: the deceased; any will; how the minor comes to be the person entitled to the grant; whether there is any person or local authority having, or deemed to have, parental responsibility and why that person or authority cannot or will not act; whether there have or have not been any proceedings under the Children Act 1989 relating to the minor and the result of any such proceedings, or if any proceedings are contemplated; whether the minor has or has not been made a ward of court; the relationship, if any, of the proposed grantees to the minor; where the minor resides and who has *de facto* care of him. The affidavit should conclude with a request for the order. For form of affidavit see Form A1.57, page 424.

The order

5.61   The order will appoint the applicants for the purpose of obtaining the grant. The order will not appoint guardians. The order will authorise the persons named to take letters of administration for the use and benefit of the minor(s) until he/she/one of them attains 18 years of age. The grant will also be so limited. It follows that it ceases to be effective upon the minor or one of several minors attaining 18.

Application under Rule 35(4) (person entitled mentally incapable)

Persons entitled in priority

5.62   Where the person entitled in priority to a grant of representation is mentally incapable of managing his affairs, the provisions of Rule 35 apply.

Rule 35(1) provides that unless the District Judge or Registrar otherwise directs, no grant shall be made under the Rule unless all persons equally entitled as the incapable person have died or renounced.

The order of priority is prescribed by Rule 35(2): first, the person authorised by the Court of Protection; then, failing any such person, the lawful attorney acting under a registered enduring power of attorney; and, finally, failing any attorney, or should the attorney renounce title on behalf of the patient, the person entitled to the residuary estate. See also CHAPTER 10 at paragraph 10.60.

No person entitled in priority

5.63   Where there is no person entitled in the order of priority set out above, application must be made on affidavit for the appointment of such other person (see Rule 35(4) as amended with effect from 14 September 1998) to take administration for the use and benefit of the incapable person. Notice of the proposed application must be given to the Court of Protection (Rule 35(5)) and the acknowledgment of such notice lodged with the affidavit to lead the order or with the grant application.

The affidavit

5.64   The affidavit is made by the proposed grantee and must contain details of: the deceased; the incapable person; how any persons entitled in priority are cleared off and also clearing those persons of equal entitlement who would usually be preferred as the applicants; the incapacity of the person entitled (exhibiting appropriate medical evidence from a responsible medical officer or general practitioner showing that the patient is mentally incapable of managing his affairs and is not likely to recover his capacity within three months); whether the Court of Protection has made a receivership order and who the receiver is, or whether an application for such order is pending or contemplated; and the relationship (if any) of the proposed grantees to the person entitled.

The medical evidence should be in the form of a certificate from a Responsible Officer if the patient is in an institution. The evidence from a general practitioner may be by certificate or letter.

The acknowledgment of notice given under Rule 35(5) (see paragraph 5.63 above) may be exhibited to the affidavit or lodged with it.

The affidavit concludes with a request for the order (see Form A1.56, page 423 for the form of affidavit).

If satisfied, the court will appoint the proposed applicants to apply: the grant will usually be for the use and benefit of the patient and limited until further representation be granted.

Application under s 123 Supreme Court Act 1981 (subpoena to lodge will)

5.65   Rule 50(2) provides that application may be made to a District Judge or Registrar *ex parte* on affidavit under s 123 of the Supreme Court Act 1981 for a subpoena to issue requiring any person who it would appear has in his possession, custody or power any document which purports to be a testamentary document, to lodge the document in the Registry from which the subpoena issued.

The affidavit must set out the grounds of the application. For a form of affidavit, see Form A1.63, page 431; and for a form of subpoena, see Form A1.73, page 441.

The affidavit and two completed forms of subpoena must be lodged. The subpoena must be endorsed as follows: 'If you the said .... (*name of person subpoena'd*) deny the testamentary document(s) referred to is/are in your possession, custody or power, you may swear an affidavit to that effect and file it in the .... (*name of Registry which issued the subpoena*).' No fee is payable on the application for, or the issue of, the subpoena. One copy of the subpoena is returned sealed.

The subpoena must also be endorsed with a penal notice in accordance with Order 45 Rule 7(4) of the Rules of the Supreme Court, and must be served personally. Where the person subpoena'd does not have the purported testamentary document in his possession or control, he should file an affidavit accordingly in the Registry from which the subpoena issued. Failure to comply with the subpoena is enforceable by summons to a Judge issued out of the Principal Registry for the defaulter's committal to prison for contempt.

Where the will is in his possession, it must be lodged in the Registry at which the subpoena directs its lodgment within eight days of service. It may be lodged in the Registry personally or by post (the latter being at the sender's risk).

As an alternative to the issue of a subpoena, application may be made by summons in accordance with Rule 50(1) under s 122 of the 1981 Act for an order for a person's attendance to give evidence regarding the will. The initial appointment will be before a District Judge or Registrar but may be adjourned or referred to a High Court Judge. For this procedure, see CHAPTER 17, at paragraph 17.2.

Chapter 6

Renunciations

Form of renunciation

6.1   A person who wishes to give up his right to a grant of representation may do so by signing a form of renunciation (see Form A1.76, page 445). The renunciant's signature must be witnessed by a disinterested person. A renunciation is effective from the date it is signed. It may be withdrawn at any time before it is filed with the court, but thereafter may be retracted only by leave of a District Judge or Registrar. Subject to paragraph 6.2 below, the renunciation of an executor or co-executor or person with a prior entitlement to the grant, unless already filed, must be filed with the documents to lead the grant.

Where a renunciation in the English language is executed by a person in a non-English speaking country, it should be executed before a notary. Where it is not executed before a notary, it may be accepted by the Registry if the District Judge or Registrar is satisfied by other evidence that the renunciant was aware of the nature of the form he signed and the effect of the document.

A disclaimer is not effective to renounce title to a grant, its effect being to disclaim any beneficial interest in the estate.

Lodging will on renunciation

6.2   An executor who does not wish to administer his testator's estate may renounce his right to probate on the death of his testator. He cannot renounce *before* the testator's death. The renunciation may be filed at any Registry and the original will must be lodged with it. An executor renouncing his right to a grant of probate must at the same time also renounce any right to a grant to which he may be entitled in a lower capacity (for example to a grant of letters of administration (with will annexed) in his capacity as the residuary legatee and devisee in trust) under Rule 20(b).

Where there is no appointment, or no effective appointment, of an executor the will may be lodged with the renunciation of a residuary legatee and devisee or of the person next entitled in priority under Rule 20. The Registry in which the will is lodged on renunciation will record an entry in the index of pending grant applications (now maintained in the 'Probateman' computer system) which will be searched on any application for a grant. The original will will be held by the Registry in which it was lodged.

A will lodged on renunciation is not open to public inspection (until it is subsequently proved), nor can a copy be obtained as of right. Where application is made to prove such a will, the oath may be sworn and the will marked at the Registry at which it was lodged, or at another Registry. Alternatively, application may be made to a District Judge or Registrar for leave to mark a copy of the will (for which purpose a copy may be obtained from the Registry – see Rule 10(2)).

Executor's renunciation

On application for the grant

6.3   Should an executor have intermeddled in his testator's estate, he may not renounce probate. Any person entitled to a grant in any other capacity may renounce that right. The executor may be cited to take a grant of probate. Only an executor can be compelled to apply for a grant (see paragraph 16.13 below). If the executor is reluctant to take a grant, application may be made for an order passing over such executor under s 116 Supreme Court Act 1981 (see paragraph 5.27 above).

Rule 37 provides that the renunciation of probate by an executor does not operate as a renunciation of any right he may have to a grant in a lower capacity (for example, as a residuary legatee or devisee in trust to a grant of letters of administration (with will annexed)). Where an executor wishes to renounce all his entitlement to a grant in whatever capacity, the form of renunciation must expressly state this. The form of renunciation need not include renunciation in a lower capacity if probate is to be taken by another executor, that executor's title being superior in any event.

When an executor files a renunciation of probate of his testator's will, that executor also renounces his right of executorship of any will of which his testator had been executor. Any chain of representation under s 7 of the Administration of Estates Act 1925 (see paragraph 7.24 below) is thereby broken. If an executor does take probate, he cannot thereafter abrogate his responsibility as executor under a chain of representation.

After issue of the grant

6.4   Where a grant of probate has issued with power reserved to an executor, that executor may renounce his right by lodging a renunciation in the Registry from which the grant issued. Neither the original grant nor any copy need be lodged: no copy other than the record copy (i.e. the copy grant retained by the Registry) is noted. The Registry will endorse a note on the record copy grant that the executor has filed his renunciation. Where the Registry file has been transferred to the Probate Records Centre a memorandum will be sent for the renunciation to be noted on the copy grant lodged there.

Administrator's renunciation

6.5   Any person entitled to apply for a grant of letters of administration (with or without will) may renounce his right to that grant. The renunciation must state the capacity in which the renunciant was entitled. Rule 37(2) provides that, except with the leave of a District Judge or Registrar, a person who has renounced administration in one capacity may not obtain a grant in any other capacity.

Renunciation by attorney

6.6   Provided a power of attorney specifically authorises the attorney to renounce the donor's right to a grant, the attorney may renounce such right whatever the donor's entitlement. Where an attorney is acting under a registered enduring power of attorney he may renounce the donor's right to the grant (see Rule 35(2)(c) at paragraph 10.60 below): this will enable the residuary beneficiary to apply.

Renunciation by minor or person mentally incapable

As executor

6.7   Rule 34(1) provides that where a minor is appointed an executor, his right to a grant of probate on attaining his majority may not be renounced by any person on his behalf. Where representation was granted during the minor's minority, he may renounce on attaining his majority.

As administrator

6.8   Rule 34(2) provides that where a minor is entitled to a grant of administration (with or without will) his right may be renounced only by a person appointed by a District Judge or Registrar under Rule 32(2) and authorised to renounce on behalf of the minor (see paragraph 5.58 above).

Subject to the provisions of Rule 34(1) (see above), renunciation on behalf of a mentally incapable person may be made only by a person authorised by the Court of Protection in that respect. Where the incapable person is also a minor, the minor's right cannot be renounced until he attains his majority. In the absence of any person authorised to renounce, application may be made under s 116 of the Supreme Court Act 1981 (see paragraph 5.27 above) to pass over the person entitled to the grant.

Renunciation as personal representative

6.9   Any person entitled to a grant of administration by virtue of his being the personal representative of a deceased person who would have been entitled to a grant, if alive, may renounce his right in that capacity and in any other capacity in which he would have been entitled in his own right. This applies whether the personal representative is executor or administrator. Where there are two or more persons constituted personal representatives under a grant of letters of administration, one of them may renounce to enable application to be made by the other(s) (subject to any requirement for there to be more than one grantee where a life or minority interest arises). Where two or more executors have taken the 'leading grant', those who do not apply need not renounce or consent to enable administration to be taken by the other(s).

Renunciation by trust corporation

6.10   A trust corporation may renounce its right to a grant through its properly authorised officer; alternatively the form of renunciation must be sealed with the seal of that corporation. If the corporation does not have a seal, then the renunciation must be signed by two directors or a director and the company secretary (see s 36A Companies Act 1985). Where renunciation is made through an authorised or nominated officer the renunciation should state that the officer is authorised or nominated by a resolution, a copy of which has been lodged with the Senior District Judge and that the resolution is still in force. Alternatively, a copy of the resolution authorising the officer to act on behalf of the corporation must be lodged. As to trust corporations generally, see CHAPTER 11.

Renunciation by partners of a firm

6.11   Rule 37(2A) was introduced with effect from 14 September 1998. The new paragraph provides for two partners in a firm of solicitors or any other trading partnership, where all the partners were appointed executors, to renounce probate (and administration with will) on behalf of and with the authority of the other partners. The renunciation must recite the authority. For a form of renunciation see Form A1.77, page 446.

Retraction of renunciation

6.12   Rule 37(3) provides for a renunciation to be retracted at any time on the order of a District Judge or Registrar, but that only in exceptional circumstances may an executor retract his renunciation of probate if a grant has been made to another person entitled in a lower degree (see paragraph 5.26 above).

Similarly, a retraction of a renunciation by a person other than an executor may be made only where the circumstances of the case warrant it (for example on the death or incapacity of all other persons entitled to and able to complete the administration).

Application to retract a renunciation is made, pursuant to Rule 37(4), *ex parte* on affidavit setting out the facts of the case. The application may be made to the District Judge or Registrar of the Registry where the renunciation was lodged. The original grant (if a grant has issued – see paragraph 6.2 above), or a copy of it, should be lodged with the affidavit. Rule 37(2A), mentioned at paragraph 6.11 above, also allows retraction by two partners on behalf of, and with the authority of, their other partners.

Where leave to retract is granted, a form of retraction (Form A1.78, page 446) should be lodged with the application for the further grant.

Chapter 7

Grants of probate

Appointment of executors

7.1   A grant of probate issues to the executor (or executors) who prove(s) the deceased's will. Executors may be appointed:

(a)   expressly by name in the will (see paragraph 7.3 below);

(b)   by description in the will, such as 'the partners at the date of my death in AB and Co my solicitors or the firm which at that date has succeeded to or carries on their business' (see paragraph 7.4 below);

(c)   by the tenor of the will indicating in terms sufficiently setting out a person's duties that it was the testator's wish that that particular person act in the administration of his estate (see paragraph 7.5 below);

(d)   by the testator authorising by his will a named person to nominate an executor (see paragraph 7.6 below);

(e)   by the appointment of a person through the official title he holds, for example the Manager, Piggy's Bank, Anytown (see paragraph 7.7 below).

An executor's powers arise from the will and not from the grant of probate. The executor(s) appointed has/have a priority of entitlement over all others to prove the will by applying for the grant.

No prohibition on acting

7.2   A person capable of making a will is capable of being an executor. An executor properly appointed may act as such notwithstanding he is an undischarged bankrupt, is insolvent, is in prison or has been convicted of a serious crime. However, in such circumstances, it may be desirable for the executor not to act, and, unless he renounces his title to the grant, application may be made under s 116 of the Supreme Court Act 1981 (see paragraph 5.27 above) to pass over his prior title.

Appointment by name: change of name

7.3   Where executors are appointed expressly by name, all those who survive the deceased, provided they are not under a disability (that is, they are not minors and are mentally capable), may prove the will; have power to take a grant of probate reserved (see paragraph 7.16 below); or, if they do not wish to act, may renounce their right to a grant (see CHAPTER 6). Any difference between their true name(s) and the name(s) given in their appointment in the will must be recited in the oath. Where there has been a change of name, the manner of the change should be set out (for example, having changed her name on marriage; having reverted to her maiden name after her divorce; having changed his name by Deed Poll). Where the District Judge or Registrar is not satisfied that the identity of any executor is sufficiently established in the oath, confirmation of the true name may (at the court's discretion) be given by a letter, accompanied by a copy marriage certificate or Deed, from the extracting solicitors certifying such name. The court may make a direction for an affidavit of identity, dealing with the discrepancies, to be filed. For the form of such an affidavit, see Form A1.51, page 418.

Appointment by description

7.4   Where an appointment is by description as in paragraph 7.3 above, it must be clear who it is intended should take the grant. An appointment contained in the phrase 'the firm of XY and Co, Solicitors' is construed as an appointment of all the members (that is, partners) of that firm at the date of the will, unless the will expressly directs otherwise. Where the description is not clear the appointment may be void for uncertainty (but see paragraph 7.11 below) (see also *Re Horgan [1971] P 50, [1969] 3 All ER 1570, [1970] 2 WLR 393* referring to *Re Fernie (1849) 6 Notes of Cases 657).*

Executor according to the tenor of the will

7.5   An executor according to the tenor of the will is a person not specifically appointed an executor, but to whom the duties assigned by the testator are those which would normally be performed by an executor. For example where the will contains a statement directing a named person 'to pay all my debts' or 'to distribute my estate', this may be considered sufficient to constitute the named person an executor according to the tenor. An appointment of '"A" to be my personal representative' would also qualify 'A' to be an executor according to the tenor. The directions of the District Judge or Registrar should be taken on the sufficiency of the appointment.

Nominated executor

7.6   Where the will authorises a person to nominate another person as executor, the nominated person must lodge his authorisation (in the form of a signed nomination) with the oath to lead the grant and recite the details in the oath. An example is to appoint as executors 'such [two] partners in the firm of AB and Co at the date of my death as shall be nominated by the senior partner of that firm at that time'. The senior partner nominates the partner or partners as may be necessary (to the number specified, if there is a specified number). Unless there is a contrary statement the senior partner is, in the example given, taken to be the senior partner of the firm and not the senior partner by date of admission as a solicitor.

Executor by official position

7.7   Where the appointment is through a person's official title, for example, 'The Vicar of St Xavier's Church ...' without naming the incumbent, the appointment is held to be of the holder of the office at the date of death, unless the will contains an express wish to the contrary, that is the appointment was of the holder of the office at the time the will was executed. The oath to lead the grant should recite the fact that the applicant was the holder of the office at the appropriate time.

Where the appointment is of a trust corporation, application is made by a person authorised by resolution of that corporation either by name or by the position held, for example 'assistant manager of ...' (see CHAPTER 11).

Limited appointments

Limitation to part of the estate

7.8   An executor may be appointed to administer part only of the deceased's estate, for example his personal estate. Where the deceased left assets in more than one country, then the appointment may be limited to estate in a particular country. The testator may also appoint executors for specific purposes, for example (i) to deal with his literary estate or (ii) to administer settled land, and executors generally to administer the remaining estate. There is no longer provision for a grant of probate including settled land. If there is settled land to be administered, any special executors appointed for its administration will take a separate grant (of administration). See Rule 29 and paragraph 10.24 below.

Where the testator leaves a business, he may appoint an executor to carry on that business and another executor for the remainder of his estate. Each executor will prove the will: application may be made for one grant to include the particular limitation of the appointment for each executor. To make administration easier, however, it is probably preferable to take separate grants for each part of the estate. The first proving executor will prove the original will, and a copy (with the leave of the court) may be marked for the second grant application. If the grant applications are made contemporaneously, the original will should be marked by all proving executors.

Limitation to time

7.9   The appointment may be limited in other ways, for example as to time. A will may appoint an executor for a specific period after the testator's death or for the duration of a child's minority. Similarly, an appointment may be made to commence at a particular time. Where such an appointment leaves a period of time when there is no executor appointed to take up the administration of the estate, application may be made for a grant of letters of administration (with will annexed) by the person entitled thereto in accordance with Rule 20 (see paragraph 8.2 below); such a grant would be limited until the appointment of the executor becomes effective. Similarly, where the executor's appointment ceases to be effective because of the effluxion of the specified period of time, and estate remains unadministered, letters of administration (with will annexed) may be granted to the person next entitled under the rule.

Minor appointed

7.10   Where a minor is appointed sole executor, application may be made for a grant of letters of administration (with will annexed) limited for his use and benefit until he shall attain the age of 18 years. The application may be made by the person entitled to the residuary estate (unless a District Judge or Registrar otherwise directs) where the minor has no interest therein; or where the minor has a beneficial interest by a parent who has, or is deemed to have parental responsibility for him in accordance with paragraphs 12, 13 or 14 of Schedule 14 to the Children Act 1989 or a guardian of the minor appointed under s 5, or a person with parental responsibility pursuant to a residence order made under s 8 or a local authority to whose care the child has been committed under s 31(1)(a) of the Children Act 1989. (See also paragraph 10.48 below.)

Void appointments

7.11   Where there is uncertainty or ambiguity as to the appointment of executors the appointment may be void unless there is definitive evidence of the intention of the testator. Affidavit evidence of the testator's intention may be filed to clarify the appointment. The appointment of 'one of' or 'two of' the partners in a firm of solicitors without naming him or them is void for uncertainty (see *Re Baylis's Goods (1862) 2 SW & Tr 613* and *Re Blackwell's Goods (1877) 2 PD 72*). It is generally the case that the testator intended to appoint *all* the partners but also intended that only 'one' or 'two' of them should act.

Section 20 of the Administration of Justice Act 1982 empowers the court to order that a will be rectified so as to carry out the testator's intentions, where the court is satisfied that the will, *prima facie*, fails to carry out those intentions as a result of a clerical error or the failure to understand the testator's instructions. This section applies to an error in a bequest contained in the will in the same way as it applies to the appointment of executors.

Application to rectify is made *ex parte* on affidavit to a District Judge or Registrar and must clearly show that the error arose from circumstances within the ambit of s 20. For the procedure on rectification, see paragraphs 5.21–5.24 above.

Similarly, s 21 of the Administration of Justice Act 1982 empowers the court to accept extrinsic evidence, including evidence of the testator's intention, to assist in the interpretation of a will in so far as:

(a)   any part of it is meaningless;

(b)   the language used in any part of it is ambiguous on the face of it; or

(c)   evidence other than evidence of the testator's intention, shows that the language used in any part of it is ambiguous in the light of the surrounding circumstances.

It is the usual practice of the District Judges and Registrars to apply s 21 to an appointment of executors which is uncertain, i.e. to interpret the appointment in accordance with the testator's intention.

Application for a direction as to interpretation is made *ex parte* on affidavit to the District Judge or Registrar of the Registry to which it is intended to apply for the grant. See paragraph 5.25 above.

Executor appointed on condition: substituted appointment

7.12   Where an executor is appointed on a condition, for example 'that "A" remains my husband at the date of my death', he must satisfy the court that the condition has been met by including an appropriate statement in the oath to lead the grant. Where the condition is that the executor proves within a prescribed period, his appointment fails unless application is made within the prescribed time. A testator may appoint another executor to be substituted if the first named executor predeceases the testator, fails to apply within a prescribed time or is unable or unwilling to prove the will and administer the estate. This may continue through a series of conditional appointments.

Two appointments

7.13   Where a will contains two appointments of executors and the later appointment describes the executor as 'sole executor' the earlier appointment is revoked. Similarly, an appointment of a sole executor in a codicil serves to revoke the appointment of executors in the will or another earlier codicil. This applies even though there are no expressed words revoking the former appointment. The directions of the court should be obtained before application for a grant.

Executor a non-trust corporation

7.14   Where a testator has appointed as his sole executor a corporation which is a non-trust corporation, that corporation cannot take a grant of probate (see Rule 2(1), and paragraph 11.2 below for the definition of a trust corporation and as to trust corporations generally).

A grant of letters of administration (with will annexed) may issue to a nominee of the corporation, or its lawfully constituted attorney (see Rule 36(4)), provided the corporation has power under its constitution to take such a grant through its nominee or attorney.

However, if the appointment is of a corporation and an individual, that individual has a prior right to the grant (which would be a grant of probate). Application may be made for probate by the individual with power reserved to the corporation (that corporation's ability to take probate being decided at the time of any subsequent application for double probate).

If the corporation is to apply through its nominee, the individual's prior right must be cleared by reciting his predecease if that is the case, or by his renouncing title.

The oath to lead the grant must recite the fact that the corporation is not a trust corporation as defined by Rule 2(1) but is empowered by its constitution to take the grant. A copy of the constitution or the relevant extract may be called for but usually the sworn statement in the oath is now accepted as sufficient. The resolution authorising the nominee or the power of attorney must, however, be lodged.

Appointment of firm as executors

7.15   Where the will appoints a firm (for example, AB and Co, solicitors, or XY and Co, accountants) as executors, unless the will contains an express direction to the contrary (at the date of my death) the appointment is construed as an appointment of all the partners at the date of the will. The oath to lead the grant must account for all non-proving partners at the relevant date by reciting their predecease, renunciation or having power reserved.

However, if the will omits the express direction but contains an appointment of a successor firm, the appointment is usually interpreted as being of the partners at the date of death.

Where the appointment is of all the partners in a firm but that firm has changed its constitution so that there are 'directors' instead of partners, the appointment is regarded as being void: there now being no 'partners' in the firm.

Reserving power to non-proving executors to take a grant

7.16   Where several executors are appointed in a will any one or more of them, up to a maximum of four, may prove the will (s 114(1) Supreme Court Act 1981). Those who do not prove may renounce their right to apply or elect to have power reserved to them to take a grant at a later stage.

Executors for different parts of the estate

7.17   Where the testator appointed four (or more) general executors, and an executor or executors limited to a particular aspect of his estate the administration of which was excluded from the power given to the general executors, the normal limitation of four executors to whom probate may be granted may be exceeded, but only to the extent that there can never be more than four executors acting in respect of the same part of the estate (for example, there could be four general executors and four literary executors).

Subsequent application by executors who had power reserved

7.18   The grant applied for by an executor to whom power had been reserved is a grant of double probate (see paragraph 10.19 below). Application for the further grant (of double probate) may be made at any time after the grant of probate has issued and usually occurs when a vacancy arises, either through death or incapacity, in the executors who originally proved the will. At no time may the number of executors acting under the original grant and the grant of double probate exceed the maximum permitted (four) in respect of the same part of the estate.

Should power have been reserved to more than one executor, but only one seeks the grant of double probate and power is still to be reserved to the other, a statement to this effect should be endorsed on the oath (see Form A1.3, page 345 for the form of oath, and see below).

Notice under Rule 27

7.19   Rule 27(1) now provides, subject to paragraphs (1A), (2) and (3) (see below), that the proving executor or executors must give notice of their application to all non-proving executors who are having power reserved to them, and a statement to this effect must be included in the oath. The manner of giving such notice is a matter for the proving executors.

Rule 27(1A) as amended from 14 September 1998 provides that where power is to be reserved to executors who are partners in a firm notice need not be given to them under paragraph (1) of the rule if probate is applied for by another partner in that firm. There is no need for the non-proving partners to be named in the oath (Registrar's Direction, 12 June 1990), the oath simply reciting that power is reserved to *all* the remaining partners in the firm at the date of death (or as the case may be).

Rule 27(2) provides that where power is to be reserved to partners in a firm and notice has to be given under paragraph (1), then notice of the application may be given by sending it to the firm at its principal or last known place of business.

Dispensing with notice under Rule 27

7.20   Rule 27(3) allows a District Judge or Registrar to dispense with the giving of notice where it is impracticable to do so, or where to do so would result in unreasonable delay or expense. Application to dispense with the giving of such notice should be made before the application for the grant, as the oath must recite that the giving of such notice to the other executor(s) (or any one of them) has been dispensed with. Application to dispense with the giving of notice may be made by letter setting out the reasons for dispensation (Registrar's Direction 21 December 1987). These provisions apply equally to original grants and to grants of double probate.

Executor incapable

7.21   A grant of probate will not be given to an executor who is mentally incapable of managing his affairs, nor will it be given to a minor child; in other words, unless a person has testamentary capacity he cannot act as an executor (see paragraphs 10.47 and 10.60 below).

Where there are two or more executors, those capable may prove the will, and power may be reserved to the incapable executor should he regain his mental capacity.

Where the sole or surviving executor is mentally incapable, it is usual for administration (with will annexed) to be taken for the executor's use and benefit. Application for an order under Rule 35 for the use and benefit of an incapable executor is dealt with in CHAPTER 5 at paragraph 5.62 above. However, under s 116 of the Supreme Court Act 1981 (see paragraph 5.27 above) application could be made to pass over the executor. Application is made under s 116 where it is considered that the executor should be deemed unfit to act not through mental incapacity but, for example, by virtue of his being bankrupt or in prison or having a conflict of interest with the beneficiaries under the will.

Where the executor is physically incapable of acting, he may renounce or appoint an attorney. If he fails to do either, then application may be made under s 116 as referred to above.

Renunciation

7.22   An executor may renounce his right to take a grant of probate at any time after his testator's death provided he has not intermeddled in the estate. Generally, to be considered to have intermeddled, an executor must have assumed some duty or performed an act which would normally only be attributable to a person assuming the mantle of executorship. As an intermeddling executor cannot renounce he must take probate but, where he refuses to do so, application may be made to pass over his title under s 116 of the Supreme Court Act 1981 (see paragraph 5.27 above and see *Re Biggs' Estate [1966] 1 All ER 358*). Such an application is generally preferable to citing the executor to take or refuse probate. See CHAPTER 16 as to citations. Renunciation by partners (on behalf of other partners) in a firm, and renunciation generally, are dealt with in CHAPTER 6.

Chain of executorship

Creation of the chain

7.23   If a sole or last surviving executor who has proved a will dies testate before he has completed the administration of the estate, the unadministered estate may be dealt with by the executor's executor. This chain of representation exists provided the executor appointed in the will of the sole or last surviving executor proves his testator's will. It will not be necessary for a fresh grant to be applied for to deal with the unadministered estate, the original grant and the grant to the executor's estate being used together to administer the unadministered estate (see s 7(1) Administration of Estates Act 1925).

Breaking of the chain

7.24   A chain of representation may continue through several sole or last surviving proving executors, but will be broken should such an executor die intestate, fail to appoint an executor in his will or an appointment of executor otherwise fails (e.g. predecease of executor), or fail to take a grant of probate (see s 7(3) of the Act). Where the original grant was taken by one of two or more executors with power reserved to the non-proving executors, a chain continues through the proving or last surviving proving executor. The chain through the original proving executor will be broken should be non-proving executor take a grant of double probate (see paragraph 10.19) below).

Chain through resealed grant

7.25　The chain may continue through grants issued by courts of states or countries to which the Colonial Probates Act 1892 applies, provided the grants have been resealed (see CHAPTER 15). Similarly, the chain may continue through a grant issued by a court in Northern Ireland provided the testator died domiciled there (see s 7(1) of the 1925 Act). However, the chain does not pass through a Scottish confirmation.

Effect of an impounded grant

7.26　A chain may continue through a grant which has been impounded (see paragraph 18.18 below for the practice on impounded grants) through the sole or last surviving executor becoming mentally incapable. On such an executor dying testate without recovering his capacity the impounded grant may be handed out on application therefor by his executor.

Effect of limited grant

7.27　The chain is not broken by a grant limited to part of the estate or a temporary grant, for example a grant of administration *ad colligenda bona* (see paragraph 10.5 below), provided a full grant of probate is taken, the chain passing through those who take the full grant. Executorship is not transmitted if the executor's appointment is limited in time; nor is a chain of representation created through an administrator added after the grant's issue (see paragraph 9.2 below). An executorship transmitted through a chain carries the same rights as those held by the original executor.

Each grant forming the chain of executorship must be produced as evidence to administer estate.

Time limit for grant

7.28　Rule 6(2) provides that, except with the leave of a District Judge or Registrar, no grant of probate may issue within seven days of the death of the deceased. The papers may be lodged with the Registry before the seven days have expired but the Registry, unless leave to expedite is granted, will not allow the grant to issue until that period has expired. The day of death is excluded when calculating the prescribed period.

Application to abridge the time limit may be made by letter, or exceptionally on affidavit, setting out the reason(s) why the grant's issue is required earlier, for example where contracts to sell real property have been exchanged and the grant is required to enable completion to be effected, or to exercise voting rights in a stock or share transaction.

Citation to accept or refuse probate

7.29   If an executor appointed by a will refuses or neglects to prove the will he may be cited to accept or refuse probate. The citation may be issued at the instance of any person who would himself be entitled to a grant should the executor renounce (Rule 47(1)). An executor to whom power was reserved may be cited to accept or refuse a grant by the proving executor(s) or the executors of the last survivor of deceased executors who have proved the will (Rule 47(2)). Where he does not enter an appearance to the citation, application may be made for an order for a grant of letters of administration (with will annexed) to be made to the citor, being the person next entitled in priority (see paragraph 8.2 below for the order of priority and paragraph 16.17 below for the procedure on citations).

Oath to lead application

Executors

7.30   Rule 8 provides, *inter alia*, that every application for a grant of probate must be led by an oath sworn, or affirmed, by every executor applying for the grant. Rule 3 applies the provisions of Order 41 of the Rules of the Supreme Court 1965 (note: the Rules of the Supreme Court 1965 still apply to applications made within the Non-Contentious Probate Rules) as to the form of any oath or affidavit used in non-contentious probate business. Where a deponent is taking probate in a professional capacity, for example as a solicitor or accountant, his business address may be given. Otherwise the full *permanent* address must be given. The business address of a trust corporation is usually shown in the grant: the grant will, unless otherwise requested, show the address given in the oath. Former addresses are unnecessary except where such address assists in establishing the identity of the executor. The occupation or, if none, the descriptions of each deponent must be inserted, although the omission of the occupation or description would not cause the oath to be rejected.

The order of executors appearing in the oath will be repeated in the grant unless there is a specific request to change the order. Titles of the nobility and ecclesiastical appointments should be recited.

Any difference between the executor's true name and that appearing in the appointment must be stated and explained, for example 'Mary Smith in the will called Mary Jones having changed her name on marriage' or 'by Deed Poll'. Alternatively, a separate affidavit of identity may be filed (see Form A1.51, page 418, which should be adapted as the circumstances require).

Where an executor is having reserved to him power to take a like grant, the oath must recite that notice of the application has been given to him (subject to Rule 27(1A) – see paragraph 7.19 above), or that the giving of such notice has been dispensed with by District Judge's or Registrar's direction under Rule 27(3).

Testamentary documents

7.31   The will and any codicils must be recited (for example 'the last will and testament with a codicil thereto'), and each document being proved, including any documents being treated as incorporated (see paragraphs 2.44–2.48 above), must be marked with the signatures of the deponents and the solicitor or other authorised person before whom the oath was sworn.

Testator's name(s) and address

7.32   Additionally, the executor's oath must account for any difference between the testator's true name and any alias and give the reason(s) why any alias is required to appear in the grant (for example that a specific asset, which must be identified, is held in a different name; or that the testator made his will in a different name; see Rule 9). The testator's last permanent address and any former address appearing in the will or last codicil, if different, must be stated. It is no longer the policy of Probate Registries to include a former address in the grant as a matter of course. If, for identification or any other relevant purpose a former or second address is required to appear in the grant, this must be specifically requested. The postcode of the last permanent address must be included (President's Practice Direction 22 March 2002).

Dates of birth/death

7.33   The date of death appearing in the death certificate and the age of the deceased must be inserted or, where this cannot be precisely sworn, an approximation, for example 'over 65' (see paragraph 3.4 above) may be given. Where the deceased's death was registered in the United Kingdom, his date of birth as it appears in the death certificate must be given (Practice Direction 12 January 1999).

Domicile

7.34   Unless otherwise directed by a District Judge or Registrar, the state or country in which the deceased died domiciled must be given in the oath (Rule 8(2)). It is imperative that the correct domicile is inserted; the court's jurisdiction to entertain the application in the form made is determined by the deceased's domicile.

Settled land

7.35   The oath must also contain a statement as to whether or not there is any settled land in accordance with Rule 8(3).

Status of deponents

7.36   The designation of the deponent(s), for example 'two of the surviving executors named in the said will', must be given in the oath.

Estate values

7.37   The oath should conclude with a statement of the duties of personal representatives as prescribed by s 25 of the Administration of Estates Act 1925; and a statement of the gross and net values of the estate and that, if appropriate, it is not a case in which an Inland Revenue Account is required to be delivered. For the form of oath and further instructions on completion, see Form A1.1, page 340; see also CHAPTER 13.

Delivery to Registry

7.38   The oath, original will (and any codicil(s)), Form D18 (if appropriate) (see CHAPTER 12) and any other necessary documents (such as an affidavit of due execution) may be sent or delivered to any Probate Registry or sub-Registry (see APPENDIX 3), together with the appropriate fee (see APPENDIX 2).

Chapter 8

Grants of letters of administration (with will annexed)

A grant of letters of administration (with will annexed) issues to the person, other than an executor, who proves the will.

Circumstances in which a grant will issue

8.1   A grant in this form will issue:

(a)   where there is no executor appointed by the will;

(b)   where the appointment of the executor in the will is void for uncertainty;

(c)   where the executor appointed by the will cannot prove the will because he is a minor or is mentally incapable of managing his affairs or applies through his lawfully constituted attorney (an executor may apply for a grant through his attorney irrespective of whether he is resident in England and Wales or elsewhere) (applications by attorneys are dealt with at paragraph 10.32 below);

(d)   where the executor appointed by the will has renounced his entitlement to prove the will or has been cited to accept or refuse probate and has not entered an appearance to the citation;

(e)   where the executor appointed by the will has predeceased the testator or has survived the testator but died without proving the will;

(f)   where, in respect of deaths on or after 1 January 1983, the sole executor, or sole surviving executor, appointed by the will is the testator's former spouse (their marriage having been dissolved or annulled) and such appointment is omitted by virtue of s 18A(1)(a) of the Wills Act 1837 (see paragraph 2.76 above);

(g)   where the executor's appointment relates only to the administration of estate outside the jurisdiction of the court;

(h)   where the court, on request, exercises its discretion under s 116 Supreme Court Act 1981 to pass over the executor named in the will (see CHAPTER 5 at paragraph 5.27 above);

(i)   where the sole executor appointed is a corporation or charitable or other organisation but not within the definition of a trust corporation (see paragraph 11.2 below), when the grant will issue to the corporation's nominee or lawfully appointed attorney (applications by non-trust corporations are dealt with at paragraph 11.17 below).

The grant cannot issue to more than four persons in respect of the same part of the estate (see paragraph 7.16 above) (s 114(1) Supreme Court Act 1981).

Where a life or minority interest arises in the estate, there must be at least two grantees, unless the District Judge or Registrar directs otherwise (s 114(2) Supreme Court Act 1981).

Except with the leave of a District Judge or Registrar, the grant cannot issue within seven days of the testator's death (Rule 6(2)). Application for leave to abridge the time limit is made by letter setting out the reason(s) why the grant is required to issue earlier, for example to complete the sale of real property, contracts having already been exchanged.

To whom the grant may be made

8.2   Rule 20 provides that the person or persons entitled to a grant of probate or letters of administration (with will annexed) shall be determined in accordance with the following order of priority:

(a)   the executor (save that where a corporation, not being a trust corporation, is appointed jointly with an individual, the provisions of Rule 36(4)(d) shall not apply unless the right of the individual has been cleared off; see paragraph 11.17 below for the provisions of Rule 36(4));

(b)   any residuary legatee or devisee holding in trust for any other person;

(c)   any other residuary legatee or devisee (including one for life) or, where the residue is not wholly disposed of by the will, any person entitled to share in the undisposed of residue (including the Treasury Solicitor when claiming *bona vacantia* on behalf of the Crown), provided that:

   (i)   unless a District Judge or Registrar otherwise directs, a residuary legatee or devisee whose legacy or devise is vested in interest shall be preferred to one entitled on the happening of a contingency; and

   (ii)   where the residue is not in terms wholly disposed of, the District Judge or Registrar may, if he is satisfied that the testator has nevertheless disposed of the whole or substantially the whole of the known estate, allow a grant to be made to any legatee or devisee entitled to, or to share in, the estate so disposed of, without regard to the persons entitled to share in any residue not disposed of by the will;

(d)   the personal representative of any residuary legatee or devisee (but not one for life or one holding on trust for any other person), or of any person entitled to share in any residue not disposed of by the will;

(e)   any other legatee or devisee (including one for life or one holding in trust for any other person), or any creditor, provided that, unless a District Judge or Registrar directs otherwise, a legatee or devisee whose legacy or devise is vested in interest shall be preferred to one entitled on the happening of any contingency;

(f)   the personal representative of any other legatee or devisee (but not one for life or one holding in trust for any other person), or of any creditor.

Entitlement

Oath to set out 'clearings'

8.3   Whoever applies for the grant of letters of administration (with will annexed) must establish his title to the grant in the oath to lead the grant. All surviving persons with a higher entitlement to that of the applicant must be cleared off by renunciation, consent or citation (see paragraphs 6.3, 11.9 and 16.13), and the manner in which they are cleared must be set out in the oath (see Rule 8(4)).

A sole or last surviving executor who does not wish to act must renounce his right to the grant of probate; he cannot merely consent to the grant being given to an individual. He can appoint an attorney to apply for a grant for his use and benefit (see paragraph 10.32 below for attorney applications) and, with the consent of the residuary beneficiaries, a grant may issue to a trust corporation. Where the executor (or trustee or beneficiary) is a corporation, but not a trust corporation as defined by Rule 2(1), the corporation may take administration (with will annexed) through its properly authorised nominee or lawfully appointed attorney.

Renunciation by trustee

8.4   Where a sole or last surviving executor does not wish to take a grant and he is also the (or one of the) residuary legatee(s) or devisee(s) in trust, he must also renounce his right to a grant of letters of administration (with will annexed), he being the person next entitled in his capacity as a trustee (Rule 20(b)). It should be noted that before an executor (or any other person) is constituted a residuary legatee or devisee in trust the will must contain a specific gift to be held in trust for another; it is insufficient for him to be so constituted by the testator appointing him 'my executor and trustee'.

Number of grantees

8.5   Any number of persons, subject to the limitation of four persons, of equal class of entitlement may apply for the grant without reference to others of the same class (see Rule 27(4)). For example, where the residuary estate is divided between two beneficiaries, either may apply without reference to the other. No notice of the application is required to be given, as in the case for non-proving executors.

Dispute between persons of equal entitlement

8.6   Where a dispute arises between two persons of equal entitlement, the matter may be brought before a District Judge or Registrar on summons (see paragraph 17.1 below and Rule 27(6)).

Preference of 'live' interest

8.7   Unless otherwise directed by a District Judge or Registrar, administration will be granted to a living person in preference to the personal representative of a deceased person who would have been entitled in the same degree had he been alive (Rule 27(5)). This means, for example, that where the deceased was survived by his two residuary legatees, one of whom then dies, the survivor is entitled in preference to the now deceased beneficiary's personal representative (the person who has taken the grant to his estate).

Grant to assignees

8.8   Where persons beneficially interested in the deceased's estate assign all their interest to another or others, the assignee(s) replace(s) those persons in the normal order of priority for a grant under Rule 22 (paragraph 9.28 below) (see generally Rule 24).

Residuary legatees or devisees

Definition

8.9   A residuary legatee is the person to whom the residue of the personal estate passes; a residuary devisee is the person to whom the residue of the real estate passes. Generally, this is one and the same person. To be a residuary legatee or devisee in trust the will must clearly state that the residue of the testator's estate is held on a declared trust for another (see paragraph 8.4 above).

Determining disposition of residue

Absence of specific gift of residue

8.10   Difficulties frequently occur in determining whether a will disposes of the residuary estate. In the absence of a specific gift of residue the will must be considered as a whole and the testator's words considered in an endeavour to ascertain his intentions. To constitute a residuary gift the words used must be sufficiently clear so as to lead to the conclusion that the testator intended by those words to dispose of everything that was not otherwise disposed of by the will.

Phrases and words accepted as gifts of residue

8.11   Where the term 'money' or 'moneys' is used, the whole of the phraseology of the will must be considered to determine whether the testator intended the expression to represent 'possessions'. This may constitute a gift of residue.

It is generally accepted that phrases such as 'all I possess'; 'the rest of my money'; 'after these the remainder'; 'all my estate or property'; 'all my belongings'; 'everything I own' are sufficient to constitute a gift of the residue of the estate and for those named as beneficiaries of such gifts to be entitled as residuary legatees/devisees (see *Perrin v Morgan [1943] 1 All ER 187* and *Re Schott's Will Trust (1968) 112 Sol Jo 335*). The will should be considered as a whole, and the words used given their usual grammatical meaning. Although there may be no specific use of the words 'residue' or 'remainder', there may be sufficient to infer (i.e. an 'inferential gift') the disposition of the residuary estate.

Relatives

8.12   Consideration must be given not only to the words used to frame the gift of residue, but also to the words used to indicate the intended beneficiaries.

A gift to 'my relatives' has been held to be a gift to those persons entitled to share under an intestacy. Similarly a gift to 'my next of kin' has been held to be to the person(s) entitled under an intestacy.

A gift to 'my children' has been held to mean a gift to issue living at the date of death. 'Children', as a class, includes all issue living at the date of death so would include grandchildren, great-grandchildren and so on. However, a gift to 'children of our marriage' means a gift to children only, excluding grandchildren. 'Issue' also includes any illegitimate children of the deceased and any child adopted by him. Any child of the deceased adopted away from him becomes the child of his adopters and would not receive any benefit – see s 39(2) of the Adoption Act 1976.

'Adoption' includes orders made abroad which are recognisable under Part IV of the Act. 'Family' has, however, been held to be the children of the deceased.

Double gift of residue

8.13 Where there is an apparent double gift of the residue, that is where the will makes a gift of all the estate to a named person, then specific bequests followed by a gift of the remainder, it has been held that the earlier gift takes precedence, the later being intended to deal with any lapsed specific gifts. (See *Re Gare, Filmer v Carter [1951] 2 All ER 863.*) Where any doubt arises, the views of a District Judge or Registrar should be sought before application for a grant (but see also paragraph 8.24 below).

Residue not wholly disposed of

8.14 The District Judge or Registrar may, if he is satisfied that notwithstanding the residue is not in terms wholly disposed of but that there is a disposition of the whole or substantially the whole known estate, allow a grant to issue to any legatee or devisee entitled to, or to share in, the estate which is disposed of. The directions of a District Judge or Registrar should be sought if there is a disposition of substantially the whole estate.

The importance of establishing whether there is or is not a gift of residue is that from the determination follows title to the grant. The Probate Registries construe purported residuary gifts simply to determine title to the grant.

Secret trust

8.15 Difficulties may also occur in determining whether a gift to trustees is sufficient to make them residuary legatees or devisees in trust (see paragraph 8.3 above). In the absence of an effective gift on trust the 'trustee's' title is lost. It is accepted that a gift to trustees of 'all my estate to deal with in accordance with my wishes', although *prima facie* a secret trust, is sufficient to constitute them residuary legatees and devisees in trust. Where the wording contained in the will raises doubt as to entitlement to the grant the matter should be referred to a District Judge or Registrar for directions before any application for a grant is made.

Gifts to charity or to hospitals

Charities

8.16 Frequently, wills contain gifts to charities which are not named or are improperly named, giving rise to doubt as to the intended beneficiary.

Similarly, wills often contain gifts 'for charitable purposes'; 'to charity'; 'for cancer research'; or 'for use in famine relief'. Where there is doubt as to which charity was intended to benefit, the directions of the Attorney-General (through the Treasury Solicitor) should be obtained. If title to apply for the grant depends on the determination of the intended charitable beneficiary the matter should be referred to the Treasury Solicitor before any application for a grant is made. The Attorney-General possesses the sole right to represent the beneficial interest of any charity or charitable organisation.

Enquiry of the Attorney-General should be addressed to:

The Treasury Solicitor (Charities Team)
Queen Anne's Chambers
28 Broadway
London
SW1 9JS
DX: 123240 St James's Park
Tel: 020 7210 3000

A gift of residue in a will to a church at a particular place which has closed has been held to be a gift to the church charity payable to its trustees: see *Re Broadbent (2001) Times, 27 June.*

Hospitals

8.17 A gift to a hospital within the National Health Service remains effective provided that the purpose for which the hospital was founded remains. Such a gift would now pass to the Hospital Management Committee unless there is a specific reference to a part of the hospital or purpose for the gift. The Management Committee, if not a trust corporation, would apply for a grant through its nominee authorised by resolution or lawful attorney.

Where doubt arises because the hospital is now contained within a National Health Trust, it should be referred to a District Judge or Registrar for directions.

Section 33 Wills Act 1837

8.18 Where the deceased died on or after 1 January 1983, s 33 as now enacted provides that:

'(1) Where:

(a) a will contains a devise or bequest to a child or remoter descendant of the testator; and

(b) the intended beneficiary dies before the testator, leaving issue; and

(c)   issue of the intended beneficiary are living at the testator's death,

then, unless a contrary intention appears by the will, the devise or bequest shall take effect as a devise or bequest to the issue living at the testator's death.

(2)   Where:

(a)   a will contains a devise or bequest to a class of persons consisting of children or remoter descendants of the testator; and

(b)   a member of the class dies before the testator, leaving issue; and

(c)   issue of that member are living at the testator's death,

then, unless a contrary intention appears by the will, the devise or bequest shall take effect as if the class included the issue of its deceased member living at the testator's death.

(3)   Issue shall take under this section through all degrees, according to their stock, in equal shares if more than one, any gift or share which their parent would have taken and so that no issue shall take whose parent is living at the testator's death and so capable of taking.

(4)   For the purposes of this section—

(a)   the illegitimacy of any person is to be disregarded; and

(b)   a person conceived before the testator's death and born living thereafter is to be taken to have been living at the testator's death.'

Where the applicant relies on the provisions of s 33 for his entitlement to the grant, this fact and the details of his predeceasing parent must be recited in the oath. Form A1.17, page 369, may be adapted for use in this application.

It should be noted that a specific legacy or bequest to a person other than a child or remoter descendant of the testator, who dies in the testator's lifetime, fails, and falls into the residue, unless there is a specific saving clause to the bequest.

Absolute gifts: gifts over

For a comprehensive exposition of the law relating to the interpretation of gifts of residue, see *Tolley's Administration of Estates, Part E.*

Life interest: grantee(s)

8.19   Where the residue of the estate is left to a person for that person's life (see paragraph 8.26 below), the grant of administration (with will annexed) will normally issue to at least two grantees or a trust corporation. The Probate Registry's concern is to establish (a) whether there is a life interest requiring there to be at least two grantees or a trust corporation as grantee (see s 114 Supreme Court Act 1981) and (b) whether there is sufficient evidence to support an application for the court's directions under s 114 to allow a grant to issue to a sole grantee.

Implied gift over

8.20   Where a will makes an apparent absolute gift and then implies a gift over, there is a general rule that the absolute gift takes priority over the gift over, thereby not creating a life interest. However, there are occasions when the terms of the will are such that an absolute gift is reduced to a life interest and, *vice versa*, an apparent life interest is considered an absolute gift. The intentions of the testator as a whole must be considered within the words used in making the gift. The principle, supported by case law, is that a gift once given cannot then be made the subject of a course of devolution.

Gift over on contingency

8.21   Where there appears from the terms of a will an absolute gift but subject to a contingency, the determining factor is the occurrence of the contingency. For example, a gift to a widow 'until she shall remarry' would be deemed to be an absolute gift if the widow died unmarried. With effect from the coming into force of s 22 Administration of Justice Act 1982 (1 January 1983), there is a presumption that where a testator devises or bequeaths property to his *spouse* in his will, in terms which in themselves would give an absolute interest to the spouse, but by the same instrument purports to give his *issue* an interest in the same property, the gift to the spouse is absolute notwithstanding the purported gift to the issue. This provision does not apply to gifts to persons other than a spouse or gifts over to persons other than issue. However, where the testator's intention is clear from the plain English meaning of the words used, the gift may be treated similarly. A gift of 'all the remainder of which I am possessed to my sister and thereafter to her issue' was held to be an absolute gift of residue to the sister (see *Re Gouk, Allen v Allen [1957] 1 All ER 469*).

Residue substantially disposed of

8.22   Where the executors and residuary legatees or devisees in trust have been cleared off, application may be made by a residuary legatee or devisee, including one for life. If the residue is not wholly disposed of, but the District Judge or Registrar is satisfied that the whole or substantially the whole known estate is disposed of, application may be made by any legatee or devisee entitled to, or to share in, the estate so disposed of without regard to the persons entitled to share in any residue not disposed of by the will (see Rule 20(c)(ii)).

There is no general rule as to what constitutes 'substantially the whole known estate'. Where application is to be made on this basis it is preferable to submit the facts, including the values of the estate disposed of and the total known values to the court, as a pre-lodgment enquiry, for directions.

Person(s) entitled to undisposed of estate

8.23   Where the residue of the estate is not disposed of, or the residuary gift fails, then on clearing off any executor those persons entitled to share in the estate now undisposed of may apply for the grant. The undisposed of estate passes to those who would be entitled to benefit under a total intestacy and accordingly the order of priority to apply follows Rule 22 (see paragraph 9.28 below).

Where the person entitled to the undisposed of estate is the surviving spouse, the statutory legacy prescribed by s 46 (as amended) of the Administration of Estates Act 1925 applies. The spouse is currently entitled to £125,000 if issue also survive, and £200,000 if there are no issue surviving. It follows that a life and/or minority interest may arise in respect of the undisposed part of the estate, requiring there to be two grantees.

If the surviving spouse subsequently dies, his personal representative is entitled to take a grant (see Rule 20(d)).

Rule 38 provides for notice of an application for a grant to be given to the Treasury Solicitor where it appears the Crown is or may be beneficially interested in the deceased's estate, that is, where there are no known kin entitled to (share in) the estate undisposed of by the will. The Treasury Solicitor's acknowledgment of the notice must be lodged with the papers to lead the grant. If the Treasury Solicitor does claim *bona vacantia*, he has an entitlement to the grant which, if he does not apply, must be cleared by renunciation.

Vested interest preferred to contingent interest

8.24   A legatee or devisee, whether residual or otherwise, whose interest is vested, has preference of entitlement to the grant over that of a legatee or devisee whose interest is contingent upon the happening of any event, for example attaining 25 years of age. (See Rule 20(c)(i) and 20(e) at paragraph 8.2 above.) The court has a discretion to override this preference if the circumstances of a particular case so justify.

Conditional gift

8.25   Where a gift is subject to a condition, the condition must be a fulfillable condition to make the gift effective. If the wording of the condition is unclear, the condition may be void for uncertainty and the court must decide whether the gift is effective.

It is not the function of the Probate Registries to be a court of construction to determine vested, contingent or conditional interests, except where it is necessary to construe a gift to determine entitlement to apply for the grant. Generally, questions of construction fall to be determined in the Chancery Division.

Grant to assignees

8.26   Rule 24 provides that where the person(s) entitled to the estate assign their whole interest to one or more other persons, the assignees take the place of the assignors in the order of priority under Rule 20 and may take administration (with will annexed). Clearly all those with a prior entitlement under the Rule must be cleared off before the assignees may apply. The original Deed of Assignment should be lodged with the Registry and a copy provided for the court's retention, the copy being certified as a true and complete copy and signed by a person authorised to sign in the firm's name.

Life or minority interest: number of personal representatives

Required number of grantees

8.27   If a life or minority interest arises under the terms of the will (or as a result of a partial intestacy because the residue is not (fully) disposed of, or those entitled to the residue predeceased the deceased), there must either be at least two applicants for the grant, or application may be made by a trust corporation, with or without an individual joining in.

Application for grant to sole grantee

8.28   On application being made, a District Judge or Registrar, having taken into account all the circumstances, may consider it expedient to allow the grant to issue to one person and make a direction accordingly (see s 114(2) Supreme Court Act 1981). Since there are now no provisions in the Rules for an administration guarantee to be directed, the court will always require evidence and sufficient cause to be shown before allowing a grant to issue to an individual alone. Application for the direction under s 114 is made *ex parte* on affidavit, but subject to the court's discretion may be made by letter setting out the facts. Where there is only one person of the higher class entitled, a person of a lower class of entitlement may be added as joint administrator (see paragraph 9.28 below for the order of priority of entitlement).

Addition of personal representative after grant's issue

8.29   Section 114(4) of the 1981 Act provides for an additional personal representative to be appointed to act during the minority of a beneficiary or while a life interest subsists. This may occur when one of the original grantees dies or becomes incapable of continuing the administration. It sometimes occurs that a life or minority interest arises only after the grant has issued (to a sole grantee). Application to appoint an additional personal representative is made to a District Judge or Registrar *ex parte* on affidavit by the applicant, supported by the consent of the proposed additional representative (see Rule 26). The District Judge or Registrar may direct the filing of such other evidence as he requires. On any such application the District Judge or Registrar may direct that a note be made on the original grant of the addition of another personal representative, or he may impound or revoke the grant or make such other order as the circumstances of the case require.

Loss of beneficiary's entitlement to grant

Attesting witness

Loss of right to grant

8.30   Section 15 of the Wills Act 1837 provides that a person taking any beneficial interest under a will loses that benefit if he or his spouse was an attesting witness to the will. Not only is the benefit lost, but the right to the grant if it derives from the beneficial interest in the normal order of priority is also lost.

A charging clause in a will providing for a professional person to charge for services in administering an estate was held to equate with a legacy and would therefore be forfeit (*Re Pooley (1888) 40 Ch D 1*) if the will is witnessed by that person or another partner in the firm. This is no longer the case. Section 28(4) of the Trustee Act 2000 provides that a charging clause contained in a will is not regarded as a gift for the purposes of section 15 of the 1837 Act. Such charges are now regarded as administrative expenses. This applies to wills *proved* after 1 February 2001.

Saving of right to grant

8.31   If such an attesting witness is also appointed executor, his right in that capacity is not forfeit. If the will was attested by three or more witnesses, the benefit is not lost, as the normal requirement of at least two attesting witnesses is maintained by the other witnesses; this provision applies only to deaths occurring after 30 May 1968 irrespective of the date the will was executed (Wills Act 1968). Rule 21 provides that a loss of entitlement as a beneficiary named in the will in priority to the grant because a person was a witness does not preclude that person from taking the grant if he is entitled in another capacity, for example as a person entitled to share in any estate undisposed of by the will.

Effect of codicil

8.32   An attesting witness to a will does not lose any benefit derived from a codicil unless he has also attested that codicil. Similarly, a benefit derived from a will is not lost by the attesting witness to a codicil provided he did not also attest the will.

Effect of beneficiary and witness subsequently marrying

8.33   The benefit is not lost if a beneficiary marries an attesting witness after the execution of the will. Where the grant is applied for the beneficiary in this circumstance, the Registry should be appraised of the marriage to avoid the application being 'stopped'.

Oath to lead grant

8.34   In all cases where a right to take a grant is lost by virtue of s 15 of the Act the oath to lead the grant should recite this fact in clearing the applicant's title to apply, for example 'that ..., the residuary legatee and devisee, was also one of the attesting witnesses to the said will and whose benefit thereunder is lost by virtue of s 15 of the Wills Act 1837, I am a legatee named in the said will'.

Death by murder or manslaughter

Loss of benefit and loss of title to grant

8.35   Where the death of the deceased was caused by a person who has been convicted of the murder or manslaughter of the deceased, that person is precluded on the grounds of public policy from receiving any benefit from the deceased's estate (see *Re Crippen's Estate [1911] P 108*). This rule is qualified by the murderer being found insane at the time of the offence. However, this is subject, in the case of a conviction for manslaughter, to the beneficiary applying for relief under s 2 of the Forfeiture Act 1982. Consideration has to be given to whether moral culpability is a relevant factor in determining whether the forfeiture rule should apply (see *Re K [1986] Ch 180, [1985] 2 All ER 833, [1985] 3 WLR 234, CA*). If entitlement to the grant depends on the beneficial entitlement to the estate, then the convicted person loses his right to the grant.

See also *Re DWS and EHS, TWGS (a child) v JMG [2001] 1 All ER 97*, *CA*, referred to at paragraph 9.19 below.

Renunciation or passing over

8.36   Where the convicted beneficiary renounces his right to a grant, application may be made by the person next entitled in priority. Where the convicted beneficiary refuses or neglects to execute a renunciation, application may be made for an order under s 116 Supreme Court Act 1981 (see paragraph 5.27 above) passing over that beneficiary and for an order for the grant to issue to the person next entitled or, if the circumstances dictate, to someone with no title to a grant in the normal order of priority. Similarly, application may be made under s 116 if the person entitled has been charged but not convicted with the crime and there is a need to administer the estate or some part of it now. Where there is no conviction, consideration should be given to an application to the District Judge or Registrar *ex parte* on affidavit for a discretionary order to lead the issue of a temporary grant, a grant *ad colligenda bona* limited to preserving the estate (or in whatever way the court considers appropriate) until a full grant can be taken following determination of the accused's trial (see paragraph 10.5 below).

Oath to lead the grant

Clearing executors

8.37   The oath to lead the grant must clear off all executors or account for there being no executor appointed, for example 'that AB and CD the executors named in the will died in the lifetime of the deceased'; 'that the said deceased did not appoint any executor in his will'; or 'that . . . the executor named in the said will has renounced probate . . .'. Where appropriate, the oath must also clear off all residuary legatees or devisees and others with a higher entitlement (in the order prescribed by Rule 20; see paragraph 8.2 above) than the person(s) making the application.

Statement of title

8.38   The deponent(s) must state the capacity in which they apply (for example 'I am [one of] the residuary legatee[s] . . .'), and if this entitlement derives from s 15 of the Wills Act 1837 or Rule 21 or from an order made under s 116 of the Supreme Court Act 1981, the appropriate fact or details of the order must be recited.

Where the application is based on substantially the whole known estate being disposed of by the will, the relevant values must be recited, thus 'that £ ... of the total known value of £ ... is disposed of by the said will'.

Where the applicant's title derives from his being a personal representative of a residuary beneficiary, details of the grant of representation to the beneficiary's estate must be recited.

Similarly, where title derives from the applicant's being a person entitled to the (or to a share in the) undisposed of estate, his relationship to the deceased, and clearing of possible closer kin, must be recited to establish this title.

The oath must also state whether or not a life interest or a minority interest arises and contain the usual statement as to settled land required by Rule 8.

The general information required in the oath to lead a grant of probate must also be given. See APPENDIX 1 for the forms of oath.

Chapter 9

Letters of administration

Necessity for grant

9.1   Where a person dies domiciled in England and Wales wholly intestate, a grant of letters of administration may be required to administer his estate in the United Kingdom. Where the value of the estate is small, it may be collected in and distributed without the authority of a grant (see CHAPTER 4 at paragraphs 4.9–4.10).

The grant will issue to a person or persons who have a beneficial interest in the estate in priority in accordance with Rule 22(1) (see paragraph 9.28 below) or to their lawfully appointed attorneys. Where there is no estate, a grant may be required (a 'nil estate' grant) for the purpose of constituting a personal representative, in order, for example, to take or defend legal proceedings on behalf of the deceased's estate or, as is more common, to perfect title to real property. For the procedure where the deceased died domiciled outside England and Wales, see CHAPTER 14.

A grant of letters of administration may be required to deal with settled land remaining settled after the deceased's death (see paragraph 10.22 below).

Maximum and minimum number of applicants for grant: life or minority interests: additional personal representative/trustee

9.2   As for grants of probate and letters of administration (with will annexed), the maximum number of persons who may apply for a grant of letters of administration is four (s 114(1) of the Supreme Court Act 1981).

Where under the intestacy a life or minority interest arises, there must be at least two grantees, unless the grant is taken by a trust corporation either alone or with an individual. A District Judge or Registrar may direct that, in the particular circumstances of the case, the grant may issue to a sole grantee (see s 114(2) of the 1981 Act). A life interest will arise where the net value of the estate, after deductions (see paragraph 9.29) below), exceeds the statutory provision (see paragraph 9.11 below) for the surviving spouse.

Where, after a grant has issued, one of the grantees dies and the life or minority interest still subsists, application may be made to a District Judge or Registrar *ex parte* on affidavit by the surviving grantee for the addition of a further personal representative. The consent of the proposed administrator must also be lodged, together with such other evidence as the court may direct. The District Judge or Registrar may direct that a note be made on the original grant of the addition of a further personal representative, or he may impound or revoke the grant or make such other order as the circumstances of the case require (see s 114(4) of the 1981 Act and Rule 26).

Where it is found that a life or minority interest exists only after the grant has issued to a sole grantee, application may, similarly, be made to add a second administrator. Administrators of an estate who have obtained administration, whether with or without will annexed, hold the deceased's estate as trustees for the beneficiaries and have power, under s 36 of the Trustee Act 1925, to appoint new trustees.

Failure to prove testamentary document

Citation

9.3   Where the deceased died leaving what purported to be a testamentary document, letters of administration will be granted to the citee(s) (the person(s) entitled under an intestacy) when the person(s) entitled to a grant or having an interest under the testamentary document if it were proved (the executor(s) and beneficiar(y)(ies)) have all been cited to propound that document and have not appeared to the citation (see Rule 48(2) and paragraph 16.12 below for the procedure on citations).

Failure to act under the citation and enter an appearance is taken to be an admission that the purported testamentary document is invalid. The oath will recite that the deceased died intestate.

After claim to determine validity

9.4   Similarly, where a Part 57 probate claim has been tried in the Chancery Division and judgment has been given pronouncing against the validity of a purported testamentary document, and there is no other valid testamentary document, letters of administration will be granted to the person(s) entitled thereto in the order of priority prescribed by Rule 22 (see paragraph 9.28 below).

Details of the citation or judgment must be recited in the oath.

Effect of revocation of all testamentary documents

9.5   If the deceased died leaving a properly executed document, the sole effect of which was to revoke all previous testamentary documents, his estate will pass as on an intestacy, and a grant of letters of administration will issue on application therefor by the person(s) entitled under Rule 22 (see paragraph 9.28 below).

The document should be lodged with the oath to lead the grant, but will not be annexed to the grant. The grant will be noted by the court as to the effect of the documents filed.

Representative 'leading' grants

When required

9.6   Where the person who would have been entitled to apply for a grant survives but dies without taking such grant, it may be necessary to obtain a 'leading grant', that is a grant in the estate of the last to die, to constitute personal representatives to apply in the estate of the first to die.

This may occur under a will, for example, where the sole executor and residuary beneficiary survives the deceased but dies without obtaining a grant. A grant will be necessary to the beneficiary's estate to give title to apply for administration (with will annexed) of the first to die. Similarly under an intestacy if the whole estate passes to one person who dies without taking the grant, for example an only sister of the deceased, then the person(s) entitled to a grant to the sister's estate (whether under a will or intestacy) must take a 'leading grant'.

If several persons survived and died, each in turn being the lone person entitled to benefit and to a grant, there may be a need for a succession of leading grants. However, if each leading grant is only required to establish title (there being no estate to be administered), application may be made for a discretionary order under s 116 of the Supreme Court Act 1981 (see paragraph 5.27 above). The order will provide for direct title to the grant, thus avoiding the intermediate grants. This is more likely to occur when there is a need for several leading grants.

Title

9.7   An executor, who may be one of several executors who proved his testator's will, may apply for a grant of administration to an estate for which his testator would, if alive, have been able to apply. Application may be made without notice to any other proving executor. However, where the proposed administrator's title to apply for the second or subsequent grant derives from a grant of administration, notice of the application should be given to all other co-administrators. He may still obtain administration alone provided those who were his co-administrators in the leading grant renounce their title or consent to the application.

Surviving spouse

9.8 Where a deceased's surviving spouse was entitled to the whole of the estate, but died without taking a grant, application may be made for a grant by his personal representative(s) (see Rule 22(4)). Application must be made for a 'leading grant' to the estate of the survivor and, once that grant has issued, application may be made for a grant to administer the estate of the first to die.

However, where the deceased's surviving spouse was not entitled to the whole of the estate, application for a grant may be made by (one of) the other person(s) entitled in priority to share in the estate, for example a child. There will be no requirement for a 'leading grant'. The oath should recite the death of the surviving spouse, state that there is *now* no life interest in the estate and describe the applicant as one of the, or the only, person(s) *now* entitled to (share in) the deceased's estate, as appropriate. Where a member of a lower class of kin is beneficially entitled to share the estate and survives, that person is preferred to the personal representative of a beneficiary who survived the deceased but has since died (see Rule 27(5)).

Where the surviving spouse and all other kin entitled to share die without obtaining representation, the personal representative of the surviving spouse has the first entitlement to apply, in preference to the personal representatives of others entitled to share (see proviso to Rule 22(4)). However, where the surviving spouse's beneficial entitlement under the statutory legacy was wholly satisfied, application may be made by the personal representative of another entitled to share, the oath stating that the spouse's beneficial entitlement was satisfied.

Renunciation in one capacity

9.9 If a person having a beneficial interest other than the surviving spouse renounces administration of the survivor's estate, he cannot apply for administration of the estate of the first to die, Rule 37(2) stating that a person who has renounced in one capacity cannot apply if entitled in another capacity.

Lodging applications

9.10 The oath in these applications must recite the fact that the applicant(s) is/are the personal representative(s) by virtue of the leading grant, which has already issued, to the estate of the survivor who was the only person entitled to the deceased's estate.

It is however, permissible for both sets of papers to be lodged together, the oath in the estate of the first to die reciting the applicant's title as 'the executor/ administrator of the estate of ...., application for a grant thereto being made contemporaneously with this application'. The Registry will ensure the leading grant issues first, the second grant usually issuing the day after the leading grant issues.

Grant to surviving spouse

9.11   Where the net value of the estate does not exceed the statutory sum to which a surviving spouse is entitled (see the table at paragraph 9.28 below); or where no life or minority interest arises under the intestacy; or where a life interest does arise but the reversioners assign all their interest to the surviving spouse, a surviving spouse may apply for a grant alone.

The Law Reform (Succession) Act 1995, in force in respect of deaths occurring on or after 1 January 1996, provides, *inter alia*, that a surviving spouse will only attain a vested interest in his/her deceased spouse's estate if he/she survives the deceased spouse by at least 28 days. Strictly, therefore, no grant should issue to the surviving spouse of an intestate until 28 days have elapsed since the date of death. The practice, however, is to allow grants to issue before the 28-day period has elapsed, treating the estate as vesting subject to divesting. If the survivor dies before obtaining the beneficial interest, then the grant will be treated as being of no effect and a new grant may be taken by the person(s) next entitled.

Statutory sum

9.12   Where the gross value of the estate exceeds the statutory sum to which a surviving spouse is entitled (see the table at paragraph 9.28 below), s 46 of the Administration of Estates Act 1925 provides for the following deductions from the gross value to be made to discover whether the net value exceeds the statutory sum:

  (i) the value of the personal chattels of the deceased as defined by the Administration of Estates Act 1925 s 55(1)(x);

 (ii) any debts and funeral expenses;

(iii) costs incurred or to be incurred in obtaining the grant and administering the estate;

 (iv) capital transfer or inheritance tax;

  (v) the fees payable to the Probate Registry on the application for the grant.

Should any of the above deductions be made to reduce the net estate to below the statutory sum, they must be set out in the oath to lead the grant following the statement of the gross value. Usually the value of the estate at the date of death is accepted in order to determine entitlement to the grant, although the Act provides for the statutory payment to be based on the value of the estate at the time of payment or appropriation.

Where a change in value occurs between the date of death and lodging the application, thereby creating a life interest, so that the surviving spouse cannot take the grant alone without leave under s 114 of the Supreme Court Act 1981, details of such change in value must be included in the oath.

Accretion

9.13   Where the net value does not exceed the statutory sum payable to the surviving spouse he or she may renounce his/her right to the grant. Application may then be made by the person next entitled to benefit under the intestacy notwithstanding that he has no immediate beneficial interest in the estate but who may have a beneficial interest in the event of an accretion to the estate or by a creditor (see Rule 22(3)). For example, a child of the deceased may apply on the basis that if the estate increased in value so as to exceed the statutory sum he would obtain a beneficial interest. (For a form of oath, see Form A1.29, page 385.) The surviving spouse retains his/her beneficial interest in the estate.

This procedure may be used where the surviving spouse does not wish to act and does not want to appoint an attorney.

Assignment of life interest

9.14   A surviving spouse who has a life interest under an intestacy may assign his interest to those entitled thereto (the reversioner(s)) on his death. Similarly, the reversioners may assign their interest to the life tenant. Assignment is made by deed, the original of which must be produced for inspection on the application for the grant, and details of it be recited in the oath. A copy of the deed must be lodged for retention by the Registry pursuant to Rule 24(3). Where the life tenant has assigned his interest to the reversioner(s) the renunciation of the life tenant's right to the grant must be lodged with the application for a grant by the reversioner(s). No renunciation by the reversioner(s) is required on application by the life tenant to whom their interest has been assigned.

Redemption of life interest

9.15   Where the deceased died on or after 1 January 1953 intestate and the surviving spouse has a life interest in part of the residuary estate, he may require the intestate's personal representative to redeem the life interest to which he is entitled by the payment of the capital value thereof (s 47A(1) of the Administration of Estates Act 1925). The surviving spouse may only elect redemption if the part of the residuary estate to be redeemed consists of property in possession. An election to redeem is given by written notice to the personal representative(s) and the right must be exercised within one year of the date of issue of the grant of representation, unless the court is satisfied that to insist upon this limitation would operate unfairly (see s 47A(3) and (5) of the Act).

Where the life tenant is also the sole personal representative an election to redeem the life interest is given by written notice to the Senior District Judge of the Family Division, Principal Registry of the Family Division, First Avenue House, 42–49 High Holborn, London WC1 6NP, within the one-year time limit (for the form of notice, see Form A1.79, page 447) (s 47A(7)). The notice may be lodged (in duplicate) at the District Registry from which the grant issued, for transmission to the Principal Registry.

By virtue of s 47A(3A) of the Act the calculation of the capital value of the life interest is prescribed: currently by the Intestate Succession (Interest and Capitalisation) Order 1977.

See also Rule 56.

Renunciation of life tenant: application by persons of lower or no entitlement

9.16 Where the surviving spouse, who is entitled to a life interest under an intestacy, renounces his right to the grant, application for letters of administration may be made by any two other persons entitled in priority in accordance with Rule 22 (see section 2 above and s 114(2) of the Supreme Court Act 1981).

Where there is only one person of the lower entitlement in a particular class, that person may, with leave, be joined by another of even lower entitlement (for example, an only child of the deceased may be granted administration together with a parent of the deceased (see also section 10)). Alternatively, on renunciation, and with the consent of all persons entitled, application may be made by a trust corporation (see CHAPTER 11). Application may also be made in accordance with Rule 31 by the lawfully constituted attorney of the person entitled (see paragraph 10.32 below). The need for two administrators under the 1981 Act may be resolved by appointing two attorneys.

Living interests: minority interests: preference

9.17 Unless otherwise directed by a District Judge or Registrar, administration will be granted to a living person entitled thereto in preference to the personal representative of a deceased person who, if alive, would be entitled to a grant in the same degree; for example where the deceased died a bachelor without issue or parent, but was survived by a brother, his sister having predeceased him, the grant may be taken by the brother in preference to the personal representative of the sister (see Rule 27(5)). Where it is desired that the grant be taken by the personal representative, all 'living interests' must be cleared by those persons renouncing their right to the grant. In the absence of renunciation, application for directions may be made (by letter) to a District Judge or Registrar.

Similarly, under the same rule provision, administration will be granted to a person of full age in preference to the guardian of, or person with parental responsibility for, a minor who, if of full age, would be entitled in the same degree.

Attorney applications

9.18   Rule 31 provides that the lawfully constituted attorney of a person entitled to a grant may apply for a grant of representation for the use and benefit of the person entitled and until further representation be granted. Any person entitled to administration in the order of priority set out at paragraph 9.28 below may appoint an attorney (or attorneys) to obtain letters of administration without the leave of the court. See paragraph 10.32 below for attorney applications, and Form A1.31, page 388 for the form of oath.

Unlawful killing: loss of benefit

Renunciation

9.19   Where a beneficiary under a will has been found guilty of the murder or manslaughter of the testator he loses his right to that benefit. The same principle applies to a beneficiary found guilty of the murder or manslaughter of a person dying intestate (see *Re Crippen's Estate [1911] P 108*). In such a circumstance, where the beneficiary is the person first entitled in priority to apply for the grant he must renounce his entitlement to the grant if application is to be made by a person of a lower class of priority. This may allow a person of lower entitlement to take a grant and administer the estate but does not necessarily pass the beneficial entitlement. It was held in *Re DWS and EHS, TWGS (a child) v JMG [2001] 1 All ER 97, CA* that where a son had been convicted of the murder of his parents, the parents' estate did not pass to the grandson (the son of the murderer). For the grandson to inherit, his father had to predecease the deceased. His forfeited benefit could not pass to remoter issue under s 46 of the Administration of Estates Act 1925.

Refusal to renounce

9.20   Where the beneficiary refuses or neglects to execute a renunciation, application may be made for a discretionary order under s 116 of the Supreme Court Act 1981 passing over that person's prior entitlement to the grant and directing that administration be granted to the next person entitled or, indeed, to any person that the court approves on the application as being a fit and proper person to administer the estate (see paragraph 5.27 above).

Prior notice to others of equal entitlement

9.21   Rule 27(4) provides that a grant of administration may be made to any person entitled thereto without prior notice being given to any other person of equal entitlement. In the event of a dispute arising (which cannot be amicably resolved) between persons of equal entitlement as to which of them should take the grant, application must be made on summons to a District Judge of the Family Division at the Principal Registry, or to a District Registrar (see Rule 27(6)), for a direction to whom the grant shall issue. The summons should issue out of the Registry in which (one of) the grant application(s) is pending. Through the national computer system, an entry will be made in the record of pending grant applications that a summons has issued at the issuing Registry. If a grant application is pending at another Registry, that Registry's record will also be noted. No grant will issue until a decision as to entitlement has been made (see Rule 27(8)), provided that the issue of the summons is known to the other Registry.

Inheritance (Provision for Family and Dependants) Act 1975

9.22   Where the statutory provision prescribed under the intestacy rules is considered inadequate by the person entitled to that provision, application may be made for an increase in the provision out of the estate. Similarly, where the marriage of a person who dies intestate has been dissolved or annulled, the former spouse has no claim to the deceased's estate save on application under the Act.

The Act allows a claim by, *inter alia*, a former spouse who has not remarried, where the intestate died on or after 1 April 1976. (Where the death occurred before that date, application could have been made under s 26 of the Matrimonial Causes Act 1965.) As well as husbands or wives, application may be made for provision, or greater provision, by (i) a former wife or husband who has not remarried; (ii) any person, other than a husband or wife, who during the period of two years immediately preceding the date of the deceased's death was living with him/her in the same household as husband or wife; (iii) any child of the deceased; (iv) a person not the child of the deceased but who was treated as being a child of the family in relation to any marriage to which the deceased was at any time a party; or (v) a person other than those mentioned above who immediately before the death was being maintained wholly or partly by the deceased. Those in (ii) above were added by the Family Law (Succession) Act 1995 in respect of deaths occurring on or after 1 January 1996.

Application must be made within six months of the issue of the grant of representation. Application may be made after that time provided good cause can be shown for the application being made after the prescribed time limit has elapsed. Application is made by claim in the High Court (to either the Family Division or the Chancery Division) or by claim to a county court. Application may now be made to a county court irrespective of the value of the estate (High Court and County Courts Jurisdiction Order 1991, with effect from 1 July 1991). Part 57 of the CPR 1998 applies to such applications made on or after 2 December 2002.

Application may also be made under the Act to vary the provisions contained in a will where such provision is considered inadequate.

There is no bar on the claimant for relief under the Act also being the personal representative, proceedings under the Act being essentially an application to redistribute the estate and not proceedings requiring the personal representative to defend the estate (see Notes to Part 57 CPR 1998 in *Civil Procedure*).

The Act applies only to estates of deceased persons dying domiciled in England and Wales.

Effect of divorce or separation

Effect of divorce granted in England and Wales

9.23   The former spouse of a person dying intestate, their marriage having been dissolved or annulled, has no right to benefit under the intestacy and therefore no entitlement to apply for a grant. When the deceased's marriage has been dissolved or annulled, the oath to lead the grant should recite this fact, and give details, including the date of the decree absolute, the court which granted the decree, and the fact that the deceased had not remarried. The deceased should be described as 'a single man' or 'a single woman' as appropriate where the marriage was dissolved; or as a bachelor or spinster as the case may be (that is, status before marriage) where the marriage was annulled (see paragraphs 9.57 and 9.58 below). There is no requirement to lodge a copy of the decree absolute, the statement in the oath being accepted as sufficient.

Effect of divorce outside England and Wales

9.24   If the divorce or annulment took place outside England and Wales the decree may be recognisable as valid in this country provided the conditions set out in ss 45 and 46 of the Family Law Act 1986 are met. Generally, this means the decree will be recognised as valid provided it was obtained by means of judicial or other proceedings; is effective under the law of the country in which it was obtained; and at the date of the institution of those proceedings either spouse was habitually resident in, was domiciled in, or was a national of the foreign country. Decrees granted by other courts in the British Isles are recognised as valid (see s 44 of the Act). Details of the foreign proceedings and the decree, order or pronouncement should be included in the oath if such a decree is relied on.

Effect of judicial separation

9.25   Section 18(2) of the Matrimonial Causes Act 1973 provides that:

'if while a decree of judicial separation is in force and the separation is continuing either of the parties to the marriage dies intestate as respects all or any of his or her real or personal property, the property as respects which he or she dies intestate shall devolve as if the other party to the marriage had then been dead.'

In effect the grant will be taken by issue or other surviving kin entitled in priority under Rule 22 (see below) on the basis that the other spouse had predeceased the intestate. This section does not, however, apply to orders made by magistrates' courts which include a non-cohabitation clause (see s 18(3) of the Act).

Grant to former spouse for use and benefit of minors

9.26   Where the deceased died divorced, leaving children the only persons entitled to his estate who are all minors, the surviving former spouse as surviving parent may take letters of administration. The grant will be for the use and benefit of the minors until one of them attains the age of 18 years. The surviving parent has parental responsibility under s 2(1) of the Children Act 1989 and priority of entitlement to the grant.

Deceased divorced: no issue

9.27   (Where the deceased died divorced, leaving no issue but remoter kin, the kin are entitled to the grant in the normal order of priority – see below.)

Persons entitled to a grant

9.28   The following table sets out the persons entitled to the estate and the persons entitled in priority, in accordance with Rule 22, to a grant, where the deceased died intestate on or after 1 January 1953:

Intestate dies leaving	*Person(s) entitled to the estate*	*Person(s) entitled to a grant*
1 *Surviving spouse and issue:*		
a *Net estate not exceeding:*		
● £5,000 where death occurred on or after 1 January 1953 but before 1 January 1967;		
● £8,750 where death occurred on or after 1 January 1967 but before 1 July 1972;		
● £15,000 where death occurred on or after 1 July 1972 but before 15 March 1977;		
● £25,000 where death occurred on or after 15 March 1977 but before 1 March 1981;		
● £40,000 where death occurred on or after 1 March 1981 but before 1 June 1987;		
● £75,000 where death occurred on or after 1 June 1987 but before 1 December 1993;		
● £125,000 where death occurred on or after 1 December 1993	Surviving spouse*	Surviving spouse

b   *Net estate exceeding:*

£5,000, £8,750, £15,000, £25,000, £40,000, £75,000 or £125,000 (see *a* above for appropriate dates)

The surviving spouse receives personal chattels and £5,000, £8,750, £15,000, £25,000, £40,000, £75,000 or £125,000 (see *a* above for appropriate dates) free of costs and duty/tax, with interest, currently at 6%† p.a., together with a life interest in half of the remainder of the estate with reversion to issue. The issue receive the other half absolutely

Surviving spouse and a child**

2   *Surviving spouse without issue:*

a   *Net estate not exceeding:*

● £20,000 where death occurred on or after 1 January 1953 but before 1 January 1967;
● £30,000 where death occurred on or after 1 January 1967 but before 1 July 1972;
● £40,000 where death occurred on or after 1 July 1972 but before 15 March 1977;
● £55,000 where death occurred on or after 15 March 1977 but before 1 March 1981;
● £85,000 where death occurred on or after 1 March 1981 but before 1 June 1987;
● £125,000 where death occurred on or after 1 June 1987 but before 1 December 1993;
● £200,000 where death occurred on or after 1 December 1993

Surviving spouse*

Surviving spouse

b *Net estate exceeding:* £20,000, £30,000, £40,000, £55,000, £85,000, £125,000 or £200,000 (see *a* above for appropriate dates)	The surviving spouse receives personal chattels and £20,000, £30,000, £40,000, £55,000, £85,000, £125,000 or £200,000 (see *a* above for appropriate dates) free of costs and duty/ tax, with interest, currently at 6%† p.a., together with half of the remainder absolutely. As to the other half of the remainder, if there are surviving parents, to the parents absolutely. If no parents survive, the other half of the remainder is shared equally between brothers and sisters of the whole blood, the issue of such brothers and sisters as have predeceased the intestate receiving the share to which their parent would have been entitled	Surviving spouse**
3 Surviving spouse without issue, parent, brother or sister of the whole blood or their issue, irrespective of the value of the estate	Surviving spouse	Surviving spouse
4 No surviving spouse but issue	Issue who attain 18 years of age or marry under age in equal shares; lawful issue of predeceasing issue receiving the share to which their parent would have been entitled (NB Issue includes illegitimate children if the death occurred on or after 1 January 1970)	Issue**

5	No surviving spouse or issue but both parents	Both parents in equal shares	Either or both parents
6	No surviving spouse or issue but a parent	The parent	The parent
7	No surviving spouse, issue or parent but brothers and sisters of the whole blood and the issue of such brothers and sisters as have predeceased the intestate	Brothers and sisters of the whole blood in equal shares, the issue of such brothers and sisters as have predeceased the intestate receiving the share to which their parent would have been entitled	A person or persons entitled to share in the estate**
8	No surviving spouse, issue or parent or brothers or sisters of the whole blood or their issue but brothers and sisters of the half blood and the issue of such brothers and sisters as have predeceased the intestate	Brothers and sisters of the half blood in equal shares, the issue of such brothers and sisters as have predeceased the intestate receiving the share to which their parent would have been entitled	A person or persons entitled to share in the estate**
9	No surviving spouse or other closer relative as in 8 above, but grandparents	The grandparents in equal shares	Either or both grandparent(s)
10	No surviving spouse or other closer relative as in 8 or 9 above, but uncles and aunts of the whole blood and the issue of such uncles and aunts as have predeceased the intestate	Uncles and aunts of the whole blood in equal shares, the issue of such uncles and aunts as have predeceased the intestate receiving the share to which their parent was entitled	A person or persons entitled to share in the estate**
11	No surviving spouse or other closer relative as in 8, 9 or 10 above, but uncles and aunts of the half blood and the issue of such uncles and aunts as have predeceased the intestate	Uncles and aunts of the half blood in equal shares, the issue of such uncles and aunts as have predeceased the intestate receiving the share to which their parent was entitled	A person or persons entitled to share in the estate**

12 No blood relation with an interest as set out in 1 to 11 above	(i) the Crown (ii) The Duchy of Lancaster (iii) The Duchy of Cornwall	(i) Treasury Solicitor (ii) Solicitor for the Lancaster (iii) Solicitor for the Duchy of Cornwall
13 A creditor		The creditor (upon the renunciation or clearing off of all persons with a prior right to the grant, including the Crown)

* Provided that the spouse survives for 28 days (Law Reform (Succession) Act 1995) in respect of deaths on or after 1 January 1996.

** Where a minority or life interest arises there must be at least two applicants for the grant unless a trust corporation applies or a District Judge or Registrar directs otherwise under s 114(2) Supreme Court Act 1981.

† The current rate of interest (6%) on the statutory legacy until payment applies to estates of intestates dying on or after 1 October 1983. Where the deceased died before 1 October 1983 but after 15 September 1977 the former rate of interest (7%) in force between those dates will apply to the legacy for the appropriate part of that period. For the rates of interest applicable before 15 September 1977 see the Intestate Succession (Interest and Capitalisation) Order 1977 and s 46(1) of the Administration of Estates Act 1925.

Note: With effect from 4 April 1988, the date of the coming into force of the Family Law Reform Act 1987, entitlement to benefit, and therefrom entitlement to apply for a grant, is not affected by the fact that the relationship to the deceased was not lawful, except as regards a surviving spouse. Where the death occurred after the above date, it is not necessary in the oath to describe the relationship as 'lawful' or 'natural', except when application is made by the surviving lawful spouse.

Grant to surviving spouse

Life or minority interests

9.29   Where an intestate dies and is survived by his spouse, the latter is entitled to the grant of letters of administration in preference to all others. However, where a life or minority interest arises under the intestacy, a second person or a trust corporation must apply with the surviving spouse, or, with appropriate renunciations and consents, a trust corporation alone may apply (see also paragraph 11.10 below). For the form of oath see Form A1.43, page 407.

A life interest arises where the intestate is survived by his spouse *and issue* and the net estate exceeds the statutory legacy to which the surviving spouse is entitled; this is currently, in respect of deaths occurring after 1 December 1993, £125,000 (but see para 1(b) of the table set out above). A life interest does not arise where the intestate is survived by his spouse and kin more remote than issue.

A minority interest arises when the intestate is survived by issue or remoter kin entitled to benefit who are under the age of 18 years. Where a spouse also survives, the estate must exceed the statutory legacy to allow issue to share. Where a minor is entitled to benefit, and would also be entitled to take the grant if of full age (for example, where the deceased is survived by his wife and a minor), the parent who has, or is deemed to have, parental responsibility for the minor in accordance with s 2(1), 2(2) or 4 of, or paragraph 4 or 6 of Schedule 14 to, the Children Act 1989 or under an adoption order within the meaning of s 12(1) of the Adoption Act 1976 (see Rule 32(1)(a)), or the person who has parental responsibility by virtue of a residence order made under s 8 of the Children Act 1989 (see Rule 32(1)(aa)); or the guardian of the minor who is or is deemed to have been appointed in accordance with s 5 of, or paragraph 12, 13 or 14 of Schedule 14 to, the Children Act 1989 (Rule 32(1)(b)), may nominate any person considered fit and proper to act as co-administrator (Rule 32(3) and see Form A1.83, page 450 for a form of nomination).

Application by surviving spouse alone, notwithstanding life or minority interest

9.30   Where the net value of the estate exceeds the statutory legacy by a small amount, or the minority interest will exist for a short period only, or there is other good reason, application may be made to a District Judge or Registrar seeking the exercise of his discretion under s 114(2) of the Supreme Court Act 1981 to allow the grant to issue to the surviving spouse alone.

Child en ventre sa mère

9.31   Where a man dies intestate survived by his wife who is pregnant at the date of his death, a possible minority interest may arise in respect of the child *en ventre sa mère*. The unborn child has the same entitlement as issue living at the date of death. It is usual for the grant to be taken by the surviving spouse alone (even if the estate exceeds the spouse's statutory legacy and there is no other child of age to join in the application) under s 114(2), referred to above. Where estate remains unadministered after the child's birth a second administrator may be added under Rule 25(2) (see paragraph 9.37 below).

Where the mother was not married to the deceased, consideration should be given to the issue of a limited grant *ad colligenda bona* to preserve the estate or if there is a need to administer the estate or part of the estate before the child is born (see paragraph 10.5 below).

Grant to children or other issue

Lawful issue (see also paragraph 9.33 below)

9.32   Where an intestate dies leaving no surviving spouse, the child(ren) of the deceased, or the issue of any such child who has died in the lifetime of the deceased, is/are entitled to apply for the grant of letters of administration, the grandchildren of the deceased being entitled to the share to which their predeceased parent would have been entitled.

This is, of course, subject to the child applying having attained the age of 18 years. Even if the child has married under the age of 18 years his entitlement to apply for a grant is restricted during his minority.

Where the deceased was survived by two or more children, one of whom has since died, preference is given to the surviving children over the personal representative of the child who has died (see Rule 27(5)). For the form of oath see Form A1.22, page 376.

Illegitimate issue

9.33   In respect of deaths before 1 January 1970, section 9(1) of the Legitimacy Act 1926 entitled the illegitimate child to take the same interest as a legitimate child in the estate of his intestate mother. Where the illegitimate child of the deceased predeceased him leaving *lawful* issue, those children are entitled to the share of their parent and are entitled to apply for the grant. This does not apply where the child of the deceased's illegitimate children was also illegitimate.

As regards deaths occurring on or after 1 January 1970 but before 4 April 1988, illegitimate children of the deceased have the same entitlement as legitimate children to the estate of either parent (s 14(1) Family Law Reform Act 1969 which replaced s 9 of the 1926 Act). Where a child born illegitimate is subsequently legitimated, by the marriage of his parents or otherwise, his rights of succession equate with those of a lawful child (see Legitimacy Act 1976).

Where the applicant claims to be an illegitimate child of a man who has died, evidence of paternity must be produced in the form of an affiliation order containing a finding of paternity; or a birth certificate in which the deceased is named as the applicant's father and was the informant; or other affidavit evidence. Such evidence will not be necessary in an application relating to the child's mother's estate. It may be necessary to petition the court (High Court or county court) for a declaration of parentage under s 56 of the Family Law Act 1986 (as substituted by the Family Law Reform Act 1987). The oath to lead the grant should describe an illegitimate child as the 'natural son' or 'natural daughter' as appropriate.

With effect from 4 April 1988, in respect of deaths occurring on or after that date, s 18 of the Family Law Reform Act 1987 provides that there is no difference as regards succession whether the parents, of any child or other issue, were married to each other at any time. On application for a grant there is no longer any requirement to describe children of the intestate as 'lawful' or 'natural'; for example 'I am the son/daughter of the deceased and (one of) the (only) person(s) entitled to share in the estate' is now sufficient in all cases.

Child conceived by artificial insemination

9.34   Section 27 of the 1987 Act, effective from 4 April 1988, provides that where a woman who is married (and her marriage still subsists) gives birth to a child as the result of artificial insemination with the semen of a person not a party to the marriage, then, unless the court is satisfied the other party to the marriage did not consent to the insemination the child shall be treated as a child of the parties to the marriage.

Adopted children

9.35   The right to succeed to estate between adopters and adopted children was brought into force by the Adoption Act 1950 and subsequently re-enacted in the Adoption Act 1958. The specific rights to succeed are contained in these Acts. In respect of deaths occurring on or after 1 January 1976, an adopted child has the same entitlement as if he were the lawfully born child of the adoptive parent(s) (see s 39 Adoption Act 1976).

The oath should recite details of the adoption order, including the court which made it and the Act under which it was made, and confirm that the order still subsists. It also follows that the estate of an adopted child on his death devolves as though he were the lawful child of his adoptive parents and his estate will pass to those entitled under the usual intestacy provisions – to the adoptive parents, or, if they predeceased, to any of his adoptive parents' lawful or other adopted children (assuming the adopted child had not married and had no issue).

Where a child is adopted *after* the death of a parent, the child ceases to be a child of that parent and becomes the child of his adopters. Any entitlement to benefit from his natural parent's estate is lost – see s 39(2) of the 1976 Act.

Adoption orders made in the designated countries set out in the Adoption (Designation of Overseas Adoptions) Order 1973 have the same effect as orders made under the Adoption Act 1976. Evidence of such adoption is proved by the production of a certified copy of the entry made in a public register in accordance with the law of the place where the adoption was effected *or* by a certificate signed by a person authorised by the law of the place where the adoption was effected stating that the adoption was effected.

For a form of oath see Form A1.23, page 378.

Children of a void marriage

9.36   The child(ren) of a marriage, whenever born, are treated as the legitimate child(ren) of their parents provided that at the time of conception or the insemination resulting in their birth – or at the time of the marriage, if later – either or both the child(ren)'s parents believed the marriage to be valid (see s 1 Legitimacy Act 1976). The belief that the marriage was valid may derive from a mistake as to the law by a party to it.

The above applies in respect of children born after 4 April 1988 (s 28 Family Law Reform Act 1987).

Where a marriage is annulled in respect of a voidable marriage, the decree takes effect from the date of it. Any child born during the subsistence of the marriage is legitimate.

Death of surviving child

9.37   Where the deceased died intestate without a surviving spouse and his only child survives him but then dies, and provided the child attained an absolute interest in the estate (that is, he must have achieved 18 years of age or married under that age), application may be made by the child's personal representative. If the child did not achieve an absolute interest, the estate passes as though the deceased died without issue, to those next entitled under Rule 22.

Grant to parents

9.38   Where an intestate dies leaving no surviving spouse or issue, either or both the parents who survive the intestate, or the surviving parent, is/are entitled to apply for the grant of letters of administration. For the form of oath see Form A1.24, page 379.

Evidence of paternity

9.39   If the intestate was illegitimate and died on or after 1 January 1970, his parents or either of them, if surviving, is/are entitled to apply

141

for the grant as if the intestate had been born legitimate (see s 14(2) Family Law Reform Act 1969). Evidence of paternity is required on application by the person claiming to be the father of an illegitimate child, in the same way as it is required by an illegitimate child claiming an interest in his putative father's estate (that is, birth certificate or affiliation order (see paragraph 9.33 above)).

Section 14 of the Act of 1969 was repealed from 4 April 1988, by the Family Law Reform Act 1987. As from that date s 18 of the Act of 1987 came into force and, in respect of any person dying on or after that date, any person whose mother and father were not married to each other at the date of his birth shall be presumed not to have been survived by his father or any person related to him only through his father unless the contrary is shown. Section 21 of the 1987 Act provides that for the purpose of entitlement to a grant of representation of the estate of a person dying intestate on or after the above date, it is presumed the deceased was not survived by any person related to him whose parents were not married to each other at the time of his birth or by any person whose relationship with him is deduced through a person whose parents were not married to each other at the time of that person's birth. Subject to this presumption, it appears therefore that the mother of an illegitimate child dying after 4 April 1988 is the only person entitled to his estate.

Where application is made by a person who claims to be the father of a child who died before 4 April 1988, evidence to establish paternity must be lodged. Where the deceased died after this date evidence to establish paternity will be required only in exceptional circumstances.

Grant to personal representative of parent(s)

9.40   Where the deceased was survived by a parent who subsequently died without obtaining letters of administration, application may be made by the personal representative of the surviving parent. Where both parents survived and died, application may be made by the personal representative of either.

The personal representative must constitute himself as such by taking the appropriate grant to the surviving parent's estate. If no grant has been obtained he must apply for the grant as a representative ('leading') grant (see paragraph 9.6 above) to give him title to apply. Title comes from taking a grant in the estate of the last to die.

Adoptive parents

9.41   Adoptive parents have the same right to a grant in respect of a child adopted by them who dies intestate as the parents of a lawfully born child, the child becoming the child of the adopters from the date of the adoption order (see s 39 Adoption Act 1976).

Grant to brothers and sisters or their issue

9.42   Where an intestate dies leaving no surviving spouse, issue or parent, the brothers and sisters of the whole blood are entitled to apply for the grant of letters of administration. Equally entitled *per stirpes* are the issue of brothers and sisters of the whole blood (nephews and nieces of the deceased) whose parent has predeceased the intestate, such nephews and nieces sharing equally the share to which their parent would have been entitled if (s)he had survived.

If there are no brothers and sisters of the whole blood or their issue surviving, the grant may issue to the brothers and sisters of the half blood, or to their issue *per stirpes* if their parent has predeceased the intestate. Where application is made by brothers or sisters of the half blood the oath must clear not only a spouse, issue and parents, but brothers and sisters of the whole blood *and* their issue.

Brothers and sisters of the whole or half blood and their issue need only be *lawful* if the intestate died before 4 April 1988. From that date there is no requirement that the relationship to the intestate be lawful (s 18(1) Family Law Reform Act 1987). This is subject to the rebuttable presumption that an illegitimate person was not survived by his father or anyone related to him through his father (s 18(2) of the Act). This presumption is rebutted by the statement of title contained in the oath to lead the grant. For the form of oath see Form A1.25, page 380.

Grant to grandparents

9.43   Where an intestate dies leaving no surviving spouse, issue, parents, brother or sister of the whole or half blood or their issue, the grandparents of the deceased, or any one of them, is/are entitled to apply for the grant of letters of administration.

See paragraph 9.32 above as to when the relationship must be lawful.

Grant to aunts and uncles or their issue

9.44   Where an intestate dies leaving no surviving spouse, issue, parent, brother or sister of the whole or half blood or their issue or grandparent, the aunts and uncles of the whole blood (they being the brothers and sisters of the whole blood of a parent of the intestate) may apply for the grant of letters of administration. Equally entitled *per stirpes* are the issue of such aunts and uncles (cousins) whose parent has predeceased the intestate. If there are no aunts or uncles of the whole blood or their issue surviving, application may be made by aunts and uncles who are brothers and sisters of the half blood of a parent of the intestate, or their issue if their parent has predeceased the intestate.

The oath must state the applicant's precise relationship to the deceased and clear off all persons with a higher priority. A cousin of the deceased is described as the 'cousin german of the whole or half blood (as appropriate)'; for example, 'I am the cousin german of the whole blood of the deceased being the daughter of (*name*) an uncle of the whole blood of the deceased who died in the deceased's lifetime'. There is no beneficial entitlement to second cousins (i.e. children whose parents were cousins) and consequently no right to the grant. For the forms of oath, see Forms A1.27–A1.28, pages 383–384.

See paragraph 9.32 above as to when the relationship must be lawful.

It should be noted that to qualify (as shown above) as such, an uncle or aunt of the deceased must have been a sibling of a parent of the deceased. Great uncles or aunts and the issue of great uncles or aunts are outside the degrees of consanguinity entitled to benefit from the intestate's estate (see s 46 of the Administration of Estates Act 1925).

Grant to the Crown

9.45   Where the intestate dies leaving no person with a beneficial interest to his estate, application for a grant of letters of administration may be made by the Crown if the Treasury Solicitor claims *bona vacantia* on its behalf (see Rule 22(2)). The Treasury Solicitor represents the Crown in its capacity of the Duchy of Lancaster and the Duchy of Cornwall. Normally, where it is known the intestate had kin, but the whereabouts of such kin are unknown, the Treasury Solicitor will seek to trace those kin, including the placing of advertisements. Where no response is received, application is made to a District Judge or Registrar under s 116 of the Supreme Court Act 1981 (see paragraph 5.27 above) for a discretionary order passing over such kin and allowing the grant to issue to the Crown. Where surviving kin are discovered after a grant has issued, the Treasury Solicitor will apply for the revocation of the grant to enable a grant to issue to the surviving kin.

Rule 38 provides that notice must be given to the Treasury Solicitor by the applicant in any case where it is possible the Crown may have a beneficial interest in the deceased's estate. The District Judge or Registrar may direct that no grant shall issue within 28 days after the notice to the Treasury Solicitor has been given. Where the Treasury Solicitor accedes to the application for a grant notwithstanding the Crown's interest, or disclaims any interest, the Treasury Solicitor should renounce his right to the grant, but a letter from the Treasury Solicitor consenting to the applicant's extracting a grant is acceptable and should be lodged with the oath to lead the grant.

Grant to a creditor

Clearing

9.46   Where all the persons entitled to share in the intestate's estate have been cleared off by death, renunciation or citation (see CHAPTERS 6 and 16) (including the Treasury Solicitor, if appropriate), any person who is a creditor of the deceased may apply for a grant of letters of administration (see Rule 22(3)). A creditor may apply for a grant to recover his debt notwithstanding that the creditor is statute barred by virtue of the Limitation Act 1980 from taking proceedings to recover his debt. For the form of oath see Form A1.34, page 392.

Surviving spouse

9.47   Where the deceased is survived by a spouse, on the spouse's renunciation alone a creditor may apply for the grant. This is subject to the estate not exceeding the spouse's statutory legacy (see paragraph 9.28 above). No renunciation or citation is required to clear those persons entitled in the event of an accretion to the estate, i.e. to those who would acquire a benefit if the value of the estate increased so as to exceed the spouse's statutory legacy.

Where the estate value exceeds the spouse's statutory legacy, those others beneficially entitled must renounce or be cited before a creditor may take the grant.

Assignee or non-trust corporation

9.48   The assignee of a creditor is not entitled to a grant under Rule 24, the creditor not being a person having an interest in the whole estate. Where the creditor is a non-trust corporation, for example a building society, the creditor may apply for a grant through its duly authorised nominee or lawfully appointed attorney (see paragraph 11.17 below).

Trust corporation

9.49   It sometimes occurs that the creditor is a trust corporation, e.g. a bank. The trust corporation may apply in the usual way (see CHAPTER 11) clearing prior entitlement to the grant. Some local authorities qualify as trust corporations and may apply as such to recover any care home fees due.

Undertaker's expenses

9.50   An undertaker is not a creditor of the deceased; he is a creditor of the deceased's estate. He therefore has no title to apply, in respect of the funeral expenses incurred, as a creditor. Such expenses are a first charge on the estate under ss 33 and 34 of the Administration of Estates Act 1925 and fall to be paid by the person who contracted the undertaker, or by the administrator. An undertaker cannot cite those entitled to take representation as he is not next entitled in priority to take the grant. Where the person(s) entitled to apply for the grant refuse(s) or neglect(s) to apply the undertaker may apply for a discretionary order under s 116 Supreme Court Act 1981 (see paragraph 5.27 above). This will enable him to take a grant and recover his debt from the estate.

Partnership firm a creditor

9.51   Where a partnership firm, such as a firm of accountants or solicitors, is a creditor, application may be made by such of the partners (subject to there being not more than four grantees) as wish to apply. The oath to lead the grant should confirm that the partners not applying concur in the application.

Minority interest

9.52   When a minority interest arises in the estate, then two applicants (together constituting the creditor) or two creditors should apply. Where a single creditor wishes to apply, it may be appropriate for the District Judge or Registrar (on application therefor) to dispense with the need for two grantees (see s 114 Supreme Court Act 1981). Although, strictly, application for leave for the grant to issue to a sole grantee should be made on affidavit, application may be made, with the court's approval, less formally by letter.

Joinder of administrator

When leave required

9.53   Where there is a life or minority interest, two grantees are required. A person entitled to a grant of administration in a lower class may apply for such a grant jointly with the person entitled thereto in priority, with the consent of that person and without the leave of the court if there is no other person with a prior right to a grant who wishes to apply, or if every such other person has renounced his right to apply (Rule 25(1)). For example, if the deceased dies leaving a surviving spouse and issue beneficially entitled to share, and a life interest is created in favour of the surviving spouse, the surviving spouse and a child may apply for the grant.

An application to join with a person entitled to a grant of letters of administration another person entitled in a lower class in accordance with Rule

22 (see paragraph 9.28 above), or with no entitlement, is made *ex parte* on affidavit to a District Judge or Registrar by the first person entitled. The consent of the proposed second administrator, and such other evidence as the court may require, must be lodged with the affidavit (see Rule 25(2)).

When leave not required

9.54 Unless a District Judge or Registrar otherwise directs, application need not be made where the proposed second administrator is:

(a)   a person nominated by the person with parental responsibility for, or the guardian of, a minor where the grant is to be taken for the use and benefit of that minor under Rule 32(3) or a person nominated by the person entitled to apply for the grant for the use and benefit of a mentally incapable person under Rule 35(3) (see also paragraphs 10.48 and 10.60 below);

(b)   a trust corporation (see CHAPTER 11).

(See Rule 25(3).)

Application by assignee

Whole estate to be assigned

9.55 Where all persons entitled to the estate of the deceased have assigned their whole interest to one or more other persons, the assignee(s) take the place in the order of priority for a grant of the assignor(s), or of the assignor with the highest priority. Where there are two or more assignees, application for the grant may be made by any one or more of them with the consent of the other(s). Where the deceased was survived by his spouse and other kin entitled to share in the estate (including those entitled to benefit only in the event of an accretion to the estate), all must join in the assignment to enable application to be made by an assignee.

Where an assignee is a minor the grant must be taken by two or more assignees (there being a minority interest) unless a District Judge or Registrar otherwise directs. Where the sole assignee is a minor, the grant may be taken by the person(s) with parental responsibility for the minor. Where there is only a person with parental responsibility, that person may nominate their co-administrator (see paragraph 10.58 below).

Deed to be lodged

9.56 An application for a grant by an assignee must be accompanied by the original assigning document which will be returned after examination; a copy for retention by the Registry must also be lodged. An assignment may be effected by those entitled to the deceased's estate irrespective of whether he died testate or intestate (see Rule 24). The deed may be a deed of assignment, variation or family arrangement provided the effect of the deed is to transfer all the assignors' interest in the whole estate to the assignee(s).

Stamp duty: A deed of assignment produced on an application for a grant of representation must either:

(a) be stamped to the effect that the correct amount of duty payable to the Inland Revenue has been paid on the deed; or

(b) should bear a certificate in writing which may be included in the deed; it may be endorsed thereon or physically attached to it, showing that the deed is exempt from duty by virtue of its falling into a category set out in the list below. Where the certificate does not form part of the deed or is not endorsed thereon it should contain a description of the deed to which it refers. The exempt categories are as follows:

- the vesting of property subject to a trust in the trustees of the trust on the appointment of a new trustee, or in the continuing trustees on the retirement of a trustee;

- the conveyance or transfer of property the subject of a specific devise or legacy to the beneficiary named in the will (or his nominee);

- the conveyance or transfer of property which forms part of an intestate's estate to the person entitled on intestacy (or his nominee);

- the appropriation of property within s 84(4) of the Finance Act 1985 (death: appropriation in satisfaction of a general legacy of money) or s 84(5) or (7) of that Act (death: appropriation in satisfaction of any interest of surviving spouse and in Scotland also of any interest of issue);

- the conveyance or transfer of property which forms part of the residuary estate of a testator to a beneficiary (or his nominee) entitled solely by virtue of his entitlement under the will;

- the conveyance or transfer of property out of a settlement in or towards satisfaction of a beneficiary's interest, not being an interest acquired for money or money's worth, being a conveyance or transfer constituting a distribution of property in accordance with the provisions of the settlement;

- the conveyance or transfer of property on and in consideration only of marriage to a party to the marriage (or his nominee) or to trustees to be held on the terms of a settlement made in consideration only of the marriage;

- the conveyance or transfer of property within s 83(1) of the Finance Act 1985 (transfers in connection with divorce, etc.);

- the conveyance or transfer by the liquidator of property which formed part of the assets of the company in liquidation to a shareholder of that company (or his nominee) in or towards satisfaction of the shareholder's rights on a winding-up;

- the grant in fee simple of an easement in or over land for no consideration in money or money's worth;

- the grant of a servitude for no consideration in money or money's worth;

- the conveyance or transfer of property operating as a voluntary disposition *inter vivos* for no consideration in money or money's worth nor any consideration referred to in s 57 of the Stamp Act 1891 (conveyance in consideration of a debt, etc.);

- the conveyance or transfer of property by an instrument within s 84(1) of the Finance Act 1985 (death: varying disposition).

The court, however, retains the right to require adjudication if in doubt as to the correctness of the certificate.

Oath to lead the grant

Contents of oath

9.57   In common with all other oaths to lead grants, the oath to lead a grant of letters of administration must state:

- the applicant's full name, address and occupation or status,

- the full name and last address of the deceased,

- the date of birth and death as they appear in the death certificate and the age of the deceased at death,

- the deceased's domicile at death (Rule 8(2)),

- whether there is any settled land vested in the deceased which was settled before his death and remains settled notwithstanding his death (Rule 8(3)),

- whether any life or minority interest arises in the estate (Rule 8(4)), and

- the necessary clearings of kin with prior entitlement (Rule 8(4)).

Clearings

9.58   Clearings are effected by:

(i)   giving the status of the deceased, for example 'a bachelor'; 'a widow'; 'a widower without issue', and where the title requires the clearance of issue and others who might be entitled, for example adopted children, the additional words 'or any other person entitled in priority to share in his/her estate by virtue of any enactment'; and

(ii) by giving the status of the applicant, for example 'the lawful husband of the deceased'; 'the daughter of the deceased and [one of] [the only] person[s] entitled to [share] in the estate'. Where the applicant is the surviving spouse and the net estate does not exceed the statutory sum (see paragraph 9.28 above) the words 'the only person now entitled to the estate' must be added.

Descriptions

9.59   Where the deceased died on or after 4 April 1988, the only relationships which must be described as lawful are those of husband/wife and of adopted children, thus 'lawful wife'; 'lawful adopted son'. Where the deceased died a single man or woman (the marriage having been dissolved) the oath must also contain a statement, as appropriate to the case, 'that the marriage between x and y was dissolved by the final decree of the ...... Court in England and Wales dated the .... day of .... 20 .. and the deceased did not thereafter remarry'. There is no longer any requirement for an office copy decree absolute to be lodged with the oath. Otherwise 'I am the sister of the whole blood' or 'I am the lawful cousin german of the whole blood once removed being the son of X who was a cousin of the whole blood who was the daughter of Y who was an uncle of the whole blood and that both X and Y predeceased the deceased'.

Citations, renunciations or consents

9.60   Where the application follows a citation to propound a will (see CHAPTER 16) or a judgment of a court in a probate claim, details of the citation or judgment must be recited. Similarly, any renunciation and/or consent must be recited and the appropriate document lodged with the oath.

Any alias of the deceased required to appear in the grant must be justified by a statement in the oath deposing to his true name and specifying the asset or assets held in the alias name, or any other reason for the alias to be included. (See Rule 9.)

Statement of duties and of estate values

9.61   The oath must conclude with a statement of the duties of a personal representative as prescribed by s 25 of the Administration of Estates Act 1925; and of the gross and net values of the estate; and, if the case is one in which an Inland Revenue Account is not required to be delivered, it must contain a statement to that effect. See APPENDIX 1 for forms of oath and CHAPTER 12 for when an account is required and for the 'excepted estate' limits in relation to the date of death.

Chapter 10

Limited grants

Grants pending determination of a probate claim

When required

10.1   Where there are pending proceedings in the Chancery Division relating to a disputed will or entitlement to a grant and it is necessary to prevent loss to or otherwise to protect the estate, s 117 of the Supreme Court Act 1981 provides for a limited grant of letters of administration to issue by order. The order will direct to whom the grant shall issue, usually to a person upon whom the disputing parties agree, or, in default of agreement, to a person nominated by the court.

Application for order

10.2   Application for the order is made on application notice in the probate claim (Part 57 CPR 1998: Practice Direction) to a Master of the Chancery Division or to a District Judge of one of the Chancery District Registries (Birmingham, Bristol, Cardiff, Leeds, Liverpool, Manchester, Newcastle-upon-Tyne and Preston). Application for the order cannot be made until a Part 57 probate claim has begun. Application may be made by a party to the claim or any person interested in the estate as a beneficiary or creditor. If satisfied as to the need for the grant, the Master or District Judge will direct the appointment of an administrator, who may be a sole administrator notwithstanding there may be a life or minority interest arising.

Application for the grant

10.3   Application for the grant must be made to the Principal Registry (see Rule 7(1) which prevents a grant issuing out of a District Probate Registry until any contention is disposed of). A copy of the order and, where necessary, an Inland Revenue Account, must be delivered and any inheritance tax paid. The fee of £50 payable on any application for a grant must be paid. Where tax is paid this will be transferred to the Account delivered with the application for the full grant.

The grant remains in force until an order is made determining the claim.

The administrator has the same authority to collect in estate as an administrator under a full grant, but has no power to distribute.

Application for the full grant following the determination of the claim may be made to the Principal or a District Probate Registry. A copy of the judgment or order must be lodged with the oath and the oath must give details of the judgment and of the first grant. The full grant, being a second grant in the same estate, carries a fee of £15.

Grant limited to commencing or defending a claim

10.4   Application may be made for an order for a grant limited to a claim when the persons entitled in the usual order of priority, whether as executors to probate or beneficiaries to letters of administration, refuse or neglect to take a grant – this neglect or refusal having the effect that the estate cannot sue or be sued.

Application for an order for the grant will be made under the court's discretionary powers contained in s 116 of the Supreme Court Act 1981. See CHAPTER 5 at paragraph 5.27 above.

The grant following the order will be of letters of administration and will follow the limitation in the order, i.e. reciting the claim or proposed claim and the purpose for which the grant issues. As mentioned above, the grant may be limited to commencing or defending proceedings, for example 'limited to commencing a claim for damages in the Queen's Bench Division' or 'limited to being the respondents in proposed proceedings under section 1 of the Inheritance (Provision for Family and Dependants) Act 1975'. The grant will not convey authority to collect in or distribute other estate.

The court has power to dispense with the need for a grant. Where the deceased had an interest in the matter in question but has no personal representative, the court may direct the proceedings continue in the absence of a representative or appoint a person solely for the purpose of representing the estate (see Rule 19.8 of CPR 1998).

Grants *ad colligenda bona*

When application necessary

10.5   Where the deceased's estate requires the protection afforded by a grant of representation, but there is difficulty in making application for a full grant to the estate, for example because:

● of doubt about who should be the personal representative; or

- the proposed personal representative is unable to apply; or

- the full value of the estate cannot be ascertained; or

- there is an undetermined dispute affecting the application for the grant or in relation to the estate,

application may be made for an order directing a grant of letters of administration *ad colligenda bona* to issue to any person who can show to the court that he has an interest in protecting the deceased's estate, for example where the deceased's business will suffer unless dealt with; where a house must be sold without delay; where a grant is required to deal with stocks and/or shares; or where there is undue delay in applying for a grant (see *IRC v Stype Investments (Jersey) Ltd* and *Re Clore [1982] Ch 456, [1982] 3 All ER 419*). The procedure for applying for the order to lead the grant is set out in CHAPTER 5 at paragraph 5.34.

Application for the grant

10.6   Application for the grant will be made on oath in the usual way. The oath must recite the details of the order under Rule 52 which leads the grant and set out the limitation contained in the order. The grant will always be a grant of letters of administration even if the deceased died testate. Unless there are special requirements the usual limitation imposed is 'limited for the purpose only of collecting and getting in and receiving the estate and doing such acts as may be necessary for the preservation of the same but no further or otherwise.' The grant will also be limited until further representation be granted. The limitation is a matter for the District Judge or Registrar when making the order.

The oath need not recite whether the deceased died testate or intestate and the grant will also be silent as to this fact; neither need the oath contain any clearings of entitlement to the grant. The values to be shown in the oath are those applicable to the 'excepted estate' provisions if appropriate or appearing in the Inland Revenue Account. Only the value of the estate passing under this grant need be included. If inheritance tax is payable, the tax payable on that part of the estate passing under the grant only need be paid (with the agreement of IR Capital Taxes). At the time of applying for the order, IR Capital Taxes should be approached. There is power to dispense with the delivery of an Account or pay tax at this stage: this is a matter in the discretion of IR Capital Taxes. Form D18 showing that the tax has been paid must be lodged in the usual way. Where the grant is limited to a purpose for which there is no estate value, e.g. to representing the estate at a share distribution meeting, no fee is payable. Where the estate passing under the grant exceeds £5,000, the usual £50 fee is payable (for the form of oath see Form A1.40, page 401).

Where there develops a need for a further temporary grant in respect of another part of the estate, but still no full grant can be taken, application may be made for a further order for a second grant to deal with the estate now requiring administration but outside the ambit of the original grant.

Subsequent application for full grant

10.7   Application for a full grant may be made by the person(s) entitled when the purpose of the limited grant has been achieved or the impediment to application for a full grant has been removed. The oath to lead the full grant must recite details of the *ad colligenda bona* grant. On the issue of the full grant the limited grant ceases notwithstanding that it may not have achieved the full purpose for which it was issued. If application for the full grant is made to a Registry other than the Registry which issued the *ad colligenda bona* grant, a copy of that grant must be lodged with the oath.

Grants *de bonis non*

10.8   Where a grant of representation has issued and the grantee dies, or is incapacitated in some way, leaving the estate unadministered or partially unadministered, and there is no chain of executorship or executor to whom power was reserved willing to take a grant of double probate, application may be made for a grant *de bonis non* in respect of the unadministered estate.

Deceased testate

Executor with power reserved

10.9   Where the deceased died testate and probate has issued in respect of his estate to an executor or executors with power reserved to another or other executors, the latter may apply for a grant of double probate to continue the administration if the proving executor(s) die(s) or cannot continue the administration (see paragraph 10.19 below).

Application by beneficiary

10.10   Where there are no executor(s) to continue the administration, application for a grant of letters of administration (with will annexed) *de bonis non* may be made by a residuary legatee or devisee or other person entitled in accordance with the order of priority contained in Rule 20 (see paragraph 8.2 above) provided that, where the original grant was one of probate, there is no chain of representation through the sole or last surviving proving executor (see paragraph 7.23 above), or such a chain has been broken, or no grant of probate has been taken to the sole or last surviving proving executor's estate leaving the chain in abeyance. All executors, including those to whom power was reserved on the original grant, must be cleared off by death, renunciation or citation, and each clearing recited in the oath to lead the grant. Similarly, the manner in which a chain of executorship is broken – for example by the proving executor dying intestate – and the clearing of persons with a higher entitlement must be recited in the oath. On clearing all persons with a prior beneficial interest in the estate, application may be made by those entitled in a lower degree of priority in accordance with Rule 20. Where a chain of representation is in abeyance, the grant will be limited until probate of the sole or last surviving proving executor's will is granted.

Person equally entitled

10.11 Where the original grantee was one of several persons entitled (for example one of the residuary legatees and devisees), application may be made by another residuary legatee and devisee. Where the original grant issued to a person entitled to share in estate undisposed of by the will, application may be made by another also entitled to share in the undisposed of estate.

Personal representative

10.12 Where the original grant was of letters of administration (with will annexed) and issued to the sole residuary legatee and devisee, application should be made by his personal representative. Application for a 'representative grant', sometimes referred to as a 'leading grant' (see paragraph 9.6 above), to the estate of the sole residuary legatee or devisee may be necessary to establish title to apply for the grant *de bonis non*, that is unless such grant has already issued.

Where the original grantee was the only person entitled in whatever capacity, or those equally entitled survived the deceased but predeceased the grantee, application may be made by their personal representative(s). The personal representative of a person entitled who renounced his title or did not enter an appearance to a citation may apply for a *de bonis non* grant.

As can be seen from the above, the order of priority to apply for a second grant (*de bonis non*) is the same as for an original grant (Rule 20).

Deceased intestate

10.13 Where the deceased died intestate, application may be made for a grant of letters of administration *de bonis non* by those beneficially entitled to the estate in accordance with Rule 22 (see paragraph 9.28 above). Where the whole estate vested in the original administrator, application for the *de bonis non* grant must be made by the personal representative of that administrator (see Rule 22(4)). This may also require an application for a 'representative grant' (see paragraph 9.6 above) to the estate of the original administrator, that is unless such a grant has already issued.

Others beneficially entitled

10.14 Rule 22(4) also states that where there are kin taking a beneficial interest in the estate, their interest is to be preferred in priority to that of the personal representative of a spouse who has died without taking a beneficial interest in the whole estate as ascertained at the time of the application for that grant; that is, where the value of the estate exceeded the statutory sum accruing to the surviving spouse (see paragraph 9.28 above), the living person(s) entitled to benefit under the intestacy (for example issue of the deceased) are to be given preference in title to the grant *de bonis non* over the personal representative of the surviving but now deceased spouse.

To determine whether the statutory legacy to which a surviving spouse is entitled (see paragraph 9.28 above) exceeds the value of the whole estate, reference should be made to the value at the time of payment or appropriation. It is usual, however, for the value as at the date of death to be used as the value to determine whether the statutory legacy was exceeded. Consideration should be given to this question and to the consequential entitlement to the grant where a change in value of the estate, or of one particular asset, has occurred.

Where the deceased was not married or was not survived by his spouse but by issue or remoter kin, one of whom took the original grant, another child or member of the same class of remoter kin may apply for the grant *de bonis non*.

Application

The oath

10.15 The preference for a living person as applicant to the personal representative of a deceased person of equal entitlement as prescribed by Rule 27(5) also applies to grants *de bonis non* (see paragraph 10.14 above). Application for a *de bonis non* grant may be made to any Registry, not necessarily the Registry from which the original grant issued. The provisions of s 114(2) Supreme Court Act 1981, requiring at least two grantees or application by a trust corporation alone or with an individual, apply to grants *de bonis non* where a life or minority interest still exists. The oath must recite details of the original grant and the death of the original grantee, and refer to the value of the unadministered estate.

Marking will

10.16 Where the grant is of administration (with will annexed) the original or an office copy of the original will issued by the proving Registry, must be marked by the applicant. Where the original will is to be marked, it must be so marked and the oath sworn in the Registry from which the original grant issued, as the will cannot be released out of the Registry. If the probate copy, that is the copy included in the original grant, is marked then that grant will be retained by the Registry.

Inland Revenue Account

10.17 Although this is a 'second' grant in the estate, the provisions of the Inheritance Tax (Delivery of Accounts) (Excepted Estates) Regulations 2002 to constitute the estate as 'excepted' – and so making the delivery of an Account unnecessary – apply provided the criteria allowing the estate to be treated as 'excepted' are met. This will generally be the case where the criteria were met on the first grant.

The oath to lead the grant should state that the gross and net value of the unadministered estate does not exceed £xxx (these being the figures on the original grant).

Where on an application for the first grant an Account was delivered, an Account must now also be delivered dealing only with the unadministered estate. Where a change in value takes the unadministered estate outside the excepted estate limit, an Inland Revenue Account will be necessary. Where an Account must be delivered, the Account will be in Form A-5C where the estate to be covered by the new grant was covered by the original grant. Form A-5C is lodged *in the Probate Registry* on the application for the grant, *not* sent to IR Capital Taxes.

The fee for a *de bonis non* grant is £15, it being a second grant to the estate. For the form of oath, see Form A1.41, page 403.

Cessate grants

10.18 Where a grant ceases to operate because:

(a) the limitation imposed in it has been fulfilled;

(b) the grantee dies or ceases to be competent, leaving the limitation outstanding or the estate unadministered;

(c) the original will is found, a copy or reconstruction having been previously proved;

(d) a minor, to whose parent(s), guardians or persons appointed by order the grant has issued, achieves his majority;

(e)   a person, formerly mentally incapable, recovers his ability to administer the estate; or

(f)   the original grant issued to an attorney and the donor of the power of attorney now wishes to obtain a grant himself or through another attorney,

a *cessate* grant, which is a grant to the whole estate unlike a *de bonis non* grant which is a grant to the unadministered estate only, will issue for the purpose of dealing with the estate or any estate remaining unadministered. The circumstances in (a)–(f) above are dealt with in detail below.

(a)   Where a limitation (for example where an executor was appointed for a prescribed period) is fulfilled, application may be made by the person next entitled, who may be a substituted executor or the person next entitled in priority under Rule 20 (see paragraph 8.2 above). Where the grant issued for the purpose of taking or defending court proceedings, that grant ceases on the determination of the proceedings. In either of these circumstances, a *cessate* grant will be necessary to administer the estate or any estate remaining unadministered.

(b)   Where a limited grant issued and the grantee dies or ceases to be capable of managing his affairs, leaving the limitation remaining, a *cessate* grant may be required to continue the limited administration. It may be that the circumstances have now changed and that a full grant may be taken.

(c)   Where a copy or reconstructed will was proved the limitation in the grant would have been 'until the original will or a more authentic copy is proved'. If the original or a more authentic copy is found, the original grant remains in force until the original is proved. Should the copy be exactly the same as the original there is no obligation to prove the original; however, where there is a material difference the original should be proved and on the issue of the new grant the original grant will cease to be effective.

The oath to lead the new grant should recite details of the first grant and the discovery of the original, or more authentic copy of the, will. The original or more authentic copy should be marked with the oath.

If the original grantee has died the new grant should be taken by the person(s) next entitled in priority, the relevant facts being deposed to in the oath.

(d)   Where a grant of administration (with will annexed) was issued for the use and benefit of a minor executor, the grant would have been limited until he (the minor executor) attained the age of 18 years or further representation was granted. On attaining his majority the executor may apply for probate, the grant ceasing to operate on the minor attaining 18 years.

Where the grant was of letters of administration (with will annexed) and issued for the use and benefit of a minor beneficiary under the will or was a grant of letters of administration for the use and benefit of a minor entitled under an intestacy, the grant would have been limited in the same way and a *cessate* grant will be necessary on the beneficiary attaining his majority to deal with the estate remaining unadministered.

If there was more than one minor for whose use and benefit the grant issued, the grant would have been limited until one of them attained the age of 18 years. On the first minor attaining his majority, a *cessate* grant will be necessary to deal with any unadministered estate. Subsequent grants may be necessary as each child attains 18 years. If a minority interest still exists there will be a requirement for a further administrator by virtue of s 114(2) of the Supreme Court Act 1981. Unless otherwise directed, the *cessate* grant will be limited until further representation be granted. It cannot be for the use and benefit of the remaining minor(s) as (one of) the grantee(s) is now entitled to the grant. The oath must recite details of the former grant and the date the child attained his majority. For the procedure dealing with the addition of a personal representative after the issue of a grant see paragraph 5.26 above.

(e) Where a grant issued for the use and benefit of a person mentally incapable of managing his affairs (see paragraph 10.60 below) and that person recovers his capacity, he may apply for a *cessate* grant in whatever entitlement he originally had (for example an executor to probate or beneficiary to administration). Evidence of the recovery of his capacity must be filed, either in the form of an authority from the Court of Protection if the original grantee was authorised to apply by that court, or, if not, in the form of medical evidence from a doctor. Unless a District Judge or Registrar otherwise directs, the consent of the original grantee to the issue of the new grant should be obtained.

Where the grant was limited 'and during his incapacity' it ceases to have effect on his recovering his capacity, but if the grant was limited 'until further representation be granted' it will remain in force until the further grant issues either to the recovered person or another entitled.

Should the original grantee die before the incapable person, and estate remains unadministered, a second grant may be taken, to the whole estate; the evidence for and authorisation of the new grantee will be as required for an original grant.

(f) Where the donor of a power of attorney wishes, he may apply for a *cessate* grant in the capacity in which he was originally entitled. The original grant, which will have been limited until further representation be granted, will cease on the issue of the new grant.

Where the attorney dies before the donor of the power of attorney –

or another attorney is appointed, the original power being revoked – leaving estate unadministered, application may be made by the donor or by the other attorney. If, however, the donor of the power of attorney dies before administration is complete, a *de bonis non* grant should be applied for in respect of the unadministered estate.

In all the cases described above, the oath to lead the grant must give details of the original grant and the reason for its ceasing to be effective. The deponent swears to administer *all* the estate, but the amount inserted in the oath will be the value of the unadministered estate. Where necessary, an Inland Revenue Account in form IHT 200 must be delivered to Inland Revenue Capital Taxes and form D18 lodged in the Registry. If the excepted estate criteria applied on the original grant application, they may still apply to the *cessate* grant application. The estate values at the date of death of the deceased will apply.

This being an application for a second grant in the same estate, a fee of £15 is payable. See Form A1.42, page 405 for the form of oath.

Grants of double probate

10.19   Where a grant of probate issued to one or some of the executors appointed and power was reserved to others, a grant of double probate may issue to one or more of those others to whom power was reserved.

Number of executors

10.20   Where probate was granted to four executors application may be made only when a vacancy occurs in the original executors who proved the will, since the normal requirement of not more than four proving executors must be observed (s 114(1) Supreme Court Act 1981).

The oath to lead the grant must contain details of the original grant and how the vacancy in the executorship has arisen (for example by the death of a proving executor). Subject to the maximum number of grantees, application may be made at any time for a grant of double probate by *any* executor to whom power was reserved on the application for the original grant.

Effect of grant

10.21   A grant of double probate runs concurrently with the original grant (provided an original proving executor is still alive), and confers the same rights on the proving executor as those held by the original proving executor. The original grantee need not be notified of the application, and the original grant is not noted. Application for a grant of double probate, as with a grant of letters of administration (with will annexed) *de bonis* *non,* requires the applicant to mark either the original will or an office copy of it (see paragraph 10.16 above).

An office copy of the original grant must be lodged with the papers to lead the grant if application is made to a Registry other than the Registry which issued the original grant.

A grant of double probate is a grant to the whole estate, but the amount appearing in the oath and on the grant is the value of the unadministered estate.

An Inland Revenue Account in Form A-5C should be completed where the criteria to bring the estate within the definition of an 'excepted estate' are not met. If the original grant issued as an 'excepted estate' case the grant of double probate will now generally also be in respect of an 'excepted estate'. The oath should depose to the fact that the gross value of the unadministered estate 'does not exceed £.....', the appropriate value being inserted. Form A-5C is delivered to the Probate Registry with the grant application.

Where power to take a like grant is to be reserved again to other non-proving executors, notice of the application must be given to them, and the oath must recite details (subject to Rule 27(1A)). Application may be made to a District Judge or Registrar to dispense with the giving of such notice where it is impracticable to do so, or where to require notice to be given will result in unreasonable delay or expense (see Rule 27(1) and (3)).

A fee of £15 is payable on application for a grant of double probate. See Form A1.3, page 345 for the form of oath.

Settled land grant

10.22 Where land was vested in the deceased at the date of his death which was settled prior to his death (and not by his will if he died testate), and which remains settled land notwithstanding his death, a settled land grant may be necessary to administer such land according to the settlement.

Definition

10.23 Settled land is any immovable property, as defined by the Settled Land Act 1925, which is not held upon an immediate trust for sale, and may include leasehold property. Land may be settled by a deed, trust instrument or will which entitles the tenant to enjoy the use of it for his life. The land must have been vested in the life tenant before he died, and remain settled after his death, before a settled land grant will be necessary. It follows, therefore, that where land passes to a single life tenant for his life only, it will not be settled land but simply a life interest.

Vesting is effected by the execution of a 'vesting deed' or 'vesting assent'. The statutory owner of the land is the trustees of the settlement who, generally, where there is no tenant for life, have the powers of the tenant for life (see s 117(1) of the Act). If it has not been vested in the life tenant, the land is not settled.

A settled land grant is necessary to transfer or vest title in land in accordance with the trust instrument. A settled land grant will not be necessary where land, the subject of a settlement, has been sold and the value is now held as a capital sum, although the capital sum is held subject to the settlement. Where the capital sum is used to purchase new property, the new property may become settled land under the trust instrument. Where land is settled by the deceased's will, a settled land grant will not be necessary until the death of the life tenant beneficially entitled under that will.

Rule 29: order of entitlement

10.24   Rule 29 was amended with effect from 14 October 1991, to read as follows:

'(1) In this rule "settled land" means land vested in the deceased which was settled prior to his death and not by his will, and which remained settled land notwithstanding his death.

(2)   The person or persons entitled to a grant of administration limited to settled land shall be determined in accordance with the following order of priority:

(i)   the special executors in regard to settled land constituted by section 22 of the Administration of Estates Act 1925;

(ii)   the trustees of the settlement at the time of the application for the grant; and

(iii)   the personal representatives of the deceased.

(3)   Where there is settled land and a grant is made in respect of the free estate only, the grant shall expressly exclude the settled land.'

It follows therefore that from 14 October 1991 only grants of administration limited to settled land issue where there is settled land. There is no longer any provision for issuing a grant of probate limited to settled land to special executors, nor will a grant issue including settled land. A separate grant of administration will issue in respect of the settled land and, where necessary, a separate grant in the appropriate form to deal with free estate (see below). A grant may therefore issue to the free estate 'excluding' settled land.

Special executor

10.25   The persons first entitled to the grant are the special executors in regard to the settled land. If they have not been appointed executors, either generally or specially, by the will, their appointment will be deemed as special executors limited to settled land (see s 22 Administration of Estates Act 1925). Their powers are basically those held by general executors, but no chain of representation will exist. The special executors may also be trustees and are entitled in either capacity to the grant. As the grant is of administration, any appointed executor who does not join in the application cannot have power reserved to him. Although the life tenant's will is not proved on the settled land grant application, it may be called for to establish who are the special executors.

Trustees of the settlement

10.26   If no trustees of the settlement are alive at the date of death of the deceased, or such trustees as survive the deceased renounce their right to a grant, a grant of letters of administration will be necessary to administer the settlement. Such a grant will issue to any trustees of the settlement appointed since the date of the death of the tenant for life, or if they are cleared off, to the personal representatives of the deceased tenant for life. Where no trustee of the settlement or personal representative exists, any other person interested in the transfer of the property may apply for an order under s 116 of the Supreme Court Act 1981 for a discretionary grant (see paragraph 5.27 above). The applicant is usually the 'remainderman', that is the person in whom the beneficial interest in the land ultimately vests. Where the tenant for life died wholly intestate, a grant of letters of administration limited to settled land may be made to trustees of the settlement at the time the grant is applied for, or to the persons entitled in order of priority to such a grant. A settled land grant may issue to an individual notwithstanding there is a life or minority interest in the land.

Land ceasing to be settled

10.27   Land which is settled land and may remain settled through a succession of life tenants, may cease to be settled by the execution of a 'disentailing deed'. This is a deed executed by the current tenant for life and his successor as tenant. On the death of the current tenant the land vests absolutely in the successor. The land will also cease to be settled land on the death of the last life tenant: it then falls to be dealt with under the terms of the original settlement.

The Trusts of Land and Appointment of Trustees Act 1996 provides that no settlement created after the commencement of the Act (1 January 1997) may be a settlement for the purposes of the Settled Land Act 1975. It follows therefore that only settled land which was settled before the commencement of the Act falls to be dealt with by way of settled land grants under the provisions set out above.

Form of grant

10.28   Where a grant issues in respect of settled land, it will expressly state that it is so limited. Where a general grant issues excluding settled land it will include the phrase 'save and except settled land'. Where a full grant has already issued without a notation 'save and except', it should be returned to the issuing Registry for amendment.

The oath by administrators to lead a grant in respect of settled land is set out as Form A1.44, page 409. All relevant vesting documents and assents, together with any appointment of trustees, must be lodged with the oath. The grant, being of administration only, will not require proof of the tenant for life's will (if any). If the tenant for life died testate, his will will be proved on application for the grant (save and except settled land) to his free estate. The grant limited to settled land will not therefore state whether the life tenant died testate or intestate.

The usual grant fee of £50 is payable on an application for a settled land grant.

Grant limited to part of estate: insolvent estate

Power to sever estate

10.29   Section 113 of the Supreme Court Act 1981 enables the court to issue a grant of representation in respect of part of the deceased's estate and to limit the grant in any way considered appropriate. Where the deceased's estate is known to be insolvent, the grant to the estate shall not be severed (that is issued in respect of part thereof), except as regards a trust estate in which the deceased had no beneficial interest. Section 113 does not enable the court to issue a grant in respect of part of the estate to a person not entitled in priority under Rules 20 or 22 (see paragraphs 8.2 and 9.28 above). Application by a person not entitled should be made under s 116 of the Act (see paragraph 5.27 above).

Application for order

10.30   Rule 51 provides that where a grant in respect of part of the estate is required under s 113, application for an order is made *ex parte* on affidavit to the District Judge or Registrar of the Registry at which the application for the grant will be made if the order is made. The procedure for applying for the order is set out in CHAPTER 5 at paragraph 5.43.

Grant where there is trust property

10.31   Where there is trust property but no other estate vested in the deceased, application should be made for a full grant, but for a 'nil estate', that is, a grant in the normal form taken by the person entitled to it under the normal order of priority contained in the rules but under which no estate will pass. The fact that there is trust property requiring a grant to perfect title should be recited in the oath. This will be sufficient to enable a 'nil estate' grant to issue.

Where the deceased died testate, his will must be proved and a grant of probate or letters of administration (with will annexed), as appropriate, will issue with the appropriate limitations.

Attorney grants

10.32   Rule 31(1) provides that where a person entitled to a grant as executor or administrator so wishes, administration may be granted to his lawfully constituted attorney for the use and benefit of the person entitled. The grant will be limited until further representation be granted, but may be further limited as the District Judge or Registrar may consider appropriate.

Rule 31(2) provides that where the donor is one of several executors, notice of the application should be given to every other surviving executor unless a District Judge or Registrar dispenses with the giving of such notice (see paragraph 10.33 below).

Rule 31(3) provides that where the donor is now mentally incapable of managing his affairs and the attorney is acting under an enduring power of attorney, the provisions of Rule 35 (which deal with applications on behalf of mentally incapable persons; see paragraph 10.60 below) shall apply. The enduring power of attorney, to be effective in this situation, must have been registered with the Court of Protection (still referred to as such in the Rule, but now the Protection Division of the Public Guardianship Office).

There is no longer any provision which limits attorney applications to cases where the donor of the power (the person entitled to apply for the grant) resides outside England and Wales, or requires a direction from a District Judge or Registrar before application can be made on behalf of a person resident within the jurisdiction. The rule allows any person entitled to apply for a grant to appoint an attorney to obtain a grant for their use and benefit. Similarly, there is no requirement that the attorney should be resident in England and Wales. The rules make no provision for requiring an administration guarantee to be obtained where application is made by an attorney. All these former provisions were contained in the

Non-Contentious Probate Rules 1954 and were revoked by the 1987 Rules with effect from 1 January 1988.

Executor's attorney

Notice

10.33   Where the person applying is the attorney of one of the executors, notice of the application must be given to all other surviving executors (see Rule 31(2)), unless a District Judge or Registrar dispenses with such notice. Notice need be by letter only sent to the last known address(es) of the executor(s).

Limitation in grant

10.34   Where there are several executors but only one executor applies through his attorney, the grant will be limited until further representation be granted but the District Judge or Registrar may direct that the grant should be limited until the executor who is applying – or one or all of the remaining executors – prove(s) the will. Where the applicant is the attorney of all the executors, the grant will similarly be limited until further representation be granted or until *all* the executors prove the will.

Form of grant

10.35   Probate is not granted to an executor's attorney; the grant will be of letters of administration (with will annexed). It follows therefore that an executor and the attorney of an executor cannot apply together for a grant, the former being entitled to a grant of probate and the latter only to administration (with will annexed). One of them must agree to application in the manner proposed by the other. If agreement cannot be reached, both executors may prove the will in that capacity and thereafter the executor who wishes to act through his attorney may appoint the attorney for the purpose of administering the estate. This will again require the agreement of all executors who prove. For a form of oath, see Form A1.10, page 357. See also paragraph 10.41 below where more than one attorney is appointed.

Administrator's attorney

10.36   Any person entitled in priority under a will or intestacy to administration may appoint an attorney to apply for the grant without giving prior notice to any other person of equal entitlement. (For a form of oath, see Form A1.31, page 388.)

Life or minority interests

10.37   Where a life or minority interest arises under a will or an intestacy, the usual requirement for two grantees will apply (see s 114 Supreme Court Act 1981). This is so even where the attorney appointed derives his power from an executor. Thus:

(i)   two attorneys will have to be appointed; or

(ii)   application may be made by the attorney and another person of equal entitlement; or

(iii)   where there is no other person entitled, either equally or in a lower degree, application may be made to a District Judge or Registrar for a co-administrator to be appointed, or to dispense with a second administrator.

The discretion vested in the court under s 114(2) of the Act to allow the grant to issue to a sole administrator may be exercised when the court considers it expedient, but is used only in exceptional circumstances.

Alternatively, a trust corporation alone may be appointed attorney.

The power of attorney

General power of attorney

10.38   A general form of power of attorney given in accordance with the Powers of Attorney Act 1971 is sufficient authorisation for the attorney to take a grant of representation for the use and benefit of the donor. Alternatively, a power limited to taking out the grant may be given (see Form A1.68, page 435).

Where the power is limited to taking out a grant in respect of *part* of the deceased's estate the matter should be referred to a District Judge or Registrar for directions before lodging the papers to lead the grant. Where the power appoints more than one attorney who may act jointly or severally, then any one or more of them may apply for the grant.

Where several persons are entitled to a grant, as executors or otherwise, they may all appoint the same attorney or different attorneys to take the grant.

The power must be signed by the donor in the presence of a disinterested witness. Where the power of attorney is written in a foreign language, it must be accompanied by a translation properly certified by a person competent to translate the power. If the power was executed in English in a non-English speaking country, the power will be acceptable if witnessed by a notary or British Consul. If the power is in English but not witnessed by a notary or Consul it will be acceptable if the extracting solicitors can certify that the donor understood English, or there is sufficient other evidence to satisfy the District Judge or Registrar that the donor understood English.

Acceptance of copy power of attorney

10.39   It is usual for the original document to be lodged with the papers to lead the grant. A power of attorney limited for the purpose of obtaining the grant remains in the Registry, the original of which must be lodged. However, the Registry may accept a copy of the power of attorney:

(a)   if it contains a certificate by a solicitor at the end of the document stating that the copy is a true and complete copy of the original;

(b)   where the power consists of more than one page, if each page contains a certificate by a solicitor at the end of each page that that page is a true and complete copy of the original page; or

(c)   where a power has been deposited with a notary or court of the place where the deceased died domiciled, (i) a notarised copy provided there is affidavit evidence stating that the notarised copy is acceptable as valid by the court of the place of the domicile, or (ii) a court certified copy.

Where a general power of attorney has been lodged but is required for other purposes, it may be released on application made in that respect, provided a properly certified copy is lodged in substitution.

Enduring power of attorney

10.40   The Enduring Powers of Attorney Act 1985 came into force on 10 March 1986. Section 1 of the Act provides that where there is an enduring power of attorney within the meaning of the Act that power is not revoked by any subsequent mental incapacity of the donor, but until the power is registered with the Court of Protection, the attorney has only limited rights under the power and the Act.

A power of attorney executed in the form of an enduring power of attorney (see Form A1.69, page 436) will normally also be an ordinary power of attorney.

Section 4 of the Act provides that the attorney acting under an enduring power of attorney should apply for registration of the instrument creating the power with the Court of Protection as soon as practicable after he is aware the donor is or is becoming mentally incapable. The Court of Protection will register the power unless it is satisfied of any of the grounds of possible objection set out in s 6 of the Act. Once registered the power cannot validly be revoked by the donor until the Court of Protection confirms the revocation. That court may also, in certain circumstances, cancel the registration; it also has power to determine any question of the meaning and effect of the registered instrument and to give directions in respect of it.

An application for a grant by an attorney acting under a registered enduring power of attorney must be supported by the filing of the original or an office copy of the instrument registered under the Act. A copy certified in accordance with s 3 of the Powers of Attorney Act 1971 may be accepted only when supported by evidence of registration. A copy of the registered power endorsed with the Court of Protection seal and then certified to be a true and complete copy will be accepted.

More than one attorney appointed

10.41   Where two (or more) persons entitled to a grant each appoint their own attorney to apply for a grant for each of their benefits, the grant will be limited for the use and benefit of those entitled during the joint lives of the donors and the attorneys and until further representation is granted. The oath should recite, for example, that 'A' is the attorney of 'B' and 'C' is the attorney of 'D' for the use and benefit of 'B' and 'D' during the joint lives of 'A', 'B', 'C' and 'D'.

Grant to person entitled and the attorney of another person equally entitled

10.42   Letters of administration may issue to a person entitled under the intestacy and the attorney of another equally entitled, for example to a brother and the attorney of a sister. As there is a person entitled taking the grant, it will not be for the use and benefit of the donor but will be limited until further representation be granted. The oath to lead the grant should contain the consent to the limitation of the applicant who is entitled to apply. The consent (in writing) may, however, be given separately.

Attorney's authority

10.43   The properly appointed attorney has the same status as the donor of the power. If the donor dies, the grant ceases to be operative, as will be the case if the attorney dies (see paragraph 10.45 below). Where the donor was an executor no chain of representation (see paragraph 7.23 above) will be created through his attorney. The chain will be in abeyance during the duration of the grant. The chain may not be broken and can be recreated by the donor (executor)'s obtaining probate. A power of attorney may contain an authority for the attorney to appoint another attorney to take the grant. In such circumstances, both powers should be lodged with the application.

No further authority will be required by a Probate Registry from the donor of a power of attorney to enable his attorney to apply for a grant in another estate to which he is entitled by being the personal representative of the deceased. Thus if a person dies intestate leaving two siblings one of whom takes letters of administration through an attorney, on the death of the other surviving sibling intestate the attorney may take a grant in that estate as the personal representative. The grant will usually be limited until further representation is granted in the estate of the first to die.

Renunciation by attorney

10.44 An attorney acting under a registered enduring power of attorney may renounce title to the grant on the patient's behalf. An attorney acting under any other form of power of attorney may only renounce if specifically authorised so to do in the power of attorney.

Death of donor of power of attorney

10.45 Where the donor of the power of attorney dies before the administration of the estate is complete, the donee's power to act ceases. No liability is incurred by the donee if he continues to act in ignorance of the donor's death (see s 5(1) of the 1971 Act). A grant *de bonis non* to deal with the unadministered estate will be necessary (see paragraph 10.8 above).

Consular officers

10.46 Section 1 of the Consular Conventions Act 1949 allows a consular officer to take a grant on behalf of a national of a state to which the Act has been applied where that national is entitled to a grant of representation but is resident outside England and Wales.

The oath to lead the grant should set out that the applicant is a consular officer of the country or state to which the Act applies; that the national is resident outside England and Wales; the national's title to the grant; and that no application has been made by an attorney on the national's behalf. The consular officer may apply without the consent of or any other authority from the national. A consular officer may apply alone notwithstanding a life or minority interest arises in the estate. The grant will issue to the consular officer (by his official title) and his successors in office.

The Act applies to the following countries or states:

Austria, Belgium, Bulgaria, Czechoslovakia, Denmark, The Federal Republic of Germany, France, Greece, Hungary, Italy, Japan, Mexico, Mongolia, Norway, Poland, Spain, Sweden, USSR and Yugoslavia.

The Act applies to the Federal Republic of Germany, Czechoslovakia and Yugoslavia as the former countries they were but not to the new countries/states which have evolved since the former countries split or, in the case of Germany, its merger with East Germany. No new Orders in Council have been made in the names of any of the new countries.

Grants for the use and benefit of minors

10.47 A grant of representation may not issue to a minor, that is a person under 18 years of age. The age of majority, formerly 21 years, was reduced to 18 by s 1 of the Family Law Reform Act 1969 with effect from 1 January 1970.

Entitlement to

10.48 Unless otherwise directed by the court, administration for the use and benefit of the minor, where the person entitled to the grant is a minor, shall be granted to:

'(a) a parent of the minor who has, or is deemed to have, parental responsibility for him in accordance with:

  (i) s 2(1), 2(2) or 4 of the Children Act 1989;

  (ii) para 4 or 6 of Sch 14 to the Act; or

  (iii) an adoption order within the meaning of s 12(1) of the Adoption Act 1976; or

(aa) a person who has, or is deemed to have, parental responsibility for the minor by virtue of s 12(2) of the Children Act 1989 where the court has made a residence order under s 8 of that Act in respect of the minor in favour of that person; or

(b) a guardian of the minor who is appointed, or deemed to have been appointed, in accordance with s 5 of the Children Act 1989 or in accordance with paras 12, 13 or 14 of Sch 14 to that Act; or

(c) a local authority which has, or is deemed to have, parental responsibility for the minor by virtue of s 33(3) of the Children Act 1989 where the court has made a care order under s 31(1)(a) of that Act in respect of the minor and that local authority is designated in that order;

provided that where the minor is sole executor and has no interest in the residuary estate of the deceased, administration for the use and benefit of the minor limited as aforesaid shall, unless a District Judge or Registrar otherwise directs, be granted to the person entitled to the residuary estate.'

(Rule 32(1) as amended from 14 September 1998).

The grant will be limited for the use and benefit of the minor child until he attains the age of 18 years. Where the grant issues for the benefit of several minors, the limitation will be for their use and benefit until one of them shall attain the age of 18 years (see Rule 32(1)). It should be noted that there is no longer any requirement for *both* parents to apply: para (a) above states 'a parent'. 'Parent' or 'parents' includes adoptive parents.

Sub-paragraph (aa) above, added by the Non-Contentious Probate (Amendment) Rules 1998, now enables a person, other than a parent or guardian, having parental responsibility by virtue of a residence order made under s 8 of the Act, provided the order remains in force, to apply for a grant for a minor's use and benefit.

Paragraph (c), also added by the 1998 Rules, allows a local authority having parental responsibility by virtue of a care order made under s 31(1)(a) of the Act to take a grant for the use and benefit of the minor whose care has been committed to it. The local authority will apply and the oath will be sworn by the person nominated or otherwise authorised to act for the authority, usually the Director of Social Services. The local authority may qualify as a trust corporation and may apply as such.

Where a minor and a person of full age are equally entitled, Rule 27(5) provides that the adult person will be preferred as grantee to the guardian of the minor, unless the court directs otherwise. Application to avoid the preference is made to a District Judge or Registrar. Usually application by letter is accepted but an affidavit of facts may be called for. A second grantee will still be required because of the minority interest (see paragraph 10.49 below).

Number of grantees

10.49 By s 114(2) of the Supreme Court Act 1981, where a life or minority interest arises in an estate, a grant of administration must be made to two or more persons, or to a trust corporation with or without another person, unless a District Judge or Registrar considers it expedient in all the circumstances to direct otherwise.

Section 114(4) of the Supreme Court Act 1981 provides that if at any time during the minority of a beneficiary under a will or intestacy there is only one personal representative (not a trust corporation) and estate remains unadministered, the court may appoint one or more additional personal representatives to act while the minority interest subsists. Application to add a co-administrator is made *ex parte* to a District Judge or Registrar on affidavit by the applicant, with the consent of the person proposed to be added as personal representative. The 'applicant' may be the existing personal representative, any person interested, or the guardian or receiver of such person. (See CHAPTER 5 at paragraph 5.41 for application under Rule 26.)

Minor appointed executor

10.50   Section 118 of the Supreme Court Act 1981 provides that where a minor is appointed an executor, the appointment shall not operate to vest the estate or any part of it in the minor, or to constitute him a personal representative for any purpose unless and until probate is granted to him on application by him after he has attained his majority.

Where the sole executor is a minor with no beneficial interest in the residuary estate, the person entitled to the residuary estate may take letters of administration (with will annexed) for the use and benefit of the minor, limited until he attains the age of 18 years. (Rule 32(1), proviso.) Where the minor executor also has a beneficial interest, his parents, other persons or local authority having parental responsibility for him may apply for the grant for the minor's use and benefit until he achieves his majority. Where there are no such persons or body, application must be made under Rule 32(2) for the appointment of persons to apply (see CHAPTER 5 at paragraph 5.57).

Rule 33(1) provides that where one executor of several appointed is a minor, application may be made by the adult executors with power reserved to the minor until he shall attain his majority. Where the adult executors renounce or otherwise fail to prove the will, application may be made by the person(s) or body with parental responsibility (see Rule 32(1), paragraph 10.48 above).

No person or body having parental responsibility or otherwise may renounce on behalf of a minor executor the right to take a grant of probate on attaining his majority (Rule 34(1)). On attaining the age of 18 years, the minor executor himself may renounce.

Minor beneficially interested in estate and entitled to administration

10.51   Where the minor is a residuary beneficiary, the grant of letters of administration may be taken by the person or body with parental responsibility for him.

Where a minor is entitled to a grant of letters of administration (with or without will annexed) his right thereto may be renounced only by a person authorised to do so and appointed under Rule 32(2) for that specific purpose (see Rule 34(2)).

Grant to a trust corporation

10.52   Where all executors appointed under a will are minors, a grant limited for their use and benefit and until one of them shall attain the age of 18 years may issue to a trust corporation. The consent of all persons entitled to the residuary estate is a prerequisite to the application. Where all persons entitled to the residuary estate under a will, or to a grant of administration on an intestacy, are minors, application for a limited grant may be made by a trust corporation on the consents of the person(s) having or deemed to have parental responsibility for the minors, or of the guardian(s) of the minors. Where there is/are no such persons living, or such persons do not consent, application for a direction to allow administration to be granted to a trust corporation may be made to a District Judge or Registrar. (See CHAPTER 11 at paragraph 11.12.)

Parental responsibility

10.53   Where a child's parents were married to each other at the time of his birth, both parents have parental responsibility for the child (s 2(1) of the Children Act 1989). Where they were not so married, parental responsibility vests in the child's mother (s 2(2) of the Act).

Where the child's parents were not married to each other at the time of the child's birth, his father may acquire parental responsibility either:

(a)   by applying to the court for an order that he should have parental responsibility; or

(b)   by the mother and father of the child agreeing that the father shall have parental responsibility and registering such agreement, in accordance with the Parental Responsibility Agreement Regulations 1991, in the Principal Registry (s 4 of the Act).

Where, before the Children Act 1989 came into force (14 October 1991), an order under s 4(1) of the Family Law Reform Act 1987 had been made giving the father of a child parental rights and duties in relation to that child, then such order is deemed to be an order under s 4 of the Children Act 1989, giving the father parental responsibility (para 4 Sch 14 to the Act).

Where the child's parents were married to each other at the time of his birth and there is an existing order, that is, an order made before 14 October 1991, in respect of the child, each parent shall have parental responsibility for the child, but the fact that a person has parental responsibility does not entitle him to act in any way incompatible with the existing order. Where the parents were not so married and the father has custody or care and control by virtue of an existing order, then the court shall be deemed to have made a parental responsibility order in his favour (para 6 Sch 14).

Where a child has been adopted by an order under the Adoption Act 1976, the adoptive parents have parental responsibility for the child (s 12 of the 1976 Act as amended by s 88 of the 1989 Act in accordance with Part I of Sch 10 to the Act).

The above covers those with parental responsibility under Rule 32(1)(a).

With effect from 14 September 1998 a person who has a residence order in respect of the minor in his favour made under s 8 of the Act has parental responsibility for him and may apply for the grant for the use and benefit of the minor. The above covers those with parental responsibility under Rule 32(1)(aa).

Guardians

10.54   The court (that is, the High Court, a county court, or a magistrates' court) may appoint an individual to be a guardian of a child if the child has no parent with parental responsibility for him, or a residence order has been made in favour of a parent or guardian who has died while the order was in force and there is at that time no other surviving parent in whose favour the residence order was made (s 5(1) of the Act). A residence order is defined by s 8 of the Act as an order settling the arrangements to be made as to the person with whom the child is to live.

A parent who has parental responsibility for his child may appoint another individual to be the child's guardian in the event of his death. A guardian of the child may in turn appoint another individual to take his place if he dies. Any such appointment shall not have effect unless it is in writing and is dated and signed by the person making the appointment; or where the appointment is made in a will not signed by the testator but at the direction of the testator, is in accordance with s 9 of the Wills Act 1837; or, in any other case, is signed by the person making the appointment in the presence of two witnesses who each attest his signature (s 5(3), (4) and (5) of the Act).

Where there was in existence, that is before 14 October 1991, an order appointing a person guardian of a child then the guardian shall be deemed to have been appointed guardian after that date, having effect as though appointed under s 5 of the Act (para 12 Sch 14 to the Act).

Any appointment of a person as guardian of a child made by order under ss 3 to 5 of the Guardianship of Minors Act 1971 which had not taken effect before 14 October 1991 shall take effect in accordance with s 5 of the Act (para 13 Sch 14 to the Act).

For the purposes of the Wills Act 1837 and the Children Act 1989, where a will contains any disposition or devise of the custody and tuition of any child made before 14 October 1991, such disposition or devise shall be deemed to be an appointment by will of a guardian of the child (para 14 Sch 14 to the Act).

In respect of deaths on or after 1 January 1996, s 4 of the Law Reform (Succession) Act 1995 provides, *inter alia*, that, on a divorce or annulment of a marriage, any appointment by one of the former spouses of the other former spouse as guardian of a child is revoked unless a contrary intention appears from the appointment.

The above covers those with parental responsibility under Rule 32(1)(b).

Care order to local authority

10.55 With effect from 14 September 1998, where the court has made a care order under s 31(1)(a) of the Act, the local authority to whose care the child has been committed has parental responsibility for the minor and may apply for a grant for the minor's use and benefit.

Application for the grant will be made through the authority's duly authorised nominee. If the authority qualifies as a trust corporation (see paragraph 11.1 below), no second administrator will be necessary.

The above covers the body with parental responsibility under Rule 32(1)(c).

Appointment of a person to obtain administration

10.56 A District Judge or Registrar may by order appoint a person to obtain administration for the use and benefit of a minor. The person may be appointed to act in default of, or jointly with, or to the exclusion of, any person or body who has parental responsibility, or is deemed to have parental responsibility, for the minor child, or who is or is deemed to be a guardian of the child; that is, a person having such responsibility under Rule 32(1) (see paragraph 10.48 above).

Application to be appointed is made *ex parte* on affidavit by the person intending to be appointed. Application is usually made where there is no person or body with parental responsibility or such person or body neglects, or refuses, to apply for the grant. See paragraphs 5.57–5.61 where the procedure for such applications is set out.

Election or nomination of guardian

10.57 There is no longer any provision in the Rules enabling a minor child who has attained the age of 16 years to elect or nominate his next of kin or, if female, her husband, as guardian. Even though a minor child may have attained the age of 16, application must now be made by the person(s) or body retaining parental responsibility for the minor in accordance with Rule 32(1) or by (a) person(s) appointed under Rule 32(2).

Nomination of co-administrator

10.58 Where a minority interest exists, which would usually require two persons to apply for the grant (see s 114 of the Supreme Court Act 1981), but there is only one person competent and willing to take the grant under paragraph (1) or (2) of Rule 32, that person may, unless a District Judge or Registrar otherwise directs, nominate a suitable person as his co-administrator (see Rule 32(3)). The form of nomination, including a statement as to fitness of the proposed co-administrator, must be signed by the first person entitled in the presence of a disinterested witness. The form is lodged with the oath to lead the grant (for the form of nomination, see Form A1.83, page 450). Where it is necessary to appoint a person under paragraph (2) of the Rules, the District Judge or Registrar should be asked to appoint two persons, rather than appoint one person and for that person to nominate another as his co-administrator.

Where a local authority has care of the minor and applies under Rule 32(1)(c), or is appointed under Rule 32(2), no second administrator will be necessary if the authority qualifies as a trust corporation. If the local authority is not a trust corporation, it may be appropriate for the local authority to apply for the grant to issue to a sole nominee.

A person authorised by the Court of Protection to obtain a grant for the use and benefit of a mentally incapable minor may, provided his authority makes provision therefor, nominate a co-administrator. (See also paragraph 10.60 below.)

Oath to lead the grant

10.59   The oath to lead the grant must contain a statement showing the capacity in which the deponent applies:

(a)   *Where the child's mother applies*, that she is the mother of the minor and a person with parental responsibility. Whether the child's mother was married to the child's father at the time of the child's birth does not affect the mother's title.

(b)   *Where the child's father applies:*

   (i)   that he is the father of the minor and a person with parental responsibility under s 2(1) of the Children Act 1989 (it should be noted that it is a matter for the solicitor extracting the grant to satisfy himself that the mother and father of the child were married to each other at the time of the child's birth); or

   (ii)   that he is the father of the minor and a person having parental responsibility by order under s 4(1)(a) of the Children Act 1989 (A copy of the order must be produced); or

   (iii)   that he is the father of the minor and a person having parental responsibility under s 4(1)(b) of the Children Act 1989 (having parental responsibility under a duly recorded parental responsibility agreement) (A sealed copy of the agreement issued by the Principal Registry under the Parental Responsibility Agreement Regulations 1991 must be produced); or

(iv) that he is the father of the minor and a person having parental responsibility by virtue of an order made under s 4(1) of the Family Law Reform Act 1987 which was in force immediately before the commencement of Parts I and II of the Children Act 1989 (A copy of the order awarding parental rights must be produced); or

(v) that he is the father of the minor having custody or care and control of the minor under a court order which was in force immediately before the commencement of Parts I and II of the Children Act 1989 (A copy of the order must be produced); or

(vi) that he has obtained a residence order under s 8 of the Children Act 1989 (A copy of the order must be produced).

(c) Where the applicant is the adopter or one of the adopters of the minor, that he/she is the adopter by an order made within the meaning of s 12 of the Adoption Act 1976 (A copy of the adoption order must be produced).

(d) Where the applicant is a guardian appointed under s 5(1)(a) or (b) of the Children Act 1989 (see paragraph 10.54 above), that he/she is a guardian having parental responsibility by virtue of an order made under s 5 of the Children Act 1989 (A copy of the order must be produced).

(e) Where the applicant is a guardian by virtue of an appointment under s 5(3) or (4) of the Children Act 1989, that he or she is a guardian of the minor having parental responsibility by virtue of an appointment made by –

- a parent having parental responsibility for the minor, or

- a duly appointed guardian having parental responsibility for the minor by will (or by deed as appropriate).

The will or deed must be produced (or in the case of a proved will, an official copy thereof), together with such further evidence as a District Judge or Registrar may require in the circumstances of the case. The date of death of the person making the appointment must be sworn, as must the date of death of any other person upon whose death the appointment takes effect.

(f) Where the applicant is a local authority having care of the minor by virtue of an order under s 31(1)(a) of the Children Act 1989, that the local authority has parental responsibility by virtue of the order, reciting details of the court which made the order and the date of it. Where nominees of the authority apply, details of the resolution nominating those nominees must be included in the oath, or where the authority applies as custodian trustee, it must be included in the oath that it is a trust corporation as defined by Rule 2(1) and is thereby entitled to apply.

(g) *Where the applicant is a guardian by virtue of an appointment of such a kind as is referred to in paragraphs 12, 13 or 14 of Sch 14 to the Children Act 1989*, he/she must state that he/she is a guardian of the minor having parental responsibility by virtue of an appointment as guardian under the Guardianship of Minors Act 1971, or the Sexual Offences Act 1956, or the High Court's inherent jurisdiction with respect to children, which is deemed to be an appointment made and having effect under s 5 of the Children Act 1989 (A copy of the order must be produced).

(h) *Where the applicant is appointed under Rule 32(2)*, 'that I ...... (name) have been appointed by order of District Judge/Registrar ...... (name) dated the ...... (date)'. The oath must clear all persons with a prior entitlement under Rule 32(1).

For forms of oath, see Forms A1.37 and A1.38, pages 397–399.

Grants for the use of persons mentally incapable of managing their affairs

10.60 Rule 35 (as amended with effect from 14 September 1998) provides:

'(1) Unless a District Judge or Registrar otherwise directs no grant shall be made under this rule unless all persons entitled in the same degree as the incapable person referred to in paragraph (2) below have been cleared off.

(2) Where a District Judge or Registrar is satisfied that a person entitled to a grant is by reason of mental incapacity incapable of managing his affairs, administration for the use and benefit of the incapable person, limited until further representation be granted, or in such other way as the District Judge or Registrar may direct, may be granted in the following order of priority:

(a) to the person authorised by the Court of Protection to apply for a grant;

(b) where there is no person so authorised, to the lawful attorney of the incapable person acting under a registered enduring power of attorney;

(c) where there is no such attorney entitled to act (or if the attorney shall renounce administration for the use and benefit of the incapable person) to the person entitled to the residuary estate of the deceased.

(3) Where a grant is required to be made to not less than two administrators, and there is only one person competent and willing to take a grant under the foregoing provisions of this rule, administration may, unless a District Judge or Registrar otherwise

179

directs, be granted to such person jointly with any person nominated by him.

(4)   Notwithstanding the foregoing provisions of this rule administration for the use and benefit of the incapable person may be granted to such other person as the District Judge or Registrar may by order direct.

(5)   Unless the applicant is the person authorised in paragraph 2(a) above, notice of an intended application under this rule shall be given to the Court of Protection.'

Proof of incapacity

10.61   Where the person applying applies as the person authorised or as attorney (see paragraphs 2(a) and 2(b) above), no medical evidence of incapacity will be required, the Court of Protection being satisfied as to the person's incapacity before making the order or registering the power of attorney.

Where application is made by a residuary beneficiary (see paragraph 2(c) above), then evidence of incapacity must be lodged.

A person's mental incapacity must be proved by medical evidence. Where the person is a patient resident in an institution, a certificate from a responsible medical officer will be required before the application is accepted. The certificate should be in the form:

'.. (*name of institution*)

....(*name of patient*)

I certify that:

(1)   The above-named patient, who is now residing in this institution is in my opinion by reason of mental disorder incapable of managing his property and affairs;

(2)   In my opinion the above-named patient is unlikely to be fit to manage and administer his property and affairs within a period of three months

Dated this .... day of .... 20 ..

(Signed) .... Responsible medical officer.'

Where the incapable person is not resident in an institution an appropriate certificate in similar terms by that person's general practitioner will be accepted. Where a certificate cannot be obtained the directions of a District Judge or Registrar should be sought as to the evidence required to satisfy the court of the incapable person's mental condition. A letter from the general practitioner may be acceptable. Evidence will need to have been exhibited to the affidavit to lead an order (see Rule 35(4)).

Notice of the intended application should be given to the Public Guardianship Office (Protection Division), Archway Tower, 2 Junction Road, London N19 5RQ (see Rule 35(5)). The acknowledgement of that notice must be lodged on application for the grant.

Application for grant

Incapable person an executor

10.62   Where the incapable person is one of several executors, a grant of probate may be taken by the competent executors, or one or more of them, with power reserved to the others, including the incapable person.

Where the incapable person is the sole executor or the sole surviving executor, or the only person entitled to the residuary estate, there being no executors able or willing to apply, application for a grant of letters of administration (with will annexed) may be made by any person in priority in accordance with Rule 35(2) (see paragraph 10.60 above). Similarly, a grant of administration (with will annexed) may be applied for by such a person where the incapable person would, if capable, have been entitled to apply as the only person entitled to share in the residue of the estate undisposed of by the will, that is where under the terms of the will a partial intestacy is created.

Incapable person entitled under intestacy

10.63   Where the deceased died intestate and the incapable person is the only person entitled in priority under Rule 22 (see paragraph 9.28 above), a grant for his use and benefit may be taken by the person entitled under Rule 35(2)(a) or (b).

Unless a District Judge or Registrar otherwise directs, application for a grant shall be made by the person who has an entitlement equal to that of the incapable person in preference to application on behalf of the incapable person. As in any other case, any person with a higher priority must be cleared off before this provision would apply. Thus if the deceased died leaving two brothers, one of whom is incapable, application by the capable brother is preferred.

Person authorised by Court of Protection

10.64   The authority given by the Court of Protection will contain specific provisions as to the powers of the person authorised by it to obtain the grant. A receivership order is not in itself regarded as authority to obtain a grant – specific authorisation is required from the Court of Protection. Where an application is to be made for the appointment of a receiver, application for authority to apply for a grant for the patient's use and benefit may be included in the application for the first general order. Where a first general order has already been made, the receiver may apply to the Court of Protection for authority to take the grant.

The person authorised by the Court of Protection is usually given authority to apply alone or with a co-administrator with the grant limited during the patient's incapacity. The grant will contain the restrictions imposed by the Court of Protection.

Where a life or minority interest arises, requiring two grantees under s 114 of the Supreme Court Act 1981, the authority may make provision for the authorised person to nominate a co-administrator. However, Rule 35(3) enables any person entitled under Rule 35(2) (see paragraph 10.60 above), if there is no other person competent or willing to act, to nominate a co-administrator to act with him where a second administrator is necessary.

Registered enduring power of attorney

10.65 Where there is no person authorised by the Court of Protection to apply, the next person entitled in priority is the attorney of the incapable person acting under a *registered* enduring power of attorney. The power must have been registered to give the attorney title to apply.

Application by residuary legatee or devisee

10.66 Where there is no person authorised and no attorney acting under a registered enduring power of attorney, or such attorney cannot or will not apply, application may be made by the person entitled to the residuary estate.

Person authorised by order under Rule 35 (4)

10.67 Where none of the above persons entitled in priority applies, or the person entitled to the residuary estate is the incapable person, or where sufficient cause is shown to a District Judge or Registrar, it may be ordered by the District Judge or Registrar that administration be granted to such other person considered appropriate. The applicant may be the person, or one of the persons, next entitled in priority to the incapable person, or can be any person without title who is considered a fit and proper person to act. The Rule has been amended with effect from 14 September 1998 to enable application by a sole applicant. Two applicants will only now be required if a life or minority interest exists. The procedure for such applications is set out above at paragraph 5.62.

The oath

10.68   The oath to lead the grant must state that the person entitled to the grant is mentally incapable of managing his own affairs, and any orders or authorisation from the Court of Protection must be recited. Where the applicant is an attorney acting under a registered enduring power of attorney, his title should be recited in the oath. The oath should also recite that there is no one authorised by the Court of Protection to apply. If the applicant is the person entitled to the residuary estate this must be stated clearing those with prior title. Where the applicant has been appointed by order of a District Judge or Registrar, details of the order should be recited (for forms of oath, see Form A1.36, page 395). The authorisation of the Court of Protection and the original registered enduring power should be lodged. A copy enduring power certified to be a true and complete copy should also be lodged: the original power will be returned (usually with the grant). Similarly, the acknowledgment of notice given under Rule 35(5) must be lodged with the oath, as must, where appropriate, the certificate from a responsible medical officer or other medical evidence.

The grant

10.69   Where the grant is made to the person authorised by the Court of Protection, the grant will be limited in accordance with the court's order. This will usually be 'for the use and benefit of ...... and during his incapacity'. Where the grant issues to a person not so authorised, the usual limitation will be 'for the use and benefit of ...... and until further representation be granted'. The limitation must be recited in the oath.

Where a grant has issued and the estate has not been fully administered, and the personal representative then becomes mentally incapable of administering his affairs, application should be made for revocation of the grant (see paragraph 18.14 below) and application for a grant *de bonis non* applied for. For a form of oath, see Form A1.41, page 403.

Rule 35 of the 1987 Rules deals with grants in cases of *mental* incapacity and does not cover *physical* incapacity as did Rule 33 of the 1954 Rules. Where a person is considered physically incapable of administering his affairs, he may renounce his right to the grant of representation, or may appoint an attorney to apply for the grant for his use and benefit (see Rule 31 and paragraph 10.32 above).

Chapter 11

Trust corporations, institutions and approved bodies

Trust corporations

Authority

11.1   Section 115(1) of the Supreme Court Act 1981 provides that the High Court may:

'(a)   Where a trust corporation is named in a will as executor, grant probate to the corporation either solely or jointly with any other person named in the will as executor, as the case may require; or

(b)   grant administration to a trust corporation either solely or jointly with another person,

and that the corporation may act accordingly as executor or administrator as the case may be.'

Subsections (2) and (3) of s 115 provide for the grant to issue to the trust corporation and not to its authorised officer as a nominee, and for the action of such corporation's properly authorised officer to be binding on the corporation.

A trust corporation may apply for administration alone notwithstanding a life or minority interest arises in the estate.

Definition

11.2   Section 128 of the same Act defines a trust corporation as 'the Public Trustee or a corporation either appointed by the court in any particular case to be a trustee or authorised by rules made by s 4(3) of the Public Trustee Act 1906 to act as custodian trustee'. Rule 2(1) defines a trust corporation as any corporation within the definition of s 128 of the Act.

The term 'custodian trustee' is defined by Rule 30 of the Public Trustee

Rules 1912, as amended by the Public Trustee (Custodian Trustee) Rules 1975, 1976, 1981, 1987 and 1994. The definition includes, *inter alia*:

(a) the holders of certain official positions such as the Official Solicitor;

(b) corporations authorised by the Lord Chancellor to act as trust corporations in relation to charitable, ecclesiastical and public trusts;

(c) Regional, District or Special Health Authorities in relation only to any trust authorised to be held under s 90 of the National Health Services Act 1977;

(d) some local authorities;

(e) in relation to a bankrupt's property or property the subject of a deed of arrangement, the respective trustees thereof.

Where there is a question as to whether a corporation is a trust corporation, reference should be made to Rule 30 of the Public Trustee Rules.

To enable a trust corporation to apply for a grant in its corporate capacity, it must:

(a) be constituted under the law of the United Kingdom or any part thereof or under the law of a country which is a member state of the EU or any part thereof;

(b) be empowered by its own constitution to deal with trust business; and

(c) have at least one place of business in the United Kingdom.

Trust corporation appointed as an executor

11.3 A trust corporation may be appointed as an executor of a will to act alone or in conjunction with other persons appointed as executors.

Corporation appointed by name of branch office

11.4 Where a will appoints as an executor the branch of a bank which is a trust corporation, the grant will normally be taken by the bank in its full title and not in the name of the branch.

Form of application

11.5 Application for a grant and all papers required to lead the issue of that grant are made or completed by a nominated officer of the trust corporation authorised by resolution (see paragraph 11.15 below) to execute documents on behalf of the corporation. The grant of probate will issue in the corporation's name and not the nominee's.

Renunciation: power reserved

11.6   Where a trust corporation does not wish to act as an executor, it may renounce probate or have power reserved as would be the case with a named individual. Where the trust corporation is sole executor and residuary legatee or devisee in trust, it must also renounce its right to a grant of administration (with will annexed), as it will also be next entitled in that capacity under Rule 20(b) (see paragraph 8.2 above) to letters of administration (with will annexed).

Execution of renunciation

11.7   Similarly to executing the oath to take probate, the renunciation is effected through an officer of the corporation appointed by resolution. A copy of the resolution must be lodged with the renunciation (see also paragraph 11.15 below).

Administration (with will annexed) to trust corporation

Title to apply

11.8   A trust corporation may apply for letters of administration (with will annexed) where:

(i)   there is or are no executor(s) named in the will, or all executors are dead or have been cleared off by citation or renunciation, and the corporation is named in the will as residuary legatee and devisee in trust; or

(ii)   no executor(s) is or are named in the will, or all executors are dead or are minors, or have been cleared off by citation or renunciation, provided all persons entitled to a grant with an interest in the residuary estate consent to the application of the trust corporation; or

(iii)   the executors named in the will renounce probate but are also interested in the residuary estate and consent to the trust corporation applying on their behalf, provided they also renounce their right as residuary legatees and devisees, and provided all other persons entitled to a grant and all other persons interested in the residue also consent to the application of the trust corporation (where the residue is not fully disposed of by the will or there is no gift of residue, those entitled to share the undisposed of estate must also consent);

(iv)   as attorney of an executor or person entitled to administer (see below).

In (iv) above, no consent is required for the trust corporation to apply as attorney of the person entitled.

Consents required

11.9   In all cases where the consents of persons entitled to a grant, or of residuary legatees or devisees, are required (i.e. where (ii) or (iii) above is applicable), the written consent of each such person must be lodged with the papers to lead the grant. Should these consents not be forthcoming, or be unobtainable because, for example, the whereabouts of the interested person are not known, or the cost of seeking the consent of the person interested would be prohibitive in relation to the total value of the estate, the case should be referred to a District Judge or Registrar who may, if satisfied on the evidence, dispense with that person's consent on such terms (if any) as he thinks fit (see Rule 36(3)).

Intestacy

Title to apply: consents

11.10   If a person dies intestate, letters of administration of his estate may be applied for by a trust corporation either alone or together with another person, provided that all persons beneficially interested in the estate consent to the trust corporation taking the grant. A person entitled to the grant may request a trust corporation to join in the application with him in taking the grant. Where the consent of any person interested cannot be readily obtained, as for grants of letters of administration (with will annexed), the District Judge or Registrar may, if so requested, dispense with that person's consent (see Rule 36(3)). Persons having no immediate beneficial interest but who may have an interest in the event of an accretion are not required to consent.

Minors entitled

11.11   Where all the persons entitled to administration are minors, a grant may issue to a trust corporation, provided any person with parental responsibility, or any guardian, that is, any of those persons who qualify (or body which qualifies) under Rule 32(1) (as amended) and are entitled to apply for a grant for the use and benefit of those minors, consents (see paragraph 10.52 above). If there are no persons who qualify under the Rule, a trust corporation may apply for a grant of administration where the minor's next of kin refuse to apply. Such refusal must be in writing and must be lodged with the oath. The grant issued in these circumstances is discretionary and in any event will be limited until one of the minors attains the age of eighteen years and applies for and obtains a grant, or further representation is granted.

Where a minor is beneficially entitled (whether under a will or intestacy) with others of full age and as such entitled to a grant, no person may consent on his behalf, nor will the court appoint any person to consent to a trust corporation's applying. Those of full age entitled must renounce their title and consent; the grant may be taken by the trust corporation, limited until the minor obtains a grant or further representation be granted.

For the form of oath to lead the grant, see Form A1.43, page 407.

Trust corporation appointed by order

11.12   A trust corporation may be appointed for the purpose of applying for a grant for a minor's use and benefit. Application for appointment is usually confined to applications in respect of trust property devolving on a minor, by a local authority in whose area the child is. However, where good reason is shown, a District Judge or Registrar may appoint a trust corporation as a person under Rule 32(2). See paragraph 10.52 above.

Application as attorney

11.13   A trust corporation may be appointed by power of attorney to apply for administration for the use and benefit of the person entitled either under a will or intestacy. Where the person entitled is an executor, notice of the application should be given to all other surviving executors unless such notice is dispensed with by direction of a District Judge or Registrar (see Rule 31(2) and paragraph 10.32 above). No notice need be given to other persons of equal entitlement under the will or intestacy. The grant, whether of letters of administration (with will annexed) or letters of administration, will be limited for the use and benefit of the donor of the power of attorney and until further representation be granted, or in such other way as a District Judge or Registrar may direct.

Administration in mental incapacity cases

11.14   Application may be made for a grant of administration to issue to a trust corporation for the use and benefit of a person who is entitled to a grant but who is mentally incapable of managing his affairs. An application to a District Judge or Registrar will be necessary to authorise the trust corporation to obtain the grant under Rule 35(4). The procedure for such an application is the same as for an individual applying to be appointed (see CHAPTER 5 at paragraph 5.62).

Procedure for applying for grants

Resolutions

11.15 Where the trust corporation is the holder of an official position (for example the Public Trustee), any officer whose name appears on a list, filed with the Senior District Judge of the Principal Registry, of persons authorised to make affidavits and sign documents on behalf of the office-holder may act as the officer through whom the holder of the official position applies for the grant.

In all other cases a certified copy of the resolution of the trust corporation authorising the officer to make the application must be lodged unless, under the special arrangements that exist, a certified copy has been filed with the Senior District Judge in the Principal Registry and it can be sworn in the oath that the officer is therein identified by the position he holds and that such resolution is still in force. Such a resolution will authorise the officers to act generally, and is not confined to a particular case. Whatever the resolution applying, details must be recited in the oath.

The oath

11.16 A trust corporation may apply alone notwithstanding a life or minority interest exists under a will or intestacy. The oath is made in the name of the deponent as the nominated officer reciting his title or position which qualifies him under the resolution. Details of the resolution must be recited. The oath must also state the capacity in which the corporation is applying, for example 'one of the executors named in the said will', and, where the grant is of administration, clear all those with prior entitlement and recite any renunciations and consents.

Where a corporation applies as attorney the oath must recite that fact and contain the usual limitation 'for the use and benefit of ...... and until further representation be granted', or as the case may be.

The oath must also state that the corporation is a trust corporation as defined by Rule 2(1) of the Non-Contentious Probate Rules 1987 and has power to accept the grant being applied for. In addition to lodging the certified copy resolution mentioned above (where necessary), all consents and renunciations must be lodged and, where appropriate, any power of attorney. The grant issues in the name of the corporation and not the deponent to the oath.

For the forms of oath to lead the grant see Forms A1.4 and A1.43, pages 346 and 407.

Non-trust corporations

Title to apply

11.17   Rule 36(4) provides that a corporation which would, if an individual, be entitled to a grant, but which is not a trust corporation as defined by Rule 2(1) may apply for and take such a grant through its nominee or its lawfully constituted attorney, for the use and benefit of that corporation, and limited until further representation be granted.

The nominee or attorney must be expressly appointed to obtain the grant by whatever constitutes the properly authorised body exercising control of the corporation. A copy of the resolution or power of attorney sealed by the corporation or otherwise authenticated to the District Judge or Registrar's satisfaction, must be lodged with the papers to lead the grant. Where, as is usually the case now, there is no company seal, the resolution must be authenticated by whatever body or persons constitute the governing body of the corporation.

Non-trust corporation as executor

11.18   A non-trust corporation which has been appointed an executor in a will cannot take as such a grant of probate through its nominee or attorney. It may, however, apply for letters of administration (with will annexed), provided the corporation's constitution contains a power to take such a grant through its nominee or attorney. A copy of the authorising power as contained in the constitution must be lodged with the documents to lead the grant. This will not, however, be necessary where the corporation applies in its capacity as a beneficiary under the will or as a creditor of the estate.

Where the corporation is appointed executor together with other individuals it may not apply for letters of administration (with will annexed) unless the individuals appointed executors are cleared off, by pre-decease, renunciation or citation. The oath must contain a statement that the corporation is *not* a trust corporation as defined by Rule 2(1) of the Non-Contentious Probate Rules 1987. The grant will issue in the name of the nominee or attorney and will be 'for the use and benefit of [name of corporation]'; the grant will be limited until further representation be granted.

Renunciation by a non-trust corporation

11.19   Renunciation of a right to a grant by a non-trust corporation may be executed by its authorised nominee. A certified copy of the resolution appointing the nominee to renounce must also be lodged with the renunciation.

Institutions and approved bodies

11.20   By s 54 of the Courts and Legal Services Act 1990 (to come into force on a date to be appointed), certain institutions and approved bodies will be permitted to prepare papers for probate, etc. without employing a solicitor to act on their behalf in extracting a grant of representation.

By s 23(1) of the Solicitors Act 1974, unqualified persons are prohibited from preparing papers for probate. Section 54(1) of the 1990 Act disapplies s 23(1) of the 1974 Act in respect of:

(a)   a barrister;

(b)   a duly certificated notary public;

(c)   the Public Trustee;

(d)   the Official Solicitor;

(e)   any institution authorised by the Bank of England under the Banking Act 1987 to carry on a deposit-taking business;

(f)   any building society authorised to raise money from its members under the Building Societies Act 1986;

(g)   any insurance company authorised under the Insurance Companies Act 1982; and

(h)   any subsidiary (as defined by s 736(1) of the Companies Act 1985) of a body falling within (e), (f) and (g) above whose business, or part of whose business, consists of acting as trustee or executor.

Rule 4 has been amended with effect from 14 September 1998 to enable barristers and notaries public to extract grants and prepare other probate papers for proceedings under the 1987 Rules without instructing a solicitor.

By s 54(2) of the 1990 Act, those institutions mentioned in (e) to (h) must be a member of or subject to a scheme for dealing with complaints about the provision of probate services. Section 55(1) of the 1990 Act disapplies s 23(1) of the 1974 Act (see above) in respect of any person granted exemption by an 'approved body', an 'approved body' being a professional or other body approved by the Lord Chancellor.

It follows that with effect from the date ss 54 and 55 come into force, any of the bodies referred to in (c) to (h) above and any person exempted by an authorised body will become 'probate practitioners' and may apply to any Probate Registry for a grant of representation without instructing a solicitor, barrister or notary public to extract the grant. Such bodies or persons will be able to complete all the necessary documents to lead the grant themselves and such an application will be treated as a 'solicitor application', that is, not as a 'personal application'.

11.20 *Trust corporations, institutions and approved bodies*

As at the date of going to press, the commencement order for ss 54 and 55 has not been made, nor have the consequential amendments to the Rules.

Chapter 12

Inheritance tax and the Inland Revenue Account

Note: Capital transfer tax legislation was consolidated into the Capital Transfer Tax Act 1984 ('CTTA 1984'). Various amendments were effected by the Finance Act 1986 (FA 1986), which affected transfers on and after 18 March 1986. From the date of the Royal Assent on 25 July 1986 the name of the tax was changed to inheritance tax, and the name of the Act to the Inheritance Tax Act 1984 ('IHTA 1984'). Subsequent Finance Acts have incorporated further amendments. This chapter attempts to state the position as at 1 May 2003. The term 'inheritance tax' ('IHT') in this chapter should be read as 'capital transfer tax' ('CTT') when the chargeable occasion took place before 25 July 1986.

The terms 'transfer' and 'transferor' include 'death' and 'deceased'.

Requirement for an Account

12.1   When the death occurs on or after 13 March 1975, completion of an Inland Revenue Account is required to give full details of the deceased's estate for IHT purposes unless the estate falls within the excepting provisions authorised by s 256 of the IHTA 1984. When IHT is payable, the Account must be stamped to show that payment has been made before an application for a grant can proceed. Form D19 (part of IHT 200) enables the taxpayer to apply to IR Capital Taxes for confirmation that the Inland Revenue is satisfied that the information supplied to them results in no inheritance tax being due and at the same time register a reference number. Form D19 is not though a formal certificate of clearance. If a formal confirmation is required form IHT 30 must be completed (see paragraph 12.63 below).

No Account required for 'excepted estates' or 'excepted settlements'

Excepted estates

12.2   No account need be delivered for the estate of any person who has died domiciled in the UK on or after 6 April 2002 where:

(a)   the estate comprises only property which has passed under the deceased's will or intestacy, or by nomination on death, or entitlement to a single interest in possession settlement, or beneficially by survivorship;

(b)   the total gross value of the estate for tax purposes (inclusive of (c)–(e) below, as may be the case) does not exceed £220,000 (£210,000 for deaths before 6 April 2002 but after 5 April 2000, £200,000 for deaths before 6 April 2000 but after 5 April 1998, £180,000 for deaths before 6 April 1998 but after 5 April 1996, £145,000 for deaths before 6 April 1996 but after 5 April 1995, £125,000 for deaths before 6 April 1995 but after 31 March 1991, £115,000 for deaths before 1 April 1991 but after 31 March 1990, £100,000 for deaths before 1 April 1990 but after 31 March 1989, and £70,000 for deaths before 1 April 1989);

(c)   not more than £75,000 (£50,000 for deaths before 6 April 2002 but after 5 April 1998, £30,000 for deaths before 6 April 1998 but after 5 April 1996, £15,000 for deaths before 6 April 1996 but after 31 March 1989, £10,000 for deaths before 1 April 1989 but after 31 March 1987, £10,000, and for deaths before 1 April 1987 the higher of 10% of the total gross value or £2,000) consists of property situated outside the UK; and

(d)   the deceased died and had made no lifetime gifts chargeable to inheritance tax (including potentially exempt transfers becoming chargeable on death and gifts with reservation where the reservation subsists at death or where the property ceased to be subject to the reservation in the seven years before the donor's death) excepting lifetime transfers made within seven years of the deceased's death consisting of 'specified transfers' – i.e. cash, listed shares or securities, an interest over land and furnishings and chattels enjoyed with the land and transferred at the same time – that did not exceed £100,000 (£75,000 for deaths before 6 April 2000 but after 5 April 1998; £50,000 for deaths before 6 April 1998 but after 5 April 1996; before 6 April 1996 such transfers would have ruled out the excepted estates procedure);

(e)   not more than £100,000 represents value attributable to property which, immediately before the person's death, was settled property.

No account need be delivered for the estate of any person who died on or after 6 April 2002 who was never domiciled in the UK or treated as domiciled in the UK (s 267 IHTA 1984) where:

(f)   the value of such a person's estate that is situated in the UK which is attributable to cash or quoted shares or securities that pass by will, or by intestacy, or beneficially by survivorship and does not exceed £100,000.

A grant of representation will still be required but applicants will only be required to swear as to the brackets into which the value of the estate falls.

With the IHT 200, the P26A has been replaced with form D18, which is one of the supplementary pages to the IHT 200 Account.

Estates where the deceased had an interest in settled property are not excepted estates except insofar as that property from 6 April 2002 was wholly settled property the value of which immediately before the person's death amounted to not more than £100,000. Where the value of an estate is attributable in part to property passing by survivorship in a joint tenancy, or in Scotland by survivorship, it is the deceased's beneficial interest in that property which is taken into account for the purposes of the limit in (b) above (Inland Revenue Press Release, 2 July 1987).

Excepted terminations

12.3   No account need be delivered on a termination of an interest in possession in settled property where:

(a)   the transferor has given notice to the trustees of available exemptions under s 57(3) of the IHTA 1984 (annual exemption and gifts in consideration of marriage); and

(b)   the value transferred does not exceed the amount of the exemption specified in the notice.

The Board retains the right to call for an account by written notice to the trustees. If no such notice is issued within six months of the termination, the trustees will automatically be discharged from any claim for tax at the expiration of that period (unless there is fraud or non-disclosure of material facts) (SI 1981 No 1440 and SI 2002 No 1731).

Excepted settlements

12.4   No account need be delivered in respect of an excepted settlement (i.e. one with no qualifying interest in possession) on an occasion of a chargeable event on or after 6 April 2002 where:

(a)   cash is the only property comprised in the settlement;

(b)   after making the settlement, the settlor provided no further property which became comprised in the settlement;

(c)   the trustees of the settlement are resident in the UK throughout the existence of the settlement;

(d)   the gross value of the settled property at the time of the chargeable event does not exceed £1,000; and

(e)   there are no related settlements.

The Board retains the right to call for an account by written notice to the trustees of the excepted settlement. If no such notice is issued within six months of the termination, the trustees will automatically be discharged from any claim for tax at the expiration of that period (unless there is fraud or non-disclosure of material facts) (SI 2002 No 1732).

Property to be included

12.5   The calculation of IHT payable is based on the total value of the estate, together with the cumulative total of lifetime transfers and failed potentially exempt transfers. The FA 1986 introduced potentially exempt transfers, and gifts with reservation. For IHT purposes, the 'estate' is the 'aggregate of all property to which the deceased is beneficially entitled, except that the estate of a person immediately before his death does not include "excluded property"' (s 5(1) IHTA 1984) (see paragraph 12.8 below. Accordingly, details are required of:

(a)   chargeable transfers, including failed potentially exempt transfers and gifts with reservation made within seven years of the deceased's death (or, for deaths before 18 March 1986, chargeable transfers made on or after 27 March 1974, but not more than ten years before the deceased's death);

(b)   the free estate;

(c)   nominated property; *donatio mortis causa*;

(d)   property passing by survivorship;

(e)   settled property in which the deceased had a beneficial interest;

(f)   any other property forming part of the estate.

Values

12.6   The value at any time of the property shall, for the purposes of IHT, be the price which the property might reasonably be expected to fetch if sold in the open market at that time (s 160 IHTA 1984). That is except as otherwise provided, most notably by sections 178–198 of the IHTA 1984 where there are sales of quoted securities and/or land; see paragraph 12.9 below.

Exclusions, exemptions and reliefs

12.7   The IHT legislation has provided for numerous exclusions, exemptions and reliefs, most of which are listed below.

Excluded property

12.8

(a)   Most reversionary interests that have not been purchased (s 48(1) IHTA 1984).

(b) Property situate outside the UK where the deceased is domiciled outside the UK (s 6(1) IHTA 1984).

(c) Settled property situate outside the UK, if the settlor was domiciled outside the UK when the settlement was made (s 48(3) IHTA 1984).

(d) Certain government securities issued by the Treasury with a condition that they should be exempt from taxation while in the beneficial ownership of a person not ordinarily resident in the UK at the date of death (s 6(2) IHTA 1984). Where the security is settled property the beneficiary or beneficiaries concerned must be ordinarily resident outside of the UK.

(e) When the deceased died domiciled in the Channel Islands or Isle of Man, War Savings Certificates; National Savings Certificates; Premium Savings Bonds; National Savings Bank deposits; and certified contractual savings schemes ('Save as You Earn') are excluded property (s 6(3) IHTA 1984).

Exemptions and reliefs

12.9

(a) For lifetime transfers, including potentially exempt transfers, only:

   (i) exemption for transfers of value to any one person, not in excess of £250 in any one-year period 6 April to 5 April (previously 'to the extent that transfers did not exceed £250', for the year ending 5 April 1981, or £100 in earlier years) (s 20 IHTA 1984);

   (ii) exemption for the first £3,000 in value of transfers made in any one-year period 6 April to 5 April (£1,000 for the period 27 March 1974 to 5 April 1974 and for the years ending 5 April 1975 and 5 April 1976; £2,000 for the years ending 5 April 1977 to 5 April 1981). If the exemption for the current year is exhausted, any unused exemption for the previous year only may be utilised (s 19 IHTA 1984);

   (iii) exemption for transfers comprising normal expenditure out of income, not affecting the transferor's usual standard of living (s 21 IHTA 1984);

   (iv) exemption for transfers made by gift in 'consideration of marriage' to the bride or groom to the extent that the transfers do not exceed £5,000 from a parent; £2,500 for a bride, groom, grandparent or remoter ancestor; or £1,000 from other persons (s 22 IHTA 1984).

(b) Exemption for transfers to 'exempt beneficiaries':

   Briefly, the transfers in (i) below are required to take immediate effect, or, in the case of death must not be dependent on a condition

197

that is not satisfied within twelve months. The same conditions apply to (ii), (iii) and (iv), but, in addition, the property must be the deceased's whole interest, without reservation of interest, and must be wholly applicable for the purposes of the charity, political party, or public body involved:

(i) exemption to the extent that the value transferred is attributable to property which becomes comprised in the estate of the transferor's spouse (s 18 IHTA 1984). Where the spouse of a UK domiciled transferor is domiciled outside the UK, the exemption is limited to £55,000 in respect of transfers made on or after 9 March 1982 (s 18(2) IHTA 1984);

(ii) exemption for transfers made to recognised charities established within the UK. There is no limit on the exemption in the case of transfers occurring on or after 15 March 1983 (s 23(1) IHTA 1984);

(iii) exemption for transfers made to the institutions listed in Sch 3 IHTA 1984 including the National Trust, local authorities and universities;

(iv) exemption for transfers to a body not established for profit (where the Board so directs) of various kinds of property including land, buildings and objects of outstanding interest for various reasons, e.g. national, scientific, historic (Sch 25 FA 1998);

(c) Other exemptions and reliefs:

(i) conditional exemption, which must be claimed, for such objects, land or buildings as the Board has designated as being of national, artistic, historic interest (s 30 IHTA 1984);

(ii) exemption on the death of a person who was a member of the armed forces of the Crown, or other body listed, and whose death was caused or hastened by service against the enemy or other warlike service (s 154 IHTA 1984);

(iii) conditional exemption in respect of non-agricultural woodlands, subject to an election being made within two years of the death (ss 125–130 IHTA 1984);

(iv) for transfers on or after 10 March 1981 relief for agricultural land occupied for the purposes of agriculture, subject to conditions of occupation and ownership. Land valued with vacant possession (or the right to obtain it within twelve months) is reduced in value by 100% for deaths on or after 10 March 1992; 50% for earlier deaths. By reason of FA 1995 relief at 100% will also be appropriate for farmland that is let on a tenancy *beginning* on or after 1 September 1995. Other tenanted land is reduced in value by 50% for deaths on or after 10 March 1992; 30% for earlier deaths (20% for transfers prior to 15 March 1983) (ss 115–124 IHTA 1984).

For transfers prior to 10 March 1981 there was a relief for 'working farmers' in respect of agricultural land, amounting, since 7 April 1976, to 50% of the value of the land, such relief to be claimed within two years of death (Sch 8 FA 1975 as amended).

As a transitional provision, if on 10 March 1981 the deceased/transferor would have been entitled to 50% relief under Sch 8 FA 1975 as amended, then if it had not been possible to obtain vacant possession since 10 March 1981, relief for deaths on or after 10 March 1992 will be at 100%; 50% for earlier deaths;

(v) relief in respect of 'relevant business property', subject to conditions regarding ownership. Subject to exclusions, this includes:

- sole business or partnership interest; relief is at 100% for deaths on or after 10 March 1992; 50% for earlier deaths;

- shares giving the transferor control of an unquoted company; relief at 100% for deaths on or after 10 March 1992; 50% for earlier deaths;

- 50% relief for a control holding of shares in a quoted company;

- minority shareholdings of more than 25% in companies not quoted on a recognised stock exchange; relief at 100% for deaths on or after 10 March 1992; 50% relief for deaths before 10 March 1992 but on or after 17 March 1987; (for earlier transfers relief at 30% or 20% as set out below);

- shares other than those above, not quoted on a recognised stock exchange but including those traded in the USM or AIM; relief at 100% for deaths on or after 6 April 1996; relief at 50% for deaths before 6 April 1996 but on or after 10 March 1992; relief at 30% for transfers before 10 March 1992 but on or after 15 March 1983 (20% between 27 October 1977 and 14 March 1983 inclusive);

- land, buildings, machinery and plant owned by the transferor but used by a company he controlled, or a partnership in which he was a partner; relief at 50% for deaths on or after 10 March 1992; 30% for earlier transfers;

- any land or building, machinery or plant which, immediately before the transfer, was used wholly or mainly for the purposes of a business carried on by the deceased and was settled property in which he was then entitled to an interest in possession; relief at 50% for deaths on or after 10 March 1992; 30% relief for deaths between 10 March 1981 and 9 March 1992.

(ss 103–114 IHTA 1984).

Note: Shares in companies dealt with on the Unlisted Securities Market ('USM') – before 17 March 1987 these were treated as unquoted; between 17 March 1987 and 10 March 1992 they were treated as quoted; for deaths on or after 10 March 1992 they are treated as not quoted on a recognised stock exchange for the purposes of business relief for IHT. Shares dealt with on the Alternative Investment Market ('AIM') are unquoted;

(vi) relief for successive charges, when the 'later transfer' was on or after 10 March 1981. The relief applies when the value of a person's estate was increased by a chargeable transfer ('the first transfer') made not more than five years before (i) his death, or (ii) in certain circumstances, a chargeable transfer involving settled property in which the transferor has an interest in possession. The total tax on the death estate (or on the 'later transfer' at (ii) above) is reduced by a percentage of the tax on the 'first transfer' attributable to the increase in the deceased's estate. The percentages are 100% if there is not more than a year between the 'first transfer' and 'later transfer'; 80% if the period is more than one year but not more than two; 60% if more than two years but not more than three; 40% if more than three years but not more than four; 20% if more than four years but not more than five (s 141 IHTA 1984);

(vii) relief in respect of tax paid in a foreign country with which there is a double taxation agreement, as allowed by the agreement (s 158 IHTA 1984);

(viii) unilateral relief, as set out in the statute, for tax paid in a foreign country for property chargeable to IHT (s 159 IHTA 1984);

(ix) relief in respect of quoted securities sold at a loss within twelve months of the deceased's death (for transfers on or after 17 March 1987, this includes shares dealt with on the USM). However, relief will only be given where the sale price is less than the date of death value *after* any business relief. For deaths on or after 16 March 1994, 'sales' are extended to include suspension of quotation and/or cancellation. Only the overall loss, taking all sales into account, is allowed (ss 178–189 IHTA 1984);

(x) relief whereby, subject to conditions, the sale price of all land sold within four years of the death (three years for deaths before 16 March 1990) is substituted for the date of death values (ss 190–198 IHTA 1984).

Variations of the dispositions of the property comprised in the deceased's estate

12.10 Section 142(1) of the IHTA 1984 allows variations and disclaimers in writing, dated on or after 11 April 1978 and within two years after the deceased's death, to apply for IHT purposes as if the variations had been effected by the deceased, or as if the disclaimed interest had not been given. If the statutory requirements are satisfied the variation or disclaimer will not give rise to a lifetime transfer of value, or potentially exempt transfer, for IHT purposes.

Prior to 1 August 2002 these provisions did not apply to variations unless an election was given as required by s 142(2) of the IHTA 1984, within six months of the date of the instrument (or such longer period as the Board of the Inland Revenue allowed), by written notice to the effect that s 142(1) of the IHTA 1984 was to apply. The election, for which there was no specified form, had to be signed by the persons making the instrument, and where additional tax was payable, by the personal representatives. The election should have been delivered to Inland Revenue Capital Taxes Office, and could be incorporated into the instrument effecting the variation. Section 142(1) of the IHTA 1984 will not apply to variations made for any consideration in money or money's worth (s 142(3) IHTA 1984).

For instruments after 31 July 2002 it is no longer necessary for an election to be made and the instrument itself should contain a statement as to the variation. Where the variation results in additional tax being payable, the person (or persons) making the instrument shall, within six months after the day on which the instrument is made, deliver a copy of it to the Board of the Inland Revenue and advise them of the additional tax that is due (s 120(2) FA 2002).

Variations apply to dispositions effected by the deceased's will, or intestacy, or otherwise (including survivorship), but not to interests in possession in settled property (s 142(5) IHTA 1984).

The requirements to satisfy the provisions of s 142 of the IHTA 1984 may be summarised, as indicated by the Inland Revenue:

(a)   the instrument in writing must be made by the persons or any of the persons who benefit or would benefit under the dispositions of the property comprised in the deceased's estate immediately before his death;

(b)   the instrument must be made within two years after the death;

(c)   the instrument must clearly indicate the dispositions that are the subject of it, and vary their destinations as laid down by the deceased's will, or under the law relating to intestate estates, or otherwise;

(d)   a notice of election should now be included in the instrument, applicable to instruments drawn up after 31 July 2002; and

(e)   the notice of election must refer to the appropriate statutory provisions e.g. IHT and/or CGT.

The execution of disclaimers or variations can clearly have an effect on the available reliefs and exemptions from IHT. Where execution of an instrument has been effected prior to the completion of the Inland Revenue Account, the instrument, or a copy thereof, should be filed with the Account, and reliefs and exemptions from IHT may be taken provisionally, on the basis that the instrument has effect for IHT purposes as from the deceased's death.

The forms of Account

Form IHT 202

12.11   Form IHT 202 was in use as a four-page form having the advantages of simplicity and economy, but was only used when the conditions set out in the form were satisfied. This form is no longer in use and IHT 200 and its supplementary forms are now used.

Form IHT 200

12.12   This form is for use in all other cases where an original grant is required, where the deceased is domiciled in a part of the UK, where form IHT 202 is not appropriate and the estate is not an 'excepted estate' (see paragraphs 12.2–12.4 above). Its use is also required for a second grant after the revocation of an original grant, or after a grant *pendente lite*, or for a grant limited to settled land.

Form IHT 201

12.13   This form was used in all cases where the deceased died domiciled outside the UK but has now been superseded by IHT 200 and the relevant supplementary forms.

Form A-5C

12.14   This form is for use for a grant of double probate, a grant *de bonis non*, or a grant following which an earlier grant will become *cessate*.

Obtaining the forms

12.15 Copies of these forms may be obtained from IR Capital Taxes (Pre-Grant Section), Ferrers House, PO Box 38, Castle Meadow Road, Nottingham NG2 1BB (DX 701202 Nottingham 4); Tel 0845 234 1000; Fax 0845 234 1010.

Computer-generated forms

12.16 It is possible to use computer-generated forms, please write to the Customer Service Manager at IR Capital Taxes, or phone 0115 974 2424.

Completion of the Account

12.17 An Inland Revenue pamphlet (form IHT 210) contains instructions for the completion of forms IHT 200 and IHT 201 and should be consulted.

Detailed leaflets are also available from IR Capital Taxes as follows:

IHT 2:	IHT on lifetime gifts;
IHT 3:	IHT an introduction;
IHT 4:	Notes on informal calculation of tax;
IHT 8:	Alterations to an inheritance following a death;
IHT 11:	Payment of IHT from National Savings;
IHT 12:	Excepted estates procedure;
IHT 11(s):	IHT from National Savings (Scotland);
IHT 12(s):	Excepted estates procedure (Scotland);
IHT 13:	Penalties leaflet;
IHT 14:	The personal representatives' responsibilities;
IHT 15:	How to calculate the liability;
IHT 16:	Settled property;
IHT 17:	Businesses, farms and woodlands;
IHT 18:	Foreign aspects;
IHT 19:	Delivery of a reduced IR account;
IHT 110:	Guide to completing IHT 100;
IHT 111:	Guide to completing IHT 101;
IHT 210:	Guide to completing IHT 200;
IR 45:	What to do when someone dies;
COP 1:	Putting things right when we make mistakes.

Form IHT 202

12.18   This form, which was last revised in 1993, was used as a simplified version of form IHT 200. There was no provision for foreign property, settled property, lifetime transfers of property chargeable with IHT, or for assessment of IHT. The net estate after exemptions and reliefs must not have exceeded the IHT threshold at the date of death; the gross estate must not have exceeded twice the IHT threshold. Otherwise, in general terms, the instructions below for form IHT 200 also apply to form IHT 202 which now unfortunately has been superseded by IHT 200.

Form IHT 200 and supplementary pages D1 to D21

12.19   References made in the following pages are to the latest (amendments to April 2003) editions of these forms, for use when the deceased died on or after 18 March 1986.

Page 1: Sections A to C

12.20   The first page requires such things as the address, telephone number, fax and reference of the solicitors acting; DX code (if appropriate); the name of the Registry to which application for a grant is being made; details regarding the deceased's name, dates of birth and death, occupation, last usual address, surviving relatives; the District and reference of the Inspector of Taxes concerned; National Insurance number; and the name(s) and address(es) of the executor(s) or intending administrators. Applicants acting under a power of attorney are required to sign their own names, while the fact that they are acting under a power of attorney may be mentioned. On form IHT 200, the deceased's domicile within the UK must be shown as England and Wales, or Scotland, or Northern Ireland.

Page 2: Section D – supplementary pages

12.21   Section D lists all the supplementary pages that should be completed, where appropriate, when completing the Inland Revenue Account. These will be forms D1 to D16. Form IHT 210 notes should be read in conjunction with the preparation of the relevant forms D1 to D16. Where a form is not relevant the box should be ticked 'No'. See later in this section for commentary on supplementary pages D1 to D21.

Page 3: Sections E and F – domicile and non-instalment option

12.22   Section E refers to the domicile of the deceased with regard to Scotland and also asks for the numbers of children who were under 18 or

18 years and over at the time of death. Section F requires the listing in value of assets, from forms D1 to D17, which do *not* attract the instalment option in relation to UK assets. This section will require completion after forms D1 to D17 have been totalled. See later in this chapter for forms D1 to D21.

Stocks, shares, etc

12.23   Quoted securities (stock, shares, debentures and other securities) should be valued by reference to form D7 (Notes), or included in a separate professional valuation. Where the securities are quoted on the Stock Exchange, a price of one-quarter up from the lower margin of the quotation should be adopted (e.g. for a stock quoted 40–44, a price of 41 would be appropriate). Regard should be had to any markings on the Official List, e.g. 'xd', when the net dividend should be accounted for; 'IK', the gross accrued interest should be accounted for; 'Ex captn', the new shares should be accounted for, and it should be indicated that the holding shown includes the 'Ex captn' shares; 'Ex Rights', the value of the new shares or rights should be included.

As regards securities other than quoted securities, unit trusts should be included at the managers' published list price. Shares in private companies and other unquoted shares should be included at the best estimate on the basis of information available. This could include the Alternative Investment Market (see the Stock Exchange List or *Financial Times*); over-the-counter market (see *The Times, Financial Times and The Daily Telegraph*); Rule 163 transactions (see *Financial Times and Stock Exchange Weekly Official Intelligence*). In some cases, the company secretary may suggest a price that could be adopted in the first instance (s 168 IHTA 1984).

Where National Savings Certificates are held, a form DNS 904 can be obtained from the Post Office, completed it should be sent to the Director of Savings, Savings Certificates Division, Durham DH99 1NS, stating the date of death value.

Debts due

12.24   These must be shown at the full amount due, plus any interest, except to the extent that recovery is impossible or not reasonably practicable (s 166 IHTA 1984).

Policies not on the deceased's life

12.25   In the first instance at least, these may be included at the surrender value if such a value is quoted by the insurance company.

Household goods, etc

12.26   Preferably, a valuation should be supplied, and details given for items valued. In the absence of a valuation a reasoned estimate of value must be supplied (see form D10).

Details should also be given, when exemption is claimed under s 30 of the IHTA 1984 (see paragraph 12.9 above), together with details of any previous death on which exemption has been granted.

Interest in another estate

12.27   Details of the underlying assets should be included in form D11. Where IHT was paid on an earlier death within five years of the deceased's death in relation to this property, quick succession relief may be due.

Interest in expectancy

12.28   Details and values must be shown, but unless the interest had been purchased by the deceased or some other person previously entitled to it, it will in most circumstances be excluded property and should be deducted as excluded property (s 48(1) IHTA 1984). See page 40 of IHT 210.

Other personal assets

12.29   Refunds from gas, electric etc, insurance premiums, annuity lump sums, money from the sale of real and leasehold property where contracts were exchanged before death and other assets not included elsewhere should be entered on form D17 and the total entered here. Except in the case of liability imposed by law, a liability incurred by the deceased shall be taken into account only to the extent that it was incurred for consideration in money or money's worth (s 5(5) IHTA 1984). Liabilities arising after death by way of administration expenses are (with the exception of reasonable funeral expenses) not a good deduction for IHT purposes.

A liability which is an incumbrance on any property shall, so far as possible, be taken to reduce the value of that property (s 162(4) IHTA 1984).

Debts incurred or incumbrances created on or after 18 March 1986 may be disallowed in cases where the debtor had received property from the deceased in his lifetime. The liability is disallowed to the extent that the value of any of the consideration given for it consisted of:

(a)   property derived from the deceased; or

(b) consideration (not itself being property derived from the deceased) given by anyone who was at anytime entitled to, or amongst whose resources there was at anytime included, property derived from the deceased. If such circumstances are in point, reference will be required to s 103 of the FA 1986.

Pages 4 and 5: Sections F (continued) and G – liabilities and instalment option

12.30 Section F continues on page 4 and requires the insertion of liabilities, funeral expenses and exemptions and relies that may be claimed.

Liabilities and incumbrances

12.31 Details, including the name and address of the creditor, and the asset on which the liability is charged, must be shown. Details of any mortgage protection policy should be included at section 3A on page 4.

Funeral expenses

12.32 A deduction from the value of the estate is allowed for reasonable funeral expenses (s 172 IHTA 1984). This includes the cost of a headstone, and, by concession, a reasonable amount for mourning for the family and servants.

Exemptions

12.33 Details of any exemptions and reliefs available against capital values included should be sent out, for example:

(a) reversionary interest;

(b) 'spouse' exemption – if relief in excess of £55,000 is claimed details should be entered about the domicile of the surviving spouse on form D17;

(c) 'charity exemption';

(d) 'heritage exemption';

(e) objects of national, artistic or historical interest;

(f) 'killed in war' exemption;

(g) woodland exemption;

(h) agricultural relief;

(i) business relief;

(j) exemption for settled property, previously subject to estate duty on the death of the predeceasing spouse.

All property within the UK for which there is *not* an option to pay IHT by instalments and in respect of which the grant is to be made is included in section F. In section G the option to pay IHT by instalments is available and the value of such assets should be entered.

As set out in sections 227 and 228 of the IHTA 1984, instalments are allowed for payment of IHT on (in general terms):

- land of any description, wherever situated;

- shares or securities in a company which gave the deceased control of the company immediately before his death;

- shares or securities in a company not listed on the stock exchange for transfers on or after 17 March 1987 and before 10 March 1992 shares in companies dealt in on the Unlisted Securities Market ('USM') and Alternative Investment Market ('AIM') are treated for all IHT purposes in the same way as shares in companies with a full Stock Exchange listing; however, for transfers before 17 March 1987, or on or after 10 March 1992, shares on the USM and AIM are treated for the purposes of instalments for IHT as 'not quoted on a recognised stock exchange';

- shares of a company not quoted on a recognised stock exchange, where the value for the holding exceeds £20,000 (£5,000 for deaths prior to 15 March 1983) and either the nominal value of the shares is not less than 10% of the nominal value of all shares in the company, or for ordinary shares, not less than 10% of the nominal value of all the ordinary shares in the company;

- a business, or an interest in a business (e.g. a partnership interest). This does not include either any 'business' carried out other than for gain, or assets used in a business, as distinct from the business itself.

Land, etc

12.34   On form IHT 200, this includes all land situate in the United Kingdom. Other land owned jointly should be included on form D4. A full description must be given and full details of tenancies given.

Business interests

12.35   It should be made clear how the figures included have been obtained. Schedules of assets and liabilities, or balance sheets, and, when appropriate, the articles of partnership, may be filed. The basis of calculation of goodwill should be shown, or its omission explained. The principal activity, or activities, of the business(es) and/or partnership interests(s) should be shown.

Unquoted shares

12.36   In considering whether the deceased had a control holding it is important to note that shares owned by the deceased's spouse and non free estate shares forming part of the deceased's estate for IHT purposes must be aggregated (s 161 IHTA 1984).

Page 6: Section H – summary of the chargeable estate

12.37   Prior to filling in this section the IHT (WS) working sheet should be completed so that the figures may be copied into the relevant boxes. This section requires values of assets where tax may not be paid by instalments from the UK estate, joint property, foreign property and settled property. Below this box the value of assets that may attract the instalment option should be inserted, again from the IHT (WS). In the third box on page 6 other property taken into account from IHT (WS) is to be entered to calculate the total tax payable.

Section H should be left blank if the individual applying for a grant does not have the assistance of a solicitor or other agent and does not wish to calculate the tax themselves – the individual should complete section K and L only.

Instalment option assets and non-instalment option assets have been covered at sections F and G but the third box in H relates to other property to be taken into account, specifically settled property and gifts with reservation (GWR).

In the first two boxes there is space for foreign property to which the deceased was beneficially entitled, other than settled property, and for which no grant of representation is required. There is the same division between property with and without the instalment option as set out in paragraph 12.33 above.

Details should be given showing how the foreign currency value and the sterling equivalent have been obtained.

Liabilities due to persons resident outside the UK, except so far as the liability has been contracted to be paid in the UK, or is charged, should be included. If, by reason of their foreign situation, additional administration expenses are incurred in connection with foreign assets, a deduction for those additional expenses may be claimed, limited to 5% of the value of the foreign assets (s 173 IHTA 1984).

Details are required of all property in which the deceased had an interest in possession in settled property. This includes property over which the deceased had exercised by will a general power of appointment, and property outside the UK comprised in a settlement made by a person domiciled within the UK at the time the property was settled.

If the deceased was domiciled outside the UK at the date of death, or the settlor was domiciled outside the UK when the settlement was created, then any of the settled property situated outside the UK will be excluded property for IHT purposes.

Details of the trustees and/or the agents acting should be supplied.

Details must also be provided of any property that was the subject of a gift with reservation by the deceased (see below) and any other property in which the deceased is treated as having a beneficial interest in possession immediately before death.

There is the same division between property with and without the instalment option, as set out in paragraphs 12.23–12.29 above, and the same comments apply regarding the instalment option property as were made in respect of sections F and G (see paragraph 12.33 above).

There are separate boxes in which to show the value of property where tax is to be paid/not paid on delivery of the Account. It will be noted that the liability for payment of IHT on settled property falls on the trustees of the settlement. There is therefore no requirement that the IHT on settled property be paid on delivery of form IHT 200.

Section 102 of the FA 1986 introduced gifts with reservation ('GWR') into inheritance tax. For gifts made by an individual on or after 18 March 1986, if either the donee did not have *bona fide* possession and enjoyment of the property, or the donor was not entirely excluded from enjoyment of the property, then the property given is 'property subject to a reservation'. An example is the gift of a home, where the donor continued to live rent free. If the reservation ceased before the donor's death the GWR would become a PET at the time the reservation ceased. If the reservation still subsisted at the date of death the 'property subject to a reservation' forms part of the death estate and is subject to IHT at the death rates on the value of the property as at the date of the death.

Page 7: Section J – calculating the tax liability

12.38   In this section, reference should be made to the IHT (WS) figures. In the first box the total tax payable is calculated using the table of rates for transfers on death, appropriate for date of death concerned. If the cumulative total of lifetime transfers exceeds the nil rate threshold on the table of rates as at the deceased's death, the tax assessable on the lifetime transfers (using the scale of rates for death shown on that table of rates at paragraph 12.45 below) is deducted from the tax on the death estate.

Value on which tax is now being paid

12.39   Tax must be paid on the delivery of the Inland Revenue Account on all the property that is not settled property, and/or does not have the instalment option. Tax on settled property may be paid on delivery of the Inland Revenue Account if desired.

Following discussions between the British Bankers' Association and the Building Societies' Association, the IR have agreed a process that will allow personal representatives to draw on funds held in the deceased's bank and building society accounts solely for the purpose of paying any IHT that is due before the grant of representation can be issued. They have now prepared the necessary forms and guidance and the Associations are working with their members to implement the scheme at branch level. The date for the start of the scheme was 31 March 2003. Forms D20 and D21 have been added to D1–D19 to implement this procedure (see pages 252–253).

If the Inland Revenue Account is assessed and delivered before the end of the month that is six months after the death (e.g. death on 10 August 2003, Account delivered before 28 February 2004), then no IHT need be assessed on the property with the instalment option. If the Account is delivered after this time, one (or more) instalments must be assessed.

Double taxation relief

12.40   If the deceased dies domiciled within the UK but has assets abroad, relief can be taken against the IHT on these assets for foreign tax of a similar nature to IHT that is paid on those assets. If there is a double taxation agreement/convention with the foreign authority, relief is given under the terms of the agreement/convention (s 158 IHTA 1984). In the absence of an agreement, relief for the foreign tax is given on a unilateral basis (s 159 IHTA 1984). The relief given is the amount of foreign tax paid on the foreign assets or the amount the amount of IHT payable on the foreign assets, whichever is lower. If the final figures have not been ascertained a provisional deduction may be taken, if accompanied by a reasonable estimate.

Interest

12.41   Interest accrues from six months after the end of the month in which the death occurs at:

		Days
10%	p.a. up to 5 May 1991	61
9%	6 May 1991 until 5 July 1991	61
8%	6 July 1991 until 5 November 1992	489
6%	6 November 1992 until 5 December 1992	30

5%	6 December 1992 until 5 January 1994	396
4%	6 January 1994 until 5 October 1994	273
5%	6 October 1994 until 5 March 1999	1,612
4%	6 March 1999 until 5 February 2000	337
5%	6 February 2000 until 5 May 2001	445
4%	6 May 2001 until November 2001	184
3%	thereafter	

Except in cases where interest relief is available, interest is charged on the whole tax outstanding. When tax is paid by instalments, there is interest relief on the instalments of tax on land subject to agricultural relief and business assets or shares (excluding investment holding and dealing companies). In such cases interest is only charged on individual instalments that are paid after they have become due (s 234 IHTA 1984).

Instalment property

12.42   There is also a provision for assessment of tax on the instalment option property, in one sum, or the appropriate number of tenths. If the account is delivered before the end of the month six months after the deceased's death there is no requirement to pay any IHT on the instalment option property that remains unsold on delivery of the account.

Page 8: Section K – authority for repayment

12.43   If a repayment of inheritance tax becomes necessary, the cheque will be made out in the names of all the people who have signed the form. If there is no bank account in those names, it may be difficult to cash the cheque.

To avoid this difficulty, detail here a preference in how the cheque is made out. If there are three or four executors and the cheque is to be made out to just one or two of them, write the name(s) of the people here. If a solicitor or other agent is acting and the cheque is to be made out to their firm, write the name of the firm here.

Page 9: Section L – declaration

12.44   This page contains a declaration which must be read and considered. Box L3 covers the situation where it is not possible to obtain exact values. The best estimates must be included, and an undertaking must be entered into to deliver a further Account and pay any additional IHT as soon as final values are obtained.

Finally, at the bottom of the declaration there are four boxes for the names, addresses and signatures of each person or persons delivering the account.

Forms D1–D21

Form D1

12.45   If the deceased left a will then this form should be completed and a copy of the will attached. The original will must go to the Probate Registry, Commissary Court or Sheriff Court in Scotland. If the gross value of the estate is below the tax threshold (see table) then a copy of the will is not required. Where an Instrument of Variation or Disclaimer has been made then a copy of this should be attached to the will and sent with form D1 irrespective of the value of the estate.

TRANSFERS ON DEATH AFTER 5 APRIL 2003

2003 Tax on transfers

Gross taxable transfers £	Gross cumulative totals £	Rate
First 255,000	0–255,000	Nil
Above 255,000		40% for each £ over 255,000

2003 Grossing-up of specific transfers on death which do not bear their own tax

Net transfers £	Tax payable thereon £
0–255,000	Nil
Above 255,000	Nil + 2/3 (66.666%) for each £ over 255,000

CHARGEABLE LIFETIME TRANSFERS AFTER 5 APRIL 2003

2003 Tax on gross transfers

Gross taxable transfers £	Gross cumulative totals £	Rate
First 255,00	0–255,000	Nil
Above 255,000		20% for each £ over 255,000

2003 Grossing-up of net lifetime transfers

Net transfers £	Tax payable thereon £
0–255,000	Nil
Above 255,000	Nil + 1/4 (25%) for each £ over 255,000

Box 2 of form D1 requests a note of specific legacies such as the writing off of a loan that is still outstanding at death and details should be given in the box provided. If an item mentioned in the will was given away the gift must also be detailed in the box. If there are no specific bequests etc, the box should be ticked 'N/A'. Note that if the bequest or legacy is to one of the less well known charities then the charity registration number or, in Scotland, the recognition number on the Scottish Charities Index should be entered in the box.

Form D2

12.46   This form should be filled in where the deceased was domiciled outside the UK when they died. Form D2 (Notes) explains the domicile determining factors for an individual. Box 3 deals with long term residents of the UK and states:

'Tick the box to answer this question. Long term residence in the UK for income tax purposes is another of the circumstances when a person may be treated as domiciled in the UK for inheritance tax. If you have answered 'yes' to this question, we will have to establish how long the deceased was resident in the UK over the last 20 years. Include in this box the periods that the deceased was resident. You can help us by making sure that you have completed boxes B16 to B18 on page 1 of form IHT 200.'

UK domicile determining factors are:

  (i)   the deceased was domiciled in the UK on or after 10 December 1974 and within the three years immediately preceding his death: or

 (ii)   the deceased was resident in the UK in seventeen of the twenty years prior to death; or

(iii)   only in cases where the deceased before 15 March 1983, the deceased, not being someone with a domicile of origin in the Channel Islands or Isle of Man, has, since 10 December 1974, become domiciled there, and immediately before doing so had a domicile in the UK.

Form D3

12.47   This form must be filled in if the deceased gave away or transferred any assets since 18 March 1986. This does not apply to gifts made by the deceased if these were to their husband or wife or outright gifts to any individual which did not exceed £250 in any one year or gifts that were converted by the annual exemption. In form D3 (Notes) other exemptions are detailed such as gifts out of income. However, the more complex situations are covered by this form such as gifts with reservation. Box 2 is explained as follows:

'A gift with reservation is one where the person receiving the gift does not fully own it or where the person making the gift either reserves or takes some benefit from it. Where this happens, the law says that we can include the assets as part of the deceased's estate at death. The rule only applies to gifts made on or after 18 March 1986, but there is no seven-year limit as there is for outright gifts.

One of the most common examples is where the deceased gives their house to their child but continues to live there. Another is where a bank or building society is put in the name of a child, but the interest the money produces continues to be paid to the deceased.

However, if arrangements are made, such as payment of a market rent, then the donor will not reserve a benefit and you should include the gift in section 1 of form D3.'

Care should be taken when reviewing the deceased's past gifts that this category is not overlooked. Property is one of the main areas where pre-death planning is undertaken and even though the paperwork may on the face of it point to an outright gift when investigated flaws may be uncovered by the Inland Revenue that indicate, say, the market rent paid is not in fact such and consequently the gift was made with reservation subsisting.

Form D4

12.48   This form applies to joint and nominated assets. That is assets that the deceased owned jointly with other people. Form D4 (Notes) explains the principles of 'joint tenants', 'tenants in common' and in Scotland 'special or survivorship destination'. This is primarily a valuation exercise and in some cases, such as household items, it is only possible to give estimated value. Discounts may be available and D3 (Notes) states:

'The amount of the discount will vary depending on the circumstances of each property. To give us a starting point, you may reduce the arithmetical share of the value of the whole of the property by 10%. This will give us an indication of the value of the share of the property. This figure of 10% is only to give us a starting point. The amount of the discount, as well as the value estimated for the whole of the property may need to be changed after the grant has been issued.

For example, the deceased owned a house worth £120,000 jointly with one other person. The arithmetical value of the deceased's share is £60,000 and this may be reduced by 10% or £6,000. The value to include is £54,000.

You may not deduct a discount if the other joint owner is the deceased's spouse. Special rules prevent this discount from applying, so you should include the deceased's arithmetical share of the whole value of the house or land.'

Care should be taken in the valuation, as the Inland Revenue will invariably ask the Valuation Office to pronounce on the declared value and may come up with a higher or lower figure. In the case of property it may well be advisable to obtain three independent valuations in order to arrive at the mean valuation for these purposes. Any increase in value may incur further tax and also interest.

Form D5

12.49   This form applies to assets held in trust and can include foreign trusts but will not include discretionary trusts because no one has a *right* to benefit from those trusts. The trustees should give full details of the assets and liabilities of the trust and they must pay the inheritance tax on that proportion that relates to the trust assets.

With regard to foreign trusts form D5 (Notes) states:

'If the deceased had a right to benefit from settled property where the assets are overseas and the person who set up the trust was domiciled outside the United Kingdom when the trust was created, please answer question 1 only.'

Form D6

12.50   This form applies if the deceased received or had made provision for a pension. Many pensions cease on the death of the pensioner e.g. state pension and therefore there is not value after the death. However, other pensions are guaranteed for a fixed period and they continue to be paid to the estate after death and details are required on this form.

Form D6 (Notes) covers the common situation where a 'letter of wishes' is lodged with the trustees of the pension fund and states:

'A binding nomination is different from a "letter of wishes". A letter of wishes records what the deceased would *like* to happen with the death benefit and does not bind the trustees to the deceased's wishes.

It is important to find out whether or not the deceased could bind the trustees with a nomination. Many pension schemes and policies provide a form that is called a nomination, but which usually goes on to say that the trustees are not bound to follow the deceased's wishes. If the deceased signed such a form, they have signed a letter of wishes and not a binding nomination.'

Form D7

12.51   Details of stocks and shares owned by the deceased should be listed on this form. The valuation of such stocks and shares is covered in paragraph 12.23 above. Form D7 (Notes) covers the valuation requirements for PEPs, ISAs, foreign shares and unusual shares quoted on the US NASDAQ which should be dealt with on form D15.

Form D8

12.52   This form applies if the deceased had any debts owing to them at the date of death. A separate form should be filled in for each debt owed from each different source. The debt it is assumed will be repaid in full including full outstanding capital and interest. A reduced figure may be included where it is impossible or not reasonably possible that the money will be repaid, for example where money has been loaned to a company and it is in receivership. If the deceased wrote off the loan then a copy of the Deed of Releases must be provided.

Form D9

12.53   This form should be filled in where the deceased was paying premiums on any life insurance policies. This may be on the life of the deceased or any other person. If the policy is a mortgage protection policy then the mortgage, the property and the policy are separate items on the respective forms. If the property was owned jointly then the property, mortgage and policy should be included on D4.

Joint life last survivor policies and second hand policies should be included. The former is to be detailed on form D4.

Form D9 (Notes) covers the common case where the insurance policy is taken out on the person's life but held in trust for others and states:

'Life insurance policies taken out on one person's life may be held in a trust for the benefit of others. Parents and grandparents may often take out a life insurance policy but put it in trust for their children or grandchildren. Business partners or the directors of a company may also take out insurance on their lives but for the benefit of their partners or co-directors.

So, if the deceased died whilst they were still working, or they died before their parent(s), there is a possibility that they may have a right to benefit under a policy held in trust.

If the deceased had the right to benefit under a life insurance policy held in trust, that right may be settled property. You will need to fill in form D5 giving details of the names and addresses of the trustees and, if possible details of the life insurance policies concerned.'

Form D10

12.54 This form should be completed where household or personal goods are owned, for example antiques, cars, caravans, boats, TV, video, cameras, clothes, garden equipment and tools. Items passing to the widow or widower do not have to be detailed but an estimate value may be provided and the spouse exemption on page four of the IHT 200 claimed.

On form D10 (Notes) the valuation of household goods is covered as follows:

'Remember that the value of any asset that you or your valuers give should be the price that you would expect the item to sell for in the open market. For household and personal goods, such a sale often takes place at auction. Or items might be advertised in the local paper or sold at a car boot or other such sale. If you have a professional valuation, it is only acceptable if the instructions to the valuer were for an open market value.

A valuation for a "forced sale" is not acceptable. A valuation "for insurance", although a good place to start, may be the cost to replace the items and not necessarily a realistic price for which the items might be sold.

As a rough guide, it might be worth having individual items specifically mentioned in the will and any other items that individually are thought to be worth more than £500 valued.'

Form D11

12.55 If the deceased had the right to a legacy or share in an estate of someone that died before them but had not received the share then a separate sheet should be filled in for each legacy/share. Where the person who has left the deceased a legacy/share died within five years prior to the deceased the relief from successive charges may be claimed.

Form D12

12.56 Details of all land and buildings or interests in land and buildings owned by the deceased should be entered on this form. As the District Valuer will be asked, ordinarily it is important to have a professional valuation made of the land or buildings. In cases of large areas of farmland etc, it is necessary to include a map showing the boundaries. In Box 3 it is appropriate to show any damage that may have occurred. Form D12 (Notes) states:

'If any of the properties is suffering from any major damage, its value may be affected. Things like a poor state of internal and external decoration are not so important. But if the property is damaged in a way that is covered by buildings insurance, we have to value the property in a special way.

Tick the box to answer this question. If you have answered "yes", show the item number from column A in the first column and give details of the damage in the box. If you have a survey or structural engineer's report, please provide a copy.

You should say whether the deceased's insurance policy covered all or part of the repairs and whether you will make a claim under the policy. If you are intending to make a claim under the policy, please provide a copy of any correspondence you may have had with the insurers or loss adjusters.'

Form D13

12.57 This form should be filled in where agricultural relief is being claimed and a plan of the property should accompany the form when it is sent. The relief is shown in paragraph 12.9 above. Form D13 (Notes) covers the situation where there was a binding contract for sale:

'If, before the deceased died, all or part of the property was subject to a binding contract for sale where contracts have been exchanged (or, in Scotland, when missives have been concluded), but the sale had not been completed, agricultural relief will not be due. You should give details of the sale, and clearly identify the part of the property that was sold on the plan.'

Form D14

12.58 If the deceased owned shares in a company and business relief is claimed, or owned a business (or part) or an asset used in a business it is necessary to fill in a separate form. The relief available is detailed in paragraph 12.9 above.

Form D14 (Notes) details at length how to value the different types of business asset, much of which has been covered in earlier sections of this chapter.

Form D15

12.59 This form should be filled in where the deceased had assets situated outside the UK, which were owned prior to death, The assets, for example stock/shares, property, are separated into those where tax may be paid by instalments and those where the instalment option is not available. These assets may be encumbered by mortgage or charge and may also attract reliefs and form D15 has boxes for such liabilities and reliefs.

Form D16

12.60 This form is to be completed where there are debts owed by the estate such as a loan from a close friend or relative, overdrafts, guarantees, debts, etc. Written evidence of loans from a close friend or relative should be attached to form D16.

Form D16 (Notes) also raises a complex issue, where money has been borrowed from someone by the deceased and the deceased has also made a gift to that person:

> 'The rules that apply when the deceased has both borrowed money from someone and made a gift to that same person are very complicated. You should follow the notes here and include both the debt and the gift, or just the debt alone. However, we will look at the papers in more detail after you have obtained the grant and we may need to alter either or both of the values. If this happens, we will explain what we are doing and why.'

For more detailed comment on this complicated area the Inland Revenue's Advanced Instruction Manual includes examples and calculations of typical situations.

Form D17

12.61   This form is available to add additional information or advise the Inland Revenue of further matters to be taken into account.

Form D18

12.62   If applying for a grant in England and Wales or Northern Ireland this form should be completed. Section A is to be completed if applying for a grant with the help of a solicitor or other agent otherwise it is to be left blank and only sections B and C completed.

Form D19

12.63   This form is to be filled in where it is considered that no inheritance tax is payable, confirmation of this fact is required. Within three months of the submission of the IHT 200 the Inland Revenue should, if there is no query with the figures on the IHT 200, return the D19 stamped acknowledging that there is no inheritance tax to pay in respect of the estate. The D19 is not a formal certificate of clearance. The formal clearance certificate is form IHT 30.

Form D20

12.64   When the tax that is due has been calculated, the personal representatives may complete form D20 and send it to the relevant bank or building society to transfer funds to the Inland Revenue to settle the inheritance tax earlier, but see the commentary on form D21 below.

Form D21

12.65 This form is an application for an IR reference number so that this number may be inserted on form D20 when application is made to pay IHT direct from the deceased's bank account to the Inland Revenue.

Payment of tax

12.66 When IHT has been assessed, the assessed Account and payment may be sent by DX to IR Capital Taxes, Section K, DX 701205, Nottingham 4 or by post to IR Capital Taxes, Section K, Ferrers House, PO Box 38, Castle Meadow Road, Nottingham NG2 1BB.

Payment may be made by cheque payable to 'Inland Revenue only' and crossed 'A/c payee', or by Certificates of Tax Deposit. Cheques should show the deceased's full name and date of death on the reverse. IHT can be paid by personal attendance only at the London Stamp Office on the Ground Floor of South West Wing, Bush House, Strand, London WC2, prior to lodging papers.

The personal representative's liability to tax extends to the tax on property which:

(a)   was not immediately before the death comprised in a settlement; or

(b)   was so comprised and consists of land in the UK which devolves on or vests in the deceased's personal representatives (s 200(1) IHTA 1984).

It will be noted that the deceased's personal representative's liability extends to the IHT on nominated property and the deceased's beneficial share of joint property passing by survivorship. Although this property does not vest in the personal representatives they are still liable for the IHT, but s 211(3) IHTA 1984 gives them the right to obtain reimbursement from the person in whom such property does vest (i.e. the nominee or the survivor).

Amendments

12.67 If amendments to the estate as included in the Inland Revenue Account are discovered after the grant has been obtained, details should be delivered to the IR Capital Taxes, quoting the deceased's full name and date of death, if the official reference is not known.

Amendments and adjustment can conveniently be included in a corrective Account (Cap D3).

Certificate of discharge

12.68   When there is no reason to believe that there will be any amendment to the tax payable, an application for a certificate under s 239(1) of the IHTA 1984 may be made, by completion and delivery of form IHT 30 in duplicate.

Second grant required in the UK

12.69   Where the deceased died domiciled outside the UK and left property in more than one jurisdiction in the UK, more than one grant may be required. For example, after a grant in England has been obtained, a further grant in Northern Ireland or Scotland would be required to administer shares held on Registers in Northern Ireland or Scotland. In these circumstances the appropriate Inland Revenue Account (A3 for Scotland or 201(N) for Northern Ireland) should be completed and delivered to IR Capital Taxes, Ferrers House, PO Box 38, Castle Meadow Road, Nottingham NG2 1BB (DX 701201, Nottingham 4) for certification before the application for a grant in Scotland or Northern Ireland proceeds.

Useful telephone and fax numbers for IR Capital Taxes are as follows:

IR Capital Taxes	Fax 0115 974 2432
Customer Service	Tel 0115 974 2424
Stationery	Fax 0115 974 3030
Switchboard	Tel 0115 974 2374
Inheritance Tax General Enquiries	Tel 0115 974 2400
Shares Valuation General Enquiries	Tel 0115 974 2222

Inland
Revenue
Capital Taxes Office

The Will

Name

Date of death

/ /

Give details about the latest Will made by the deceased. If a Deed of Variation has been signed before applying for a grant, fill in the form to show the effect of the Will and the Deed together. You should read form D1(Notes) before filling in this form.

1 Is the address for the deceased as shown in the Will the same as the address on page 1 of form IHT200?

No Yes

If the answer is "No", say below what happened to the property shown in the Will.

2 Are all items referred to in the Will, for example, legacies referring to personal possessions, stocks and shares, loans or gifts made by the deceased, included in form IHT200?

N/A No Yes

If the answer is "No", say below why these items are not included.

3 Does the whole estate pass to beneficiaries who are chargeable to inheritance tax?

No Yes

If the answer is "No", deduct the exemption on form IHT200.

D1 **(Substitute)(LexisNexis UK)** CTO Approval Ref No L3/00 ROG4113CTO11/99

Inland **Revenue** Capital Taxes Office	*Domicile outside the United Kingdom*

Name	Date of death
	/ /

You have said that the deceased was not domiciled in the United Kingdom. Answer the following questions and give the further details we ask for. You should read form D2(Notes) before filling in this form.

1 Write a brief history of the life of the deceased. If the deceased was female, and had married at any time on or before 1 January 1974, include a history of the life of the deceased's husband (or husbands) while she was married and up until 1 January 1974.

2 Was the deceased domiciled in the UK at any time during the 3 years up to the date of death?   No ☐ Yes ☐

3 Was the deceased resident in the UK for income tax purposes during the 3 years up to the date of death?   No ☐ Yes ☐

If the answer is "Yes" give details of any periods that the deceased was treated as resident in the UK during the last 20 years.

Please turn over

D2   **(Substitute)(LexisNexis UK)**   CTO Approval Ref No L3/00   R0H4163CTO11/99

4 Who will benefit from the deceased's estate under the law that applies in the country of domicile?

5 Do you claim surviving spouse exemption?   No [ ]   Yes [ ]

If you have answered "No" go on to question 6 below. If you have answered "Yes", provide the details we ask for below.

5a Give brief details of the property the surviving spouse will receive following the death.

5b Was a community of property established in the foreign country?   No [ ]   Yes [ ]

If you have answered "No" go on to question 6. If you have answered "Yes" give full details of the rights each party to the marriage had over property.

5c Was any property under the community situated in the UK at the date of death?   No [ ]   Yes [ ]

If you have answered "Yes" give full details of the property.

5d Has the form IHT200 been completed on the basis of the community?   No [ ]   Yes [ ]

6 Did the deceased leave any assets of any description outside the UK?   No [ ]   Yes [ ]

If so, give their approximate value.   £ [ ]

7 Do you expect the terms of a Double Taxation Convention or Agreement to apply to any or all of the foreign assets owned by the deceased?   No [ ]   Yes [ ]

8 Is any foreign tax to be paid on assets in the UK as a result of the deceased's death?   No [ ]   Yes [ ]

D2

Inland
Revenue
Capital Taxes Office

Gifts and other transfers of value

Name

Date of death

/ /

You have said that the deceased had transferred assets during their lifetime. Answer the following questions and give the further details we ask for. You should read form D3(Notes) before filling in this form.

1 Did the deceased within seven years of their death

1a make any gift or transfer to, or for the benefit of, another person? No ☐ Yes ☐

1b create any trust or settlement? No ☐ Yes ☐

1c pay any premium on a life insurance policy for the benefit of someone else other than the deceased's spouse? *(see also form D9, question 5)* No ☐ Yes ☐

1d cease to have any right to benefit from any assets held in trust or in a settlement? No ☐ Yes ☐

If the answer to any part of question 1 is "Yes", fill in the details we ask for below

Date of gift	Name and relationship of recipient and description of assets	Value at date of gift	Amount and type of exemption claimed	Net value after exemptions

Total **LT1** £

D3 **(Substitute)(LexisNexis UK)** CTO Approval Ref No L3/00

R0H4164CTO11/99

Gifts with reservation

2 Did the deceased transfer any assets during their lifetime but

2a the person receiving the gift did not take full possession of it, or
No ☐ Yes ☐

2b the deceased continued to have some right to benefit from all or part of the asset?
No ☐ Yes ☐

If the answer to either part of question 2 is "Yes", fill in the details we ask for below.

Date of gift	Name and relationship of recipient and description of assets	Value at date of death	Amount and type of exemption claimed	Net value after exemptions

Total **LT2** £ ☐

Earlier transfers

3 Did the deceased make any *chargeable* transfers during the 7 years before the earliest date of the gifts shown at boxes LT1 and LT2 above?
No ☐ Yes ☐

*If the answer to question 3 is "Yes", fill in the details below, **but do not include the value in any of the tax calculations.***

Date of gift	Name and relationship of recipient and description of assets	Value at date of gift	Amount and type of exemption claimed	Net value after exemptions

D3 (Substitute)(LexisNexis UK)

Inland
Revenue
Capital Taxes Office

Joint and nominated assets

Name

Date of death

/   /

Give details of any assets that the deceased owned jointly with another person or people. If necessary use a separate form for each item. Give details of any property that the deceased had nominated during their lifetime. You should read form D4(Notes) before filling in this form.

1 Bank and building society accounts, stocks, shares, unit trusts, household effects etc

If the value of the deceased's share is **not** the **whole** value, say

- who the other joint owner(s) is or are

- when the joint ownership began

- how much each joint owner provided to obtain the item

- who received the income or interest, if there was any

- who received the benefit of any withdrawals from bank or building society accounts, if any were made

- whether the item passes to other joint owner(s) by survivorship or under the deceased's Will or intestacy.

	Whole value	Deceased's share

• Liabilities	**Total of assets**	**JP1**	£
	Total of liabilities	**JP2**	£
	Net assets *(box JP1 less box JP2)*	**JP3**	£
• Exemptions and reliefs			
	Total exemptions and reliefs	**JP4**	£
	Net total of joint assets *passing by survivorship* where tax may not be paid by instalments *(box JP3 less box JP4)*	**JP5**	£

Please turn over
R0H4165CTO11/99

D4   **(Substitute)(LexisNexis UK)**   CTO Approval Ref No L3/00

2 **Land, buildings, business assets, control shareholdings and unquoted shares**

Do you wish to pay tax on these assets by instalments?   No ☐   Yes ☐

If the value of the deceased's share is **not** the **whole** value, say

- who the other joint owner(s) is or are

- when the joint ownership began

- how much each joint owner provided to obtain the item

- who received the income, if there was any

- whether the item passes to other joint owner(s) by survivorship or under the deceased's Will or intestacy.

	Whole value	Deceased's share

- Liabilities   Total of assets **JP6** £

Total of liabilities **JP7** £

- Exemptions and reliefs   **Net assets** *(box JP6 less box JP7)* **JP8** £

Total exemptions and reliefs **JP9** £

Net total of joint assets *passing by survivorship* where tax may be paid by instalments *(box JP8 less box JP9)* **JP10** £

3 **Nominated property**

If the deceased nominated any assets to any person, describe the assets below and show their value.

Include the assets in the appropriate box in section F of form IHT200.

D4

Inheritance tax and the Inland Revenue Account

Inland Revenue
Capital Taxes Office

Assets held in trust (settled property)

Name

Date of death / /

You have said that the deceased had a right to benefit from a trust created by a deed or under someone else's Will or intestacy. Answer the following questions and give the further details we ask for. If necessary, use a separate form for each trust. You should read form D5(Notes) before filling in this form.

1 Give the
- full name of the person who created the trust or who died before the deceased
- date the trust was created, or date of death of the person who died earlier, and
- name(s) of the trustees and the name and address of their solicitors.

2 Settled property where tax may not be paid by instalments
- Assets

Total of assets **SP1** £

- Liabilities

Total of liabilities **SP2** £

Net assets *(box SP1 less box SP2)* **SP3** £

- Exemptions and reliefs

Total exemptions and reliefs **SP4** £

Net total of settled property where tax may not be paid by instalments *(box SP3 less box SP4)* **SP5** £

D5 (Substitute)(LexisNexis UK) CTO Approval Ref No L3/00

Please turn over
R0H4166CTO11/99

230

3 Settled property where tax may be paid by instalments

Do you wish to pay tax on these assets by instalments?　　　　No ☐　Yes ☐

• Assets

| | Total of assets | SP6 £ |

• Liabilities

| | Total of liabilities | SP7 £ |

| | Net assets *(box SP6 less box SP7)* | SP8 £ |

• Exemptions and reliefs

| | Total exemptions and reliefs | SP9 £ |

| Net total of settled property where tax may be paid by instalments *(box SP8 less box SP9)* | SP10 £ |

D5

Inheritance tax and the Inland Revenue Account

Inland
Revenue
Capital Taxes Office

Pensions

Name

Date of death
/   /

Answer the following questions and give the further details we ask for about the provision for pension(s) made by the deceased. You should read form D6(Notes) before filling in this form.

1 Did any payments made under a pension scheme or a personal pension policy continue after the deceased's death?   No Yes

If the answer is "Yes" give details below

Total **PA1** £

Include the figure from box PA1 in box F15, page 3, IHT 200.

2 Was a lump sum payable under a pension scheme or a personal pension policy as a result of the deceased's death?   No Yes

If the answer is "Yes" give details below

Total **PA2** £

If the lump sum was payable as described in the notes, include the total from box PA2 in box F23, page 3, IHT 200.

3 Did the deceased, **within 2 years of the death**
- dispose of any of the benefits payable, or
- make any changes to the benefits to which they were entitled

under a pension scheme or a personal pension policy?   No Yes

If the answer is "Yes" give details below

D6 (Substitute)(LexisNexis UK) CTO Approval Ref No L3/00   R0J4121CTO11/99

232

Inland
Revenue
Capital Taxes Office

Stocks and shares

Name

Date of death

/   /

Give details about the stocks and shares included in the deceased's estate. You should read form D7(Notes) before filling in this form.

1 **Quoted stocks, shares and investments** *(see box 2 for government securities)*

Name of company and type of shares or stock, or **full** name of unit trust and type of units	Number of shares or units or amount of stock held	Market price at date of death	Total value at date of death	Dividend or interest due to date of death	For CTO use only

Total (s)		**SS1**	£	£	

Copy the total from box SS1 to box F1, page 3, form IHT200.
Include the total of all dividends and interest in box F5, page 3.

D7 (Substitute)(LexisNexis UK) CTO Approval Ref No L3/00

Please turn over
R0H4167CTO11/99

233

Inheritance tax and the Inland Revenue Account

2 | UK Government and municipal securities

Description of stock	Amount of stock £	Market price at date of death	Total value at date of death	Interest due to date of death	For CTO use only
Total (s) SS2			£	£	

Copy the total from box SS2 to box F2, page 3, form IHT200.
Include the total of all dividends and interest in box F5, page 3.

3 | Unquoted stocks, shares and investments

Name of company and type of share or stock	Number of shares	Price per share	Total value of shares	Dividend due to date of death	For CTO use only

*Include the value of the shares in box F3, page 3 **or** box G 11, page 5, form IHT200.*
Include the total of all dividends in box F5, page3.

4 | Traded unquoted stocks and shares

Name of company and type of share or stock	Number of shares	Price per share	Total value of shares	Dividend due to date of death	For CTO use only

*Include the value of the shares in box F4, page 3 **or** box G12, page 5, form IHT200.*
Include the total of all dividends in box F5, page 3.

D7

234

Inland
Revenue
Capital Taxes Office

Debts due to the estate

Name	Date of death
	/ /

Give details about any debts owed to the deceased. Use a separate form for each loan or mortgage. You should read form D8(Notes) before filling in this form.

1 On what date was the original loan made?   / /

2 What was the original value of the loan on that date?   £

3 What was the value of the loan, including any interest due, still outstanding at the date of death?   **DD1** £

Copy the total from box DD1 to box F10 or F11, page 3, form IHT200.

4 If you do not think that the value in box DD1 should be included as part of the deceased's estate, say why in the box below. If you wish to include a reduced value in box F10 or F11, page 3, form IHT200, show how that value is calculated.

5 Give the name(s) of the borrower(s) and say whether they were related to the deceased.

6 Is there evidence to prove the existence of the loan?   No   Yes
If the answer is "Yes" give details below

7 Was interest charged on the loan?   No   Yes
If the answer is "Yes" give details below

8 Was any capital repaid to the deceased during their lifetime?   No   Yes
If the answer is "Yes" give details below

D8 **(Substitute)(LexisNexis UK)** CTO Approval Ref No L3/00   R0G4112CTO11/99

Inland **Revenue** Capital Taxes	*Life insurance and annuities*

Name

Date of death

/ /

Give details about the life insurance policies and annuities that the deceased paid premiums for. You should read form D9(Notes) before filling in this form.

1 Were any sums payable by insurance companies to the estate as a result of the deceased's death? No ☐ Yes ☐

If the answer is "Yes" give details below

Total **IP1** £

2

2a Was the deceased a life assured under a joint life insurance policy which continues after death? No ☐ Yes ☐

If the answer is "Yes" give details of the policy and it's value on form D4.

2b Was the deceased entitled to benefit from a life insurance policy on the life of another person where the policy continues after death? No ☐ Yes ☐

If the answer is "Yes" give details below

Total **IP2** £

Total value for life insurance policies *(box 1P1 plus box 1P2)* **IP3** £

Copy the total from box IP3 to box F16, page 3, form IHT200.

D9 (Substitute)(LexisNexis UK) CTO Approval Ref No L3/00

Please turn over
R0H 4305 IRCT 12/02

3 Did any payments made under a purchased life annuity continue after the deceased's death?

No ☐ Yes ☐

If the answer is "Yes" give details below

Total **IP4** £ _____

Include the total from box IP4 in box F15, page 3, form IHT200.

4 Was a lump sum payable under a purchased life annuity as a result of the deceased's death?

No ☐ Yes ☐

If the answer is "Yes" give details below

Total **IP5** £ _____

Include the total from box IP5 in box F23, page 3, form IHT200.

5 Did the deceased, within 7 years of their death, pay any premium on a life insurance policy for the benefit of someone else, other than the deceased's spouse?

No ☐ Yes ☐

6 Did the deceased have some right to benefit from a life insurance policy taken out on another person's life and held in trust for the benefit of the deceased (and others)?

No ☐ Yes ☐

If the answer to either question 5 or 6 is "Yes" you should read form D9(Notes) to find out what you should do.

D9

237

Inheritance tax and the Inland Revenue Account

Revenue
Capital Taxes Office

Household
and personal goods

Name	Date of death
	/ /

Give details about the household goods or other personal property owned by the deceased. You should read form D10(Notes) before filling in this form.

1 If any household goods and other personal possessions have **already been sold**, fill in the **gross** sale proceeds below.

Gross proceeds of sale **HG1** £

Copy the value from box HG1 to box F19, page 3, form IHT200.

2 If you have obtained any valuation(s) of the household goods and other personal possessions that have not been sold, enter the total figure in the box below.

If no valuation has been obtained, give brief details of the items and their value.

Total value of household and personal goods unsold **HG2** £

Copy the value from box HG2 to box F20, page 3, form IHT200.

3 Are any of the unsold items going to be sold?   Unknown   No   Yes

4 Say below how the value for the unsold items has been established. If you have given a low total value, or the value is "Nil", say why this is so.

D10 (Substitute)(LexisNexis UK) CTO Approval Ref No L3/00   R0J4120CTO11/99

238

Inland
Revenue
Capital Taxes Office

Interest in another estate

Name	Date of death
	/ /

Give details about the right the deceased had to a legacy or share in an estate of someone else who died before them, but which they had not received before they died. You should read form D11 (Notes) before filling in this form.

1 Full name of the person who died earlier (the 'predecessor')

2 On what date did the predecessor die?   / /

3 State CTO reference of the earlier estate, if known

4 What was the deceased's entitlement from the other estate?

5 Had the deceased received any part of their entitlement before they died?   No ☐   Yes ☐

If the answer is "Yes", give details of the assets that the deceased had received before they died

6 Details of the entitlement the deceased had still to receive

Net value   UE1 £

Copy the total from box UE1 to box F21, page3, form IHT200.

D11   (Substitute)(LexisNexis UK)   CTO Approval Ref No L3/00   R0G4111CTO11/99

Land, buildings and interests in land

Inland Revenue
Capital Taxes Office

Name

Date of death
/ /

CTO reference

1 Give the details we ask for about the land included in the deceased's estate. You should read form D12(Notes) before filling in this form.

2 Name and address of the person that the Valuation Office should contact

Reference

Telephone number

A Item No.	B Full address (including postcode) or description of property	C Tenure	D Lettings/leases	E Agricultural, timber or heritage element	F Open market value
			Total(s) carried forward	£	£

Please turn over
ROH4169CTO11/99

D12 **(Substitute)(LexisNexis UK)** CTO Approval Ref No L3/00

240

A Item No.	B Full address (including postcode) or description of property	C Tenure	D Lettings/leases	E Agricultural, timber or heritage element	F Open market value
				£	£
			Total(s) brought forward		
				Total(s)	
				£	£

3 Were any of the properties subject to any damage that may affect their value? No ☐ Yes ☐

If the answer is "Yes", fill in the box below using the same item number(s) that you have used in column A above.

Item No.	Details of damage

4 Have any of the properties been sold, or do you intend to sell any of them within 12 months? No ☐ Yes ☐

If the answer is "Yes", fill in table below using the same item number(s) that you have used in column A above.

G Item No.	H Present position of sale	Sale price	J Type of sale	K Price for fixtures, carpets and curtains	L Use sale price as value

Inland
Revenue
Capital Taxes Office

Agricultural Relief

Name

Date of death

/   /

You have deducted agricultural relief on form IHT200. Answer the following questions and give the further details we ask for. If necessary, fill in a separate form for each item of property. You should read form D13(Notes) before filling in this form.

1 What is the address of the property concerned?

2a Did the deceased own and occupy the property for the purposes of agriculture *throughout* the 2 years up to the date of death?   No   Yes

If the answer is "Yes" go to question 3 and ignore question 5. If "No", go to question 2b.

2b Was the whole of the property occupied for agricultural purposes *throughout* the 7 years up to the date of death?   No   Yes

If the answer is "Yes", go to question 3 and ignore question 4. If "No", go to question 2c.

2c As you have answered "No" to questions 2a and 2b, agricultural relief would not normally be available. If you feel the relief should be due, say why below.

3 When and how did the deceased acquire the property?

4 Describe the nature and extent of the agricultural operations carried out by the deceased.

5a Who occupied the property during the 7 years up to the date of death?

5b Describe the nature and extent of the agricultural operations carried out on the land

Please turn over

D13 (Substitute)(LexisNexis UK) CTO Approval Ref No L3/00   R0K4135CTO11/99

242

5c Provide a copy of any lease, tenancy or other proprietary interest that applied to the property immediately before the deceased died. If there is nothing in writing, give details below. If the tenancy began after 31 August 1995, you need only give the date the tenancy started.

6 Did the deceased have the right to vacant possession immediately before the death, or the right to obtain it within 24 months?   No ☐ Yes ☐

If the answer is "Yes" say how the deceased would have been able to obtain vacant possession. If the answer is "No", but you feel relief is due at the higher rate, say why below.

7 Who occupied any farmhouse or cottage at the property and what was the nature of the occupation? Provide details for each building separately.

8 Was the property, or any part of it, subject to a binding contract for sale at the date of death?   No ☐ Yes ☐

If the answer is "'Yes", give details of the contract below

9 *Only answer question 9 if you are claiming agricultural relief in connection with a lifetime transfer.*

9a Was the property agricultural property immediately before the end of the relevant period?   No ☐ Yes ☐

9b Was the property owned by the person who received the gift *throughout* the relevant period?   No ☐ Yes ☐

9c Was the property occupied (by the person who received the gift or by someone else) for agricultural purposes *throughout* the relevant period?   No ☐ Yes ☐

9d Was the property subject to a binding contract for sale immediately before the end of the relevant period?   No ☐ Yes ☐

D13

Business relief, business or partnership interests

Name	Date of death
	/ /

You have deducted business relief on form IHT200. Answer the following questions and give the further details we ask for. If necessary, fill in a separate form for each business, holding of shares or business asset concerned. You should read form D14 (Notes) before filling in this form.

1 Tick one of the boxes below to show the type of business interest concerned.

☐ a holding of unquoted shares *(see question 4)*　　☐ an interest in a business *(see question 5)*

☐ the whole business, *(see question 5)*　　☐ land or buildings, plant or machinery used by a business or company *(see question 6)*

2 Did the deceased own the shares or business interest *throughout* the two years up to the death?　　No ☐　Yes ☐

If the answer is "No", business relief would not normally be due. If you feel that business relief should still be due, say why below.

3 Was the business, interest in a business, shares, assets, or any part of them, subject to a binding contract for sale at the date of death?　　No ☐　Yes ☐

If the answer is " Yes ", give details of the contract below

4 Unquoted shares and securities

4a What is the name of each company, the number, type and value of shares against which you have deducted business relief?

4b Had an order to wind up any company shown above been made, or was it otherwise in liquidation at the date of death (or date of gift, if the shares had been transferred)?　　No ☐　Yes ☐

If the answer is " Yes ", please give details in the box above.

D14　(Substitute)(LexisNexis UK)　CTO Approval Ref No L3/03

Please turn over
R0H4263 IRCT 7/01

5 Business or interest in a business

5a What is the value of the deceased's business or interest in a business at the date of death?

BR1 £ [   ]

Include the total from box BRI in either box G7 or G8, page 5, IHT200.

5b What is the name and the main activity of the business? How has the value for the business or interest in a business been calculated?

5c Is the business an interest in a partnership?　No ☐　Yes ☐

If the answer is "Yes" give details below.

5d Is the business or interest in a business to be sold as a result of the death?　No ☐　Yes ☐

6 Asset(s) owned by the deceased and used by a business or company

6a Describe the assets owned by the deceased and used by a business or a company and give their value.

Include the value(s) in the appropriate boxes at G9, page 5, form IHT200.

6b What is the main activity of the business or company concerned and what was the extent of the deceased's interest in the business or company?

7 *Only answer question 7 if you are claiming business relief in connection with a lifetime transfer.*

7a Was the business, interest in a business, shares or asset concerned owned by the person who received the gift throughout the relevant period?　No ☐　Yes ☐

7b Would the business, interest in a business, shares or asset concerned have qualified for business relief if *the person who received the gift* had made a transfer of the property at the date of death?　No ☐　Yes ☐

7c Was the business, interest in a business, shares or asset concerned subject to a binding contract for sale immediately before the end of the relevant period?　No ☐　Yes ☐

D14

Inheritance tax and the Inland Revenue Account

Inland
Revenue
Capital Taxes Office

Foreign assets

Name

Date of death

/   /

Give details about any assets situated outside the UK that the deceased owned. You should read form D15(Notes) before filling in this form.

1 **Assets outside the UK where tax may not be paid by instalments**

- Assets

Stocks, shares and securities

Total **FP1**

Other foreign assets

Total **FP2**

Total of assets *(box FP1 plus box FP2)* **FP3** £

- Liabilities

Total of liabilities **FP4** £

Net assets *(box FP3 less box FP4)* **FP5** £

- Exemptions and reliefs

Total exemptions and reliefs **FP6** £

Net total of foreign property where tax may not be paid by instalments *(box FP5 less box FP6)* **FP7** £

Please turn over

D15 (Substitute)(LexisNexis UK) CTO Approval Ref No L3/00

R0K4134CTO11/99

246

2 Assets outside the UK where tax may be paid by instalments

Do you wish to pay tax on these assets by instalments?　　No　Yes

- Assets

Total assets　FP8 £

- Liabilities

Total　FP9 £

Net assets *(box FP8 less box FP9)*　FP10 £

- Exemption and reliefs

Total exemptions and reliefs　FP11 £

Net total of foreign property where tax may be paid by instalments
(box FP10 less box FP11)　FP12 £

D15

Inland
Revenue
Capital Taxes Office

Debts owed
by the estate

Name

Date of death

/ /

You have deducted certain types of debts against the estate. Give the details of the debts we ask for below. You should read form D16(Notes) before filling in this form.

1 Debts due to close friends or relatives

2 Loans and overdrafts

3 Guarantee debts

4 Debts created on or after 18 March 1986

D16 **(Substitute)(LexisNexis UK)** CTO Approval Ref No L3/00 R0G4110CTO11/99

Revenue
Inland
Capital Taxes Office
Continuation sheet for additional information

Name

Date of death

/   /

Use this form as a continuation sheet or to give any additional information that we ask for. Show the box number on form IHT200 or the supplementary page number the information relates to. You should read form D17(Notes) before filling in this form.

Box or page number	Additional information	£

Please turn over

D17   **(Substitute)(LexisNexis UK)** CTO Approval Ref No L3/00   R0H4171CTO11/99

Inland Revenue
Capital Taxes Office

Probate summary

Fill in this page to give details of the estate that becomes the property of the personal representatives of the deceased. It is this property for which the grant of representation is to be made. You should read form D18(Notes) before filling in this form.

A Name and address

Probate registry

Date of grant
(for probate registry use)

B About the person who has died

Title

Surname

First name(s)

Last known usual address

Date of death

Domicile

Postcode

C Summary from IHT200
Add the value of any general power property on form D5 to boxes PS1-PS5

Gross assets, section F, box 24 — **PS1** £

Gross assets, section G, box 13 — **PS2** £

Gross value to be carried to Probate papers *(box PSI plus box PS2)* — **PS3** £

Liabilities, section F, box F27 — **PS4** £

Liabilities, section G, boxes G14 plus G15 — **PS5** £

Net value to be carried to Probate papers *(box PS3 less box PS4 less box PS5)* — **PS6** £

Tax and interest paid on this account, section J, box J19 — **PS7** £

Signature of person or firm calculating the amount due

Contact name and /or reference

Date

(For CTO use only)

CTO reference

EDP

Cashier's reference

CTO Cashiers

D18 (Substitute)(LexisNexis UK) CTO Approval Ref No L3/00   R0G4109CTO11/99

Inheritance tax and the Inland Revenue Account

Confirmation that no Inheritance tax is payable

Only fill in this form if you consider that there is no inheritance tax to pay as a result of the death and you would like confirmation of this.

Your name and address

Your reference

You should hear from us (by the return of this form or otherwise) within 3 months of the date you send form IHT200 to us. But we can only send this form back if you fill in all the white boxes.

About the person who has died

Full name

Date of death

Date IHT200 signed

On the basis that the information contained in this Inland Revenue Account is correct, we have no enquiries and can confirm that there is no inheritance tax to pay as a result of the death.

However, this may not apply if there is anything that you have not told us, or if there is a change in value to any other assets that are part of the estate, for example, lifetime gifts or assets held in trust.

Please remember also that you **must** tell us about any

- changes in the value of the estate, or
- new assets that you find out about after you have sent the account to us, **or**
- other changes to the circumstances of the estate

if they might mean that there is some tax to pay after all.

This letter is not a formal certificate of clearance. You do not have to get formal clearance; but if you want formal confirmation that no inheritance tax is payable you can apply for a certificate of clearance by filling in form IHT30. You can get this form from our website at www.inlandrevenue.gov.uk/cto/forms5.htm or by telephoning our stationery orderline on 0845 2341000; fax 0845 2341010.

Our ref

D19 (Substitute)(LexisNexis UK)

Application to transfer funds to pay inheritance tax

Fill in this form if you want to pay the inheritance tax that is due on delivery of form IHT200 by transferring money from the deceased's bank or building society account(s). You should read form D20(Notes) before filling in this form.

1

Name of deceased

IR CT reference

Date of death / /

I/We, the person(s) entitled to apply for a grant of representation/Confirmation to the estate of the above named deceased request

Name of deceased's bank **TR1**

Branch address **TR2**

to transfer the sum of

TR3 **TR4** £

to

" ✓ "

TR5

Bank of England	10-00-00	23430303
Royal Bank of Scotland	83-06-08	00132961
Bank of Ireland	90-21-27	23350265

in payment of the inheritance tax now due.

The money should be transferred from the following account

Sort code	Account number	Amount
TR6		£

The deceased's surname and IR CT reference number must be quoted on the transfer.

I/We certify that the amount shown above is required to pay all or part of the tax now due under s.226(2) IHTA 1984. If, before a grant has been issued, it proves necessary to refund the tax transferred hereunder I/we authorise Capital Taxes to return the money to the account shown in box TR6 above.

Full name and address

Signature Date

Full name and address

Signature Date

Full name and address

Signature Date

Full name and address

Signature Date

(Substitute)(LexisNexis UK)

D20

252

Inland
Revenue
Capital Taxes

Application for
Capital Taxes reference

Fill in this form if you need a Capital Taxes reference number so you can pay inheritance tax by transferring money from the deceased's bank or building society account(s). You should apply for a reference number at least two weeks before you intend to send form IHT200 to us.

Full name of deceased

Any other names that
the deceased was
known by

Date of death   /   /   Date of birth   /   /

When you have filled in this form, you should send it to the Capital Taxes office where you intend to send form IHT200. Our addresses are on page 2 of the guide IHT210 *"How to fill in form IHT200"*. You should send the form to

- our Nottingham office, if you intend to apply for a grant of representation in England & Wales *other than at the Newcastle District Probate Registry*

- our Edinburgh office, if you intend to apply for Confirmation in Scotland, or for a grant of representation at the Newcastle District Probate Registry

- our Belfast office, if you intend to apply for a grant of representation in Northern Ireland.

Remember to fill in the boxes below with the name of the deceased and your return address.

Name and address to return this form to

Name of deceased

IR CT reference

D21   (Substitute)(LexisNexis UK)

253

Chapter 13

Procedure for obtaining a grant

Where application made

13.1   Generally, application for any grant of representation may be made to the Principal Registry of the Family Division, a District Probate Registry or a sub-Registry. The only exception to this general rule is an application for a grant of administration pending determination of a probate claim (see paragraph 10.1 above), for which application must be made to the Principal Registry, it being provided by Rule 7(1) that no grant may issue from a District Probate Registry in any case in which there is contention, until the contention is disposed of. Where a claim is pending there is obvious unresolved contention.

See APPENDIX 3 for a list of District Probate Registries and sub-Registries and their addresses.

Who may make application

13.2   The application may be made personally, through a solicitor or probate practitioner (as defined by Rule 2(1) i.e. a barrister or notary public). Each Registry or sub-Registry maintains a Personal Application Department or section. The Principal Registry has a Personal Application Department in First Avenue House.

Personal applications

13.3   In respect of personal applications, Rule 5 (as amended from 14 September 1998) provides:

'(1)   A personal applicant may apply for a grant at any Registry or sub-registry.

(2)   Save as provided for by Rule 39 a personal applicant may not apply through an agent, whether paid or unpaid, and may not be attended by any person acting or appearing to act as his adviser.

(3)   No personal application shall be received or proceeded with if –

(a)   it becomes necessary to bring the matter before the court by action or summons unless a judge, district judge or registrar permits;

(b)   an application has already been made by a solicitor or probate practitioner on behalf of the applicant and has not been withdrawn;

(c)   the District Judge or Registrar so directs.

(4)   After a will has been deposited in a Registry by a personal applicant, it may not be delivered to the applicant or to any other person unless in special circumstances the District Judge or Registrar so directs.

(5)   A personal applicant shall produce a certificate of the death of the deceased or such other evidence of the death as the District Judge or Registrar may approve.

(6)   A personal applicant shall supply all information necessary to enable the papers leading the grant to be prepared in the Registry.

(7)   Unless the District Judge or Registrar otherwise directs, every oath or affidavit required on a personal application shall be sworn or executed by all the deponents before an authorised officer.

(8)   No legal advice shall be given to a personal applicant by any officer of a Registry and every such officer shall be responsible only for embodying in proper form the applicant's instructions for the grant.'

Note: Rule 39, referred to in (2) above, deals with resealing grants.

Person entitled

13.4   If the person entitled to a grant wishes to make his application without the aid of a solicitor or probate practitioner, he may apply personally to any Registry or sub-Registry. He will be required to attend at the Registry or sub-Registry, or at a Probate Office attached to a Registry, for at least one appointment for the oath to lead the grant to be administered to him. On request by post, telephone or personal attendance, an explanatory booklet and a set of personal application forms will be supplied to the applicant. The forms will include an application form (Form PA1) which requires details of the deceased, his executor(s) if any, and his kin; Inland Revenue Forms (Forms IHT 205 and 206 (which is an explanatory booklet dealing with the completion of Form IHT 205 and when an Account is required) both issued by IR Capital Taxes) which require details of the assets comprising the estate and any debts or encumbrances. These forms may be downloaded from the Internet on *www.courtservice.gov.uk*. A list of Registries and the Probate Offices controlled by those Registries, at which a personal applicant may attend to swear to the oath to lead the grant, is also sent.

13.5   *Procedure for obtaining a grant*

Delivery of forms

13.5   The completed forms (and the original will, if any) may be sent by post or delivered personally to the Registry (or sub-Registry) which the applicant wishes to deal with the application. Under no circumstances should they be sent to a Probate Office. The Registry will check the forms received and ensure the application is in order. The oath to lead the grant and any affidavits necessary to validate a will, any power of attorney, renunciation or other document will be drawn up in the Registry. All communications regarding inheritance tax must be sent to IR Capital Taxes at Ferrers House, PO Box 38, Castle Meadow Road, Nottingham NG2 1BB (tel: 0115 974 2400; DX 701201 Nottingham 4).

Swearing to the veracity of the application

13.6   Unless otherwise directed by a District Judge or Registrar every oath or affidavit in a personal application must be sworn before an officer of a Probate Registry authorised in that behalf (Rule 5(7)). The Registry will arrange an appointment for the applicant to attend, either at the main Registry or sub-Registry, or at one of the Probate Offices administered by the Registry, according to the applicant's preference. Where there are two or more applicants from different locations, arrangements may be made for each to attend the Registry or Office nearest to them. In straightforward cases, the papers may be sworn on the first attendance, but where difficulties arise a further appointment may be necessary.

An additional fee (Fee No 2), over and above the fee payable for the grant, is charged by the Registry for the preparation of the oath and other papers (see APPENDIX 2). The District Judge or Registrar has a discretion to remit the fee wholly or in part, but there must be extenuating financial circumstances.

In any case where the District Judge or Registrar considers it appropriate (for example where it is likely to be beyond the power of the applicant to obtain the necessary evidence to enable the case to progress without professional guidance from a solicitor or probate practitioner or there is doubt as to the applicant's ability to administer the estate), he may direct that the application shall not proceed as a personal application (see Rule 5(3)(c) above). Where such a direction is made the applicant must instruct a solicitor or a probate practitioner to act on his behalf if he wishes to pursue his application.

Applications through a solicitor or probate practitioner

13.7   Rule 4, as amended with effect from 14 September 1998, provides for an application through a solicitor or probate practitioner to be made at any Registry or sub-Registry; in such a case the solicitor or probate practitioner must give an address for service in England and

Wales. Probate Offices, which are situated in most major towns and cities, are opened at regular intervals for the attendance only of personal applicants *by appointment*. No case which is being dealt with through a solicitor or probate practitioner can be dealt with at a Probate Office.

Pre-lodgment enquiries: settling oaths, etc.

Pre-lodgment enquiries

13.8   Where a solicitor or probate practitioner has any doubt about the validity of a will, or whether evidence will be required, or if he requires the directions of the court as to the manner in which the application should proceed, or who should apply, he may make an enquiry of the District Judge or Registrar, preferably by letter.

Where a discretionary order of the District Judge or Registrar will be required before the application for the grant can be made, similarly a pre-lodgment enquiry as to the evidence required, and the form of such evidence may be made. In the Principal Registry, such enquiries should, at first instance, be made to the manager of the Probate Department. Provided there is no contention in the matter, that is, there is unlikely to be a dispute brought before the court on summons, the Registry will advise the proper procedure and direct what evidence will be necessary and in what form. Where appropriate, to avoid protracted correspondence, or where there is some urgency, an appointment may be arranged for the matter to be discussed on personal attendance before a District Judge or Registrar. In cases proceeding in the Principal Registry the appointment is likely, initially at least, to be with the manager of the Probate Department.

Settling documents: approving affidavits

13.9   Where, in an application other than an personal application, it is desired that an oath, or other document required to lead the grant, should be settled or approved by the Registry before it is sworn or engrossed, a draft of the oath or other document may be submitted to the Registry to which it is intended the application for the grant will be made. The draft oath or other document when settled, or affidavit when approved, with, if necessary, any amendment required by the District Judge or Registrar, will be returned marked 'settled' or 'approved'. After engrossment and swearing, the draft document (as approved) should be lodged with the other documents to lead the grant.

Affidavits to lead discretionary orders are not settled by the Registry, although where it is thought difficulty may arise, any affidavit may be submitted for a District Judge or Registrar's directions and approval before swearing. This may be a preferable procedure; it allows all the evidence to be submitted in the form required by the court and invariably avoids delay and additional costs. Urgent matters may be submitted by fax. Each Registry's fax number is included with the other details in APPENDIX 3. Where an oath or other document is settled or approved by the Registry, a fee of £10 *per document* settled or approved is payable.

Documents required

13.10   The papers required to lead the grant are:

(a)   where the deceased died testate, the original will and any codicils;

(b)   a sworn oath appropriate to the application;

(c)   where appropriate, Form D18 endorsed as appropriate by IR Capital Taxes and stamped to show that no tax is payable or that all tax due has been paid;

(d)   any affidavits required by the Registry (for example, an affidavit of due execution);

(e)   any relevant order made by a court or authorisation from any other court (for example, the Court of Protection); and

(f)   any other documents required in the particular circumstances of the application (such as renunciations, powers of attorney, consents, resolutions, nominations).

The procedure for the delivery of an Inland Revenue Account changed from April 1999. On all *original* applications for a grant where an Account is required to be delivered, Form IHT 200 must be delivered to IR Capital Taxes and Form D18 lodged with the grant application (see paragraph 13.20 below).

Marking the will

13.11   The will and any codicil must be marked by the signature of the applicant and the commissioner or solicitor before whom the applicant swore the oath in accordance with Rule 10.

Engrossment of will

13.12   Where the District Judge or Registrar considers that a facsimile of the original will would not be satisfactory for record purposes he may require an engrossment suitable for facsimile reproduction to be lodged (see Rule 11(1) and paragraph 19.1 below). Similarly, where a will contains unauthenticated alterations which cannot be admitted to proof, an engrossment of the will in the form to be admitted should be lodged; the engrossment should reproduce the punctuation, spacing and division into paragraphs of the original will and it should be continuous from page to page on both sides of the paper (Rule 11(2) and (3)). The engrossment will be endorsed with the District Judge's or Registrar's 'fiat' and copied to make the probate and record copies.

The oath

13.13 Rule 8(1) provides that every application for a grant must be supported by an oath in the form applicable to the circumstances of the case. A comprehensive selection of draft forms of oath and affidavits is set out in APPENDIX 1.

Inland Revenue Account

13.14 Where an Inland Revenue Account is required, Form IHT 200 must be delivered to IR Capital Taxes, properly completed and signed by the applicant(s). As to completion of the Account, see CHAPTER 12. Where tax is payable, this must be paid before the grant may issue. The receipted Form D18 should be lodged with the grant application. An Inland Revenue Account or a corrective Account may be found to be necessary after the grant's issue. Any amendment to the figures appearing in the grant, required because of an under- or over-estimate, is effected by the Capital Taxes Office – an application for such amendment must be made to that Office.

Fees

13.15 The appropriate court fees, calculated on the assessed *net* value of the estate passing under the grant, together with the fees for additional copies of the grant and any copies of the will (see APPENDIX 2, Fee Nos 1 and 8) should be paid at the time of lodging the documents and must in any event be paid before the grant may issue. Cheques should be made payable to 'Her Majesty's Paymaster General'; 'HMPG' is an acceptable abbreviation. All cheques in payment of fees should have the deceased's name written on the reverse.

No receipt for the fee paid is now issued by the Registry, the issue of the grant now being regarded sufficient acknowledgment that the fee has been fully paid. Where the wrong fee is submitted a request for the balance, or a refund as appropriate, will be made by the Registry.

No fee is payable for the grant where the net estate does not exceed £5,000. A fee of £50 is payable on application for every original grant where the net estate exceeds £5,000. Where estate which does not pass under the grant (for example, property which passes by survivorship) is included in error, there is no provision for refunding the fee.

Lodging the papers

Delivery of documents

13.16 The documents and fees may be sent by post or delivered personally to the Registry; all the Registries are members of the Document Exchange, and therefore that service may be used. All documents necessary should be lodged at the same time. Any papers sent through the post are sent at the sender's own risk.

In Principal Registry cases the documents should be lodged with, or sent to, the Probate Department, Principal Registry of the Family Division, First Avenue House, 42–49 High Holborn, London WC1 6NP (DX 941 London/Chancery. In District Probate Registry matters the documents should be sent to or lodged with the probate manager.

On receipt of the documents to lead the grant, they are examined and any will or codicils are photocopied and copies prepared for attachment to the grant of probate or letters of administration (with will annexed) (the probate copy), and, in District Registry cases, for transmission to the Probate Records Centre (the record copy).

Registry procedure

13.17 Where the papers lodged are defective the Registry will contact the solicitor or probate practitioner by telephone if the defect can be remedied easily; where the defect is more substantial and may require further evidence or an oath resworn, the Registry will notify the solicitor or probate practitioner by letter. Care should be exercised to ensure that the proper documents to lead the grant, properly completed, are lodged, together with the will and codicils (if any). Care should also be taken to ensure that all testamentary documents have been marked by the signature of the applicant and the commissioner/solicitor who swore the oath in accordance with Rule 10. Any defect will cause delay in the issue of the grant. (See Checklist, APPENDIX 4.)

Proof of death

13.18 In personal applications the applicant is required to lodge the death certificate, or such other evidence as may be allowed, as proof of death (Rule 5(5); see paragraph 13.3 above). However, where application is made other than personally, it is for the solicitor or probate practitioner to be satisfied as to the death; in such cases the Registry will accept the oath, containing the date of death, as sufficient proof.

The Practice Direction of 12 January 1999 requires the oath to contain the deceased's name, date of birth and date of death as they appear in the death certificate. The Direction applies only to UK registered deaths.

Referral for directions

13.19   Where several questions arise, or a complicated question arises, the District Judge or Registrar may request the solicitors or probate practitioners to attend the Registry. Rule 7(1) provides that no grant shall issue from a District Probate Registry in any case in which there is contention until that contention is disposed of. The District Probate Registrar may refer to a District Judge at the Principal Registry any case in which it appears to him that a grant ought not to be made without the directions of a District Judge or a Judge. Any matter referred to a District Judge at the Principal Registry may be dealt with as he deems fit; that District Judge may give directions as to the future course of the case; confirm the matter be referred to a Judge and give directions accordingly; direct the District Probate Registrar to proceed in accordance with his instructions; or direct the District Probate Registrar to take no further action in the case. Rule 61 allows a District Judge or Registrar to direct that any matter be brought before a District Judge or Registrar or Judge on summons. Rule 62A, added with effect from 14 September 1998, enables one Registrar to exercise another's jurisdiction (see also CHAPTER 17).

Inheritance tax

13.20   All pre-grant enquiries relating to the payment of tax and as to whether an Inland Revenue Account will be required in a particular case should be directed to IR Capital Taxes, Ferrers House, PO Box 38, Castle Meadow Road, Nottingham NG2 1BB (DX 701201 Nottingham 4); Tel 0115 974 2400; Fax 0115 974 3030, and *not* to the Probate Registry.

Section 109 of the Supreme Court Act 1981 prevents any grant from issuing and any grant made outside the United Kingdom from being resealed until the court is satisfied that the inheritance tax payable on the delivery of the Account has been paid or that no such tax is payable.

Enquiries relating to the postponement of payment or part payments are also made to IR Capital Taxes at Ferrers House.

Taxable estates (see also CHAPTER 12**)**

Solicitor or probate practitioner applications

13.21   Where a non-instalment liability for inheritance tax arises, such tax has to be assessed and paid before a grant may issue. Where application is made by a solicitor or probate practitioner and tax is payable, the Account and a cheque for the amount of tax due as assessed under the self-assessment scheme, should be sent to IR Capital Taxes at Nottingham (address above). Alternatively, the amount due may be paid in person to the Inland Revenue Department at Somerset House. Form D18, stamped by IR Capital Taxes to show that the tax now due has been paid, should be lodged with the grant application. To minimise interest accruing on money borrowed to pay the tax, it is suggested the Account and tax be sent to IR Capital Taxes at the same time as the papers are lodged in the Registry. The grant can then issue immediately Form D18 is lodged.

The oath to lead the grant should recite the exact gross and net values of the estate appearing in the summary of the Account and on Form D18. The Registry will question the figures if they do not agree.

Personal applications

13.22 *Taxable estates:* In personal applications the forms supplied by the Probate Registry or from the Internet indicate when an Account must be delivered. All enquiries relating to tax and forms required are dealt with direct by IR Capital Taxes. IR Capital Taxes will assess the liability for tax and issue a receipted Form D18. The same procedure applies as for a solicitor application. The Probate Registries no longer have any responsibility for preparing the Account.

Non-taxable estates: Where no tax is payable and the application does not qualify as an excepted estate (see below), an Inland Revenue Account in Form IHT 200 must be delivered to IR Capital Taxes and Form D18 certified 'NIL' tax to pay lodged in the Registry.

Excepted estates

13.23 The Inheritance Tax (Delivery of Accounts) (Excepted Estates) Regulations 2002 came into force on 1 August 2002 and replaced all the former regulations dealing with excepted estates. The Capital Transfer Tax (Delivery of Accounts) Regulations 1981 provided for a grant to issue without the delivery of an Account for deaths on or after 6 April 1981. Any grant now issuing in respect of the estate of a person dying before 6 April 1981 will require an Account to be delivered. An excepted estate is defined as the estate of a person immediately before his death where:

(i)   the value of the estate for tax purposes is attributable wholly to property passing under that person's will or intestacy or under a nomination of an asset taking effect on death or under a single settlement in which he was entitled to an interest in possession in settled property or by survivorship in beneficial joint tenancy;

(ii)   the total gross value of that property did not exceed £25,000 where the death occurred on or after 1 April 1981 but before 1 April 1983, £40,000 where the death occurred on or after 1 April 1983 but before 1 April 1987; £70,000 where the death occurred on or after 1 April 1989; £100,000 where the death occurred on or after 1 April 1989 but before 1 April 1990; £115,000 where the death occurred on or after 1 April 1990 but before 1 April 1991; £125,000 where death occurred on or after 1 April 1991 but before 6 April 1995; £145,000 where death occurred on or after 6 April 1995 but before 6 April 1996; £180,000 where death occurred on or after 6 April 1996 but before 6 April 1998; £200,000 where death occurred on or after 6 April 1998 but before 6 April 2000; £210,000 where death occurred on or after 6 April 2000 but before 6 April 2002; and £220,000 where death occurred on or after that date;

(iii) of that property not more than 10% of the total gross value or £1,000 (whichever is higher) where the death occurred on or after 1 April 1981 but before 1 April 1983; 10% of the total gross value or £2,000 (whichever is higher) where the death occurred on or after 1 April 1983 but before 1 April 1987; or £10,000 where the death occurred on or after 1 April 1987; or £15,000 where the death occurred on or after 1 April 1989; or £30,000 where the death occurred on or after 6 April 1996; or £50,000 where the death occurred on or after 6 April 1998; or £75,000 where the death occurred on or after 6 April 2002, represented value attributed to property then situated outside the United Kingdom;

(iv) the deceased died without having made any chargeable transfer during the period of seven years ending with his death other than specified transfers (i.e. transfers of cash or quoted shares or securities or, with effect from 6 April 2002, an interest in or over land (and furnishings and chattels disposed of at the same time to the same donee and intended to be enjoyed with the land provided that sections 102 and 102A(2) of the Finance Act 1986 apply to the transfer of the land or the land (or furnishings or chattels) became settled property on that transfer)) where the aggregate value transferred did not exceed £50,000 where the death occurred on or after 6 April 1996; or £75,000 where the death occurred on or after 6 April 1998; or £100,000 where the death occurred on or after 6 April 2002; and

(v) that person died on or after 1 April 1981 domiciled in the United Kingdom *without having made any chargeable transfer during his lifetime* (words in italics apply to deaths before 6 April 1996).

Notwithstanding that the case may be an excepted estate, an Inland Revenue Account appropriate to the case may be delivered. Where an Account is delivered, the oath should recite the gross and net values of the estate passing under the grant appearing in the Account. These figures will appear in the grant.

In an excepted case, the gross value should be stated as not exceeding £220,000, £210,000, £200,000, £180,000, £145,000, £125,000, £100,000, £70,000, £40,000 or £25,000 depending on the date of death (see (ii) above); and the net value should be stated as not exceeding the actual net value rounded up to the nearest £1,000 (see Practice Direction 22 March 2002); the oath must conclude with a statement that 'this is not a case in which an Inland Revenue Account is required to be delivered'.

Non-taxable non excepted estates

13.24 Where the criteria prescribed by the Inheritance Tax (Delivery of Accounts) (Excepted Estates) Regulations set out in paragraph 13.23 above do not apply and where there is no tax payable, Form IHT 200 must be delivered to IR Capital Taxes and Form D18, certified that no tax is payable, must be lodged with the grant application.

Foreign domicile

13.25 Where the death occurred on or after 6 April 2002, the excepted estates provisions apply to a person dying domiciled outside the United Kingdom provided that he was never domiciled in the United Kingdom or treated as domiciled in the United Kingdom by s 267 of the Finance Act 1984 and the value of that person's estate in the United Kingdom is wholly attributable to cash or quoted shares or securities passing under his will or intestacy or by survivorship in a beneficial joint tenancy the gross value of which does not exceed £100,000.

Where the deceased died domiciled outside the United Kingdom, and an Account is required, the Account must be controlled by the Inland Revenue before the grant may issue. The Account, in Form IHT 200, must be controlled and Form D18, stamped to show it has been controlled, must be lodged in the Probate Registry.

Second or subsequent grants

13.26 Where application is made for a second or subsequent grant in the same estate, and provided the criteria set out in paragraph 13.23 above were met for the first grant, the application may be treated as an 'excepted estate' case. Where the criteria are not met, an Account in Form A5C must be delivered. The Account *must* be lodged with the Probate Registry with the other papers to lead the grant, not submitted to IR Capital Taxes.

Address for service

13.27 Every oath to lead a grant should be endorsed, in the top right hand corner, with the name and address and postcode of the solicitor or probate practitioner extracting it. The name, address and any reference quoted will appear at the foot of the grant. It is of assistance to the Probate Registry if professional advisers on a Document Exchange insert their DX Number and location after their address and reference. The postcode is used by the Registries' computers to generate the professional adviser's name and address to appear on the grant. As a personal applicant's name and address appear in the body of the grant the foot of the grant will merely note that the grant was extracted 'personally'.

Grants

Time limit before issue

13.28   Rule 6(2) provides that no grant of probate or letters of administration (with will annexed) may issue within seven days of the death of the deceased, and that no grant of letters of administration may issue within fourteen days of the death of the deceased, except with the leave of a District Judge or Registrar.

Application for such leave is made *ex parte* on affidavit (or in such other written form as the District Judge or Registrar may direct), setting out the reasons, or by evidence supplied on personal attendance, why expedition is necessary. Usually leave to expedite will be given where some part of the estate requires urgent administration, for example where contracts to sell the deceased's house have been, or are about to be, exchanged.

Section 1 of the Law Reform (Succession) Act 1995 provides that a spouse must survive for 28 days before acquiring a beneficial interest in an intestate spouse's estate. The Registrars, with the approval of the Senior District Judge, allow grants to issue to surviving spouses before the 28-day survival period has elapsed. The estate is treated as vested subject to divesting if the survivor fails to survive for the required period.

Provided all the papers to lead the grant are in order and the fee and tax, if any, are properly paid, a grant will normally issue within seven working days of receipt of the application.

Addresses to appear in the grant

13.29   The deceased's last permanent residential address should be given in the oath, and this will appear in the grant. The postcode for the address should be included (Practice Direction 22 March 2002). Only on request and when good reason can be given will former addresses or more than one address be shown in the grant.

The full residential address(es) of the grantee(s) should be shown in the oath. If a postcode is given, this will usually appear in the grant (although the practice varies in some Registries). A grantee acting in a professional capacity (for example, as a solicitor or accountant) may give his business address.

Error or omission in grant

13.30   Where a grant contains an error or omission made by the Registry, provided that it is returned to that Registry for correction within 28 days of sealing, and provided that it has not been registered (that is, produced to a bank or insurance company or other asset holder to establish title and marked accordingly by them), a new grant will be prepared. All copies which have been issued must, where possible, also be returned. However, if the error is not discovered within the 28-day period or the error in the grant was not occasioned by the Registry, any amendment must be effected by a District Judge's or Registrar's order.

Where the error is not an 'official' error, application to amend is made by affidavit (usually by the grantee(s)). At the discretion of the District Judge or the Registrar, less formal application may be accepted, i.e. by letter. Depending on the seriousness of the error, consideration may be given to revocation and the issue (on application therefor) of a new grant. Amendments to the values of the estate shown in the grant are not, save in exceptional circumstances, made by the Probate Registry. Such changes are effected by IR Capital Taxes. (See CHAPTER 18, and Form A1.65, page 432 for a form of affidavit to lead the amendment.)

Search for previous grant, conflicting application or caveat

13.31   Sections 107 and 108 of the Supreme Court Act 1981 provide that no grant may issue where there are conflicting applications, and for caveats to be entered in the index of pending grant applications (although the Act has not yet been amended to take into account the 1998 rule changes).

Rule 57(1), as substituted with effect from 14 September 1998, provides that the Senior District Judge shall maintain an index of every pending grant application. The index is now computerised and maintained on linked computers by every Registry. By virtue of Rule 57(2) it is provided that before any grant issues, a search is made in the indexes of grants to ensure that no prior grant has been made or no other application is pending relating to the same estate; and that no caveat (see CHAPTER 16) has been entered against the grant issuing. Where a will has been lodged for safe custody (see CHAPTER 20), or a will has been lodged on renunci-ation, or a previous grant has issued, or an application is pending or a caveat has been entered, or there is a summons or application for a discre-tionary order pending, the applicant's solicitor will be so informed and given the details by the Registry to which the application was made.

Calendars of grants issued in England and Wales are available for public inspection at the Principal or any District Registry. District Registries hold calendars from at least 1948 (this may vary from Registry to Registry but a Registry will always hold records dating back at least 50 years), up to and including September of the previous year. Since 9 November 1998 all records of grants are retained by computer record: the computer has all records from 1 January 1996 to date. The calendars, in book form or microfiche, or the computer may be searched by any intending applicant before applying to check whether any impediment to the grant's issue exists.

Issue of grant

13.32   A form of grant appropriate to the application is prepared by the Registry from the information contained in the oath. When the grant issues, it is sent through the Document Exchange or by post to the extracting solicitor or probate practitioner (the applicant in a personal application) unless, at the request of the solicitor or applicant, arrangements are made to collect the grant personally.

Although application for a grant may be made to a sub-Registry, the papers, after examination, will be sent to its District Registry, from which the grant will issue. Each grant is signed by a District Judge or Registrar or authorised Probate Officer and sealed with the impressed seal of the Registry from which it issues. The grant is invalid unless it bears the impressed seal: the same applies to copies of the grant. A copy of the grant and, where appropriate, of the proved will, is sent by the District Registry to the Probate Records Centre for record purposes.

Grantees

More than one application

13.33   Rule 27(4) allows an applicant to apply for a grant of administration to which he is entitled without prior notice to any other person of equal entitlement.

If a dispute arises between two applicants of equal entitlement a summons, for hearing by a District Judge of the Principal Registry or a Registrar of a District Probate Registry, should be issued, under Rule 27(6), to determine who may have the grant. The issue of such a summons is recorded in the index of pending grant applications, pursuant to Rule 27(7). The grant may not issue until the summons is finally disposed of (Rule 27(8)).

It should be noted that although the rule refers to 'persons entitled to a grant in the same degree', an application to determine which of several executors may take probate may be determined in the same way as a dispute between proposed administrators. Where a dispute arises between executors, either may apply on notice to the other under Rule 27(1).

Death of applicant

Death before grant

13.34   Where an application for a grant has been lodged but the proposed grantee dies, the matter will be treated as though it has been withdrawn, provided the grant has not been sealed when the Registry is notified of the death, and provided the proposed grantee was the only applicant.

If the proposed grantee was one of two applicants and provided the grant may issue to a sole grantee (where no life or minority interest arises), the grant will issue to the surviving applicant.

A grant is deemed to be issued, i.e. that it has 'passed under the seal', at 10.00 am on the day on which it is dated. If the grantee dies at 10.01 am, the grant stands subject to revocation (see below).

Death after grant

13.35   Where the grant has been sealed, it will stand unless application is made for it to be revoked (see Rule 41 and CHAPTER 18). Where the grant is of probate and there is a surviving executor prepared to apply, application for revocation and for the new grant may be made simultaneously. This practice may also be followed on the death of one of the applicants for letters of administration where the survivor's title to apply is unaffected. Otherwise application for revocation should be made prior to application for the new grant. Application will then have to be for a *cessate* grant (see paragraph 10.18 above) by the person next entitled. Depending on the circumstances, and when the proposed grantee died, it may be possible for the oath to lead the grant and the Inland Revenue Account to stand in the application for the new grant, and, if necessary, a separate oath from a further applicant lodged.

Evidence of the death should be lodged with the District Judge or Registrar; a letter from a solicitor is usually sufficient but the District Judge or Registrar has a discretion as to further requirements.

Chapter 14

Foreign domicile

Domicile

Domicile of origin

14.1   The question of the deceased's domicile must be determined to establish both the validity of the will (if any), the entitlement to the grant and succession to the estate. The deceased's domicile is not always the deciding factor in the inheritance of estate in other countries. The law of the country concerned may apply the law of nationality. For this court's jurisdiction the place of domicile is of prime importance.

Generally, a child takes the domicile of his father and retains that domicile of origin even when his father changes his domicile; he does not become capable of having an independent domicile until he attains the age of 16 years or marries under that age (see s 3 Domicile and Matrimonial Proceedings Act 1973). If a child is illegitimate he takes the domicile of his mother. If a minor child's parents are living apart and the child lives with his mother, he similarly takes his mother's domicile. The child will retain that domicile when no longer living with his mother.

A married woman's domicile is independent of her husband's and is determined by reference to the same factors as for any other individual capable of having an independent domicile (see s 1 of the Act).

Even if a testator states in his will his intention to retain a particular domicile, on his death different factors regarding his residence and intention of residence may lead to the assumption of a different domicile.

Domicile of choice

14.2   On attaining the age of 16 years, or on marriage if he (or she) marries under age, or at any time thereafter any person may take a domicile of choice. Such a domicile is acquired by residing in a country or state, and intending to reside there, either permanently or for an indefinite period, and voluntarily deciding to acquire such a domicile. A domicile of choice is not acquired by a person merely residing or working in a country other than that in which he was originally domiciled; he must also show a desire to

14.2   *Foreign domicile*

change his domicile. A domicile of choice may be given up in favour of the domicile of origin or another domicile of choice: the same necessary factors relating to residence or intention of residence are relevant.

Statement in oath

14.3   Every oath to lead a grant must state the deceased's domicile, unless a District Judge or Registrar directs otherwise (Rule 8(2)). Where the province, state or territory in which the deceased died domiciled has a different or separate system of law from other parts of the country of which that province, state or territory is part, the province or otherwise must be stated in the oath, for example 'died domiciled in the state of Texas, United States of America'. The law to be applied (where appropriate) will be that of the particular province, state or territory.

Domicile in Scotland or Northern Ireland

Representation granted

14.4   Where the deceased died domiciled in Scotland or Northern Ireland a confirmation or grant issued from the appropriate courts of those countries operates to administer estate throughout the United Kingdom, provided such confirmation or grant contains a statement of the domicile and the document issues from the court of that domicile (s 1 Administration of Estates Act 1971).

Representation not granted

14.5   Where the deceased died domiciled in Scotland or Northern Ireland, but no form of representation has issued from the court of the country of domicile, application may be made in England and Wales for a grant appropriate to the case.

The oath to lead the grant must specifically state that no form of representation has issued from the court of the place of domicile. The grant will be 'limited to estate in England and Wales and until representation be granted in ......'; this is to avoid dual representation.

Where the deceased held assets in different parts of the United Kingdom, it is preferable to obtain appropriate representation from the court of the place of domicile, one document then serving to administer the estate wherever situate.

Evidence required if intestate

14.6   If the deceased died testate with his will in English or Welsh, application may be made for probate by an executor, or for administration (with will annexed) by the executor's attorney. Where the deceased died intestate, evidence of the law of the country of domicile will be necessary to lead an order under Rule 30(1)(b) or (c). However, where all or substantially the whole of the estate is immovable property, Rule 30(3)(b) will apply, that is the law of England and Wales will apply (see paragraphs 14.34–14.39 and 14.41 below).

Inland Revenue Account

14.7 As the deceased died within the United Kingdom, an Inland Revenue Account in Form IHT 200 should be used. The excepted estate provisions (see paragraph 13.23) apply as the deceased died domiciled in the United Kingdom. The Inheritance Tax (Delivery of Accounts) (Excepted Estates) Regulations 2002 apply to such domicile.

To whom a grant may issue

14.8 Where the deceased died domiciled outside England and Wales, the normal order contained in Rules 20 and 22 (see paragraphs 8.2 and 9.28) as to priority of right to a grant of representation does not apply. The practice is governed by Rule 30 which provides:

'(1) Subject to paragraph (3) below where the deceased died domiciled outside England and Wales a district judge or registrar may order that a grant, limited in such way as the district judge or registrar may direct, do issue to any of the following persons:

(a) to the person entrusted with the administration of the estate by the court having jurisdiction at the place where the deceased died domiciled; or

(b) where there is no person so entrusted, to the person beneficially entitled to the estate by the law of the place where the deceased died domiciled or, if there is more than one person so entitled, to such of them as the district judge or registrar may direct; or

(c) if in the opinion of the district judge or registrar the circumstances so require, to such person as the district judge or registrar may direct.

(2) A grant made under paragraph (1)(a) or (b) above may be issued jointly with such person as the district judge or registrar may direct if the grant is required to be made to not less than two administrators.

(3) Without any order made under paragraph (1) above –

(a) probate of any will which is admissible to proof may be granted –

(i)   if the will is in the English or Welsh language, to the executor named therein; or

(ii) if the will describes the duties of a named person in terms sufficient to constitute him executor according to the tenor of the will, to that person, and

(b)   where the whole or substantially the whole of the estate in England and Wales consists of immovable property, a grant in respect of the whole estate may be made in accordance with the law which would have been applicable if the deceased had died domiciled in England and Wales.'

It should be noted that the rule as amended allows the court to impose such limitation considered appropriate.

Evidence of foreign law

Affidavit of law

14.9   Rule 19 provides that where evidence of the law of any foreign country or territory is required on any application for a grant, an affidavit from a person suitably qualified to give expert evidence on the law in question, having regard to the particulars of that person's knowledge or experience, may be accepted as such evidence. The affidavit of law must state the deponent's qualifications, knowledge and experience which enable him to make the affidavit. The affidavit of law does not necessarily have to be by a legal practitioner in the country of domicile, but he must show from his qualifications, knowledge or experience that he is in a position to make the affidavit.

Notarial statement

14.10   Alternatively, the District Judge or Registrar may accept a certificate by, or an act before, a notary practising in the country, state or territory concerned, of the law as it applies to the circumstances of the case. The notary giving a certificate, or before whom an act was done, must practice in the country, state or territory of domicile.

Evidence from person entitled to grant

14.11   Where the person entitled to the grant by virtue of Rule 30 (above) is able to give evidence of the relevant foreign law, an affidavit from that person, setting out his qualifications, knowledge or experience to give such evidence, may be accepted. It follows therefore that there is no automatic bar to evidence of beneficial entitlement being given by the person beneficially entitled (see s 4 of the Civil Evidence Act 1972). The acceptance of such evidence is in the District Judge's or Registrar's discretion. For the form of affidavit of foreign law, see Form A1.61, page 428.

Alternative to English grant

14.12   Where the deceased died domiciled in a country to which the Colonial Probates Acts 1892 and 1927 apply (see CHAPTER 15), and a grant has already issued in, or representation will be necessary to administer estate in, that country, it may be preferable for a grant to be obtained in that country. Application may then be made for that grant to be resealed and used to administer estate in England and Wales. This may prove less expensive than obtaining evidence to validate a will and/or of beneficial entitlement to the deceased's estate to lead an order under Rule 30(1)(b) (see paragraph 14.8 above).

Sometimes there are difficulties obtaining a proper sealed grant from the issuing country sufficient to be resealed. Resealing may be the least expensive option, but where there are multiple assets it may be easier to obtain evidence of foreign law to lead a full grant here.

Where the deceased died domiciled in Scotland or Northern Ireland and a confirmation or grant has issued from the country in which he died domiciled, s 1 of the Administration of Estates Act 1971 provides for that confirmation or grant to be used to administer estate in England and Wales (see paragraph 14.4 above).

Validity of foreign will

14.13   Section 1 of the Wills Act 1963 provides that a will, or other testamentary instrument or act, shall be treated as properly executed if its execution conformed with the internal law (that is the law which would apply in a case where no question of the law in force in any other territory or state arises) in force:

(a)   in the territory where it was executed;

(b)   in the territory where the testator was domiciled either at the time the will was executed or at the time of his death;

(c)   in the territory where the testator had his habitual residence either at the time the will was executed or at the time of his death;

(d)   in a state (that is, a territory having its own law of nationality) of which the testator was a national either at the time of executing his will or at the time of his death.

Section 2 of the Act provides that a will shall be treated as properly executed:

(a)   if it was executed on board a vessel or aircraft of any description, provided the execution conformed with the internal law in force in the territory with which, having regard to the registration (if any) and any other relevant circumstances, the vessel or aircraft may be taken to have been most closely associated;

(b)   in so far as it disposed of immovable property, provided its execution conformed with the internal law in force in the territory where the property is situated;

(c)   in so far as it revoked a will which under the Act would be treated as properly executed, or revoked a provision which under the Act would be treated as comprised in a properly executed will, if the execution of a later will conformed to any law by reference to which the revoked will or provision would be so treated;

(d)   in so far as it exercised a power of appointment, if the execution of the will conformed to the law governing the essential validity of the power.

Section 2(2) of the Act provides that a will, so far as it exercises a power of appointment, shall be treated as properly executed notwithstanding that its execution was not in accordance with any formal requirements contained in the instrument creating the power.

The Wills Act 1963 applies to the wills of persons dying on or after 1 January 1964.

Admissibility to proof

Generally

14.14   Generally, where the will of a person dying domiciled outside England and Wales has been accepted as a valid testamentary document by the court of the country, state or territory within which the deceased died domiciled, it will be admitted to proof in England and Wales. It will not be admissible if it is limited to estate outside England and Wales (see paragraph 14.18 below). Where a will has not been proved or recognised as valid in the territory or country within which the deceased died domiciled, the District Judge or Registrar will require an affidavit of law of the country concerned, or certificate by, or an act before, a notary practising in the country, state or territory concerned (see s 1 of the Act, at paragraph 14.13 above), stating that the will is valid in that territory, state or country.

If the will was not executed in the country, state or territory of domicile at death, evidence of the law of the place where it was executed, or where the deceased was domiciled at the time of execution, may be obtained as an alternative. Either is sufficient to validate the will. There is no requirement that the will must dispose of estate in England and Wales for it to be admitted to proof in England and Wales, although this is usually the case. For a form of affidavit, see Form A1.62, page 430; see also paragraph 14.21 below.

Deceased a British national

14.15   Where the deceased was a British national either at the time of executing his will or at his death, validity of his will may be established by:

(i)   an affidavit made by a person qualified to speak to his nationality at either of the times; or

(ii)   a statement in the oath to lead the grant that he was a British national at either of the times.

Generally it is easier to use method (ii) above, but in either case as well as establishing British nationality a closer connection with the law of England and Wales must be established. Although the nationality is British, there are two distinct systems of law, English and Scottish. Obviously, a connection with English law must be established. This may be done by making a statement that the deceased 'was most closely connected with the system of law in force in England and Wales because', for example, he was born here, held property here, maintained bank accounts here, or whatever is the reason for the claim to the closer connection.

Will in English form: Practice Direction 20 November 1972

14.16   Where a will is properly executed in accordance with s 9 of the Wills Act 1837 (see paragraph 2.18) it is deemed to be in 'English form'. Any such will, under the authority of the Practice Direction, may be accepted without evidence where the deceased died domiciled in Australia, Canada, New Zealand, Northern Ireland or the Republic of Ireland. Where doubt arises as to proper execution, affidavit evidence of due execution will be required, as for a will executed in England and Wales.

Scottish wills

14.17   A will executed in Scotland may be accepted as valid to proof in England and Wales provided it meets the requirements set out in Chapter 2 (at paragraph 2.77) and note especially now the requirement of only one witness to a will in 'Scottish form'. Where the will has been proved by the Scottish court and a confirmation issued, the will may be accepted for proof in England and Wales without further evidence. However, it is unlikely that such proof will be necessary if the domicile was also in Scotland, the confirmation being sufficient to administer *all* estate in the United Kingdom.

14.17   Foreign domicile

Where the will has been 'recorded' or 'registered' in the Books of Council but no confirmation has issued, evidence of validity may be required. This is rarely necessary if the will has been properly executed according to Scottish form. Where the original of a Scottish will is retained as registered or recorded, a sealed official copy, sometimes in the form of an 'extract', may be accepted for proof.

Two or more wills

Wills expressed to take effect separately

14.18   Where a testator has made more than one will, each dealing with property in different countries, and it is clear that he intended his wills to take effect separately, the will relating to property in England and Wales may be proved alone. Suitably verified copies (and translations, if appropriate) of the will or wills dealing with property elsewhere should be lodged in the Registry where application for the grant is made, for the court to determine that such will does not affect the will sought to be proved.

Doubt as to the effect of wills

14.19   Where a will disposes of property in England and Wales, and another will disposes of the deceased's worldwide estate, it is normal practice for both wills to be proved. Any question of incompatibility between the wills as to the distribution of the estate is a matter to be dealt with on administration. Where a dispute cannot be resolved, the matter must be brought before the court for determination of interpretation/construction by probate claim commenced in the Chancery Division. In all cases where doubt arises as to the document(s) to be proved, the directions of the District Judge or Registrar should be sought as a preliminary to the grant application.

Will disposing of foreign assets

14.20   As is often the case, a person purchasing property abroad is obliged to make a will in that country disposing of his estate there.

Where the deceased has made only one will in the form required by the foreign country in which it was made but which disposes only of property in that foreign country, he may be intestate as to estate outside that country. The will, in these circumstances, will not be proved in England and Wales. On evidence of beneficial entitlement under the intestacy law of the country of domicile, an order under Rule 30(1)(b) and grant of letters of administration may be obtained.

Will not in English

Verification of translation

14.21   Where a will is in a foreign language, a translation of it and of any other documents attached or related to it must be supplied with the original will when application for proof is made. The translation must be verified by an English notary public, British Consul, or other person conversant with English and the language of the will. Where the translation was effected other than by a notary or consul, an affidavit by the translator deposing to his qualifications, and verifying the translation will, subject to the District Judge's or Registrar's discretion, be required.

Marking will

14.22   The original will, or the properly certified copy (that is, certified by the court which proved it or retains it, or a notarially certified copy) thereof (not the translation), must be marked in accordance with Rule 10 by the applicant for the grant and the solicitor or other person before whom the oath is sworn. The authenticated translation should not be marked.

Wills in Welsh

14.23   Where the will is in the Welsh language a certified translation may be obtained from the Probate Registry of Wales (see APPENDIX 3 for the address). A charge of £1.00 per folio of 72 words is payable for the translation. See also paragraph 14.14 above.

Notarial wills: exclusion of non-testamentary words

14.24   Where the will was taken before a notary, there are frequently other words or phrases not relevant included in the statement containing the will. Where such words or phrases cannot easily be excluded from the probate and record copies (which are produced by photocopying), the District Judge or Registrar may direct an engrossment be made, containing only those parts which constitute the will. Where possible, the Registry will note those parts which are testamentary and are to be copied, and from them produce the probate and record copy will.

Original will not available

14.25   Where the original will cannot be produced because it has been retained by a foreign court or deposited with a notary, Rule 54(2) allows a copy, duly authenticated by the court or notary, to be accepted for proof by the District Judge or Registrar without obtaining an order giving leave to admit a copy.

If the original will is lost or has been destroyed and no copy is available, the provisions relating to lost wills of persons dying domiciled in England and Wales apply (see paragraph 5.9 *et seq*).

Entitlement to grant

Will in English or Welsh

14.26 Rule 30(3)(a)(i) (see paragraph 14.8 above) provides that where a will is admissible to proof (that is, valid by virtue of s 1 of the Wills Act 1963) and is in the English or Welsh language, irrespective of the deceased's domicile, any executor named is accepted as having the full rights of executorship and no order will be required for him to obtain the grant. Once validity has been established, the executor may apply for probate in the usual way or appoint an attorney to take administration (with will annexed) for his use and benefit.

Executor according to tenor

14.27 Regardless of the language in which the will is written, provided it is admissible to proof in England and Wales, and sets out the duties of a person named therein sufficiently to constitute him an executor *according to the tenor of the will* (it is normally accepted that there is no equivalent to the word 'executor' in a foreign language, the word and definition being peculiarly English), that person may apply for probate without first obtaining an order (Rule 30(3)(a)(ii)). Where doubt arises as to the sufficiency of the duties described to constitute him executor according to the tenor, preliminary application should be made to a District Judge or Registrar for directions. The appointment of a named person as personal representative is regarded as sufficient.

Where an executor is appointed, or a person's duties imposed in the will are sufficient for him to be constituted an executor according to the tenor of the will, he may apply for and obtain a grant in England and Wales notwithstanding that he has renounced probate or refused to take a grant in the country in which the deceased died domiciled. Where there is more than one executor appointed, those who survive and do not apply must renounce their right to the grant or have power reserved to them.

Attorney of executor

14.28 An executor appointed in the will may himself apply for a grant of probate, or, through an attorney, for letters of administration (with will annexed), notwithstanding another person has been entrusted with the administration of the deceased's estate by the court of the country where the deceased died domiciled. The person entrusted with administration by the court of the deceased's domicile, and entitled to apply for an order under Rule 30(1)(a) (see below), may apply for such an order and obtain the grant without clearing off any executor(s) appointed in the will. If the person entrusted with administration by the foreign court is an executor it would be preferable for him to apply in his capacity as executor or through his attorney by virtue of Rule 30(3)(a), to obviate application for an order under Rule 30(1)(a).

Application under Rule 30(1)(a)

14.29   (See paragraph 14.8 above for the full text of Rule 30.)

Entrusting document

14.30   Where the law of the country of domicile requires a grant to issue to enable administration of the deceased's estate in that country, and such grant has issued, an order under Rule 30(1)(a) may be obtained and application for a grant of letters of administration in England and Wales made by the person entrusted with the administration of the estate by the court of the foreign country.

The entrusting document may be in the form of a grant recognisable as such by comparison with an English grant, or may be a decree or order of the foreign court. Whatever the document issued by that court, it must give the person entrusted the same, or substantially the same, authority as an English grant. The document must contain authority to realise assets *and* distribute the estate. Whether the deceased died testate or intestate, the criteria to be applied to the sufficiency of an entrusting document are the same. The entrusting document must be issued by a court: an authorisation from a notary is insufficient.

If a limitation as to time is imposed on the powers of the person entrusted by the foreign court, a similar limitation will, if the District Judge or Registrar is satisfied that the limitation is proper for administering the estate in England and Wales, be imposed in the English grant.

Orders to administer and/or elections to administer taken by the Public Trustee of New Zealand or the Public Trustee of the relevant state in Australia are sufficient to constitute entrusting documents. In some circumstances the order or election, depending on its terms, may be suitable for resealing (see CHAPTER 15, and in particular paragraph 15.2).

Executor not the person entrusted

14.31   Under Rule 30(3)(a)(i), an executor who is not the person entrusted with the administration of the estate, may apply for a grant of probate. Where there is doubt about the sufficiency of the grant, decree or order of the foreign court, it should be referred to a District Judge or Registrar for adjudication. Generally, no affidavit of law will be necessary – nor will it be necessary to establish validity of the will, the will having been accepted and proved by the court of the place of domicile.

Application may be made under Rule 30(1)(a) for an order allowing a grant to be made to the person entrusted with the administration of the estate of the deceased by the court whose jurisdiction covers the place where the deceased died domiciled. Such a person may apply for a grant in England and Wales, notwithstanding that the will appointed an executor (who is a person other than the person entrusted) who has not applied for a grant in England and Wales or renounced his right, without having to obtain such a renunciation.

Attorneys

14.32   A person entrusted, whether or not resident abroad, and similarly a foreign corporation appointed as executor, may appoint an attorney to obtain a grant of administration (with will annexed) for the use and benefit of that person or corporation and until further representation be granted (see paragraph 10.32 for attorney grants).

Application for order

14.33   Application may be made by lodging any affidavit required; the original grant, order or other official document issued by the foreign court, or an officially certified copy (together with a notarised or otherwise authenticated translation, if necessary), and if the foreign grant does not contain a copy of the will, a court certified copy with a translation, if necessary, notarially or otherwise authenticated; and any other relevant documents, as a preliminary application for the District Judge's or Registrar's order before application is made for the grant. Where the grant and will are separate documents, there must be sufficient reference to establish that the grant relates to the will.

However, it is not essential for an order under Rule 30(1)(a) to be made *before* application for the grant and therefore application for the order may be made by lodging the appropriate documents at the same time as the oath to lead the grant (the request for the order being contained in the oath). Usually, an application for an order under Rule 30(1)(a) is included in the application for the grant. If the order is made on application before application for the grant, the oath must recite details of the order.

If the papers are defective, the Registry will notify the solicitor of the defect. Where the papers are in order and the District Judge or Registrar is satisfied, an order for the grant's issue will be drawn by the Registry and, if the application for the order was made simultaneously with the application for the grant, the grant will issue in due course and will include any appropriate limitation.

Where a life or minority interest arises in the estate, application for the order must be made by at least two proposed grantees, unless a District Judge or Registrar directs otherwise (see s 114(2) Supreme Court Act 1981 (see paragraph 9.2 above)). Rule 30(2) provides that where the grant is required to be made to not less than two administrators a District Judge or Registrar may direct the grant issue jointly with such other person as he deems fit.

For the form of oath see Form A1.46, page 412.

Application under Rule 30(1)(b)

Person beneficially entitled

14.34 Application under Rule 30(1)(b) may be made for an order for a grant, where there is no person entrusted by the court of the place where the deceased died domiciled, to be issued to the person beneficially entitled to the estate of the deceased by the law of the place in which the deceased died domiciled. If there is more than one person beneficially entitled to share the estate the grant may issue to such one or more of them as a District Judge or Registrar may direct. Any person(s) beneficially entitled may appoint an attorney to obtain a grant for their use and benefit (see paragraph 10.32 for attorney grants).

No person entrusted

14.35 Application under Rule 30(1)(b) will always be necessary where there is no person entrusted (in countries where a grant is normally required to administer the estate), or the deceased died domiciled in a 'non grant issuing' country, or the grant, decree or order issued by the foreign court is insufficient to constitute an entrusting document.

Even if there is an executor appointed in the will, unless he has taken a grant (i.e. become the person entrusted) there is no need to 'clear' his entitlement to a grant.

Forming evidence

14.36 An affidavit of foreign law (see Form A1.61, page 428 for a form of affidavit) or a certificate by, or an act before, a notary practising in the country or territory concerned will be required by the District Judge or Registrar. The evidence must clearly show who is beneficially entitled to the deceased's estate by the law of the place of domicile.

The affidavit, provided it clearly defines the beneficial entitlement to the deceased's estate and provided the deponent by his knowledge, experience and qualifications shows he is entitled to make the affidavit, will be accepted by the District Judge or Registrar without further enquiry or evidence as to that law. Similarly, a notarial certificate will be accepted without further enquiry (see Rule 19).

Where the person applying is one of several persons entitled, the evidence must set out their order of priority of entitlement to benefit if there is one. There is a discretion vested in the District Judge or Registrar to direct who may apply for the grant when there is more than one person beneficially entitled.

Where the deceased died testate, evidence to validate the will (see paragraphs 14.13 and 14.14 above) must be lodged.

Application for order

14.37   The procedure for making the application is as for an order under Rule 30(1)(a), that is application may be made either before application for the grant or with the application for the grant (being contained in the oath to lead the grant). If application is made before the grant application, details of the order must be recited in the oath.

Where a life or minority interest arises, Rule 30(2) provides for the District Judge or Registrar to direct that the grant be taken by an additional applicant to be appointed at the court's discretion.

Application under Rule 30(1)(c)

When application appropriate

14.38   Application is made under this provision where, in the opinion of the District Judge or Registrar, the circumstances require the grant should issue to such person as he may direct. Even if application could be made under Rule 30(1)(a) or (b), the District Judge or Registrar may make an order for a grant to such other person as is thought fit under Rule 30(1)(c). Similarly, an order under Rule 30(1)(c) will be necessary where the person entitled to apply under paragraphs (1)(a) or (b) cannot or will not apply, or in the unlikely circumstance that there is no such person.

Although the evidence often shows that there are persons beneficially entitled, application may be made for an order under Rule 30(1)(c) if it can be shown that it is impossible or difficult for the beneficiaries to take a grant or even appoint attorneys. This situation can arise because of a difficult political system in the country of domicile. Where there are communication or language problems, Rule 30(1)(c) may provide an answer – Rule 30(1)(c) may be applied whether the deceased was testate or intestate.

Rule 30(1)(c) has the same effect for a foreign domiciled deceased as has s 116 of the Supreme Court Act 1981 for an English domicile – the court has discretionary power to grant representation to whomsoever it considers an appropriate person, overriding other persons' entitlements as executors, persons entrusted or beneficiaries.

Application for order

14.39   Where application for an order under this paragraph is made, application *must* be made as a preliminary to the application for the grant, the order providing the applicant's title to apply. The oath to lead the grant must recite details of the District Judge's or Registrar's order. As well as an affidavit of law or notarial certificate dealing, *inter alia*, with beneficial entitlement, evidence will be required of the facts of the case and the particular circumstances making it necessary to pass over the person(s) entitled to apply under paragraphs (1)(a) or (b) of Rule 30 and why such person will not or cannot apply or stating that there is no such person. The District Judge or Registrar may direct application be made by two persons under Rule 30(2) where two administrators are required, i.e. where the evidence shows that a life or minority interest arises.

Where application under this provision is necessary, it is invariably preferable to seek the court's directions by way of pre-lodgment enquiry. The District Judge or Registrar's requirements as to further evidence by affidavit(s) will be notified by the Registry. When the District Judge or Registrar is satisfied on the evidence, the order will be drawn and served by post by the Registry.

Estate consisting of immovable property in England and Wales

14.40   Under Rule 30(3)(b), irrespective of whether the deceased died testate or intestate, where the whole or substantially the whole estate in England and Wales consists of immovable property, a grant in respect of the whole estate may be made in accordance with the law which would have been applicable if the deceased had died domiciled in England and Wales. That is, the order of priority of entitlement is determined in accordance with Rule 20 or 22 (see paragraphs 8.2 and 9.28).

The validity of any will may be determined in accordance with s 9 of the Wills Act 1837 (see paragraph 2.18), but if this section cannot apply, evidence to validate the will in accordance with s 1 of the Wills Act 1963 will be necessary.

An affidavit of law or a notarial certificate will not normally be necessary, but the oath to lead the grant must specifically depose to the whole or substantially the whole estate consisting of immovable property in England and Wales. There is no general definition of what constitutes 'substantially the whole estate'. It could be argued that more than 50% could constitute 'substantially the whole estate'. The application of this part of the rule and the interpretation of it come within the discretion of the District Judge or Registrar to whom the point falls to be considered. Where the application is based on substantially the whole estate being real estate, the oath must set out details of the values of the separate parts to show that the real estate is indeed the substantial part.

As the provisions of this part of the Rule allow the grant application to proceed on the more commonly used basis, it is preferable, where possible, that it should be used. The directions of the court in the particular circumstances of each case should be sought as a pre-lodgment enquiry.

Oath to lead the grant pursuant to Rule 30

Domicile

14.41   The oath must specify the country within whose jurisdiction the deceased died domiciled. Where that country has states, territories or provinces which operate different systems of law, the relevant state, territory or province within which the deceased died domiciled must also be stated. If the deceased died domiciled in Northern Ireland or Scotland, the oath should recite that no grant or confirmation has issued from the courts of those countries.

The applicant

14.42   The oath should describe the applicant as the person entrusted where an order under Rule 30(1)(a) has been made or is sought; or the person or one of the persons beneficially entitled where an order under Rule 30(1)(b) has been made or is sought.

The order

14.43   Details of the order made under Rule 30(1)(a) or (b) should be recited. Where an order under Rule (30)(1)(c) has been obtained, details of the order must be recited in the oath and the applicant described as the person authorised by the order. Where no order under Rule 30(1)(a) or (b) has been made, a request for the order sought must be included in the oath. For a form of oath see Form A1.46, page 412. As the grant will only issue in respect of estate in England and Wales, other estate outside the jurisdiction should be excluded from the values inserted in the oath.

Rule 30(2) provides that where a grant issues pursuant to an order made under Rule 30(1)(a), (b) or (c) a District Judge or Registrar may (for example where a life or minority interest arises) direct the grant be issued jointly with such other person as the District Judge or Registrar directs. Any order made will specify the persons who may apply. They must all join in deposing to the facts contained in the oath.

Attorney application

14.44 Any person entitled to apply for an order under Rule 30(1)(a) or (b) may apply for the order and for the grant through an attorney. Any order made will direct the grant to issue to the attorney. Such order, and the grant when issued, will contain a limitation that the grant is for the use and benefit of the person(s) entitled. Where application is made for an order under paragraph (1)(c), the applicant should be the proposed grantee: there should be no need for an attorney.

Where the donor of the power is one of two or more executors, the grant will usually still be limited until further representation be granted, but may be limited for the executor's use and benefit and until he, or one of the other executor(s), shall obtain probate of the will, as the District Judge or Registrar shall direct. There is power, where the circumstances so justify, for the District Judge or Registrar to impose such further or other limitation as he deems necessary.

For powers of attorney executed abroad, see paragraph 10.38.

Inland Revenue Accounts

14.45 Where the deceased died domiciled outside the United Kingdom and:

(a) was never domiciled in the United Kingdom or treated as domiciled in the United Kingdom by s 267 of the Inheritance Tax Act 1984; and

(b) the value of the deceased's estate in the United Kingdom is wholly attributable to cash or quoted shares or securities passing under his will or intestacy or by survivorship in a beneficial joint tenancy; and

(c) the gross value of the estate does not exceed £100,000; and

(d) the deceased died on or after 6 April 2002,

the excepted estates provisions apply and no Inland Revenue Account need be delivered. The oath to lead the grant must recite the facts set out above.

In all other cases of foreign domicile, an Inland Revenue Account in Form IHT 200 must be delivered. The Account must also be submitted for control by IR Capital Taxes before the grant may issue, whether or not tax is payable. The Account should be submitted direct to IR Capital Taxes who will return Form D18 with a note of any tax due or certified that none is payable. Form D18, endorsed with a receipt for the tax paid or with a certificate that no tax is payable, should be lodged with the oath and other documents. The Account should deal with all the assets in the United Kingdom and not merely those in England and Wales.

The Inland Revenue may consider a person domiciled in England and Wales for tax purposes, but this may not necessarily be the deceased's domicile for the purpose of establishing validity of a will or as supporting evidence to lead an order under Rule 30.

The Treasury Solicitor

14.46   Where there is doubt that any estate in England and Wales will pass to kin or other persons or body beneficially entitled, notice should be given to the Treasury Solicitor under Rule 38 (see paragraph 9.45) for a decision to be made on a claim for *bona vacantia*.

Chapter 15

Resealing grants

15.1   Rule 39 provides for application to be made to the Principal Registry, any District Probate Registry or sub-Registry for the resealing of a grant of probate or administration made by the court of a country or territory to which the Colonial Probates Acts 1892 and 1927 apply. The Acts are applied by an Order in Council. Once resealed, the grant has the same power and effect to administer estate in England and Wales as if the grant had been made by a court in England and Wales.

The District Judge or Registrar has a discretion whether to accept a grant for resealing and may refuse the application and direct application be made for an original grant in England and Wales.

Only grants issued in the English language (or in English and the foreign language – for example South African grants) may be resealed.

Countries and territories to which the Colonial Probates Acts apply

15.2   By the Colonial Probates Act Application Order 1965, the Acts apply to:

Aden (provided the grant issued before 30 November 1967)	New Hebrides
Alberta	New South Wales
Antigua	New Zealand
Australian Capital Territory	Newfoundland
Bahamas	Nigeria
Barbados	Norfolk Island
Belize (formerly British Honduras)	Northwest Territories of Canada
Bermuda	Northern Territory of Australia
Botswana (formerly Bechuanaland)	Nova Scotia
British Antarctic Territory	Ontario

British Columbia

British Sovereign Base Areas in Cyprus

Brunei

Cayman Islands

Christmas Island (Australian)

Cocos (Keeling) Islands

Cyprus (Republic)

Dominica

Falkland Islands

Falkland Islands Dependencies

Fiji

Gibraltar

Grenada

Gambia

Ghana

Guyana (formerly British Guyana)

Hong Kong

Jamaica

Kenya

Kiribati (formerly Gilbert Islands)

Lesotho (formerly Basutoland)

Malawi

Malaysia

Manitoba

Montserrat

New Brunswick

New Guinea Territory

Papua (New Guinea)

Prince Edward Island

Queensland

St Christopher (Kitts) Nevis and Anguilla

St Helena

St Lucia

St Vincent

Saskatchewan

Seychelles (Republic)

Sierra Leone

Singapore

Solomon Islands

South Africa

South Australia

Sri Lanka (formerly Ceylon)

Swaziland

Tanzania (provided grant issued in Tanganyika before 26 April 1964)

Tasmania

Tortola (formerly British Virgin Islands)

Trinidad & Tobago (Republic)

Turks & Caicos Islands

Tuvalu (formerly Ellice Islands)

Uganda

Victoria

Western Australia

Zambia

Zimbabwe (formerly Southern Rhodesia)

The countries, states and territories listed above are those which reciprocate by their courts resealing grants issued in England and Wales.

Who may apply

15.3   Rule 39(3) provides for application to be made by:

(a)   any person entrusted with the administration of the estate by the court having jurisdiction at the place where the deceased died domiciled, that is to a person to whom a grant could have been given by order under Rule 30(1)(a); or

(b)   the person, or one of the persons, beneficially entitled to the estate by the law of the place where the deceased died domiciled, that is to a person to whom a grant could have been given by order under Rule 30(1)(b) subject to evidence of beneficial entitlement being lodged on affidavit or by material statement, i.e. the same evidence as would be necessary to lead an order, under this part of the Rule, for a full English grant;

(c)   in respect of a will in the English or Welsh language admissible to proof in England and Wales, that is, valid under s 1 of the Wills Act 1963, the executor named in the will or, whatever the language of the will, the person given the duties in the will which are sufficient to constitute him executor according to the tenor, that is to the person to whom a grant could have been given under Rule 30(3)(a).

The provisions of (b) and (c) above need only be invoked when the colonial grant issued out of the court of a country other than the country in which the deceased died domiciled (for example, the deceased died domiciled in Zimbabwe but the grant issued out of the court in South Africa);

(d)   where the grantee does not qualify under (a) to (c) above, by the leave of a District Judge or Registrar.

(For Rule 30 see paragraph 14.8.)

Elections or orders to administer

15.4   An election to administer or order to administer granted to the Public Trustee in New Zealand may be accepted for resealing, the election or order being deemed to equate with a grant. It must be certified that the election or order remains in force and that no further step will be taken to administer the estate if further estate in New Zealand is discovered which takes the election over the statutory limit for such election or order.

Similarly, elections to administer from other countries or territories, for example some Australian and Canadian states, to which the 1892 and 1927 Acts relate may be accepted for reseal. In the applications evidence must be filed of the law of the country or territory concerned to show that any such election has the same force and validity as a grant.

Authority to apply

15.5   Where the original grantee does not himself apply, application may be made by a person authorised in writing by the original grantee to apply on his behalf. Such authorisation must be in writing but, except where application is made by an attorney, need not be in the form of a power of attorney.

A power of attorney authorising the donee to obtain representation in England and Wales is unacceptable as authority to apply for a reseal unless the terms of reference are such that authority is inferred, but if the power contained authority to apply for either a full grant in England and Wales or for resealing, it is acceptable.

Where the grant issued to the attorney of the person entitled, the grant is accepted as evidence of the validity of the power of attorney, and the power or a certified copy need not be lodged on application to reseal.

Questions of doubt about the sufficiency of the authorisation or power of attorney should be referred to the District Judge or Registrar before lodging the application to reseal.

Application by foreign corporation

15.6   Although a grant could not be obtained in England and Wales, application for reseal may be made by a trust corporation notwithstanding that its principal place of business is out of England and Wales and a grant made to such a corporation may be resealed. Where application is made by a trust corporation no resolution appointing the nominee to take the steps necessary for resealing need be lodged.

Number of applicants

15.7   Where the grant issued to more than one person, all surviving grantees must apply for resealing, or must consent in writing to the one of them who is making the application applying alone or to the person authorised by one of them acting. Where the grant issued to two or more persons one of whom has since died, the survivor may apply for resealing. A direction from the District Judge or Registrar will be necessary to reseal the grant.

It is not the general practice (as it contravenes s 114 of the Supreme Court Act 1981) to reseal a grant which issued to more than four grantees, but this remains in the discretion of the court.

Procedure

15.8   Application may be made by personal attendance or by post to the Principal Registry or to a District Probate Registry or sub-Registry. The documents required are:

(a)   the original grant; or a duplicate sealed by the issuing court; or a certified copy (certified as correct by the court of issue but not necessarily under seal); or an exemplification provided it contains the essential parts of the grant; or an election or order to administer having the same effect as a grant provided it is endorsed with or accompanied by the necessary certificate to validate it, that is the document which may be resealed by virtue of s 2(1) and (4) of the 1892 Act;

(b)   a copy of the will and any other testamentary document to which the grant relates, if any, properly certified as correct by or under the authority of the granting court, if a copy is not included in the grant (see Rule 39(5));

(c)   a plain copy of the grant and a plain copy of the will;

(d)   if the applicant is not the grantee, the authorisation of the grantee which may be in the form of a letter of authority if the applicant is not the grantee's attorney. Where an attorney applies the power of attorney (containing specific or other sufficient authority to apply to reseal the grant) should be lodged; if the original power of attorney is required to be returned a copy for retention by the court should be lodged, the copy certified as a 'true and complete copy';

(e)   an Inland Revenue Account in the form appropriate to an application being made for a grant in England and Wales where the deceased died domiciled abroad (that is, in Form IHT 200). The 'excepted estate' provisions may now apply to applications to reseal where the criteria set out at paragraph 13.23 apply.

There are no longer provisions requiring an order to lead the reseal, or an administration guarantee. No oath is required.

Domicile

15.9   Unless doubt arises, the statement of domicile contained in the Inland Revenue Account is accepted without other evidence as sufficient to satisfy s 2(2) of the 1892 Act. If the estate is 'excepted', no statement of domicile will be necessary. The court has power to require evidence of domicile if there is any question on the matter.

Nil estate

15.10   Where there is no estate in England and Wales, evidence of the reason for resealing must be lodged.

Postal application

15.11   Although it is usual for application to be made through a solicitor, probate practitioner or other authorised person with an address in England and Wales, an application for a resealed grant may be made by the grantee or through a foreign lawyer or person resident outside the jurisdiction.

Personal application

15.12   Application may be made by the grantee, or the person he has authorised to act on his behalf, as a personal application. A personal attendance at that Registry by the grantee or his properly authorised agent may be required.

Inland Revenue Accounts

15.13   Where an Account must be delivered, the Account, in Form IHT 200, dealing with the deceased's estate in the United Kingdom should be submitted to IR Capital Taxes for control before the documents are lodged in the Registry. Where tax is payable, the Account should be submitted to IR Capital Taxes at Nottingham in the same way as for an application for a full grant in England and Wales.

Fees

15.14   Where the estate is below £5,000, no fee is payable but where the estate exceeds £5,000 the same fee is payable as on an application for an original grant (see APPENDIX 2). The additional fee (the Departmental fee) payable on personal applications (see APPENDIX 2) applies to applications to reseal.

Sealing

15.15   The District Judge or Registrar, if satisfied that the documents lodged are in order, will authorise the resealing of the grant. The grant is resealed with the seal of the Family Division of the High Court. The grant when resealed will be returned to the applicant. The Registry will inform the issuing court abroad that its grant has been resealed.

Wills

15.16   Every grant submitted for resealing must contain, or be accompanied by, a properly certified (that is, certified by the court in which it was proved) copy of the will or other testamentary document to which the grant relates (see Rule 39(5)).

Where the will to which the grant relates was a joint will, the usual requirement to supply details of the date of birth/death of the testator/testatrix, other than the one to which the grant relates, applies.

Restrictions

15.17 It should be noted that a grant limited to estate outside the United Kingdom cannot be resealed. A grant limited in any other way, or a grant of a temporary nature, may be resealed only with the leave of a District Judge or Registrar (see Rule 39(4)). Such leave will be granted only if the court is satisfied that full and proper administration of the estate in England and Wales can be carried out notwithstanding the limitation. Where a grant has been resealed in error the court may cancel the resealing on application by the grantee or a person interested, or may cancel the resealing of its own motion.

Recognition of grants throughout the United Kingdom

15.18 Since the coming into force of the Administration of Estates Act 1971, it is no longer necessary for grants issued in England and Wales or Northern Ireland, or confirmations issued in Scotland, to be resealed in order to be valid to administer estate in the United Kingdom elsewhere than the country of issue, provided the grant or confirmation issued from the court of the country where the deceased died domiciled (see s 1 of the Act). To be effective, the grant or confirmation must recite the domicile of the deceased. Where the grant or confirmation issued before the coming into operation of the Act (1 January 1972), a statement noting domicile may not appear in the grant. Application in respect of English and Welsh grants for a note of domicile to be appended to the grant is made to the Probate Manager of the Principal Registry.

Where the deceased died domiciled in Northern Ireland or Scotland leaving estate in England and Wales, application may be made for a grant in England and Wales if no grant or confirmation has issued from the court of the country of domicile. To avoid a duplication of grants effective to administer estate in the United Kingdom, the grant issued in England and Wales will be limited to the estate situated there and until further representation is granted from the court of the country of domicile.

Chapter 16

Caveats and citations

Caveats

Definition

16.1 A caveat is a notice to the court in writing filed in a Probate Registry by a person who wishes to show cause against a grant issuing.

Rule 2(1) includes in the definition of a grant any grant made by any court outside England and Wales produced for resealing. The provisions discussed in this chapter therefore apply to grants submitted for resealing as they do to original grants.

For the purpose of Rule 44 (which deals with caveats) there is no nominated Registry. The Leeds District Probate Registry is therefore the effective Registry for the purposes of entering warnings and appearances (see Rule 44(15), added with effect from 14 September 1998).

Entry of caveat

16.2 Rule 44(1) provides that any person (a caveator) may enter a caveat if he wishes to show cause against a grant of representation being sealed. Where two or more persons wish to prevent the issue of a grant, a separate caveat must be entered in the name of each of those persons. The caveat may be entered in the Principal Registry, or any District Probate Registry or sub-Registry, by any person or by a solicitor or probate practitioner on his behalf. A fee of £15 is payable on the entry or renewal (see paragraph 16.5 below) of a caveat.

Effect of caveat

16.3 Rule 44(4), as substituted with effect from 14 September 1998, provides that an index of caveats entered in any Registry must be maintained, and on receipt of an application for a grant of representation the index must be searched to determine, *inter alia*, whether a caveat has been entered to prevent the sealing of the grant. The index is contained on the Probateman computer system as part of the pending grant application index.

Rule 44(1) also provides that a District Judge or Registrar shall not allow a grant (other than a grant *ad colligenda bona* or a grant under s 117 of the Supreme Court Act 1981 (grant pending determination of a probate claim); see paragraphs 10.5 and 10.1) to be sealed where he knows of an effective caveat, except where the caveator is also the applicant for the grant.

A caveat will not, however, operate to prevent the sealing of a grant where that caveat is entered on the day the grant is sealed. Each grant is deemed to be sealed with the Registry seal immediately before 10 am on the date of the grant. Thus any caveat entered after 10 am on that date does not prevent the grant's issue being effective.

A grant which has been sealed will remain operative until revoked by the court. When a caveat is entered, its entry is recorded immediately on the index by the Registry at which it is entered.

Form of caveat

16.4   Rule 44(2) and (3) provide that any person who wishes to enter a caveat may do so by attending personally, by his solicitor or probate practitioner at any Registry or sub-Registry, and completing a notice (Form 3 of the Schedule to the Rules; the form of caveat is set out as Form A1.70, page 440) in the caveat book of that Registry. The caveat may alternatively be entered by post at any Registry.

The deceased's full true name must be stated and any possible alias(es) given, together with the deceased's last address and postcode. Where the deceased's death was registered in the United Kingdom, this information should be contained in the death certificate (see Practice Direction 12 January 1999). Failure to provide this information accurately may result in the caveat's being ineffective to prevent the issue of the grant.

Where a caveat is entered by a solicitor or probate practitioner on behalf of the caveator, that caveator's name shall be stated in the form. Where a caveat is entered by post, it is sent at the caveator's risk. A receipt acknowledging the entry of the caveat is provided by the Registry. The receipt should be retained, as it will have to be produced if application is made to withdraw the caveat.

Duration of caveat

16.5   Rule 44(3)(a) provides that a caveat remains in force for a period of six months beginning with the date it is entered (but see below). Rule 44(3)(b) provides that application may be made for a caveat to be extended or renewed; such application must be made within the last month before the caveat expires, by written request (quoting the caveat number) to the Registry at which it was entered, or by personal attendance at that Registry, to endorse the caveat book accordingly.

Provided the time limit is observed, a caveat may be extended as many times as necessary (Rule 44(3)(c)). Each extension shall be for a period of six months commencing at the date the caveat would have expired or from the date the extended caveat would have expired.

In respect of citation proceedings, Rule 46(3) provides that unless a District Judge of the Principal Registry, or the Registrar of the Registry at which the proceedings were commenced, by order made on summons (see paragraph 17.1 for the procedure on summonses) otherwise directs, any caveat in force at the commencement of citation proceedings shall, unless it is withdrawn under Rule 44(11) by a caveator who has not entered an appearance to a warning (see paragraph 16.9 below), remain in force until an application for a grant is made by the person shown to be entitled thereto by the decision of the court in such proceedings. On application being made for the grant, following the determination of the citation proceedings, any caveat entered by a party who had notice of the proceedings shall cease to have effect.

Any caveat in respect of which an appearance to a warning has been entered remains in force until the commencement of the probate claim, unless a District Judge of the Principal Registry directs. Where application to discontinue a caveat, after an appearance has been entered to a warning, is made *by consent*, the District Probate Registrar of the Registry where the grant application is pending may direct the discontinuance of the caveat (Rule 44(13)).

Unless a District Judge of the Principal Registry otherwise directs, the commencement of a probate claim shall, whether or not any caveat has been entered, operate to prevent the sealing of a grant (other than a grant under s 117 of the Supreme Court Act 1981 – a grant pending determination of a probate claim, see paragraph 10.1), until application for a grant is made by the person shown to be entitled thereto by the decision of the court in such claim. On application for the grant being made, any caveat entered by the plaintiff in the claim, and any caveat in respect of which notice of the claim had been given, shall cease to have effect (Rule 45(3) and (4)).

Where a caveat subsists, and the caveator dies during its subsistence, application to remove the caveat must be made by way of summons to a District Judge or Registrar. The summons must be served on the caveator's personal representative or the person(s) entitled to be constituted as such.

Withdrawal of caveat

16.6   At any time after the entry of a caveat the caveator may give notice to the Registry in which his caveat was entered that he withdraws the caveat. Where a warning has issued, provided the caveator has not entered an appearance to the warning, the caveat may be withdrawn on notice to the Registry at which it was entered; the caveat thereupon ceases to have effect.

Notice to the Registry may be given on personal attendance or by post. In either case, the receipt acknowledging the entry of the caveat must be produced (see Rule 44(11)).

Where the caveat is withdrawn the caveator must forthwith give notice of withdrawal to the person warning. Where an appearance has been entered the caveat cannot be withdrawn (see paragraph 16.5 above). A District Judge of the Principal Registry (or District Probate Registrar where application is by consent) may direct the caveat do cease to have effect on a summons issued seeking such a direction.

Any caveat in force when a summons for directions under Rule 44(6) is issued remains in force until the summons is disposed of or until the caveat is withdrawn (Rule 44(8)). Where an application for a grant is prevented from proceeding because of the caveat, and the caveat is subsequently withdrawn, the Registry at which the caveat was entered will note the Probateman computer record giving clearance for the grant to issue. The Registry at which the grant application is pending will automatically have its record updated to show the caveat has been withdrawn, and will so notify the applicant for the grant, or the extracting solicitor or probate practitioner. At the same time, the Registry will ask if the application for the grant should now continue, and, where some time has elapsed since the making of the application, may request confirmation that the facts deposed to when the application was lodged remain the same.

Further caveat

16.7   Where a caveat has expired, and application for an extension has not been made, the caveator may enter a further caveat. However, without the leave of a District Judge of the Principal Registry, a further caveat in an estate may not be entered by the same caveator where:

(a)   the original caveat is still in force; or

(b)   a warning to the first caveat was issued and the caveator failed to appear to that warning or failed to issue a summons for directions under Rule 44(6); or

(c)   following the decision of the court in proceedings by way of citation or in a probate claim, the caveator had had notice of such proceedings or action (see Rule 44(14)).

Where leave to enter a further caveat is granted, such caveat will remain in force for six months from the date of its entry.

Warning to caveat

16.8   Where an application for a grant is stayed by the entry of a caveat the applicant or any person having or claiming to have an interest in the estate, may issue a warning by lodging Prescribed Form 4 (Form A1.71, page 440) at the Leeds District Probate Registry. The warning informs the caveator that he must enter an appearance at the Leeds District Probate Registry (see paragraph 16.9 below) to that warning within eight days, including the day of service, setting out his interest, or claim to an interest, in the deceased's estate (see Rule 44(5)); or, if he has no contrary interest but wishes to show cause against the sealing of a grant to the person warning, to issue and serve within the same eight-day period, a summons for directions (Rule 44(6) and see below).

The warning must state the interest of the person warning the caveat in the estate of the deceased, whether under a will or codicil or an intestacy, and requires the caveator to give particulars of any contrary interest in the estate. The warning, or a copy thereof, must be served on the caveator forthwith. Where the caveator has no interest contrary to that of the person warning but wishes to show cause against the sealing of the grant he may, within eight days of service of the warning upon him (inclusive of the day of service), or at any time thereafter provided no affidavit in accordance with Rule 44(12) has been filed (see paragraph 16.10 below), issue and serve a summons for directions (see Rule 44(6)). On the hearing of such summons the District Judge or Registrar may direct the caveat do cease to have effect (see Rule 44(7)).

Service of the warning is effected personally or by post at the address for service on the caveator given in the caveat. Service must be effected forthwith after issue. Rule 67 provides that service be effected in accordance with Rules of the Supreme Court O 65 r 5. This means that service may be effected through a document exchange box where the number is given in the caveat. Where the caveator and the person warning are represented, service may be by fax in accordance with para (2B) of Rules of the Supreme Court O 65 r 5. Service by fax is subject to the recipient solicitor or probate practitioner agreeing, and to service being effected as soon as possible thereafter by any of the other prescribed methods of service.

There is no fee payable on the issue of a warning.

Where the person warning and the caveator are persons of equal entitlement to a grant and each disputes the issue of the grant to the other, a summons to determine who shall take the grant may be issued for hearing before a District Judge at the Principal Registry or the Registrar of the District Probate Registry at which the grant application is pending (see Rule 27(6)).

Appearance to warning

16.9 If the caveator has an interest contrary to that of the person warning and maintains his opposition to the issue of the grant after he has been served with the warning, he may within the eight days prescribed (inclusive of the day of service), enter an appearance to the warning at the Leeds District Probate Registry, by lodging notice in Prescribed Form 5 (Form A1.72, page 441). An appearance may be entered after the prescribed time has expired, provided no affidavit has been filed pursuant to Rule 44(12) (see Rule 44(10) and paragraph 16.10 below). By entering an appearance, the caveator prevents a grant issuing to anyone other than himself, until the caveat is removed by order made on summons, or at the conclusion of a probate claim.

The person entering the appearance must be able to show that he has an interest contrary to that of the person warning, otherwise the entry of the appearance may be refused. Where the interest arises from a will or codicil, the date of the document(s) must be stated.

An appearance may be entered by post to, or the personal attendance of the caveator or his solicitor or probate practitioner at the Leeds District Probate Registry; the form of appearance may be obtained from the Registry. The appearance must be served forthwith on the person who warned the caveat.

There is no fee payable on entering an appearance to a warning.

Subsequent procedure

16.10 Where there is no interest shown contrary to that of the person warning, a summons for directions seeking to show cause why the grant should not issue to the person warning should be issued, returnable before a District Judge or Registrar. Such summons is normally issued out of the Registry in which the grant application is pending. However, under the provisions of Rule 62A – added with effect from 14 September 1998 – such summons may be heard and determined by any Registrar.

Where an appearance to a warning has been entered and the parties concerned reach a compromise, a summons for an order of discontinuance should be issued for hearing before the Registrar of the District Probate Registry at which the grant application is pending or a District Judge of the Principal Registry. If no agreement is reached, application under Part 57 of the Civil Procedure Rules should be issued in the Chancery Division.

Where no appearance is entered to the warning, and no summons has been issued for directions, the person warning may at any time after eight days of service of the warning upon the caveator (inclusive of the day of service), file an affidavit as to such service in the Leeds District Probate Registry (see Rule 44(12)); the caveat shall thereupon cease to have effect.

Any caveat in force when a summons for directions is issued will remain in force until the summons has been disposed of or until there is a direction that it shall cease to have effect. Similarly, any caveat in respect of which an appearance to a warning has been entered will remain in force until removed by order or a probate action is commenced.

The issue of any summons under Rule 44(6) must be recorded by the Registry at which it issues in the caveat index (Rule 44(9)).

Search for caveat

16.11   Before making application for a grant, or for any other reason, application may be made for a search of the computer index to check whether a caveat remains effective against the issue of a grant.

Application may be made by personal attendance or by letter to any Registry or Sub-Registry.

No fee is payable for the search but the fee for a copy document (£5) will be payable if a copy caveat is supplied.

Probate claims

16.12   On being informed of the commencement of a probate claim by the court in which it was commenced, the Leeds District Probate Registrar on behalf of the Senior District Judge of the Family Division gives notice of the commencement to every caveator (other than the claimant) in respect of each caveat then in force. Where a caveat is entered after the commencement of the claim, notice is given to the caveator of the existence of the claim (Rule 45(1) and (2)).

Unless otherwise directed by a District Judge of the Principal Registry, by order made on summons, the commencement of a probate claim operates to prevent the sealing of a grant, other than a grant pending determination of a probate claim under s 117 of the Supreme Court Act 1981, until application for a grant is made by the person shown to be entitled thereto by the decision of the court in such claim. On application for the grant by the person entitled pursuant to such decision of the court, any caveat entered by the claimant and any caveat in respect of which notice has been given ceases to have effect (Rule 45(4)).

No further caveat may be entered by or on behalf of a caveator whose caveat has ceased to have effect by virtue of Rule 45(4) without the leave of a District Judge of the Principal Registry (Rule 44(14)).

Probate claims may be commenced in the Central Office in London, the Chancery District Registries at Birmingham, Bristol, Cardiff, Leeds, Liverpool, Manchester, Newcastle-upon-Tyne and Preston. If the claim is suitable to be heard in a county court it may be issued in the county court at those places having a Chancery District Registry (see Practice Direction Part 57 Civil Procedure Rules 1998).

Citations

Definition and issue

16.13   A citation is a document issued by the court, at the instance of any person with an interest in the estate (who is usually the person entitled to a grant if the person cited renounces his title), calling upon another person to perform some act. A citation may issue from the Principal Registry or any District Probate Registry, and must be settled by a District Judge or Registrar before being issued.

Where a citation refers to a will, the original will, if available, must be lodged in the Registry before the citation issues. Every averment in a citation, and such other information as the District Judge or Registrar may require, must be verified by an affidavit sworn by the person issuing the citation. Where there are special circumstances the District Judge or Registrar may accept an affidavit sworn by the solicitor or probate practitioner acting for the person issuing the citation (Rule 46(2)).

As a general rule the court will not entertain the issue of a citation unless the citor has a beneficial interest in the estate.

Citation to take a grant of probate

16.14   Where an executor appointed in a will has intermeddled in his testator's estate, but has not proved the will within six months of the testator's death, Rule 47(3) provides that he may be cited to show cause why he should not be ordered to take a grant, by any other person with an interest in the testator's estate. Such a person is generally the, or one of the, residuary legatees and devisees, being the person next entitled to a grant after the executor. It is inappropriate for such an executor to be cited to *accept or refuse* a grant. The executor cannot renounce because he has intermeddled.

The citation may issue provided there are no proceedings pending to determine the validity of the will of the deceased. Generally, an executor who has intermeddled will be cited to take a grant. The affidavit in support of the citation should give details of the alleged intermeddling. Application may be made to pass over an intermeddling executor by order under s 116 of the Supreme Court Act 1981 (*Re Biggs' Estate [1966] P 118, [1966] 1 All ER 358, [1966] 2 WLR 536*) (see paragraph 5.28).

Citation to accept or refuse a grant

16.15 Rule 47(1) provides for any person who would be entitled to apply for a grant, but for there being a person or persons with a prior right of entitlement, to cite that person or persons to accept or refuse a grant. This applies irrespective of whether the deceased died testate or intestate. This form of citation is normally necessary where a person with a prior right of entitlement delays in applying for a grant or will not renounce his right to it.

All persons with a prior right to that of the citor, who do not renounce, must be cited. Where there is no executor appointed in a will, or any executor predeceased the deceased, a specific legatee or devisee may cite a residuary legatee or devisee to take or refuse a grant. A creditor must cite all persons with a beneficial entitlement to the (or to a share in the) estate. If there is no known kin, a creditor should cite the Treasury Solicitor or the solicitor for the Duchy of Cornwall as representatives of the Crown (as appropriate). However, the Crown will usually apply for the grant where there is or may be *bona vacantia* without having to be cited, on being informed that there is no known kin and provided that the estate is solvent.

By Rule 47(2) an executor to whom power was reserved in a grant may be cited to accept or refuse a grant by the executors who proved the will, to enable the chain of executorship (see paragraph 7.23) to continue.

If the whereabouts of the person with a prior entitlement to the grant is unknown, application may be made for an order under s 116 Supreme Court Act 1981 to pass over that person (see paragraph 5.27). Citation proceedings in these circumstances may be commenced with service by advertisement. However, as such service is usually ineffective and always expensive, citation is usually inappropriate.

Citation to propound a will or other testamentary document

16.16 Rule 48 provides for a person with an interest in an estate under an intestacy or earlier will to cite the executors and all persons interested under a later will to propound that will, that is to take the steps necessary to prove it.

The citation to propound a testamentary document must cite the executors appointed, if any, and all persons beneficially interested under the document. Such citation may be issued only at the instance of a person having an interest contrary to that of the executor(s) or other interested persons either under another testamentary document or under an intestacy (see Rule 48(1)).

The will in question, if in the custody of the citor, must be lodged in the

Registry in which the citation is to issue. If it is not held by the citor, its whereabouts must be accounted for.

It is often preferable, and easier for enforcement purposes, to apply for the issue of a *subpoena* to produce the document (see paragraph 16.21 below).

Issuing a citation

16.17   Before a citation may issue, a caveat must be entered. Unless otherwise directed by a District Judge of the Principal Registry, any caveat in force at the commencement of citation proceedings will remain in force, unless withdrawn by a caveator who has not entered an appearance to a warning (see Rule 44(11)) and subject to the provisions of Rule 61 (which provides for the court to direct any application be made by summons), until application is made for a grant by the person shown to be entitled thereto by the decision of a court in such proceedings.

On application for the grant any caveat entered by a party who had notice of the proceedings ceases to have effect (Rule 46(3)). Except by leave of a District Judge of the Principal Registry no further caveat may be entered by or on behalf of any caveator whose caveat has ceased to have effect by virtue of an order for a grant made in citation proceedings (Rule 44(14)).

The following documents must be lodged in the Probate Department of the Principal Registry, or a District Probate Registry, or sent to the Registry by post, for the citation to be settled by a District Judge or Registrar:

(a)   the draft citation;

(b)   any will referred to in the draft citation, except where the will is not in the citor's possession and the District Judge or Registrar is satisfied that it is impracticable to lodge it;

(c)   a draft affidavit by the citor setting out the facts of the case and the necessity for the citation. Every averment in the citation must be verified by the affidavit. A District Judge or Registrar may, where there are special circumstances, allow the affidavit to be made by the citor's legal representative (see Rule 46(1), (3) and (5)).

Once settled, the draft documents are returned to the citor's legal representative for the affidavit to be sworn and a fair copy of the citation prepared.

The sworn affidavit and the fair copy citation, together with the drafts, should be sent to the Registry for issue. A fee of £10 is payable for settling a citation, but there is no fee payable on issue. After signing by the District Judge or Registrar, and sealing, the citation will be returned for copies to be prepared for service.

If it is known that a life or minority interest arises in the estate which will require two grantees, the citor should state who the co-grantee is to be and his entitlement to apply. Alternatively, application may be made, when it is known who is to apply, for a District Judge's or Registrar's direction that the grant issue to a sole grantee under s 114(2) Supreme Court Act 1981 or for a co-grantee to be appointed under Rule 25 (see paragraph 5.26).

Service of citation

16.18   Unless otherwise directed by a District Judge or Registrar, a citation must be served personally on the citee. The citation must, after service has been effected, be endorsed with a certificate of service. Where the circumstances of the case are such that personal service cannot be effected, a District Judge or Registrar may, on application made in this respect, direct another mode of service. Where advertisement is ordered, directions as to the newspaper(s) to be used, the number of insertions, and the time to be allowed for entering an appearance will also be given (see Rule 46(4)). It is unlikely that the court will direct service by advertisement unless it is assured that there is a more than reasonable chance that such advertisement will come to the notice of the citee.

Where the citee is under a disability, for example he is a minor, application should be made, applying Order 80 of the Rules of the Supreme Court, for the appointment of a guardian *ad litem* to accept service and thereafter act on the citee's behalf.

Where a creditor wishes to issue a citation in a case where there are no known blood relations of the deceased, the citation should be served on the Treasury Solicitor or the Solicitor for the Duchy of Cornwall or Lancaster who may wish to apply as *bona vacantia* (see paragraph 9.45).

Where the citee is resident abroad the citation should be served in the normal way except that where he is represented by a solicitor or other agent resident within the jurisdiction, a copy should also be served on him. The affidavit of service should indicate he has also been served or, if it be the case, that no other person has been served.

The affidavit of service must be made by the server and show the manner in which the citee was identified. The original citation, endorsed with a certificate as to service, should be exhibited to the affidavit.

Appearance to citation

16.19   Within eight days of service, inclusive of the day of service, or, if service is effected by advertisement, within the time directed from the date of the advertisement, the citee must enter an appearance in the Registry from which the citation issued. The form of appearance

(Prescribed Form 6) (Form A1.75; see page 444) may be obtained from the Registry.

Subsequent procedure

16.20

(i) *Where the citation is to take a grant of probate* and the citee enters an appearance, he may apply, on affidavit showing that he is willing to take the grant, to a District Judge or Registrar for an order that a grant be made to him (Rule 47(4)).

● Where an appearance is entered by the citee but he takes no further action within a reasonable time thereafter, the citor may apply on summons to the District Judge or Registrar of the Registry from which the citation issued, supported by an affidavit setting out the facts of the matter (for example that the citee has been served and appeared but has not proceeded). The summons may ask for an order that the citee apply for a grant within a specified period, or that in default thereof the grant be made to the citor or any other specified person. The summons and affidavit must be served on the citee (see Rule 47(7)).

● If no appearance is entered to the citation and the time for so doing has expired, the citor may, by summons supported by affidavit, seek an order that the citee do take the grant within a specified time, or for an order that the grant be made to himself or to some other specified person. Again, the summons and affidavit must be served on the citee (see Rule 47(5)(c) and (7)(c)). An affidavit of service of the citation on the citee must be lodged (Rule 47(6)).

(ii) *Where the citation is to accept or refuse a grant* and the citee enters an appearance and is willing to take a grant, he may apply to a District Judge or Registrar of the Registry from which the citation issued on affidavit for an order that the grant be made to him (Rule 47(4)).

● If the citee enters an appearance but does not proceed, or if he does not appear, the citor may apply by summons, which must be served on the citee, supported by affidavit setting out the details of service, seeking an order for a grant to himself (Rule 47(5)(a) and (7)(a)). Where the citee renounces his right, application for a grant may be made by the citor, if entitled thereto, without taking any further step in the citation proceedings. The caveat entered by the citor will not prevent the grant issuing to him.

● Where the citee was an executor to whom power had been reserved in a previous grant, and the citee appears but does not proceed, or does not enter an appearance, the citor must apply by summons seeking an order striking out that appearance (if any) and for the previous grant to be noted that that executor has been cited and that all his rights in respect of the executorship have ceased (see Rule 47(5)(b) and (7)(b)).

(iii)

- *Where the citation is to propound a testamentary document* and the citee does not appear, the citor may apply to a District Judge or Registrar of the Registry from which the citation issued for an order for a grant as if the testamentary document sought to be propounded were invalid; or where the citee appears but does not proceed, the citor may apply to a District Judge or Registrar of the Registry from which the citation issued by summons, which must be served on every person cited, supported by an affidavit showing that the citation was duly served, for an order that the grant be made to the person entitled as if the document sought to be propounded were invalid.

- Where the citee appears to the citation and wishes to commence an action, a writ against the citor must be issued in the Chancery Division.

Subpoena

16.21   Rule 50(1) provides that application may be made by summons under s 122 of the Supreme Court Act 1981 (see paragraph 5.65) for an order requiring a person to attend before a High Court Judge of the Family Division to be examined as to his knowledge of any testamentary document. It is now common practice for the initial attendance to be fixed before a District Judge or Registrar. Application for the order to attend is made to a District Judge of the Principal Registry or any District Probate Registrar.

The order will fix an initial date before the District Judge or Registrar who may then direct an attendance before a High Court Judge. If an order to attend is made, the date, time and place of such attendance before the Judge will be fixed on application to the Clerk of the Rules in the Royal Courts of Justice. Application for such an order may not be made where a probate claim has been commenced.

Rule 50(2) provides that application may be made to a District Judge or Registrar *ex parte* on affidavit under s 123 of the Supreme Court Act 1981 for a subpoena to issue requiring any person who it would appear has in his possession, custody or power any document which purports to be a testamentary document, to lodge the document in the Registry from which the subpoena issued.

The affidavit must set out the grounds of the application. For a form of affidavit, see Form A1.63, page 431; and for a form of subpoena, see

Form A1.73, page 441. The subpoena, properly endorsed with a penal notice in accordance with Order 45 Rule 7(4) of the Rules of the Supreme Court, must be served personally.

Where the person subpoena'd does not have the purported testamentary document in his possession or control, he should file an affidavit accordingly in the Registry from which the subpoena issued. Failure to comply with the subpoena is enforceable by summons to a Judge issued out of the Principal Registry for the defaulter's committal to prison for contempt. Where the will is in his possession, it may be lodged in the Registry personally or by post (the latter being at the sender's risk).

All summonses and applications in respect of citations are made to the District Judge or Registrar of the Registry from which the citation issued (see also CHAPTER 17).

Chapter 17

Applications on notice; removal of personal representatives; inventory and account

Applications on notice

17.1   The Civil Procedure Rules 1998 do not apply to applications made under the provisions of the Non-Contentious Probate Rules 1987 save in respect of the assessment of the costs of such applications. The Rules of the Supreme Court as in force on 26 April 1999 continue to apply. Applications requiring a hearing are made by summons supported by affidavit.

Jurisdiction and tribunal

17.2   Rule 61 empowers a District Judge or Registrar to direct any matter be brought before a Registrar or Judge by summons in chambers or in open court. Where a District Probate Registrar requires a matter to be brought before a Judge by summons, he must send a statement of the matter to a District Judge of the Principal Registry; the District Judge may refer the matter to a Judge; direct the matter be heard by a District Judge; or refer it back to the Registrar for him to determine (Rule 61(1) applying Rule 7(2)).

Generally, a District Probate Registrar has the same powers as a District Judge of the Principal Registry. However, an application under Rules 44(13) (except where application to discontinue is made by consent) and (14) and 45(3), which relate to caveats and their effect during the pendency of a probate action or citation proceedings, must be brought by summons before a District Judge of the Principal Registry. Similarly, summonses where there is a contest over the exclusion of offensive words contained in a will (see paragraph 2.60) are heard by District Judges of the Principal Registry. Applications which may be brought before a District Probate Registrar on summons are:

  (i)   a dispute between persons entitled to a grant in the same degree, under Rule 27(6);

 (ii)   for leave to sue, under s 120(3) of the Supreme Court Act 1981, a surety on a guarantee under Rule 40;

(iii)   for directions in a matter where a caveat has been entered and warned and the caveator, although having no interest contrary to the person warned, wishes to show cause against the sealing of a grant, under Rule 44(6);

(iv) where an appearance to a warning to a caveat has been entered and application to discontinue the caveat is made by consent, under Rule 44(13);

(v) where a citation has issued calling on an executor who has inter-meddled in the deceased's estate, for an order that the executor, or the citor or some other person do take a grant within a specified period, under Rule 47(5)(c) or Rule 47(7)(c);

(vi) where a citation has issued and the citee has entered an appearance thereto but failed to take a grant or prosecute his case with reason-able diligence, to strike out the appearance or for such other order as is appropriate to the particular case, under Rule 47(7)(b);

(vii) where a citation to propound a will has issued and the citee has entered an appearance but fails to propound the will with reasonable diligence, for an order for a grant as if the will were invalid, under Rule 48(2)(b);

(viii) for an order requiring a person to bring in a will or attend for exam-ination under Rule 50;

(ix) for an order requiring an executor or administrator to provide an inventory and account of the deceased's estate and his administration under Rule 61(2).

Rule 62A, added with effect from 14 September 1998, provides for a District Probate Registrar to hear and determine any matter which would normally fall to be dealt with by another Registrar.

An order for hearing at another Registry may be made by the court of its own motion or an application by a party. Where the circumstances justify, a Registrar may hear and dispose of any matter without there being any formal application.

Any summons seeking an order or directions under the above headings must issue out of the Registry in which it is to be heard (Rule 61(3)). A District Probate Registrar may make any order for costs he deems fit (Rule 63).

Where an order for costs is sought against any party, it must be claimed in the summons.

Issue and service of summons

17.3   A summons for hearing by a District Judge or Registrar shall issue out of the Registry in which it is to be heard. A summons for hearing by a Judge must issue out of the Principal Registry (Rule 61(3) and (4)). A District Judge of the Principal Registry may give directions as to the person or persons to be served with a summons for hearing in that Registry or by a Judge. A District Probate Registrar may give such directions on a summons issued out of his Registry for hearing by him (see also the reference to new Rule 62A above).

The summons should be lodged in duplicate at the Registry from which it is to issue. One copy of the summons will be retained in the Registry; the other will be endorsed with the time, date and place of the hearing, sealed and returned to the applicant's solicitors. Where counsel is to appear, the summons should be endorsed accordingly.

The summons should be supported by affidavit by the applicant setting out the facts relied on to support the application.

Unless otherwise directed, or service is dispensed with by order of a Registrar, District Judge or Judge, a summons must be served on all persons required to be served not less than two clear days before the day fixed for the hearing. Unless otherwise directed service is effected in accordance with the Rules of the Supreme Court O 65 r 5 at the appropriate person's address for service, or, if he has no known current address for service, his last known address. Service may also now be effected through a document exchange or by fax (see paragraph 16.8) (see Rules 66 and 67). No fee is payable on the issue of a summons.

Consent applications

17.4   Where the parties agree the terms of the order, a consent summons may be lodged. The summons must be endorsed with the consent of all parties and signed by the parties or their legal representatives. Unless the court otherwise directs, no attendance on such a summons will be necessary.

Court orders

17.5   All orders made on summonses dealt with in the Principal or a District Probate Registry are drawn up and served by the Registry. Generally, the order will be served by post; where any order is required to be served personally (usually for enforcement proceedings), it is for the successful party to arrange such service.

Taxation of costs

17.6   Rule 60 was substituted by the Non-Contentious Probate (Amendment) Rules 2003 in respect of proceedings commenced after 24 February 2003. Parts 43, 44 (save 44.9–44.12), 47 and 48 of the Civil Procedure Rules 1998 now apply to costs in non-contentious probate proceedings.

Every bill of costs (save a bill delivered by a solicitor to his client which falls to be assessed under the Solicitors Act 1974) shall be referred for assessment:

(i)   where the order was made by a District Judge of the Principal Registry, to a District Judge of the Principal Registry, a Costs Judge or a Costs Officer of the Supreme Court Costs Office authorised within Rule 43.2(1)(d)(iii) or (iv) of the 1998 Rules;

(ii) where the order for assessment was made by a District Probate Registrar, to that Registrar, or, if it is not possible for that Registrar to deal with the costs, to such person in (i) above as is appropriate.

Fee 10 of the Non-Contentious Probate Fees Order refers to fees payable for assessment contained in the Supreme Court Fees Order 1999.

Any appeal against the decision of a Costs Officer as defined above will lie to a Costs Judge. An appeal against the decision of a Costs Judge, District Judge or Registrar lies to a Judge of the High Court (see below).

Appeals from District Judges or Registrars

17.7   Any person aggrieved by a decision or requirement of a District Judge or Registrar may appeal against the decision or requirement to a Judge. Such appeal is brought by summons issued out of the Principal Registry.

Where any person, other than the appellant, appeared or was represented at the hearing, the summons appealing the District Judge or Registrar's decision or requirement must be issued within seven days from the giving of the decision or requirement, and served on all persons who appeared or were represented not less than two days before the return date (see Rule 65).

Where notes of evidence are required, it is for the parties' representatives to bespeak them. The Registrar's Direction of 21 February 1985 [1985] 1 All ER 896 applies to obtaining notes of evidence.

Enforcement by committal

17.8   Application to enforce an order by committal is made by summons issued out of the Principal Registry, returnable before a Judge of the Family Division. The provisions of the Rules of the Supreme Court O 52 r 4 as in force on 26 April 1999 continue to apply to such applications. Application may be made for committal to enforce an order, *inter alia*, directing an intermeddling executor to take probate; for failure to comply with a subpoena to bring in a testamentary document; for failure to attend to be examined as to a testamentary document; or for failure to deliver an inventory or account of the administration of the estate.

Inventory and account

Duties of personal representative

17.9   Section 25 of the Administration of Estates Act 1925 provides that every personal representative of a deceased person shall be under a duty to:

(a)   collect and get in the real and personal estate of the deceased and administer it according to law;

(b)   when required to do so by the court, exhibit on oath in the court a full inventory of the estate and when so required render an account of the administration of the estate to the court;

(c)   when required to do so by the High Court, deliver up the grant of probate or administration of the estate to that court.

Every oath to lead a grant must contain a statement in the terms of s 25.

The personal representative of a deceased person is under no duty to distribute the estate until a year has elapsed since the death (s 44 Administration of Estates Act 1925).

Who may apply

17.10   Where a person beneficially interested in the estate as a legatee under a will, as a person sharing under an intestacy, or as a creditor, requires details of the administration of the estate and such details are not supplied, or are insufficiently supplied, by the personal representative, and provided a reasonable period has elapsed since the grant of representation issued, he may issue a summons for the delivery of an inventory and account of the estate. There is no specific definition of 'reasonable' time. Bearing in mind the need to obtain details of creditors and other possible claims against the estate, it would not be expected for a summons to issue within six months of the grant's issue. This does, however, depend on the particular circumstances of the particular case.

Application is made on summons to a District Judge of the Principal Registry or the Registrar of the District Probate Registry from which the grant issued pursuant to Rule 61(2). The application should be supported by an affidavit.

Rule 61(1) provides that where a District Probate Registrar is of the opinion that the matter should be brought before a Judge, he shall send a statement of the matter in question to a District Judge of the Principal Registry for directions. The District Judge, if satisfied that it is appropriate for the matter to be determined by a Judge, shall direct a summons to issue accordingly (see paragraph 17.2 above for the practice relating to applications made by summons).

Rule 62A, in force from 14 September 1998, provides for a Registrar to exercise the jurisdiction of another. Although it is usual for the summons to be issued out of the Registry which issued the grant, the summons may be heard and determined by another Registrar (at another Registry, perhaps more convenient to the parties).

Failure to deliver an inventory and account in the time prescribed in the order is enforceable by committal (see paragraph 17.8 above).

The court's jurisdiction is limited to ordering the delivery of an inventory and account of the estate. It is not for the court to make any other order or direction relating to the estate's administration.

Removal of personal representative

17.11 It may be appropriate for a personal representative (either executor or administrator) to be removed from office and another substituted where there has been a failure to administer or properly administer the estate. Section 50 of the Administration of Justice Act 1985 provides that the High Court may, in its discretion:

'(a) appoint a person (in this section called a substituted personal representative) to act as personal representative of the deceased in place of the existing personal representative or representatives of the deceased or any of them; or

(b) if there are two or more existing personal representatives of the deceased terminate the appointment of one or more, but not all, of those persons.'

Where the court appoints a person to act as a substituted personal representative then:

'(a) if that person is appointed to act with an executor or executors the appointment shall (except for the purpose of including him in any chain of representation) constitute him executor of the deceased as from the date of the appointment; and

(b) in any other case the appointment shall constitute that person administrator of the deceased's estate as from the date of the appointment.'

Application under s 50 may be made by or on behalf of a beneficiary of the deceased's estate, a beneficiary being defined as a person beneficially interested in the estate whether under a will or the rules relating to intestacy.

Application is made by claim under Part 57 of the Civil Procedure Rules 1998 to the Chancery Division of the High Court. The court may, if it thinks fit, treat an application made under s 50 as an application for the appointment of a judicial trustee under the Judicial Trustees Act 1896. A certified copy of the grant or the original must be lodged with the claim. Written evidence to support the claim must also be lodged.

Unless a substituted personal representative is requested, the court cannot remove a sole personal representative, as this would leave the estate unrepresented.

Chapter 18

Amendment, revocation, impounding and notation of grants

Amendment

Official errors

18.1   Where an error of a minor nature insufficient to require revocation is discovered in a grant after it has been sealed, and the error was made by the Registry, the grant, and any copies which have issued, should be returned to the Registry from which it issued. Provided it is returned within 28 days of issue and has not been registered, that is, used as authority to receive assets and endorsed by the asset holder, a new grant in the form of an original will be produced correcting the error. No order of a District Judge or Registrar is necessary.

Applicant's error

18.2   Where the amendment required was not occasioned by an official error, application is made to the District Judge or Registrar of the Registry from which the grant issued (in the Principal Registry, the application should be lodged with the Probate Manager), *ex parte* on affidavit by the grantee(s), setting out:

(a)   the nature of the error;

(b)   how the error occurred; and

(c)   the amendment required.

Where the amendment required is of a minor nature, the court may accept application by letter rather than formal application on affidavit.

Error in deceased's name or address

18.3   Where the error is in the name of the deceased and provided it is only one of mis-spelling a forename or the omission of a second forename, or in the address or date of death, the grant may be amended. Where the error in the name is of a more serious nature, for example an incorrect surname, the grant may be revoked, or the court may exercise its discretion and allow amendment.

Application may be made for amendment to show an alias or alternate name of the deceased in addition to his true name, where for instance it is found that assets were held in a different name (see also Rule 9). Unless there is difficulty in realising the asset, there is no requirement to have the grant amended.

Error in grantee's name and address

18.4   Generally, a grant will be amended to show the correct name of the grantee and his address provided the reason for the error and need to amend can be satisfactorily explained to the District Judge or Registrar.

Other amendments

18.5   Other amendments such as the alteration of a limitation are subject to the District Judge's or Registrar's discretion but may be effected in the normal way.

Where a full grant has issued and there is settled land but the original grant failed to carry the notation that settled land was not included, the original grant may be amended. Before effecting the amendment the District Judge or Registrar will need to be satisfied that there is settled land and that a grant is to be taken to administer that land. Under no circumstances should a grant be amended otherwise than by the Registry. For the form of affidavit of facts requesting an amendment to a grant see Form A1.65, page 432.

Procedure

18.6   The original grant, and any copies, should be returned with the affidavit or, if acceptable to the court, letter. Where the amendment is to the deceased's name or date of death, a further search, with the correct information, will be made in the index of pending grant applications. Rule 41 provides that, if satisfied, the District Judge or Registrar may order the grant to be amended.

The District Judge or Registrar will not order amendment without the grantee's consent except in exceptional circumstances. If returned within 28 days, a new grant in the form of an original will be issued. Where more than 28 days have elapsed since issue, the grant will be amended in red ink by the Registry in accordance with the order and signed by the Registrar or a Probate Officer.

Error in the value of the estate

18.7   Should there have been an error in the Inland Revenue Account, and further estate has been discovered, necessitating the notation of the grant with amended value(s) of the estate, a corrective Account in IHT Form D3 (see paragraph 12.47) and the original grant should be sent to IR Capital Taxes. The notation will be effected by IR Capital Taxes. It is not the practice of the Probate Registries to amend the figures shown on the grant for the values of the estate; such amendment, where necessary, will be effected by IR Capital Taxes. It will only be necessary to amend the figures when the original figures create a difficulty with an asset holder on administration.

Where property has been included in an Inland Revenue Account in error there is generally no need to amend the grant. Similarly, where the values deposed to in the oath, in a case where no Inland Revenue Account was necessary, are found to be in error, there is no need for the grant to be amended. No extra fee or refund (as appropriate) will be occasioned where a corrective Account has to be lodged.

Where an error in a will or codicil which has been accepted for proof is discovered, provided the error does not invalidate the document, application may be made under s 20 Administration of Justice Act 1982 for rectification (see paragraph 5.20). Where the error or omission in the will is of a more serious nature, the grant may have to be revoked (see below).

Codicil subsequently found

18.8   Where a codicil to a will is found after probate of that will has been granted, the practice is to grant probate of the codicil alone rather than amend the grant. This can only be done where the codicil does not alter the appointment of executors or otherwise affect the grantee's title to the grant. See also paragraphs 2.68–2.74.

Revocation

18.9   Section 25 of the Supreme Court Act 1981 provides for the High Court to issue grants of representation. The same section enables the court to revoke grants.

When necessary

18.10   Where:

- there is an error in the grant which is serious enough to warrant revocation;

- the grant should not have issued because a caveat had been entered;

- the grantee had died before the date of issue;

- the grant had issued prematurely;

- the grant was obtained on false facts (for example that the deceased died intestate and a valid will is found or there is closer kin than the person who took the grant);

- a later will is discovered;

- the will is found to be invalid after admission to proof;

- following an order giving leave to swear death, the presumed deceased is alive; or

- one of the grantees becomes mentally incapable of administering his affairs,

the grant will be revoked.

Where further testamentary documents are found the nature of those documents will determine whether revocation is necessary. Clearly, the validity of these documents must be established before the court will consider revocation. If a later valid will is found which revokes an earlier will which has been admitted to probate, revocation will be necessary.

However, where a codicil to a proved will is found, revocation will only be necessary if the codicil alters the appointment of executors. Where it does not alter the appointment of executors, probate of the codicil alone may be obtained as a separate grant.

Procedure

18.11   Application for revocation is made *ex parte* on affidavit by the grantee or person now entitled, in similar manner to an application to amend the grant. Where application is not made by the grantee the applicant must be prepared to apply for and take the new grant. Notice may need to be given to the grantee if the District Judge or Registrar so directs.

If the circumstances are such that the original grantee's or proposed applicant's professional adviser can best speak to the facts, the District Judge or Registrar may allow the affidavit to be made by him. The affidavit setting out the facts, and the original grant, should be lodged with the Registry from which it issued. Rule 41 provides that, if satisfied, the District Judge or Registrar will order revocation, but only in exceptional circumstances will this be ordered without the grantee's consent. Where application is not made by the grantee, his consent should be exhibited to the affidavit. The Probate Registries now take a more pragmatic view of revocation of grants because of the expense to the estate of an application for revocation in the Chancery Division or application under s 50 of the Administration of Justice Act 1985 to remove an administrator. Where there is clear evidence that the grant should not have issued or, in the new prevailing circumstances, that the grantee(s) should no longer be entrusted with administering the estate, then revocation will be considered.

If the person having possession of the grant refuses to release it to the court, he may be cited to produce it (see paragraph 16.17 *et seq* for procedure on citations) or the court may revoke of its motion where the original grant is not handed in.

Where the grantee refuses to apply for or consent to revocation then, unless it is a case in which it is now clear he had no title to the grant, application for revocation must be made in the Chancery Division.

Revocation of the court's own action

18.12 Section 121 of the Supreme Court Act 1981 provides for the court, of its own motion, to call in a grant for revocation where it appears there is an error, or the grant should not have issued. The court will only revoke if satisfied that it would have done so if an application for revocation had been made by an interested party. The court may also revoke the grant where it is not possible for the grant to be called in. Similarly, the resealing of a grant, which was resealed under the Colonial Probates Acts 1892 and 1927 may be cancelled (not revoked, revocation being a matter for the court which issued the original grant) where the resealing was done in error.

Grantee wishing to be relieved of his duties

18.13 Any personal representative properly constituted under a grant of representation may only be relieved of the duties of his position for good reason. Where such person is not incapable of administering his affairs by virtue of mental incapacity but for other reasons does not wish to continue his administration of the estate, he may apply for revocation. Only in exceptional circumstances will such an application be allowed. A possible solution would be for the grantee to appoint an attorney to complete the administration on his behalf.

Where, after taking the grant, a conflict of interest arises between the grantee and the estate then the court will consider revocation.

Death of grantee

18.14 Where revocation is necessary because one of several executors who applied for a grant died before it issued, and the Registry was not aware of the death when the grant was sealed, the affidavit of facts for the order revoking the grant may also be used as the oath to lead the new grant, providing the new grant is to be made to the surviving executors.

The above does not apply when the grant was one of administration, although in this case the District Judge or Registrar does have discretion to dispense with an oath to lead the new grant, if the new grant is to be made to the surviving grantee(s) of the original grant, and he/they lodge consent(s) to the new grant being made in which he/they refer to the original oath to lead the grant.

Where the grant issued to a sole applicant who died before the grant was sealed, application for revocation and a new oath by the person now entitled must be lodged.

Where the applicant died on the day the grant was sealed evidence of the time of death will be necessary to determine whether the applicant died before or after the sealing took place. Generally, a grant is deemed to have been sealed at 10 am on the morning of the date it issues.

Where a grant issues to a sole grantee who then dies, or the last surviving grantee dies after the grant has issued but without completing the administration of the estate, application may be made either for a grant of double probate to an executor to whom power had been reserved; or for letters of administration (with or without will annexed) *de bonis non* (see paragraph 10.8). The grant of double probate will be a grant in respect of the whole estate. The grant of letters of administration (with or without will annexed) *de bonis non* will issue in respect of the unadministered estate. The original grant will not be revoked.

Incapacity of grantee

Sole grantee

18.15   Where the sole, or last surviving, grantee becomes mentally incapable of managing his affairs and unable to complete the administration, it is not necessary for that grant to be revoked, nor will it be impounded.

Application may be made by an executor to whom power had been reserved for a grant of double probate, or for letters of administration with or without will *de bonis non* by a person of equal entitlement to the original grantee, or to a person entitled in the order of priority prescribed by Rule 35 (see paragraph 10.60).

Evidence of incapacity is given on affidavit, exhibiting the medical evidence, by the proposed grantee. That affidavit may also be used as the oath to lead the new grant.

Several grantees

18.16   Where, however, one of several grantees becomes mentally incapable, application must be made for revocation and a new grant applied for by the person(s) then entitled.

Where the original grant was of probate, the new grant (of double probate) will be to the capable executor(s), and power will be reserved to the incapable executor on regaining his capacity.

Where the original was a grant of letters of administration, the new grant, whether made to a person or persons of equal entitlement (see Rule 22, and paragraph 9.28) will be a grant *de bonis non*. If the new grantee or one of them is entitled in a lower capacity, the grant will issue for the use and benefit of the incapable former grantee and be limited until further representation be granted or in such other way as the District Judge or Registrar may direct (see also Rule 35 and paragraph 10.60).

Order for revocation

18.17 Whether revocation is ordered on application or by the court of its own motion, an order will be drawn by the Registry. Any new grant will be endorsed with a note of the former revoked grant.

Impounding

18.18 Where a sole or last surviving grantee becomes incapable of managing his affairs and continuing the administration of the estate, whether he is an executor or administrator, on an application for the new grant, whether or not the new proposed grantee is authorised to apply by the Court of Protection, the original grant need not now be impounded.

Where impounding is considered necessary, application is made by the proposed new grantee, on affidavit including medical evidence of the incapacity, to the District Judge or Registrar of the Registry from which the grant issued. The original grant should be lodged with the affidavit. If satisfied, the District Judge or Registrar will make an order accordingly and allow the application for the new grant to proceed. The affidavit to lead the District Judge's or Registrar's order may, at the District Judge's or Registrar's discretion, also be used as the oath to lead the new grant.

The new grant will be of administration *de bonis non* (see paragraph 10.8) and will unless otherwise directed be limited for the use and benefit of the original grantee and until further representation be granted. It will cover the estate of the deceased then remaining unadministered.

Where the original grantee recovers his capacity the original grant may be released on application therefor on evidence, usually on affidavit with medical evidence, of the recovery of capacity. If satisfied the District Judge or Registrar will direct the original grant be released together with the second grant, the latter grant being endorsed with a note that it is no longer effective.

Where the sole or last surviving executor who took a grant loses his capacity to administer and dies without recovering his capacity, any impounded grant may be revived by his executors wishing to perpetuate a chain of executorship (see paragraph 7.23).

Notation

Inheritance (Provision for Family and Dependants) Act 1975

18.19   Where application is made under s 2 of the Act in the Chancery Division, Family Division or a county court, the original grant should be lodged with the court (Part 57 Civil Procedure Rules 1998 Practice Direction para 18.1). On making a *final* order in these proceedings, the court will forward the original grant and a copy of the order to the Probate Manager of the Principal Registry for a memorandum of the order to be endorsed. The memorandum is filed at the Registry which issued the grant, with the original will or, where there is no will, with the oath which led the grant of administration. A copy of the memorandum is endorsed on or permanently attached to the original grant and on the record copy grant held by the Probate Records Centre or the issuing Registry (the Registries now only retain files for the last two years). The original grant, after notation, is returned to the court which made the order under s 2 for return to the grantee (see s 19(3) of the Act and para 18.2 of the Practice Direction).

Additional administrator

18.20   Where an additional or substituted administrator is appointed, under s 114(4) of the Supreme Court Act 1981 (minimum number of grantees where a life or minority interest arises in the deceased's estate), the order making the appointment and the original grant should be lodged at the Registry from which the grant issued so that a notation of the order and appointment may be made on the original grant and the record copy. After notation the grant is returned to the grantees.

Redemption of life interest

18.21   Rule 56 provides that where a surviving spouse who is the sole personal representative of the deceased is entitled to a life interest in part of the residuary estate and such residuary estate is property then in possession, he may elect, under s 47A of the Administration of Estates Act 1925, to have that life interest redeemed.

Notice of the election (see Form A1.79, page 447) must be given within twelve months of the grant of representation issuing, in writing to the Senior District Judge of the Principal Registry or the District Probate Registry from which the grant issued. Where the grant issued from a

District Probate Registry, the notice of election must be given in duplicate. Where such an election is made, the original grant must be lodged with the notice, for a note thereof to be endorsed on that grant and the record copy. After notation the grant is returned to the grantee.

Administration orders

18.22   An administration order may be made under the Insolvency Act 1986 which transfers the administration of the deceased's insolvent estate from the personal representative named in the grant to the person named in the order.

A copy of any such order is sent to the Probate Manager of the Principal Registry for a notation to be made on the record copy grant. Where the grant issued from a District Probate Registry, the Probate Manager will notify that Registry of the order for a notation to be made on its record copy grant (see Part 57 Civil Procedure Rules 1998 Practice Direction).

Retraction of renunciation

18.23   Where leave is given to an executor who had renounced probate of his testator's will to retract his renunciation, the original grant will be noted to this effect. Notation is effected at the Registry from which the grant issued. The original grant will remain in the Registry from which it issued unless otherwise directed by the District Judge or Registrar.

Chapter 19

Engrossments, copies and searches

Engrossments

Copy to perpetuate

19.1 Every grant of probate or letters of administration (with will annexed) issues with a copy (usually a photocopy) of the will attached. Additional copies of the will are produced for record purposes.

Rule 11(1) provides that in a case where the District Judge or Registrar considers a facsimile copy (*sic*) of the original will would not be satisfactory for purposes of record, he may direct an engrossment (that is, a copy made up by retyping or rewriting) suitable for facsimile reproduction to be lodged by the applicant. This may be appropriate where the typing or writing of the will is faded, or it was written in pencil, or it has been folded so that parts are barely legible and the copying process cannot adequately reproduce the terms of the will in legible form.

Omitting words

19.2 Where there are alterations to the will, or it contains offensive or libellous words which are not admissible to proof, or a District Judge or Registrar has made an order under s 20(1) of the Administration of Justice Act 1982 directing that a will be rectified (see paragraphs 5.20 and 5.21), Rule 11(2) requires that an engrossment be supplied, omitting the excepted words or including or excluding words of rectification pursuant to the District Judge's or Registrar's order.

The engrossed copy must reproduce the punctuation, spelling, abbreviations, spacing and division into paragraphs of the original will. It should be made book-wise on durable paper, following continuously from page to page on both sides of the paper (see Rule 11(3)).

Inspection of wills and other documents

19.3 Section 124 of the Supreme Court Act 1981 provides that all original wills and other documents which are under the control of the High

Court in the Principal or any District Probate Registry must be deposited and preserved in such places as the Lord Chancellor shall direct, and that such documents shall, subject to the control of the High Court and to the Probate Rules, be open to inspection.

Rule 58 provides that a will or other document referred to in s 124 shall not be open to inspection if, in the opinion of a District Judge or Registrar, such inspection would be undesirable or otherwise inappropriate. It follows therefore that if a document is not open for inspection, no copy of it may be supplied.

A fee of £15 is payable for the inspection of any document; see Fee 7 in APPENDIX 2.

Copies

Wills and grants

19.4   Section 125 of the Supreme Court Act 1981 provides for office copies and sealed and certified copies of the whole, or any part, of a will open to inspection under s 124 of the Act, or of any grant of representation, to be obtained on payment of the prescribed fees (see Fee 8 in APPENDIX 2) from:

(i)   the Registry in which the will or documents relating to the grant are kept; or

(ii) the Principal Registry, if the will or other document relating to the grant is kept at a place other than a Registry; or

(iii) with the approval of the Senior District Judge of the Family Division, from the Principal Registry, where the will was proved in, or the grant issued from, a District Probate Registry.

All records have now been transferred to the Probate Records Centre. Each Registry retains the previous two years' records in addition to the current year.

Each Registry has online access to the Records Centre and copies of wills and grants may be requested as set out below.

It will save time for an applicant who knows that the will was proved in, or that the grant issued from, a District Probate Registry to apply direct to that Registry. If the Registry is not known, application should be made to York Probate sub-Registry, 1st Floor, Castle Chambers, Clifford Street, York YO1 9RG, DX 720629 York 21.

Applicants who attend in person at the Principal Registry may obtain copies of wills and grants from the Principal Registry regardless of the fact that the will may have been proved in, or the grant issued from, a District Probate Registry.

Where the records have to be searched, a fee of £3 is payable for each four-year period searched after the first four years.

Office copies

19.5 The copy will be a photocopy and will, unless a sealed and certified copy is required, be issued and marked as an office copy, and bear the seal of the Registry from which it issues.

Sealed and certified copies

19.6 A sealed and certified copy will be authenticated as a true copy by the signature of the District Judge or Registrar of the Registry from which it issues (see Rule 59).

Exemplifications

19.7 An exemplification (that is an exact copy of the will (if any) and a virtually exact copy of the grant) will be signed by the District Judge or Registrar of the Registry from which it issued.

Special copies

19.8 Special copies of grants and wills signed by the District Judge or Registrar of the Registry from which the grant issued and countersigned by the President of the Family Division, pursuant to the Hague Convention on authenticated official documents, may be obtained on request.

Exemplifications and special copies are generally required as evidence for use in foreign courts.

When requesting a copy document the form of the copy required should be stated. The full name and last address of the deceased should be stated, together with the date of death and, where known, the date of the grant.

Apostille

19.9 Application for a copy of a grant or will to be endorsed with the 'Apostille' (that is, the authentication that the document is valid and acceptable for use in those countries which were signatories to the Hague Convention) is made to the Legalisation Office of the Foreign and Commonwealth Office, Old Admiralty Building, Whitehall, London

SW1A 2LG. A fee of £12 is payable for the endorsement: a further fee of £3 ensures secure postal return to the applicant. Where copies of the grant and will are likely to be required for use in the administration of the estate, such copies, whether office, certified or exemplified, should be requested with the application for the grant.

Other documents

19.10   Copies of documents other than wills and grants (but not Inland Revenue Accounts), such as oaths, affidavits, declarations, original powers of attorney, renunciations and orders, may be obtained on request and payment of the prescribed fee, and will be issued as office copies.

Copies of a will which was not admitted to proof but marked 'Probate refused', originals of wills proved in the form of engrossments under the District Judge's or Registrar's fiat, copies of a certified copy power of attorney, and copies of revoked grants, may be obtained provided their need can be justified to a District Judge or Registrar and issued as plain copies.

Wills lodged on renunciation (see paragraph 6.2) may not be inspected, nor copies supplied, unless the applicant can show an interest in the estate. Similarly with requests for copy grants, details of the full names and address of the deceased, the date of death and the date of issue of the grant (if known) should be supplied.

Duplicate grants

19.11   Application for a duplicate grant may be made only by or on behalf of the grantee who extracted the original. The reason for requiring it, e.g. that the original grant was lost in the post from the Registry, has been mislaid or accidentally destroyed and the grant is required to be produced in its original form rather than a copy, must be included in the written application. Application is made to the Registry from which the original issued. A fee of £15 is payable for a duplicate grant. The duplicate grant is headed as such, carries the date of issue of the original and is endorsed with a marginal note of the date of issue of the duplicate.

Copies of revoked grants

19.12   When application to revoke a grant is made in a Part 57 claim in the Chancery Division, no copies may issue during the pendency of the claim without leave of a District Judge or Registrar. Should the grant be revoked, only plain copies of it may issue thereafter. Similarly, only plain copies of grants revoked by District Judge or Registrar's order may be supplied.

Searches

Searches and inspections

19.13 Details of all grants of representation issued in England and Wales since 1858 are contained in calendars (that is annual lists in alphabetical order of the names of the deceased) kept at the Principal Registry (see s 111 of the Supreme Court Act 1981). District Probate Registries have records for at least 50 years in book form covering grants up to 1980, and since then on microfilm and, from November 1998, on computer.

Searches for grants may be made personally or by post. If made by post, they may be made to the Registry from which the grant issued, or to the York Probate sub-Registry. A fee of £3 is payable for a search carried out by the Registry for each four-year period searched after the first four years. A fee of £15 (Fee No 7 in APPENDIX 2) is payable for inspecting any document.

Wills may be inspected at and copies supplied from the Registry in which they were proved. Where the will was proved more than two years before the application for the copy, arrangements for inspection must be made with the Probate Manager of the relevant Registry, the records now being held at the Probate Records Centre.

Postal applications for copies are dealt with as set out above.

Standing searches

19.14 Rule 43 provides for any person who wishes to be notified when a grant of representation in respect of a particular deceased's estate issues, to apply to any Registry or sub-Registry for the entry of a standing search. Application is made by lodging a request in writing (see Form A1.81, page 448), together with the fee of £5 (Fee No 5 in APPENDIX 2). The request must give the full name of the deceased, his address and date of death and any alias(es).

Upon receipt of the application, the Registry will search the index of pending grant applications currently maintained for a period of one year before the date of application, and if no grant is found will make an entry in the index which will record and inform the Registry which made the entry when a grant issues from any Registry.

A copy of any grant the details of which correspond with those contained in the form of request, which has issued, or issues during the six months the search remains in force, will be sent by post to the applicant by the Registry which issues the grant. The applicant may apply to extend the period of six months; the search will be extended for a further six-month period on receipt of a request in writing and on payment of a further fee of £5. The request may be lodged personally or by post and must be made or received within the last month of the period of six months during which the standing search remains in force. The standing search will then be effective for an additional period of six months from the date it was due to expire. The standing search may be extended in the same manner for further periods of six months as required.

Application for a standing search should be made by any person contemplating applying under the Inheritance (Provision for Family and Dependants) Act 1975. Any application for relief under the Act must be made within six months after the date of issue of the full grant to the estate. It should be noted that a caveat (see CHAPTER 16) should *not* be entered as this prevents the issue of the grant and will delay the making of the application.

Similarly, any person wishing to commence any other litigious proceedings against the deceased's estate, or a beneficiary wishing to know when representation is granted, should use the standing search procedure to obtain a copy of the grant. Details of the personal representatives, against whom the proceedings will be commenced, can be obtained from the grant, as can the address of their professional advisers.

Search for a caveat

19.15   Application for a search for an effective caveat against the issue of a grant of representation may be made personally or by post to any Registry. No fee is payable for the search but a fee of £5 is payable for a copy caveat. The index of pending grants and caveats is now contained in the Probateman computer system.

Production of documents for forensic examination and as evidence in other courts

19.16   Application for the production of a document (usually an original will) for inspection and examination should be made to the District Judge or Registrar of the Registry where the document is held. Where necessary, the document will be sent to the Registry nearest to the inspector/examiner to facilitate the examination. The examination will take place within the Registry, and only in exceptional cases will the document be released for examination elsewhere. Any examination is subject to the approval of and under such conditions and restrictions as the District Judge or Registrar sees fit to impose. The examiner will be obliged to sign a form of written undertaking as to the care of the document while it is in his custody, and not to subject the document to any forensic test likely to damage it.

19.16 *Engrossments, copies and searches*

Where a document is required to be produced to another court for use in other proceedings the Registry will, on request, arrange for its production and safe custody for the duration of the proceedings. It is normal practice for an officer attending from the Registry to be entrusted with the document for the duration of the proceedings. If he is obliged to leave the document in the other court, a receipt for it must be obtained. No such request is necessary when the other proceedings are in the Chancery Division, where a standing arrangement for production of documents exists.

Chapter 20

Deposit of wills of living persons

Safe-keeping

20.1   Section 126 of the Supreme Court Act 1981 provides that there shall be provided safe and convenient depositories in which a living person may deposit his will during his lifetime.

Sections 23 to 26 of the Administration of Justice Act 1982 which relate, *inter alia*, to international wills, make provision for the compulsory registration of certain wills. These sections are not yet in force but when they are brought into force, s 126 of the 1981 Act is repealed: wills deposited under s 126 of the 1981 Act will then be treated as deposited under the provisions of the 1982 Act. The place of deposit and registration will be the Principal Registry of the Family Division. The Principal Registry is, by virtue of s 24 of the 1982 Act, designated as the national body for the purposes of Registry Convention (that is the *Convention on the Establishment of a Scheme of Registration of Wills* concluded at Basle on 16 May 1972).

The Wills (Deposit for Safe Custody) Regulations 1978, which came into effect on 1 February 1979, currently regulate the procedure for deposit and withdrawal of wills. New Regulations will be necessary to regulate the procedure for deposit and registration when the relevant sections of the 1982 Act are brought into force.

The place for deposit is the Principal Registry, although wills may be lodged for deposit in a District Registry, whence they will be forwarded to the Principal Registry for deposit and safe-keeping. The present procedure for depositing a will is set out below.

A 'will' is deemed to include any testamentary document.

Every application for an original grant is checked against the register of deposited wills to ensure there is no will so deposited by the deceased. No grant can therefore issue without the deposited will being discovered, the register being contained within the Probateman computer system.

Procedure for lodging

20.2   Regulation 3(2) of the 1978 Regulations provides that a will may be deposited by:

(a)   personal attendance of the testator; or

(b)   personal attendance of an agent authorised in writing by the testator; or

(c)   post only to the Principal Registry.

Special envelopes in which the will must be enclosed and sealed by the testator are provided by the Registry. Such envelopes must bear the endorsement provided by Form 1 in the Schedule to the Regulations.

Where the testator attends to deposit his will the certificate on the envelope (see Form 1 of the 1978 Regulations) enclosing the will must be signed in the presence of an officer of the Registry, who will countersign the certificate. If the will is deposited through an agent or by post, the certificate on the envelope will be accepted at face value as the testator's signature. If deposited through an agent the District Judge or Registrar must be satisfied that the agent is authorised to deposit the testator's will (see Regulations 4 and 5).

The Registry in which the will is lodged will supply a certificate of deposit (in Form 2 in the Schedule to the Regulations) to the testator, and where the will is lodged for deposit at a District Probate Registry the sealed envelope containing the will, and a certificate of deposit, will be sent through the Document Exchange to the Principal Registry and a copy of the certificate retained. The Probate Manager of the Registry in which the will is deposited will enter details in the computer system (see Regulations 6 and 7). A fee of £15 is payable on deposit of the will (Fee No 6 in APPENDIX 2). The endorsement contained in Form 1 on the envelope containing the will requires the testator to inform the executor(s) appointed in his will of its deposit.

Withdrawal after deposit

20.3   Where a testator wishes to withdraw his will from the custody of the court after deposit for safe-keeping, he may do so on application in writing. Application must be made to a District Judge of the Principal Registry and must be accompanied by the certificate of deposit. The District Judge will authorise the return of the will provided he is satisfied of the testator's identity and that it would be proper for the will to be returned. The records will be noted accordingly. Unless the District Judge is so satisfied, the will may not be removed from the custody of the Registry until the testator's death (see Regulation 8).

No fee is payable for withdrawing the will.

Procedure on testator's death

20.4   Upon the death of the testator, the executor, or any other person who satisfies a District Judge of the Principal Registry that he intends to prove the will, must produce a certificate, or other evidence to the District Judge's satisfaction, of the testator's death and, unless otherwise directed, the certificate of deposit. Subject to any precautions thought appropriate by the District Judge (such as the retention of a copy of the will in the Registry), the envelope containing the deposited will will be opened and the will released.

Where the will has been effectively revoked, for example by the making of a later will, or there is no need to prove the will and obtain a grant of representation to administer the estate, the District Judge may release the deposited will to any person entitled to possession of it. The person to whom the will is released must sign a receipt and undertake to lodge the will on any application for a grant to the estate of the testator (see Regulation 9).

Appendix 1

Forms

Contents

Oaths

Affidavits

Forms

Preliminary note: The specimen forms given in this Appendix should be adapted as appropriate to suit the particular case. For example, where an applicant wishes to affirm, the words 'make oath and say' should be omitted and the words 'solemnly and sincerely declare and affirm' inserted in their place. The jurat should also be amended accordingly by deleting 'Sworn' and inserting 'Affirmed'. The forms use 'he', 'him', 'his', etc. for simplicity; 'she', 'her', 'hers', etc. should be substituted where appropriate.

Application of RSC Order 41

Order 41 of the Rules of the Supreme Court 1965 applies to oaths and affidavits sworn for use in Probate Registries.

Oaths

Notes:

(1) The solicitors or probate practitioners extracting the grant should insert their name, address and postcode, and, if they are a member of the Document Exchange, their DX number, and any reference they wish to appear on the grant, in the top right hand corner of the oath. The DX number and postcode are used in the Registries to generate the solicitor's full address in the Registry's computer records.

(2) All other relevant information, for example that the grant is to issue pursuant to an order or direction of the court, should be included in the oath.

(3) Where a name of the deceased other than the full, true name is required to appear in the grant, the reason for such requirement must be stated in the oath.

(4) Where a former or alternative address of the deceased or the deponent is required to appear in the grant, the reason for such requirement must be stated in the oath. The postcode of the deceased's last address must be stated.

(5) The deceased's name, address, dates of birth and death must be recited as they appear in the death certificate when the death was registered in the United Kingdom.

A1.1 Oath for executor(s): general form

IN THE HIGH COURT OF JUSTICE
FAMILY DIVISION
[Principal] [... District Probate] Registry
In the Estate of .... deceased

1. I/We, ...

Full and correct names of each of the executors applying must be given. Where any name differs from that appearing in the appointment in the will, an explanation must be given, e.g. 'A Wright, in the will called A Right'. If the executor's name has been changed by deed poll, details of the deed must be given and (a copy of) the deed included in the documents lodged. If an executrix's name has changed on marriage, she should be described as 'formerly, and in the will called ...., spinster', or as the case may be. If the will appoints 'my wife' as executrix without naming her (e.g. 'I appoint my wife sole executrix ...'), the oath must recite that she was the deceased's lawful wife at the date of the will. Where the appointment describes the executor by his initials only, or by one only of his forenames, or there is any doubt that the applicant is the appointee, an explanation of the difference must be given by the executor applying. Failure to provide a satisfactory explanation of any discrepancy in names may result in the District Judge or Registrar directing further evidence be filed.

2. of ....

The full, permanent, postal address of each executor must be given. Where an executor is applying in his professional capacity, he may give his business address. Immediately following the address each executor must state his occupation or description, e.g. 'publisher', 'of no occupation' or 'retired'. In the case of an executrix who has no occupation, her status, e.g. 'widow', 'married woman' or 'spinster', should be stated.

3. make oath and say:
   That I/we believe the paper writing now produced to and marked by me/us to be the true and original last Will and Testament

Where more than one document together constituting the last will are to be proved, the words 'as contained in the paper writings marked ...' must be added after the word 'Testament'. If there is a codicil or codicils to be proved as well as the will, the words 'together with [a codicil] [two codicils] (or as the case may be) thereto' should be added after the word 'Testament'. The documents being identified are 'marked' by the signature of each executor and the person swearing the oath.

4. of ....

The full, true, name and address (including the postcode) of the testator must be given. If the testator had been known by a different name for any length of time, the name should be given with the addition of the words 'formerly or otherwise ....'. Similarly, the same description should be used if the testator held property in a former name or under an alias. Where there is a considerable variance in names this must be explained in the oath. The reason for the alias being required to appear in the grant must be stated and any asset held in another name specified (see Rule 9). The last residential address of the testator should be given. If this differs from the address stated in the will because the testator had changed his address since making the will, the previous address should be added, prefixed by the words 'formerly of'.

5. deceased, who was born on the .... day of .... 19 ..
    and who died on the .... day of .... 20 .. aged
    .... domiciled in ....

The dates of birth and death as given in the death certificate should be inserted. It is not normally necessary to produce the death certificate, but if the deceased was a serving member of the armed forces and no death certificate has issued, the certificate of death issued by the Ministry of Defence, or where the deceased was a merchant seaman, a certificate by the Registrar-General of Shipping and Seamen, should be lodged with the other documents. The domicile of the deceased, e.g. England and Wales, must be inserted. Where the deceased's age cannot be precisely stated an approximation should be given; e.g. 'over 65'.

6. That to the best of my/our knowledge and belief there was [no] land vested in the said deceased immediately before his death which was settled previously to his death (and not by his Will (and codicil(s), *if any*)) and which remained settled land notwithstanding his death.

Where there was such land and the grant is only in respect of free estate the word 'no' should be omitted from the paragraph and the words 'save and except settled land' added in paragraph 9. A separate grant of administration limited to the settled land may be taken.

7. I am the [sole executor] [surviving executor] *or*
    We are [the executors] [the surviving executors] [two, *or as the case may be,* of the executors] named in the said will.

The applicant(s) must swear that they are the executor(s) named in the will in accordance with their appointment. Where one or more of the executors have renounced probate it is necessary to state this fact in the oath. The form(s) of renunciation must be lodged with the other documents. For forms of renunciation see Forms A1.76 and A1.77.

8. And I/we further make oath and say that notice of the application has been given to .... the executor(s) to whom power is to be reserved [save ....]

Where power is to be reserved to other executors the oath shall state that notice of the application has been given to them (see Rule 27(1)and Form A1.80). Where power is to be reserved to executors who are partners in a firm, no notice need be given to them if application is made by another partner (see Rule 27(1A)). There is no need to name all the other partners having power reserved (Registrar's Direction 12 June 1990 [1990] 2 All ER 576). Where application has successfully been made under Rule 27(3) to dispense with the giving of such notice to any executor(s) the fact that notice has been dispensed with should be recited.

If the appointment is limited in any way, the limitation should be set out, e.g. 'the executor appointed in the will to administer the deceased's estate in England and Wales'. The executor's names will appear in the grant in the order they are set out in the oath.

9. I/We will (a) collect, get in and administer according to law the real and personal estate of the said deceased; (b) when required to do so by the Court, exhibit in the Court a full inventory of the said estate and render an account thereof to the Court; and (c) when required to do so by the High Court, deliver up to that Court the grant of probate.

Where there was settled land vested in the testator the words 'save and except settled land' should be inserted after the word 'estate' in (a).

10. That to the best of my/our knowledge, information and belief the gross value of the estate passing under the grant [amounts to] [does not exceed] £ ...... and the net value [amounts to] [does not exceed] £ ...... [and that this is not a case in which an Inland Revenue Account is required to be delivered].

The value of the estate is defined as the 'free' estate and excludes joint property passing by survivorship and property in which the deceased had a limited interest only. Where there was settled land the words 'save and except settled land' should be inserted after the value of the estate. Where an Account is required under the Inheritance Tax (Delivery of Accounts) Regulations, the actual gross and net values of the estate must be inserted; where an Account is not required, insert the gross and net values the estate does not exceed, e.g. gross £25,000 where the death occurred after 1 April 1981 but before 1 April 1983; £40,000 where the death occurred after 1 April 1983 but before 1 April 1987; £70,000 where the death occurred on or after 1 April 1987 but before 1 April 1989; £100,000 where the death occurred on or after 1 April 1989, but before 1 April 1990; £115,000 where the death occurred on or after 1 April 1990 but before 1 April 1991; £125,000 where the death occurred on or after 1 April 1991 but before 6 April 1995; £145,000 where the death occurred on or after 6 April 1995 but before 6 April 1996; £180,000 where the death occurred on or after 6 April 1996 but before 6 April 1998, £200,000 where the death occurred on or after 6 April 1998 but before 6 April 2000; £210,000 where the death occurred on or after 6 April 2000 but before 6

April 2002 and £220,000 where the death occurred on or after that date. The net value should be stated as the actual value of the net estate rounded up to the nearest £1,000 (see Practice Direction 22 March 2002). If the purpose of the grant is simply to establish title and there is no estate to be administered in England and Wales, the reasons must be set out in the oath and the net value will be stated as 'nil'. An Account will be required.

Sworn by the said ....
at ....
on the ....
Before me, ...
A Commissioner for Oaths/Solicitor

A1.2 Oath for executor(s): partner(s) in firm or successor firm

IN THE HIGH COURT OF JUSTICE
FAMILY DIVISION
[Principal] [.. District Probate] Registry
In the Estate of.. deceased

1. I/We, ...

Full, true name(s) of executor(s) applying for the grant; see notes to Form A1.1, para 1, page 340.

2. of ....

Full, permanent, postal address of the executor(s) applying; see notes to Form A1.1, para 2, page 340.

3. make oath and say:
    That ....

Full name and address of testator as in Form A1.1, para 4, page 341.

    of ....
    formerly of ....
    was born on the .... day of .... 19 .. and died on the
    .... day of .... 20 .. aged ....

(see note to Form A1.1, para 5, page 341)

    domiciled in ....
    [England and Wales, *or as the case may be.*]

4. I/We believe the paper writing now produced to and marked by me/us to be the true and original last Will and Testament of the deceased

(see note to Form A1.1, para 3, page 340).

5. To the best of my/our knowledge, information and belief there was no land vested in the deceased which was settled previously to the death (and not by the Will) of the deceased and which remained settled land notwithstanding such death

(see note to Form A1.1, para 6, page 341).

6. That the said deceased appointed in the said Will [and codicil[s]] the partners at the date of his death in the firm of ....[or the firm which at that date had succeeded to and carried on their practice] *(delete if no successor firm)* to be the executors [and trustees] of the said Will.

7. That I/we am/are [one of] [two of] *(or as the case may be)* the partners in the firm of .... [being the successor firm to ....] at the date of death of the said deceased and as such [one of] [two of] *(or as the case may be)* the executors named in the said Will.

[8. That power is reserved to all the other partners in the said firm of .... at the said date of death and as such the other executors.]

Delete if no other partners and see note to Form A1.1, para 8, page 342.

9. I/We will

(i)   collect, get in and administer according to law the real and personal estate of the said deceased;

(ii) when required to do so by the Court, exhibit in the Court a full inventory of the said estate and render an account thereof to the Court; and

(iii) when required to do so by the High Court, deliver up to that Court the Grant of Probate.

10. To the best of my/our knowledge, information and belief the gross estate passing under the grant and the net estate [and this is not a case in which an Inland Revenue Account is required to be delivered]

(see note to Form A1.1, para 10, page 342).

Sworn etc.

A1.3   Oath for double probate

IN THE HIGH COURT OF JUSTICE
FAMILY DIVISION
[Principal] [.. District Probate] Registry
In the Estate of .... deceased

1.   I, ...

*Full, true name of executor applying for the grant; see notes to Form
A1.1, para 1, page 340.*

2.   of ....

*Full, permanent, postal address of the executor applying; see notes to
Form A1.1, para 2, page 340.*

3.   make oath and say:
     That ....

Full name and address of testator as in Form A1.1, para 4, page 341.

     of ....
     formerly of ....
     was born on the .... day of .... 19 .. and died on the
     .... day of .... 20 .. aged ....

(see note to Form A1.1, para 5, page 341)

     domiciled in ....
     [England and Wales, *or as the case may be.*]

4.   I believe the paper writing[s] now produced to and marked by me to
     be the [true and original] [an official copy of the true and original]
     last Will and Testament [and codicil[s]] of the deceased.

*The original will is retained in the Probate Registry which issued the
grant; to avoid an attendance at that Registry, an official copy may be
marked.*

5.   That to the best of my knowledge, information and belief there was
     no land vested in the deceased which was settled previously to his
     death (and not by his Will and codicil(s), *if any*) and which remained
     settled land notwithstanding his death.

See note to Form A1.1, para 6, page 341.

6.   That on the .... day of .... 20 .. probate of the said Will
     was granted to .... *(insert the names of the executors who
     proved the Will)* at the [Principal] [.................... District
     Probate] Registry [one, two *or as the case may be*] of the executors
     named in the said Will [power being reserved of making the like

grant to ....] *(insert names of the executor(s) to whom power was reserved)*, the other executor[s] named in the said Will.

7. That I am [the other] [one of the other] [the now surviving] executor[s] named in the said Will.

8. And I further make oath and say that notice of the application has been given to .... the executor[s] to whom power is to be reserved [save ....]

Where the power is again to be reserved to another executor a statement to this effect should be made and to the effect that notice of this application has been given to them (see Rule 27(1)); see also note to Form A1.1, para 8, page 342.

9. I will (a) collect, get in and administer according to law the real and personal estate of the said deceased; (b) when required to do so by the Court, exhibit in the Court a full inventory of the said estate and render an account thereof to the Court; and (c) when required to do so by the High Court, deliver up to that Court the grant of probate.

10. That to the best of my knowledge, information and belief the gross value of the estate now unadministered passing under the grant [amounts to] [does not exceed] £ ...... and the net value [amounts to] [does not exceed] £ ...... [and that this is not a case in which an Inland Revenue Account is required to be delivered].

The excepted estate provisions (see note to Form A1.1, para 10, page 342) on lodging an Inland Revenue Account apply to second or subsequent grants provided the criteria to constitute the case an 'excepted estate' within the meaning of the Inheritance Tax (Delivery of Accounts) (Excepted Estates) Regulations 2002 are met. Where the criteria are not met, the value the estate amounts to should be inserted and an Account in Form A5C delivered. The Account must be delivered to the Registry with the grant application. Although the executor swears to administer all the deceased's estate, the oath should show only the value of the unadministered estate.

Sworn etc.

A1.4   Oath for executors – trust corporation

IN THE HIGH COURT OF JUSTICE
FAMILY DIVISION
[Principal] [... District Probate] Registry
In the Estate of .... deceased

1. I, ...

Full name and address, which may be the business address of the corporation's nominee, and his occupation or description. See note to Form A1.1, para 1, page 340.

2. in the employ of ....
(full title of trust corporation) whose registered office is situate at
.... (full address of registered office)

3. make oath and say:
That .... of ....

(Insert full name of deceased, residence and occupation or description; see note to Form A1.1, para 2, page 340)

deceased, was born on the .... day of .... 19 .. and died on the .... day of .... 20 .. aged ....

(see note to Form A1.1, para 5, page 341)

domiciled in [England and Wales, *or as the case may be.*]

4. That I believe the paper writing now produced to and marked by me to contain the true and original last Will and Testament [and

(see note to Form A1.1, para 3, page 340)

codicil[s]] of the deceased.

5. That to the best of my knowledge, information and belief there was no land vested in the deceased which was settled previously to his death (and not by the Will [and codicil[s]] of the deceased and which remained settled land notwithstanding such death.

See note to Form A1.1, para 6, page 341.

6. That the said deceased by his said Will [and codicil[s]] appointed the said corporation [and .... *(insert full names of any executors other than the trust corporation appointed by the will)*] to be the [sole] executor[s] thereof.

7. That the said .... *(name of trust corporation)* by a resolution dated the .... day of .... 19 .. (a certified copy of which is lodged herewith) appointed me for the purpose of applying for a grant of probate of the said Will [and codicil[s]] on its behalf *or* [that the said .... *(name of trust corporation)* by a resolution dated the .... day of .... 19 .. (a certified copy of which has been lodged with the Senior District Judge and is still in force) authorised persons holding my position to apply for grants of representation] and that the said .... *(name of trust corporation)* is a Trust Corporation as defined by Rule 2(1) of the Non-Contentious Probate Rules 1987 and has power to accept the grant now applied for.

Where there is a limitation by way of terms and conditions referred to as existing at the date of the will, a further statement must be added stating that the terms and conditions do not affect the trust corporation's powers to take a full grant.

8. That the said *(name of trust corporation)* will (a) collect, get in and administer according to law the real and personal estate of the said deceased; (b) when required to do so by the Court, exhibit in the Court a full inventory of the said estate and render an account thereof to the Court; and (c) when required to do so by the High Court, deliver up to that Court the grant of probate.

See note to Form A1.1, para 9, page 342.

9. That to the best of my knowledge, information and belief the gross value of the estate passing under the grant [amounts to] [does not exceed] £ ...... and the net value [amounts to] [does not exceed] £ ...... [and that this is not a case in which an Inland Revenue Account is required to be delivered].

See note to Form A1.1, para 10, page 342.

Sworn etc.

A1.5   Oath for executor(s): lost will or reconstructed will

IN THE HIGH COURT OF JUSTICE
FAMILY DIVISION
[Principal] [... District Probate] Registry
In the Estate of .... deceased

1. I/We, ...

Full, true name(s) of executor(s) applying for the grant; see notes to Form A1.1, para 1, page 340.

2. of ....

Full, permanent postal address of the executor(s) applying; see notes to Form A1.1, para 2, page 340.

make oath and say:

3. That I/we believe the paper writing now produced to and marked by me/us to contain the last Will and Testament as contained in [the draft] [carbon copy] [photocopy] [reconstruction] *(delete as appropriate or insert the definition of the will as necessary)* exhibited to the affidavit of .... *(name of deponent to the affidavit which led the order to admit the copy etc. will)* sworn on the .... day of .... 20.. and marked ' .... '

4. of ....

Full, true name of testator; see note to Form A1.1, para 4, page 341.

5. deceased, who was born on the .... day of .... 19.. and died on the .... day of .... 20... aged .... domiciled in ....

See note to Form A1.1, para 5, page 341.

6. That to the best of my/our knowledge, information and belief there was [no] land vested in the said deceased immediately before his death which was settled previously to his death (and not by his Will) and which remained settled land notwithstanding his death.

See note to Form A1.1, para 6, page 341.

7. That by order of Mr Registrar/District Judge ..... of this Division dated the .... day of ...... 20.. it was ordered that the last Will and Testament of the said deceased be admitted to proof as contained in the said [draft] [carbon copy] *(or as the case may be).*

See para 3 above.

8. I am/We are the [sole executor] [surviving executor(s)] [executors] [two *(or as the case may be)* of the executors] named in the said Will.

See note to Form A1.1, para 7, page 341.

9. And I/we further make oath and say that notice of the application has been given to ...... the executor(s) to whom power is to be reserved [save ......].

See note to Form A1.1, para 8, page 342.

10. I/We will

(i) collect, get in and administer according to law the real and personal estate of the said deceased limited until the original Will or a more authentic copy be proved *(or whatever limitation imposed by the Registrar's/ Judge's order)*;

(ii) when required to do so by the Court, exhibit in the Court a full inventory of the said estate and render an account thereof to the Court; and

(iii) when required to do so by the High Court, deliver up to that Court the grant of probate.

11. To the best of my/our knowledge, information and belief the gross estate passing under the grant [does not exceed] amounts to [£ .... and the net estate] [does not exceed] [amounts to £ ....] [and this is not a case in which an Inland Revenue Account is required to be delivered].

See note to Form A1.1, para 10, page 342.

Sworn by the said ....
at ....
on the ....
Before me, ...
A Commissioner for Oaths/Solicitor

A1.6 Oath for special executor(s) appointed as to part of estate

IN THE HIGH COURT OF JUSTICE
FAMILY DIVISION
[Principal] [.. District Probate] Registry
In the Estate of .... deceased

1.   I/We, ...

Full, true name(s) of executor(s) applying for the grant; see notes to Form A1.1, para 1, page 340.

2.   of ....

Full, permanent postal address of the executor(s) applying; see notes to Form A1.1, para 2, page 340.

make oath and say:

3.   That I/we believe the paper writing now produced to and marked by me/us to contain the last Will and Testament

See note to Form A1.1, para 3, page 340; see also para 6, below.

4.   of ....

Full, true name of testator; see note to Form A1.1, para 4, page 341.

5.   deceased, who was born on the .... day of .... 19.. and died on the .... day of .... 20... aged .... domiciled in ....

See note to Form A1.1, para 5, page 341.

[6.   That on the .... day of .... 20.. probate of the Will of the said deceased in respect of all the estate save and except [his literary estate *(or as the case may be)*] was granted at the .... Registry to ..... his general executor(s)].

If probate of the general estate has not yet been granted, delete this paragraph. If it has, complete this paragraph and add in para 3 above after the words 'last Will and Testament' the words 'as contained in an official copy'. Alternatively, the oath may be sworn in the Registry in which the original will was proved and that will marked by the deponent(s).

7.   That I am/we are the special executor(s) in respect of the said deceased's [literary estate *or as the case may be*].

8.   That notice of this application has been given to .... the other special executor(s) to whom power is to be reserved [save ....].

See note to Form A1.1, para 8, page 342.

9.   That there was [no] land vested in the said deceased immediately before his death which was settled previously to his death (and not by his Will) and which remained settled land notwithstanding his death.

10.   I/We will

(i)   collect, get in and administer according to law the real and personal estate of the said deceased limited to the said [literary estate *or as the case may be*];

(ii) when required to do so by the Court, exhibit in the Court a full inventory of the said estate and render an account thereof to the Court; and

(iii) when required to do so by the High Court, deliver up to that Court the grant of probate.

11.   To the best of my/our knowledge, information and belief the gross estate passing under the grant limited as aforesaid [does not exceed] [amounts to] £ .... and the net estate [does not exceed] [amounts to £ ....] [and this is not a case in which an Inland Revenue Account is required to be delivered].

See note to Form A1.1, para 10, page 342.

Sworn by the above named deponent(s)
at ....
this .... day of .... 20....
Before me, ...
A Commissioner for Oaths/Solicitor

A1.7   Oath for general executor(s) save and except as to part of estate

IN THE HIGH COURT OF JUSTICE
FAMILY DIVISION
[Principal] [.. District Probate] Registry
In the Estate of .... deceased

1.   I/We, ...

Full, true name(s) of executor(s) applying for the grant; see notes to Form A1.1, para 1, page 340.

2.   of ....

Full, permanent postal address of the executor(s) applying; see notes to Form A1.1, para 2, page 340.

make oath and say:

3.   That I/we believe the paper writing now produced to and marked by me/us to contain the last Will and Testament

See note to Form A1.1, para 3, page 340; see also para 6, below.

4.   of ....

Full, true name of testator; see note to Form A1.1, para 4, page 341.

5.   deceased, who was born on the .... day of .... 19.. and died on the .... day of .... 20.. aged .... domiciled in ....

See note to Form A1.1, para 5, page 341.

[6.   That on the .... day of .... 20.. probate of the Will of the said deceased limited to his [literary estate *(or as the case may be)*] was granted at the .... Registry to ..... his special executor(s)].

If probate of the special estate has not yet been granted, delete this paragraph. If it has, complete this paragraph and add in para 3 above after the words 'last Will and Testament' the words 'as contained in an official copy'. Alternatively, the oath may be sworn in the Registry in which the original will was proved and that will marked by the deponent(s).

7.   That I am/we are the general executor(s) in respect of the said deceased's estate.

8.   That notice of this application has been given to .... the other general executor(s) to whom power is to be reserved [save ....].

See note to Form A1.1, para 8, page 342.

9.   That there was [no] land vested in the said deceased immediately before his death which was settled previously to his death (and not by his Will) and which remained settled land notwithstanding his death.

10.   I/We will

   (i)   collect, get in and administer according to law the real and personal estate of the said deceased save and except as to the said [literary estate *or as the case may be*];

   (ii)   when required to do so by the Court, exhibit in the Court a full inventory of the said estate and render an account thereof to the Court; and

(iii) when required to do so by the High Court, deliver up to that Court the grant of probate.

11. To the best of my/our knowledge, information and belief the gross estate passing under the grant save and except the literary estate *(or as the case may be)* [does not exceed] [amounts to] £ .... and the net estate [does not exceed] [amounts to £ ....] [and this is not a case in which an Inland Revenue Account is required to be delivered].

See note to Form A1.1, para 10, page 342.

Sworn by the above named deponent(s)
at ....
this .... day of .... 20....
Before me, ...
A Commissioner for Oaths/Solicitor

A1.8   Oath for executor(s): will pronounced for in a probate claim

IN THE HIGH COURT OF JUSTICE
FAMILY DIVISION
[Principal] [... District Probate] Registry
In the Estate of .... deceased

1.   I/We, ...

Full, true name of executor(s) applying for the grant; see notes to Form A1.1, para 1, page 340.

2.   of ....

Full, permanent, postal address of the executor applying; see notes to Form A1.1, para 2, page 340.

3.   make oath and say:
That ....

Full name and address of testator as in Form A1.1, para 4, page 341.

of ....
formerly of ....
was born on the .... day of .... 19 .. and died on the
.... day of .... 20 .. aged ....

(see note to Form A1.1, para 5, page 341)

domiciled in ....

[England and Wales, *or as the case may be.*]

4. To the best of my/our knowledge, information and belief there was no land vested in the deceased which was settled previously to the death (and not by the Will and codicil(s) *(if any)*) of the deceased and which remained settled land notwithstanding such death.

5. I/We believe the paper writing(s) now produced to and marked by me/us to contain the true and original last Will and Testament [and codicil(s)] of the deceased dated .... [respectively].

6. On the .... day of .... 20.... the Honourable Mr/Mrs Justice ...., one of the Justices of the Chancery Division of the High Court of Justice, in a probate claim entitled *(here set out the title and number of the claim)*, pronounced for the force and validity of the said Will [and codicil(s)] dated .... [respectively] and ordered that the said Will [and codicils] be admitted to proof and probate thereof be granted to...................... [and against the validity of the Will [and codicil(s)] dated .... [respectively]]. *(Delete if no testamentary documents pronounced against).*

7. I/We am/are [two of] the executor(s) *(or as the case may be)* named in the said Will.

8. I/We will

    (i)   collect, get in and administer according to law the real and personal estate of the said deceased;

    (ii) when required to do so by the Court, exhibit in the Court a full inventory of the said estate and render an account thereof to the Court; and

    (ii) when required to do so by the High Court, deliver up to that Court the Grant of Probate.

9. To the best of my/our knowledge, information and belief the gross estate passing under the grant [amounts to] [does not exceed] £...................... and the net estate [amounts to] [does not exceed] £...................... [and this is not a case in which an Inland Revenue Account is required to be delivered].

See note to Form A1.1, para 10, page 342.

[10. Notice   of   this   application   has   been   given   to .... the other executors named in the said Will.] *Delete if inappropriate.*

Sworn etc.

A1.9   Oath for administrators (with will annexed)

IN THE HIGH COURT OF JUSTICE
FAMILY DIVISION
[Principal] [...................................... District Probate] Registry
In the Estate of .... deceased

1.   I/We, ...

The full and correct names of each of the applicants must be given. Where there is more than one applicant they should be listed in order of the extent of interest, except where they have an equal interest when their names should appear in the same order as in the will. Their order in the oath will be the order in which they appear in the grant.

2.   of ....

The full, permanent, postal address of each applicant must be given, followed by their respective occupations or descriptions; see Form A1.1, para 2, page 340.

3.   make oath and say:
     That I/we believe the paper writing now produced to and marked by me/us to be the true and original last Will and Testament

See notes to Form A1.1, para 3, page 340.

4.   of ....

See notes to Form A1.1, para 4, page 341.

     formerly of ....

5.   deceased, who was born on the .... day of 19
     .. and died on the .... day of .... 20 .. aged ....
     domiciled in ....

See notes to Form A1.1, para 5, page 341.

6.   That no minority or life interest arises in the estate.

If such an interest does arise, the word 'no' should be deleted and the word 'a' inserted; the grant must issue to at least two persons or to a trust corporation either with or without an individual person, unless a District Judge or Registrar has directed otherwise. Where it appears from a will that a life interest exists, but at the date of the application that interest has ceased to exist, the word 'now' should be inserted before the word 'arises'. An additional paragraph should be added giving the name of the person who would have had the life interest and stating the date upon which that person died.

7.   That to the best of my/our knowledge, information and belief there

was no land vested in the deceased immediately before his death which was settled previously to his death (and not by his Will) and which remained settled land notwithstanding his death.

See note to Form A1.1, para 6, page 341.

8. [That the said deceased did not in his Will name any executor.] *or*
[That .... *(name of executor)* the sole executor named in the said Will survived the said deceased but has since died without having proved the said Will] *or*
[That .... *(name of executor)* one of the executors named in the said Will died during the lifetime of the deceased and .... *(name of executor)* the other executor named in the said Will has renounced probate thereof.] *or*
[That .... *(name of executor)* [the sole] [the surviving] executor named in the said Will has renounced probate thereof.] *or*
[That the attempted appointment of an executor in the said Will is void for uncertainty.]

Insert whichever of the above examples is appropriate. This is not a complete list of the ways in which executors may be cleared off. Whatever the manner of clearing, it must be set out.

9. [That I am/We are the residuary legatee(s) and devisee(s) in trust named in the said Will.] *or*
[That I am/We are the [residuary legatee(s) and devisee(s)] [residuary legatee(s)] [residuary devisee(s)] [substituted residuary legatee(s) and devisee(s)] [substituted residuary legatee(s)] [substituted devisee(s)].

The precise capacity in which the grant is applied for must be set out clearing off not only the executors (see paragraph 8 above), but all those with a prior entitlement to the grant pursuant to Rule 20 (see 8.2). The relationship to the deceased need only be given where it is necessary to establish title or for identification. Where there is more than one person entitled and only one of them applies, the words 'one of the persons entitled' should be added.

10. I/We will (a) collect, get in and administer according to law the real and personal estate of the said deceased *(where the grant is to be limited, e.g. 'save and except settled land', the limitation should be inserted)*; (b) when required to do so by the Court, exhibit in the Court a full inventory of the said estate and render an account thereof to the Court; and (c) when required to do so by the High Court, deliver up to that Court the grant of letters of administration (with will annexed).

11. That to the best of my/our knowledge, information and belief the gross value of the estate passing under the grant [amounts to] [does

not exceed] £ ...... and the net value [amounts to] [does not exceed] £ ...... [and that this is not a case in which an Inland Revenue Account is required to be delivered].

See note to Form A1.1, para 10, page 342.

Sworn etc.

A1.10 Oath for administrator (with will annexed): attorney of an executor

IN THE HIGH COURT OF JUSTICE
FAMILY DIVISION
[Principal] [.. District Probate] Registry
In the Estate of .... deceased

I, ...

Full and correct names of applicant.

of ....

Full, permanent, postal address of applicant.

make oath and say:

....

Full and correct name of the deceased.

1. of ....

Full, permanent, postal address including postcode.

   was born on the .... day of .... 19 .. and died on the .... day of .... 20 .. aged .... domiciled in England and Wales.

2. I believe the paper writing now produced to and marked by me to contain the true and original last will and testament [and [one] [two] *(or as the case may be)* codicil[s]] of the deceased and therein appointed .... *(name of executor)* his sole executor *(or as the case may be)*.

3. No minority or life interest arises in the estate.

See note to Form A1.9, para 6, page 355.

4. To the best of my knowledge, information and belief there was no land vested in the deceased immediately before his death (and not by the will [and *(number)* codicil[s]] of the deceased and which remained settled land notwithstanding his death.

5. I am the lawful attorney of the said .... *(name of executor)*

Where necessary, here clear off any other executor(s) appointed by reciting their predecease or renunciation.

6. I will (a) collect, get in and administer according to law the real and personal estate of the said deceased for the use and benefit of the said .... *(name of executor)* and until further representation be granted; (b) when required to do so by the Court, exhibit in the Court a full inventory of the said estate and render an account thereof to the Court; and (c) when required to do so by the High Court, deliver up to that Court the grant of letters of administration (with will annexed).

7. That to the best of my knowledge, information and belief the gross value of the estate passing under the grant [amounts to] [does not exceed] £ ...... and the net value [amounts to] [does not exceed] £ ...... [and that this is not a case in which an Inland Revenue Account is required to be delivered].

See note to Form A1.1, para 10, page 342.

Sworn etc.

Note: This form, suitably adapted, may be used where more than one executor appoints an attorney, or, where there are no executors, for the attorney of any other person entitled to letters of administration (with the will). If there were executors appointed, the manner of their clearing must be recited.

A1.11 Oath for administrator (with will annexed): person entitled to the estate undisposed of by will

IN THE HIGH COURT OF JUSTICE
FAMILY DIVISION
[Principal] [.. District Probate] Registry
In the Estate of .... deceased

I, ...

Full and correct names of applicant.

of ....

Full, permanent, postal address of applicant.

make oath and say:

....

Full and correct name of the deceased.

1.   of ....

Full, permanent, postal address including postcode.

was born on the .... day of .... 19 .. and died on
the .... day of .... 20 .. aged .... domiciled in
England and Wales.

2.   I believe the paper writing now produced to and marked by me to
contain the true and original last will and testament [and [one] [two]
(or as the case may be) codicil[s]] of the deceased.

3.   No minority or life interest arises in the estate.

See note to Form A1.9, para 6, page 355.

4.   To the best of my knowledge, information and belief there was no
land vested in the deceased immediately before his death (and not by
the will [and *(number)* codicil[s]] of the deceased and which
remained settled land notwithstanding his death.

5.   That .... *(name of executor and residuary legatee
and devisee)* died in the lifetime of the said deceased *or*
That .... *(name of executor)* has renounced probate
of the said will and that .... *(name of residuary
legatee and devisee)* died in the lifetime of the said deceased *(or as
the case may be to give title to the applicant under Rule 20(c)).*

6.   That the said deceased died a spinster without issue or parent or
brother or sister of the whole blood *(or as the case may be)* or any
other person entitled in priority to share in the estate by virtue of
any enactment.

7.   That I am the niece of the whole blood and [one of] [the only] person[s]
entitled to [share in] the estate now undisposed of by the said will.

8.   I will (a) collect, get in and administer according to law the real and
personal estate of the said deceased; (b) when required to do so by
the Court, exhibit in the Court a full inventory of the said estate and
render an account thereof to the Court; and (c) when required to do
so by the High Court, deliver up to that Court the grant of letters of
administration (with will annexed).

9.   That to the best of my knowledge, information and belief the gross
value of the estate passing under the grant [amounts to] [does not
exceed] £ ...... and the net value [amounts to] [does not exceed] £
...... [and that this is not a case in which an Inland Revenue Account
is required to be delivered].

See note to Form A1.1, para 10, page 342.

Sworn etc.

A1.12 Oath for administrator (with will annexed): legatee: whole or substantially the whole estate disposed of by will

IN THE HIGH COURT OF JUSTICE
FAMILY DIVISION
[Principal] [.. District Probate] Registry
In the Estate of .... deceased

1.   I, ...

See note to Form A1.9, para 1, page 355.

2.   of ....

See note to Form A1.1, para 2, page 340.

3.   make oath and say:
     That I believe the paper writing now produced to and marked by me
     to be the true and original last Will and Testament

See notes to Form A1.1, para 3, page 340.

4.   of ....

See notes to Form A1.1, para 4, page 341.

5.   deceased, who was born on the .... day of .... 19.. and died on
     the .... day of .... 20.. aged .... domiciled in ....

See notes to Form A1.1, para 5, page 341.

6.   That no minority or life interest arises in the estate.

See notes to Form A1.9, para 6, page 355.

7.   That to the best of my knowledge, information and belief there was
     no land vested in the deceased immediately before his death which
     was settled previously to his death (and not by his Will) and which
     remained settled land notwithstanding his death.

See note to Form A1.1, para 6, page 341.

8.   [That the said deceased did not in his Will name any executor.] *or*
     [That .... *(name of executor)* the sole executor named in the
     said Will survived the said deceased but has since died without
     having proved the said Will.] *or*
     [That .... *(name of executor)* one of the executors named in
     the said Will died during the lifetime of the deceased and
     .... *(name of executor)* the other executor named in the said
     Will has renounced probate thereof.] *or*
     [That .... *(name of executor)* [the sole] [the surviving]

executor named in the said Will has renounced probate thereof.] *or* [That the attempted appointment of an executor in the said Will is void for uncertainty.]

Insert whichever of the above examples is appropriate. This is not a complete list of the ways in which executors may be cleared off. Whatever the manner of clearing, it must be set out.

9.   [That .... the residuary legatee(s) and devisee(s) named in the said Will [has] [have] renounced letters of administration with Will annexed.] *or*
[That .... the residuary legatee(s) and devisee(s) named in the said Will died in the lifetime of the said deceased.]

The manner by which the residuary legatee(s) and devisee(s) has/have been cleared off must be set out in full, for example if one renounces and others died in the lifetime of the deceased then a combination of the above should be inserted. If the gift fails because the residuary beneficiary witnessed the will (s 15 Wills Act 1837), this fact should be recited.

10.   That I am a [legatee] [devisee] named in the said Will which disposes of [the whole] [substantially the whole] known estate. [£.............. of the total value of the known estate of £.............. is disposed of by the said Will].

The precise capacity in which the grant is applied for must be set out clearing off not only the executors (see para 8 above), but all those with a prior entitlement to the grant pursuant to Rule 20 (see 8.2). The relationship to the deceased need only be given where it is necessary to establish title or for identification. Where there is more than one person entitled and only one of them applies, the words 'one of the persons entitled' should be added.

11.   I will (a) collect, get in and administer according to law the real and personal estate of the said deceased (b) when required to do so by the Court, exhibit in the Court a full inventory of the said estate and render an account thereof to the Court; and (c) when required to do so by the High Court, deliver up to that Court the grant of letters of administration (with Will annexed).

12.   That to the best of my knowledge, information and belief the gross value of the estate passing under the grant [amounts to] [does not exceed] £ .... and the net value [amounts to] [does not exceed] £ .... [and that this is not a case in which an Inland Revenue Account is required to be delivered].

See note to Form A1.1, para 10, page 342.

Sworn etc.

Note: It is a matter for the discretion of the District Judge or Registrar to allow application in this form depending on the value of the estate disposed of as a proportion of the total. See Rule 20(c)(ii).

A1.13 Oath for administrator (with will annexed): personal representative of residuary legatee and devisee

IN THE HIGH COURT OF JUSTICE
FAMILY DIVISION
[Principal] [...................................... District Probate] Registry
In the Estate of .... deceased

1. I, ...

See note to Form A1.9, para 1, page 355.

2. of ....

See note to Form A1.1, para 2, page 340.

3. make oath and say:
    That I believe the paper writing now produced to and marked by me to be the true and original last Will and Testament

See notes to Form A1.1, para 3, page 340.

4. of ....

See notes to Form A1.1, para 4, page 341.

5. deceased, who was born on the .... day of .... 19.. and died on the .... day of .... 20.. aged .... domiciled in ....

See notes to Form A1.1, para 5, page 341.

6. That no minority or life interest arises in the estate.

See notes to Form A1.9, para 6, page 355.

7. That to the best of my knowledge, information and belief there was no land vested in the deceased immediately before his death which was settled previously to his death (and not by his Will) and which remained settled land notwithstanding his death.

See note to Form A1.1, para 6, page 341.

8. [That the said deceased did not in his Will name any executor.] *or*
    [That .... *(name of executor)* the sole executor named in the said Will survived the said deceased but has since died without having proved the said Will.] *or*

[That .... *(name of executor)* one of the executors named in the said Will died during the lifetime of the deceased and .... *(name of executor)* the other executor named in the said Will has renounced probate thereof.] *or*

[That .... *(name of executor)* [the sole] [the surviving] executor named in the said Will has renounced probate thereof.] *or*

[That the attempted appointment of an executor in the said Will is void for uncertainty.]

Insert whichever of the above examples is appropriate. This is not a complete list of the ways in which executors may be cleared off. Whatever the manner of clearing, it must be set out.

9.   [That .... [the executor(s) and] *(delete if not also executor(s))* the residuary legatee(s) and devisee(s) named in the said Will predeceased the deceased.

10.   I am [the executor of the Will of ....] [the administrator of the estate of ....], the residuary legatee(s) and devisee(s), [probate of his Will] [letters of administration of his estate] having been granted to me out of the .... Registry on the .... day of .... 20.....

11.   I will (a) collect, get in and administer according to law the real and personal estate of the said deceased; (b) when required to do so by the Court, exhibit in the Court a full inventory of the said estate and render an account thereof to the Court; and (c) when required to do so by the High Court, deliver up to that Court the grant of letters of administration (with Will annexed).

12.   That to the best of my knowledge, information and belief the gross value of the estate passing under the grant [amounts to] [does not exceed] £ .... and the net value [amounts to] [does not exceed] £ .... [and that this is not a case in which an Inland Revenue Account is required to be delivered].

See note to Form A1.1, para 10, page 342.

Sworn etc.

A1.14 Oath for administrator(s) (with will annexed): for use and benefit of executor/residuary legatee mentally incapable of managing his affairs

IN THE HIGH COURT OF JUSTICE
FAMILY DIVISION
[Principal] [... District Probate] Registry
In the Estate of .... deceased

1.   I/We ....

Full and correct names of each of the applicants.

2.   of ....

Full, permanent, postal address of each applicant and his name and description.

3.   make oath and say:

4.   That ....

Full and correct name of the deceased.

of ....

Full, permanent, postal address including postcode.

5.   who was born on the .... day of .... 19 .. and died on the .... day of .... 20 .. aged .... domiciled in England and Wales.

See note to Form A1.1, para 5, page 341.

6.   I/We believe the paper writing now produced to and marked by me/us to contain the true and original last will and testament of the deceased.

See note to Form A1.1, para 3, page 340.

7.   and thereof appointed .... *(name of executor)* to be his sole executor and *(if it be the case)* residuary legatee and devisee; *or* and thereof appointed .... *(name(s) of executor(s))* who died in the lifetime of the deceased *or* who has/have renounced probate *(or whatever the manner is to clear the executor(s))* leaving *(name of residuary beneficiary)* the residuary legatee and devisee who is now by reason of mental incapacity incapable of managing his affairs.

8.

  (i)   By order dated the .... day of .... 20 ..... of the Court of Protection I/we was/were authorised to apply for letters of administration (with will annexed) [either alone or with a co-administrator] for the use and benefit of .... *(name of executor or residuary beneficiary, as the case may be)*. *or*

  (ii) That I/we am/are the lawful attorney(s) of the said .... *(name of executor or residuary legatee, as the case may be)*, acting under an Enduring Power of Attorney which has been registered with the Court of Protection.

  (iii) By order of Mr [District Judge] *or* [Registrar] .... dated the .... day of .... 20..... made under and by virtue of Rule 35(4) of the Non-Contentious Probate Rules 1987, I/we was/were appointed to apply for letters of administration (with will annexed) limited as hereinafter described *(see para 12)*.

9. A/No minority and a/no life interest arises in the estate *(or as the case may be)*.

See note to Form A1.9, para 6, page 355.

10. To the best of my/our knowledge, information and belief there was no land vested in the deceased immediately before the death of the deceased which was settled previously to his death (and not by his will) and which remained settled land notwithstanding his death.

[11. That by a nomination dated the .... day of .... 20 ..... I *(name of first applicant)* nominated the said .... *(name of second applicant)* to be my co-administrator.]

Delete this paragraph if there is no co-administrator.

12. I/we will (a) collect, get in and administer according to law the real and personal estate of the said deceased for the use and benefit of the said .... and [during his incapacity] [until further representation be granted] *(or whatever limitation was imposed by the order)*; (b) when required to do so by the Court, exhibit in the Court a full inventory of the said estate and render an account thereof to the Court; and (c) when required to do so by the High Court, deliver up to that Court the grant of letters of administration (with will annexed).

13. That to the best of my/our knowledge, information and belief the gross value of the estate passing under the grant [amounts to] [does not exceed] £ ...... and the net value [amounts to] [does not exceed] £ ...... [and that this is not a case in which an Inland Revenue Account is required to be delivered].

See note to Form A1.1, para 10, page 342.

Sworn etc.

A1.15 Oath for administrator (with will annexed): legatee, devisee or creditor

IN THE HIGH COURT OF JUSTICE
FAMILY DIVISION
[Principal] [.. District Probate] Registry
In the Estate of .... deceased

1. I, ...

Appendix 1: Forms – Oaths

See note to Form A1.9, para 1, page 355.

2.   of ....

See note to Form A1.1, para 2, page 340.

3.   make oath and say:
     That I believe the paper writing now produced to and marked by me
     to be the true and original last Will and Testament

See notes to Form A1.1, para 3, page 340.

4.   of ....

See notes to Form A1.1, para 4, page 341.

5.   deceased, who was born on the .... day of .... 19.. and died on
     the .... day of .... 20.. aged .... domiciled in ....
     ....

See notes to Form A1.1, para 5, page 341.

6.   That no minority or life interest arises in the estate.

See notes to Form A1.9, para 6, page 355.

7.   That to the best of my knowledge, information and belief there was
     no land vested in the deceased immediately before his death which
     was settled previously to his death (and not by his Will) and which
     remained settled land notwithstanding his death.

See note to Form A1.1, para 6, page 341.

8.   [That the said deceased did not in his Will name any executor.] *or*
     [That .... *(name of executor)* the sole executor named in the
     said Will survived the said deceased but has since died without
     having proved the said Will.] *or*
     [That .... *(name of executor)* one of the executors named in
     the said Will died during the lifetime of the deceased and
     .... *(name of executor)* the other executor named in the said
     Will has renounced probate thereof.] *or*
     [That .... *(name of executor)* [the sole] [the surviving]
     executor named in the said Will has renounced probate thereof.] *or*
     [That the attempted appointment of an executor in the said Will is
     void for uncertainty.]

*Insert whichever of the above examples is appropriate. This is not a
complete list of the ways in which executors may be cleared off. Whatever
the manner of clearing, it must be set out.*

9.   [That .... the residuary legatee(s) and devisee(s) named in
     the said Will [has] [have] renounced letters of administration with
     Will annexed.] *or*

[That .... the residuary legatee(s) and devisee(s) named in the said Will died in the lifetime of the said deceased.]

The manner by which the residuary legatee(s) and devisee(s) has/have been cleared off must be set out in full, for example if one renounces and others died in the lifetime of the deceased then a combination of the above should be inserted. If the gift fails because the residuary beneficiary witnessed the will (s 15 Wills Act 1837), this fact should be recited.

10. That I am a [[legatee] [devisee] named in the said Will] [creditor of the said deceased].

The precise capacity in which the grant is applied for must be set out clearing off not only the executors (see para 8 above), but all those with a prior entitlement to the grant pursuant to Rule 20 (see 8.2). The relationship to the deceased need only be given where it is necessary to establish title or for identification. Where there is more than one person entitled and only one of them applies, the words 'one of the persons entitled' should be added.

11. I will (a) collect, get in and administer according to law the real and personal estate of the said deceased; (b) when required to do so by the Court, exhibit in the Court a full inventory of the said estate and render an account thereof to the Court; and (c) when required to do so by the High Court, deliver up to that Court the grant of letters of administration (with Will annexed).

12. That to the best of my knowledge, information and belief the gross value of the estate passing under the grant [amounts to] [does not exceed] £ .... and the net value [amounts to] [does not exceed] £ .... [and that this is not a case in which an Inland Revenue Account is required to be delivered].

See note to Form A1.1, para 10, page 342.

Sworn etc.

A1.16 Oath for administrator (with will annexed): nominee of residuary legatee and devisee – a non-trust corporation

IN THE HIGH COURT OF JUSTICE
FAMILY DIVISION
[Principal] [....................................... District Probate] Registry
In the Estate of .... deceased

1. I, ...

See note to Form A1.9, para 1, page 355.

2.   of ....

See note to Form A1.1, para 2, page 340.

3.   make oath and say:
   That I believe the paper writing now produced to and marked by me
   to be the true and original last Will and Testament

See notes to Form A1.1, para 3, page 340.

4.   of ....

See notes to Form A1.1, para 4, page 341.

5.   deceased, who was born on the .... day of .... 19.. and died on
   the .... day of .... 20.. aged .... domiciled in ....

See notes to Form A1.1, para 5, page 341.

6.   That no minority or life interest arises in the estate.

See notes to Form A1.9, para 6, page 355.

7.   That to the best of my knowledge, information and belief there was
   no land vested in the deceased immediately before his death which
   was settled previously to his death (and not by his Will) and which
   remained settled land notwithstanding his death.

See note to Form A1.1, para 6, page 341.

8.   [That the said deceased did not in his Will name any executor.] *or*
   [That .... *(name of executor)* the sole executor named in the
   said Will survived the said deceased but has since died without
   having proved the said Will.] *or*
   [That .... *(name of executor)* one of the executors named in
   the said Will died during the lifetime of the deceased and
   .... *(name of executor)* the other executor named in the said
   Will has renounced probate thereof.] *or*
   [That .... *(name of executor)* [the sole] [the surviving]
   executor named in the said Will has renounced probate thereof.] *or*
   [That the attempted appointment of an executor in the said Will is
   void for uncertainty.]

*Insert whichever of the above examples is appropriate. This is not a
complete list of the ways in which executors may be cleared off. Whatever
the manner of clearing, it must be set out.*

9.   That .... the residuary legatee and devisee named in the
   said will is not a trust corporation as defined by Rule 2(1) of the
   Non-Contentious Probate Rules 1987.

10.   By a resolution dated the .... day of .... 20.... [a
   certified copy of which is lodged herewith] I was duly appointed by

the said .... as its nominee for the purpose of applying for letters of administration (with will annexed) to the estate of the said deceased. *(If the resolution is a general authority to apply in estates on behalf of the beneficiary, this should be recited and the paragraph amended accordingly).*

11. I will (a) collect, get in and administer according to law the real and personal estate of the said deceased for the use and benefit of the said .... and until further representation be granted; (b) when required to do so by the Court, exhibit in the Court a full inventory of the said estate and render an account thereof to the Court; and (c) when required to do so by the High Court, deliver up to that Court the grant of letters of administration (with Will annexed).

12. That to the best of my knowledge, information and belief the gross value of the estate passing under the grant [amounts to] [does not exceed] £ .... and the net value [amounts to] [does not exceed] £ .... [and that this is not a case in which an Inland Revenue Account is required to be delivered].

See note to Form A1.1, para 10, page 342.

Sworn etc.

A1.17 Oath for administrator (with will annexed): gift saved by s 33 Wills Act 1837

IN THE HIGH COURT OF JUSTICE
FAMILY DIVISION
[Principal] [....................................... District Probate] Registry
In the Estate of .... deceased

1. I, ...

See note to Form A1.9, para 1, page 355.

2. of ....

See note to Form A1.1, para 2, page 340.

3. make oath and say:
That I believe the paper writing now produced to and marked by me to be the true and original last Will and Testament

See notes to Form A1.1, para 3, page 340.

4. of ....

See notes to Form A1.1, para 4, page 341.

5.   deceased, who was born on the .... day of .... 19.. and died on the .... day of .... 20.. aged .... domiciled in ....

See notes to Form A1.1, para 5, page 341.

6.   That no minority or life interest arises in the estate.

See notes to Form A1.9, para 6, page 355.

7.   That to the best of my knowledge, information and belief there was no land vested in the deceased immediately before his death which was settled previously to his death (and not by his Will) and which remained settled land notwithstanding his death.

See note to Form A1.1, para 6, page 341.

8.   [That the said deceased did not in his Will name any executor.] *or*
[That .... *(name of executor)* the sole executor named in the said Will survived the said deceased but has since died without having proved the said Will.] *or*
[That .... *(name of executor)* one of the executors named in the said Will died during the lifetime of the deceased and .... *(name of executor)* the other executor named in the said Will has renounced probate thereof.] *or*
[That .... *(name of executor)* [the sole] [the surviving] executor named in the said Will has renounced probate thereof.] *or*
[That the attempted appointment of an executor in the said Will is void for uncertainty.]

Insert whichever of the above examples is appropriate. This is not a complete list of the ways in which executors may be cleared off. Whatever the manner of clearing, it must be set out. The residuary legatee and devisee in trust, if any, must also be cleared off.

9.   That *(name of residuary beneficiary)*, the son of the said deceased and the residuary legatee and devisee named in the said Will, predeceased the deceased leaving issue who survived the said deceased.

10.   I am [one of] the issue of the said *(name of son)*, being his daughter and [one of the] person[s] now entitled to share in the residue under the said Will by virtue of section 33 of the Wills Act 1837.

The reference to issue in paragraphs 9 and 10 includes lawful, illegitimate and adopted children.

11.   I will (a) collect, get in and administer according to law the real and personal estate of the said deceased; (b) when required to do so by the Court, exhibit in the Court a full inventory of the said estate and render an account thereof to the Court; and (c) when required to do so by the High Court, deliver up to that Court the grant of letters of administration (with Will annexed).

12. That to the best of my knowledge, information and belief the gross value of the estate passing under the grant [amounts to] [does not exceed] £ .... and the net value [amounts to] [does not exceed] £ .... [and that this is not a case in which an Inland Revenue Account is required to be delivered].

See note to Form A1.1, para 10, page 342.

Sworn etc.

A1.18 Oath for administrator(s) (with will annexed): deceased divorced after date of will

IN THE HIGH COURT OF JUSTICE
FAMILY DIVISION
[Principal] [.. District Probate] Registry
In the Estate of .... deceased

1. I/We, ...

The full and correct names of each of the applicants must be given. Where there is more than one applicant they should be listed in order of the extent of interest, except where they have an equal interest when their names should appear in the same order as in the will. Their order in the oath will be the order in which they appear in the grant.

2. of ....

The full, permanent, postal address of each applicant must be given, followed by their respective occupations or descriptions; see Form A1.1, para 2, page 340.

3. make oath and say:
    That I/we believe the paper writing now produced to and marked by me/us to be the true and original last Will and Testament

See notes to Form A1.1, para 3, page 340.

4. of ....

See notes to Form A1.1, para 4, page 341.

formerly of ....

5. deceased, who was born on the .... day of .... 19 .. and died on the .... day of .... 20 .. aged .... domiciled in ....

See notes to Form A1.1, para 5, page 341.

6. That no minority or life interest arises in the estate.

If such an interest does arise, the word 'no' should be deleted and the word 'a' inserted; the grant must issue to at least two persons or to a trust corporation either with or without an individual person, unless a District Judge or Registrar has directed otherwise. Where it appears from a will that a life interest exists, but at the date of the application that interest has ceased to exist, the word 'now' should be inserted before the word 'arises'. An additional paragraph should be added giving the name of the person who would have had the life interest and stating the date upon which that person died.

7. That on the .... day of .... 20.... the marriage of the said deceased and .... the sole executor and residuary legatee and devisee was dissolved by final decree of the .... court in England and Wales and that pursuant to Section 3 of the Law Reform (Succession) Act 1995 the said Will takes effect as though the appointment of .... *(name of former spouse)* as executor was omitted and the gift to him/her has lapsed.

8. That to the best of my/our knowledge, information and belief there was no land vested in the deceased immediately before his death which was settled previously to his death (and not by his Will) and which remained settled land notwithstanding his death.

See note to Form A1.1, para 6, page 341.

9. I/We am/are the substituted residuary legatee(s) and devisee(s) *or* I/We am/are [the only] [two of the] persons *(or as the case may be)* entitled to [share] the estate now undisposed of by the said Will.

Insert whichever of the above examples is appropriate.

10. [...]

The precise capacity in which the grant is applied for must be set out. The relationship to the deceased need only be given where it is necessary to establish title or for identification.

11. I/We will (a) collect, get in and administer according to law the real and personal estate of the said deceased *(where the grant is to be limited, e.g. 'save and except settled land', the limitation should be inserted)*; (b) when required to do so by the Court, exhibit in the Court a full inventory of the said estate and render an account thereof to the Court; and (c) when required to do so by the High Court, deliver up to that Court the grant of letters of administration (with will annexed).

12. That to the best of my/our knowledge, information and belief the gross value of the estate passing under the grant [amounts to] [does not exceed] £ ...... and the net value [amounts to] [does not exceed]

£ ...... [and that this is not a case in which an Inland Revenue Account is required to be delivered].

See note to Form A1.1, para 10, page 342.

Sworn etc.

A1.19 Oath for administrator: surviving spouse

IN THE HIGH COURT OF JUSTICE
FAMILY DIVISION
[Principal] [....................................... District Probate] Registry
In the Estate of .... deceased

1. I, ...

Full and correct names of applicant.

2. of ....

Full, permanent, postal address of applicant.

3. make oath and say:
    That ....

Full and correct name of the deceased.

    of ....

Full, permanent, postal address including postcode.

4. was born on the .... day of .... 19 .. and died on the .... day of .... 20 .. aged .... domiciled in England and Wales intestate.

See note to Form A1.1, para 5, page 341.

5. That no minority or life interest arises under the intestacy.

6. That there was [no] settled land vested in the deceased immediately before the death of the deceased which remained settled land notwithstanding [his] [her] death.

7. That I am the lawful [widow] [husband] of the deceased and the only person now entitled to [his] [her] estate.

8. I will (a) collect, get in and administer according to law the real and personal estate of the said deceased; (b) when required to do so by the Court, exhibit in the Court a full inventory of the said estate and render an account thereof to the Court; and (c) when required to do so by the High Court, deliver up to that Court the grant of letters of administration.

9. That to the best of my knowledge, information and belief the gross value of the estate passing under the grant [amounts to] [does not exceed] £ .... and the net value [amounts to] [does not exceed] £ .... [and that this is not a case in which an Inland Revenue Account is required to be delivered].

See note to Form A1.1, para 10, page 342.

Sworn etc.

A1.20 Oath for administrator: child or other issue having beneficial interest: spouse survived but since died

IN THE HIGH COURT OF JUSTICE
FAMILY DIVISION
[Principal] [.................................... District Probate] Registry
In the Estate of .... deceased

1. I, ...

Full and correct names of applicant.

2. of ....

Full, permanent, postal address of applicant, and occupation or description.

3. make oath and say:
   That ....

Full and correct name of the deceased.

   of ....

Full, permanent, postal address including postcode.

4. who was born on the .... day of .... 19 .. and who died on the .... day of .... 20 .. aged .... domiciled in England and Wales intestate, leaving [his lawful widow] [her lawful husband] one of the persons entitled to share in the estate who has since died without obtaining letters of administration of [his] [her] estate.

5. That no minority and [now] no life interest arises in the estate.

6. That to the best of my knowledge, information and belief there was no land vested in the said deceased immediately before the death of the deceased and which remained settled land notwithstanding [his] [her] death.

7. I am the grandson of the said deceased and one of the persons beneficially entitled to share the estate, being the son of .... the only daughter of the said deceased who died in the lifetime of the said deceased.

This paragraph should be adapted to fit the particular circumstances of the case.

8. I will (a) collect, get in and administer according to law the real and personal estate of the said deceased; (b) when required to do so by the Court, exhibit in the Court a full inventory of the said estate and render an account thereof to the Court; and (c) when required to do so by the High Court, deliver up to that Court the grant of letters of administration.

9. That to the best of my knowledge, information and belief the gross value of the estate passing under the grant [amounts to] [does not exceed] £ .... and the net value [amounts to] [does not exceed] £ .... [and that this is not a case in which an Inland Revenue Account is required to be delivered].

See note to Form A1.1, para 10, page 342.

Sworn etc.

A1.21 Oath for administrator: spouse entitled to whole estate: survived but since died

IN THE HIGH COURT OF JUSTICE
FAMILY DIVISION
[Principal] [...................................... District Probate] Registry
In the Estate of .... deceased

1. I, ...

Full and correct names of applicant.

2. of ....

Full, permanent, postal address of applicant, and occupation or description.

3. make oath and say:
    That ....

Full and correct name of the deceased.

    of ....

Full, permanent, postal address including postcode.

4. who was born on the .... day of .... 19 .. and who died on the .... day of .... 20 .. aged .... domiciled in England and Wales intestate, leaving [his lawful widow] [her lawful husband] the only person entitled to his/her estate who has since died without obtaining letters of administration of [his] [her] estate.

5. That no minority and no life interest arises in the estate.

6. That to the best of my knowledge, information and belief there was no land vested in the said deceased immediately before the death of the deceased and which remained settled land notwithstanding [his] [her] death.

7. I am the [proposed] [executor] [administrator] of estate of *(surviving spouse)*, [probate of [his] [her] Will] [letters of administration of [his] [her] estate] [having been granted to me out of the .... [Probate] Registry on the .... day of .... 20....] [being applied for contemporaneously with this grant application].

The 'leading grant' giving title to the applicant must issue before the grant to the estate. If such grant has not yet been applied for, both applications may be lodged together; the Registry will ensure that the leading grant issues first.

8. I will (a) collect, get in and administer according to law the real and personal estate of the said deceased; (b) when required to do so by the Court, exhibit in the Court a full inventory of the said estate and render an account thereof to the Court; and (c) when required to do so by the High Court, deliver up to that Court the grant of letters of administration.

9. That to the best of my knowledge, information and belief the gross value of the estate passing under the grant [amounts to] [does not exceed] £ .... and the net value [amounts to] [does not exceed] £ .... [and that this is not a case in which an Inland Revenue Account is required to be delivered].

See note to Form A1.1, para 10, page 342.

Sworn etc.

A1.22 Oath for administrator: surviving child

IN THE HIGH COURT OF JUSTICE
FAMILY DIVISION
[Principal] [....................................... District Probate] Registry
In the Estate of .... deceased

1. I, ...

Full and correct names of applicant.

2.   of ....

Full, permanent, postal address of applicant, and occupation or description.

3.   make oath and say:
     That ....

Full and correct name of the deceased.

     of ....

Full, permanent, postal address including postcode.

4.   who was born on the .... day of .... 19 .. and who
     died on the .... day of .... 20 .. aged .... domi-
     ciled in England and Wales

See note to Form A1.1, para 5, page 341.

     intestate a [widow] [widower].

5.   That no minority or life interest arises under the intestacy.

6.   That to the best of my knowledge, information and belief there was
     no land vested in the said deceased immediately before the death of
     the deceased and which remained settled land notwithstanding [his]
     [her] death.

7.   I am the [son] [daughter] of the said deceased and [one of] the [only]
     person[s] entitled to [share] [his] [her] estate.

8.   I will (a) collect, get in and administer according to law the real and
     personal estate of the said deceased; (b) when required to do so by
     the Court, exhibit in the Court a full inventory of the said estate and
     render an account thereof to the Court; and (c) when required to do
     so by the High Court, deliver up to that Court the grant of letters of
     administration.

9.   That to the best of my knowledge, information and belief the gross
     value of the estate passing under the grant [amounts to] [does not
     exceed] £ .... and the net value [amounts to] [does not exceed] £ ....
     [and that this is not a case in which an Inland Revenue Account is
     required to be delivered].

See note to Form A1.1, para 10, page 342.

Sworn etc.

A1.23 Oath for administrator: adopted child

IN THE HIGH COURT OF JUSTICE
FAMILY DIVISION
[Principal] [... District Probate] Registry
In the Estate of .... deceased

1.   I, ...

Full and correct names of applicant.

2.   of ....

Full, permanent, postal address of applicant, and occupation or description.

3.   make oath and say:
     That ....

Full and correct name of the deceased.

     of ....

Full, permanent, postal address including postcode.

4.   who was born on the .... day of .... 19 .. and who
     died on the .... day of .... 20 .. aged .... domi-
     ciled in England and Wales

See note to Form A1.1, para 5, page 341.

intestate a [widow] [widower].

5.   That no minority or life interest arises under the intestacy.

6.   That to the best of my knowledge, information and belief there was
     no land vested in the said deceased immediately before the death of
     the deceased and which remained settled land notwithstanding [his]
     [her] death.

7.   I am the lawful [son] [daughter] of the said deceased and [one of]
     the [only] person[s] entitled to [share] [his] [her] estate.

8.   Under and pursuant to an adoption order under the authority of the
     Adoption Act [1958] [1976] *or* [the Adoption and Children Act
     2003] made by the .... court on the .... day of .... [19]
     or [20].. I was adopted by the said deceased [and .... *(insert name
     of co-adopter, if any)* which said order is still subsisting.

9.   I will (a) collect, get in and administer according to law the real and
     personal estate of the said deceased; (b) when required to do so by
     the Court, exhibit in the Court a full inventory of the said estate and
     render an account thereof to the Court; and (c) when required to do
     so by the High Court, deliver up to that Court the grant of letters of
     administration.

10. That to the best of my knowledge, information and belief the gross value of the estate passing under the grant [amounts to] [does not exceed] £ .... and the net value [amounts to] [does not exceed] £ .... [and that this is not a case in which an Inland Revenue Account is required to be delivered].

See note to Form A1.1, para 10, page 342.

Sworn etc.

A1.24 Oath for administrators: surviving parents

IN THE HIGH COURT OF JUSTICE
FAMILY DIVISION
[Principal] [...................................... District Probate] Registry
In the Estate of .... deceased

1. We, ...

Full and correct names of each of the applicants.

2. of ....

Full, permanent, postal address of each applicant, and his/her occupation or description.

3. make oath and say:
   That ....

Full and correct name of the deceased.

   of ....

Full, permanent, postal address including postcode.

4. who was born on the .... day of .... 19 .. and who died on the .... day of .... 20 .. aged .... domiciled in England and Wales

See note to Form A1.1, para 5, page 341.

   intestate a [bachelor] [spinster] without issue or any other person entitled in priority to share [his] [her] estate by virtue of any enactment.

If the deceased died a single person (i.e. divorced), insert 'a single man/woman' instead of 'bachelor/spinster' and recite details of the final decree (absolute) and the court which made it and that the deceased did not remarry. See Form A1.33, para 5, page 391.

5.   That no minority or life interest arises under the intestacy.

6.   That to the best of our knowledge, information and belief there was no land vested in the said deceased immediately before the death of the deceased and which remained settled land notwithstanding [his] [her] death.

7.   We are the parents of the said deceased and the only persons entitled to [his] [her] estate.

8.   We will (a) collect, get in and administer according to law the real and personal estate of the said deceased; (b) when required to do so by the Court, exhibit in the Court a full inventory of the said estate and render an account thereof to the Court; and (c) when required to do so by the High Court, deliver up to that Court the grant of letters of administration.

9.   That to the best of our knowledge, information and belief the gross value of the estate passing under the grant [amounts to] [does not exceed] £ .... and the net value [amounts to] [does not exceed] £ .... [and that this is not a case in which an Inland Revenue Account is required to be delivered].

See note to Form A1.1, para 10, page 342.

Sworn etc.

Note: This form may be adapted to the singular where only one parent survives or applies.

A1.25 Oath for administrators: surviving brother and sister

IN THE HIGH COURT OF JUSTICE
FAMILY DIVISION
[Principal] [.. District Probate] Registry
In the Estate of .... deceased

1.   We, ...

Full and correct names of each of the applicants.

2.   of ....

Full, permanent, postal address of each applicant, and his/her occupation or description.

3.   make oath and say:
       That ....

Full and correct name of the deceased.

of ....

Full, permanent, postal address including postcode.

4.   who was born on the .... day of .... 19 .. and who died on the .... day of .... 20 .. aged .... domiciled in England and Wales

See note to Form A1.1, para 5, page 341.

intestate [a widower] [a widow] without issue or parent or any other person entitled to share [his] [her] estate by virtue of any enactment.

5.   That no minority or life interest arises under the intestacy.

6.   That to the best of our knowledge, information and belief there was no land vested in the said deceased immediately before the death of the deceased and which remained settled land notwithstanding [his] [her] death.

7.   We are the brother and sister of the whole blood of the said deceased and [two of] the [only] persons entitled to [share] [his] [her] estate.

8.   We will (a) collect, get in and administer according to law the real and personal estate of the said deceased; (b) when required to do so by the Court, exhibit in the Court a full inventory of the said estate and render an account thereof to the Court; and (c) when required to do so by the High Court, deliver up to that Court the grant of letters of administration.

9.   That to the best of our knowledge, information and belief the gross value of the estate passing under the grant [amounts to] [does not exceed] £ .... and the net value [amounts to] [does not exceed] £ .... [and that this is not a case in which an Inland Revenue Account is required to be delivered].

See note to Form A1.1, para 10, page 342.

Sworn etc.

Note: Where there are no surviving brothers or sisters of the whole blood or their issue, application may be made by a brother/sister of the half blood adapting this form and reciting after 'without issue or parent' 'or brother or sister of the whole blood or their issue' and substituting 'half' for 'whole' in para 7.

A1.26 Oath for administrator: surviving niece

IN THE HIGH COURT OF JUSTICE
FAMILY DIVISION
[Principal] [...................................... District Probate] Registry
In the Estate of .... deceased

1.   I, ...

Full and correct name of applicant.

2.   of ....

Full, permanent, postal address of applicant, and her occupation or description.

3.   make oath and say:
     That ....

Full and correct name of the deceased.

     of ....

Full, permanent, postal address including postcode.

4.   who was born on the .... day of .... 19 .. and who
     died on the .... day of .... 20 .. aged .... domi-
     ciled in England and Wales

See note to Form A1.1, para 5, page 341.

     intestate a spinster without issue or parent or brother or sister of the
     whole blood or any other person entitled to share her estate by virtue
     of any enactment.

5.   That no minority or life interest arises under the intestacy.

6.   That to the best of my knowledge, information and belief there was
     no land vested in the said deceased immediately before the death of
     the deceased and which remained settled land notwithstanding her
     death.

7.   I am the niece of the whole blood of the said deceased and [one of]
     the [only] person[s] entitled to [share] her estate.

8.   I will (a) collect, get in and administer according to law the real and
     personal estate of the said deceased; (b) when required to do so by
     the Court, exhibit in the Court a full inventory of the said estate and
     render an account thereof to the Court; and (c) when required to do
     so by the High Court, deliver up to that Court the grant of letters of
     administration.

9.   That to the best of my knowledge, information and belief the gross
     value of the estate passing under the grant [amounts to] [does not

exceed] £ .... and the net value [amounts to] [does not exceed] £ ....
[and that this is not a case in which an Inland Revenue Account is
required to be delivered].

See note to Form A1.1, para 10, page 342.

Sworn etc.

Note: This form may be adapted for use where the person(s) beneficially
entitled is/are nephew(s) and/or niece(s) of the half blood. See note to
Form A1.25.

A1.27 Oath for administrators: surviving uncles or aunts of the half-blood

IN THE HIGH COURT OF JUSTICE
FAMILY DIVISION
[Principal] [...................................... District Probate] Registry
In the Estate of .... deceased

1. We, ...

Full and correct names of each of the applicants.

2. of ....

*Full, permanent, postal address of each applicant, and his/her occupation
or description.*

3. make oath and say:
   That ....

Full and correct name of the deceased.

   of ....

Full, permanent, postal address including postcode.

4. who was born on the .... day of .... 19 .. and who
   died on the .... day of .... 20 .. aged .... domiciled in England and Wales

See note to Form A1.1, para 5, page 341.

   intestate a bachelor without issue or parent or brother or sister of the
   whole or half blood or their issue or uncle or aunt of the whole blood
   or their issue or any other person entitled in priority by virtue of any
   enactment.

5. That no minority or life interest arises under the intestacy.

6. That to the best of our knowledge, information and belief there was no land vested in the said deceased immediately before the death of the deceased and which remained settled land notwithstanding his death.

7. We are the [uncles] [aunts] [uncle and aunt] of the half blood of the said deceased and [two of] the [only] persons entitled to [share] his estate.

8. We will (a) collect, get in and administer according to law the real and personal estate of the said deceased; (b) when required to do so by the Court, exhibit in the Court a full inventory of the said estate and render an account thereof to the Court; and (c) when required to do so by the High Court, deliver up to that Court the grant of letters of administration.

9. That to the best of our knowledge, information and belief the gross value of the estate passing under the grant [amounts to] [does not exceed] £ .... and the net value [amounts to] [does not exceed] £ .... [and that this is not a case in which an Inland Revenue Account is required to be delivered].

See note to Form A1.1, para 10, page 342.

Sworn etc.

A1.28 Oath for administrator: cousin german

IN THE HIGH COURT OF JUSTICE
FAMILY DIVISION
[Principal] [... District Probate] Registry
In the Estate of .... deceased

1. I, ...

Full and correct name of applicant.

2. of ....

Full, permanent, postal address of applicant, and her occupation or description.

3. make oath and say:
   That ....

Full and correct name of the deceased.

   of ....

Full, permanent, postal address including postcode.

4.   who was born on the .... day of .... 19 .. and who died on the .... day of .... 20 .. aged .... domiciled in England and Wales intestate a bachelor without issue or parent or brother or sister of the whole or half blood or their issue or uncle or aunt of the whole blood or any other person entitled in priority to share his estate by virtue of any enactment.

See note to Form A1.1, para 5, page 341.

5.   That no minority or life interest arises under the intestacy.

6.   That to the best of my knowledge, information and belief there was no land vested in the said deceased immediately before the death of the deceased and which remained settled land notwithstanding his death.

7.   I am a cousin german of the whole blood of the said deceased and [one of] the [only] person[s] entitled to [share] his estate.

8.   I will (a) collect, get in and administer according to law the real and personal estate of the said deceased; (b) when required to do so by the Court, exhibit in the Court a full inventory of the said estate and render an account thereof to the Court; and (c) when required to do so by the High Court, deliver up to that Court the grant of letters of administration.

9.   That to the best of my knowledge, information and belief the gross value of the estate passing under the grant [amounts to] [does not exceed] £ .... and the net value [amounts to] [does not exceed] £ .... [and that this is not a case in which an Inland Revenue Account is required to be delivered].

See note to Form A1.1, para 10, page 342.

Sworn etc.

A1.29 Oath for administrator(s): person(s) entitled on accretion

IN THE HIGH COURT OF JUSTICE
FAMILY DIVISION
[Principal] [..................................... District Probate] Registry
In the Estate of .... deceased

1.   I/We, ...

Full and correct names of each of the applicants.

2.   of ....

Full, permanent, postal address of each applicant, and his/her occupation or description.

3.   make oath and say:
     That ....

Full and correct name of the deceased.

     of ....

Full, permanent, postal address including postcode.

4.   who was born on the .... day of .... 19 .. and who
     died on the .... day of .... 20 .. aged .... domi-
     ciled in England and Wales

See note to Form A1.1, para 5, page 341.

     intestate leaving .... *(name of surviving spouse)* [his]
     [her] lawful [widow] [husband] and the only person now entitled to
     [his] [her] estate who has renounced letters of administration of the
     estate.

5.   No minority or life interest arises under the intestacy.

6.   To the best of my/our knowledge, information and belief there was
     no land vested in the deceased immediately before the death of the
     deceased and which remained settled land notwithstanding his death.

7.   [I am] [We are] the son and daughter *(or as the case may be)* of the
     said deceased and [a] [two of] *(or as the case may be)* the person[s]
     who may have a beneficial interest in [his] [her] estate in the event
     of an accretion thereto.

8.   I/we will (a) collect, get in and administer according to law the real
     and personal estate of the said deceased; (b) when required to do so
     by the Court, exhibit in the Court a full inventory of the said estate
     and render an account thereof to the Court; and (c) when required
     to do so by the High Court, deliver up to that Court the grant of
     letters of administration.

9.   That to the best of my/our knowledge, information and belief the
     gross value of the estate passing under the grant [amounts to] [does
     not exceed] £ ...... and the net value [amounts to] [does not exceed]
     £ ...... [and that this is not a case in which an Inland Revenue
     Account is required to be delivered].

See note to Form A1.1, para 10, page 342.

Sworn etc.

Note: This application may be used only where the net estate does not
exceed the spouse's statutory legacy, currently £125,000.

A1.30 Oath for administrator(s): assignee(s)

IN THE HIGH COURT OF JUSTICE
FAMILY DIVISION
[Principal] [...................................... District Probate] Registry
In the Estate of .... deceased

1. I/We, ...

Full and correct names of each of the applicants.

2. of ....

*Full, permanent, postal address of each applicant, and his/her occupation
or description.*

3. make oath and say:
   That ....

Full and correct name of the deceased.

   of ....

Full, permanent, postal address including postcode.

4. who was born on the .... day of .... 19 .. and who
   died on the .... day of .... 20 .. aged .... domiciled in England and Wales

See note to Form A1.1, para 5, page 341.

   intestate leaving .... *(name of surviving spouse)* [his] [her]
   lawful [widow] [husband] and the only person now entitled to [his]
   [her] estate.

*Where appropriate set out any other status of the deceased and necessary
clearings and title under Rule 22 (see para 9.28), e.g. 'a spinster without
issue leaving .... her lawful mother and only person entitled to
her estate'.*

5. No minority or [now] any life interest arises under the intestacy.

6. To the best of my/our knowledge, information and belief there was
   no land vested in the deceased immediately before the death of the
   deceased and which remained settled land notwithstanding his death.

7. By Deed of Assignment dated the .... day of .... 20......
   the said *(name of person entitled to estate)* has assigned to me/us
   [and to ....] all [his] [her] right and title to and interest in the
   estate of the said deceased.

8. I/we will (a) collect, get in and administer according to law the real
   and personal estate of the said deceased; (b) when required to do so

by the Court, exhibit in the Court a full inventory of the said estate and render an account thereof to the Court; and (c) when required to do so by the High Court, deliver up to that Court the grant of letters of administration.

9. That to the best of my/our knowledge, information and belief the gross value of the estate passing under the grant [amounts to] [does not exceed] £ ...... and the net value [amounts to] [does not exceed] £ ...... [and that this is not a case in which an Inland Revenue Account is required to be delivered].

See note to Form A1.1, para 10, page 342.

Sworn etc.

Note: The deed may be a deed of variation or deed of family arrangement provided it has the same effect, i.e. to pass the entire interest in the estate to another or others.

A1.31 Oath for administrator(s): attorney(s)

IN THE HIGH COURT OF JUSTICE
FAMILY DIVISION
[Principal] [.. District Probate] Registry
In the Estate of .... deceased

1. I/We, ...

Full and correct names of each of the applicants.

2. of ....

Full, permanent, postal address of each applicant, and his/her occupation or description.

3. make oath and say:
    That ....

Full and correct name of the deceased.

    of ....

Full, permanent, postal address including postcode.

4. who was born on the .... day of .... 19 .. and who died on the .... day of .... 20 .. aged .... domiciled in England and Wales

See note to Form A1.1, para 5, page 341.

intestate a widow without issue or parent *(or as the case may be)* and without any other person entitled in priority to share in their estate by virtue of any enactment leaving .... *(name of person entitled)* her sister of the whole blood *(or as the case may be)* [one of] the person[s] entitled to share in her estate.

5. No minority or life interest arises under the intestacy.

See note to Form A1.9, para 6, page 355.

6. To the best of my/our knowledge, information and belief there was no land vested in the deceased immediately before the death of the deceased and which remained settled land notwithstanding his death.

7. I am/we are the lawful attorney(s) of the said .... *(name of person entitled)*.

8. I/we will (a) collect, get in and administer according to law the real and personal estate of the said deceased for the use and benefit of the said .... *(name of person entitled)* limited until further representation be granted; (b) when required to do so by the Court, exhibit in the Court a full inventory of the said estate and render an account thereof to the Court; and (c) when required to do so by the High Court, deliver up to that Court the grant of letters of administration.

9. That to the best of my/our knowledge, information and belief the gross value of the estate passing under the grant [amounts to] [does not exceed] £ ...... and the net value [amounts to] [does not exceed] £ ...... [and that this is not a case in which an Inland Revenue Account is required to be delivered].

See note to Form A1.1, para 10, page 342.

Sworn etc.

A1.32 Oath for administrators: person entitled and attorney of another equally entitled

IN THE HIGH COURT OF JUSTICE
FAMILY DIVISION
[Principal] [.. District Probate] Registry
In the Estate of .... deceased

1. We, ...

Full and correct names of each of the applicants.

2. of ....

Full, permanent, postal address of each applicant, and his/her occupation or description.

3. make oath and say:
    That ....

Full and correct name of the deceased.

       of ....

Full, permanent, postal address including postcode.

4. who was born on the .... day of .... 19 .. and who
    died on the .... day of .... 20 .. aged .... domi-
    ciled in England and Wales

See note to Form A1.1, para 5, page 341.

       intestate a widow leaving .... and .... her son and
    daughter the only persons entitled to share her estate.

5. That no minority or life interest arises under the intestacy.

6. That to the best of our knowledge, information and belief there was
    no land vested in the said deceased immediately before the death of
    the deceased and which remained settled land notwithstanding her
    death.

7. I, the said ...., am the son of the said deceased and I,
    ...., am the lawful attorney of ...., the daughter of
    the deceased.

8. We will (a) collect, get in and administer according to law the real
    and personal estate of the said deceased limited until further repre-
    sentation be granted; (b) when required to do so by the Court,
    exhibit in the Court a full inventory of the said estate and render an
    account thereof to the Court; and (c) when required to do so by the
    High Court, deliver up to that Court the grant of letters of adminis-
    tration.

9. That to the best of our knowledge, information and belief the gross
    value of the estate passing under the grant [amounts to] [does not
    exceed] £ .... and the net value [amounts to] [does not exceed] £ ....
    [and that this is not a case in which an Inland Revenue Account is
    required to be delivered].

See note to Form A1.1, para 10, page 342.

10. I, the deponent *(name of son)*, consent to the grant being limited as
    aforesaid.

Sworn etc.

A1.33 Oath for administrator: deceased divorced person

IN THE HIGH COURT OF JUSTICE
FAMILY DIVISION
[Principal] [.................................... District Probate] Registry
In the Estate of .... deceased

1. I, ...

Full and correct name of applicant.

2. of ....

Full, permanent, postal address of applicant, and his occupation or description.

3. make oath and say:
   That ....

Full and correct name of the deceased.

   of ....

Full, permanent, postal address including postcode.

4. who was born on the .... day of .... 19 .. and who died on the .... day of .... 20 .. aged .... domiciled in England and Wales

See note to Form A1.1, para 5, page 341.

   intestate a single man without issue or parent or any other person entitled in priority to share his estate by virtue of any enactment *(or whatever the situation is)*.

5. That the marriage of the said deceased with .... *(name of former wife)* was dissolved by final decree of the .... *(name of court)* Court in England and Wales dated the .... day of .... 20.. and that the said deceased did not thereafter remarry.

Where the deceased's divorce was effected outside England and Wales, the decree or pronouncement of the foreign court must be recognisable as valid under s 46 Family Law Act 1986. Evidence to establish validity may be required depending on the particular circumstances of the case.

6. That no minority or life interest arises under the intestacy.

7. That to the best of my knowledge, information and belief there was no land vested in the said deceased immediately before the death of the deceased and which remained settled land notwithstanding his death.

8. I am the sister of the whole blood *(or as the case may be)* of the said deceased and [one of] the [only] person[s] entitled to [share] his estate.

9. I will (a) collect, get in and administer according to law the real and personal estate of the said deceased; (b) when required to do so by the Court, exhibit in the Court a full inventory of the said estate and render an account thereof to the Court; and (c) when required to do so by the High Court, deliver up to that Court the grant of letters of administration.

10. That to the best of my knowledge, information and belief the gross value of the estate passing under the grant [amounts to] [does not exceed] £ .... and the net value [amounts to] [does not exceed] £ .... [and that this is not a case in which an Inland Revenue Account is required to be delivered].

See note to Form A1.1, para 10, page 342.

Sworn etc.

A1.34 Oath for administrator: creditor

IN THE HIGH COURT OF JUSTICE
FAMILY DIVISION
[Principal] [.. District Probate] Registry
In the Estate of .... deceased

1. I, ...

Full and correct name of applicant.

2. of ....

Full, permanent, postal address of applicant, and his occupation or description.

3. make oath and say:
    That ....

Full and correct name of the deceased.

    of ....

Full, permanent, postal address including postcode.

4. who was born on the .... day of .... 19 .. and who died on the .... day of .... 20 .. aged .... domiciled in England and Wales

See note to Form A1.1, para 5, page 341.

> intestate leaving .... *(name of surviving spouse)* [his] [her] lawful [widow] [husband] and the only person now entitled to [his] [her] estate who has renounced letters of administration of the estate.

Set out here any other status of the deceased and the necessary clearings. Where the deceased died without any known kin, notice must be given to the Treasury Solicitor (BV) before a grant may be taken by a creditor.

5. That no minority or life interest arises under the intestacy.

6. That to the best of my knowledge, information and belief there was no land vested in the said deceased immediately before the death of the deceased and which remained settled land notwithstanding [his] [her] death.

7. I am a creditor of the said deceased.

8. I will (a) collect, get in and administer according to law the real and personal estate of the said deceased; (b) when required to do so by the Court, exhibit in the Court a full inventory of the said estate and render an account thereof to the Court; and (c) when required to do so by the High Court, deliver up to that Court the grant of letters of administration.

9. That to the best of my knowledge, information and belief the gross value of the estate passing under the grant [amounts to] [does not exceed] £ .... and the net value [amounts to] [does not exceed] £ .... [and that this is not a case in which an Inland Revenue Account is required to be delivered].

See note to Form A1.1, para 10, page 342.

Sworn etc.

A1.35 Oath for administrator: commorientes: by personal representative of person deemed to have survived

IN THE HIGH COURT OF JUSTICE
FAMILY DIVISION
[Principal] [..................................... District Probate] Registry
In the Estate of .... deceased

1. I, ...

Full and correct name of applicant.

2. of ....

Appendix 1: Forms – Oaths

Full, permanent, postal address of applicant, and his occupation or description.

3. make oath and say:
   That ....

Full and correct name of the deceased.

   of ....

Full, permanent, postal address including postcode.

4. who was born on the .... day of .... 19 .. and who died on the .... day of .... 20 .. aged .... domiciled in England and Wales

See note to Form A1.1, para 5, page 341.

   intestate *(set out here the deceased's status, for example bachelor without issue or parent).*

5. All possible enquiries as to survivorship have been made but it appears that the said *(name of deceased)* and *(name of other person dying with the deceased)* [his lawful brother of the whole blood] *(or as the case may be)* died in circumstances rendering it uncertain which of them survived the other.

The evidence of the deaths must be submitted to the District Judge/Registrar previously for him to be satisfied that the circumstances of survivorship are uncertain or whether further evidence is required.

6. The said *(name of person deemed to have survived)* being the younger is by virtue of Section 184 of the Law of Property Act 1925 deemed to have survived the said deceased and was the only person entitled to his estate.

7. That no minority or life interest arises under the intestacy.

8. That to the best of my knowledge, information and belief there was no land vested in the deceased immediately before the death of the deceased and which remained settled land notwithstanding his death.

9. [I am the daughter of *(name of person deemed to have survived)* and [one of] the [only] person[s] entitled to [share] his estate] applications for letters of administration being made contemporaneously with this application *or* [I am the [executor] of the estate of *(name of person deemed to have survived)*, [probate] having been granted to me out of the *(name of Registry)* on the .... day of .... 20..] *(or as the case may be).*

10. I will (a) collect, get in and administer according to law the real and personal estate of the said deceased; (b) when required to do so by the Court, exhibit in the Court a full inventory of the said estate and render an account thereof to the Court; and (c) when required to do

so by the High Court, deliver up to that Court the grant of letters of administration.

11. That to the best of my knowledge, information and belief the gross value of the estate passing under the grant [amounts to] [does not exceed] £ .... and the net value [amounts to] [does not exceed] £ .... [and that this is not a case in which an Inland Revenue Account is required to be delivered].

See note to Form A1.1, para 10, page 342.

Sworn etc.

Note: As to commoriens spouses, see now s 1 Law Reform (Succession) Act 1995 which amended s 46 Administration of Estates Act 1925 to provide that no beneficial interest is acquired unless the surviving spouse survived the other by 28 days.

A1.36 Oath for administrators for use and benefit of mentally incapable person

IN THE HIGH COURT OF JUSTICE
FAMILY DIVISION
[Principal] [...................................... District Probate] Registry
In the Estate of .... deceased

1. I/We, ...

Full and correct names of each of the applicants.

2. of ....

Full, permanent, postal address of each applicant, and his/her occupation or description.

3. make oath and say:
   That ....

Full and correct name of the deceased.

   of ....

Full, permanent, postal address including postcode.

4. who was born on the .... day of .... 19 .. and who died on the .... day of .... 20 .. aged .... domiciled in England and Wales

See note to Form A1.1, para 5, page 341.

intestate a widow without issue or parent or brother or sister of the whole blood or any other person entitled in priority to share in the estate by virtue of any enactment *(or whatever the status of the deceased was at the date of death)* leaving .... *(name of incapable person)* her niece of the whole blood who is now by reason of mental incapacity incapable of administering her affairs.

5.

[(a) That by order of the Court of Protection dated the .... day of .... 20... I the deponent *(name of first deponent)* was authorised to apply *(either alone or with another person)* for letters of administration for the use and benefit of *(name of incapable person)* and during her incapacity].

or

[(b) That no one has been authorised by the Court of Protection to apply for letters of administration. I/We am/are the lawful attorney(s) of the said *(name of incapable person)* acting under an Enduring Power of Attorney which was registered in the Court of Protection on the .... day of .... 20....].

or

[(c) That *(name of attorney)* the lawful attorney of *(name of incapable person)* acting under a Registered Enduring Power of Attorney has renounced all his right and title to letters of administration (with will annexed) and I am the residuary legatee and devisee named in the said will].

[*and, if appropriate*, By nomination dated the .... day of .... 20..... I, the deponent, *(name of second deponent)* was nominated by *(name of first deponent)* to be his co-administrator.]

[6. That no one has been authorised by the Court of Protection to apply for letters of administration for the use and benefit of .... *(name of incapable person)* and there is no one acting under a registered enduring power of attorney.]

[7. By order dated the .... day of .... 20 ..... made by District [Judge] [Probate Registrar] .... of this Division it was ordered under and pursuant to Rule 35(4) of the Non-Contentious Probate Rules 1987 that letters of administration be granted to me/us for the use and benefit of the said .... *(name of incapable person)* and until further representation be granted.]

8. No minority or life interest arises in the estate *(or as the case may be)*.

9. To the best of my/our knowledge, information and belief there was no land vested in the deceased immediately before the death of the deceased and which remained settled land notwithstanding his death.

10. I/We will (a) collect, get in and administer according to law the real

and personal estate of the said deceased limited [during his incapacity] *or* [until further representation be granted] *(delete as appropriate)*; (b) when required to do so by the Court, exhibit in the Court a full inventory of the said estate and render an account thereof to the Court; and (c) when required to do so by the High Court, deliver up to that Court the grant of letters of administration.

11.   That to the best of my/our knowledge, information and belief the gross value of the estate passing under the grant [amounts to] [does not exceed] £ ...... and the net value [amounts to] [does not exceed] £ ...... [and that this is not a case in which an Inland Revenue Account is required to be delivered].

See note to Form A1.1, para 10, page 342.

Sworn etc.

Note: Complete or delete whichever of paras 5(a), (b) or (c), 6 or 7 is appropriate or inappropriate to the case.

A1.37 Oath for administrators as person having or deemed to have parental responsibility for, or guardian or deemed to be guardian of, (a) minor(s) and nominee

IN THE HIGH COURT OF JUSTICE
FAMILY DIVISION
[Principal] [.. District Probate] Registry
In the Estate of .... deceased

We, ... *(full name of person with parental responsibility/ guardian)*

of .... *(full address of person with parental responsibility/ guardian)*

and .... *(full name of nominee)*

of .... *(full address of nominee)*

respectively make oath and say as follows:

1.   That .... *(full name of deceased)*
     of ....
     (full address of deceased including postcode) deceased, who was born on the .... day of .... 19 .. and died on the .... day of .... 20 .. aged .... domiciled in England and Wales intestate a single [man] [woman] *(or as the case may be)* leaving .... *(insert names of surviving children of*

the deceased) [his] [her] lawful *(the word 'lawful' need only be included where the deceased died before 4 April 1988)* [son[s]] [daughter[s]] and the only person[s] entitled to [his] [her] estate who [is] [are] now [a] minor[s] of the age[s] of .... [and .... respectively].

2. That the marriage of the said deceased with .... *(name of surviving parent)* [formerly .... *(former name if now known by a different name)*] was dissolved by final decree of the .... *(insert name of court)* Court dated the .... day of .... 20 .. and the said deceased did not remarry. *(Delete if deceased not married to surviving parent.)*

3. That the said .... *(name of person with parental responsibility/guardian)* is the *(here set out the relationship to the minor(s) and title under Rule 32(1), e.g. the parent of the minor with parental responsibility pursuant to s 2(1) or (2) of the Children Act 1989)* of the said minor[s] and that there is no other person with parental responsibility/appointed guardian of the said minor[s].

4. That the said .... *(name of person with parental responsibility/guardian)* has nominated by a nomination dated the .... day of .... 20 .. the said .... *(name of nominee)* to be [his] [her] co-administrator, he/she being a fit and proper person to act in that capacity.

5. That a minority [and a] [but no] life interest arises under the intestacy.

6. That there was no land vested in the said deceased which was settled previously to [his] [her] death and which remained settled land notwithstanding [his] [her] death.

7. That we will (a) collect, get in and administer according to law the real and personal estate of the said deceased for the use and benefit of the said minor[s] until [he] [she] [one of them] shall attain the age of eighteen years; (b) when required to do so by the Court, exhibit in the Court a full inventory of the said estate and when required to do so render an account thereof to the Court; and (c) when required to do so by the High Court, deliver up to that Court the grant of letters of administration.

8. That to the best of our knowledge, information and belief the gross value of the estate passing under the grant [amounts to] [does not exceed] £ ...... and the net value [amounts to] [does not exceed] £ ...... [and that this is not a case in which an Inland Revenue Account is required to be delivered].

See note to Form A1.1, para 10, page 342.

Sworn etc.

A1.38 Oath for administrators appointed to take letters of administration for minor(s)

IN THE HIGH COURT OF JUSTICE
FAMILY DIVISION
[Principal] [...................................... District Probate] Registry
In the Estate of .... deceased

We, ...

and ....

of ....

and of ....

(full name(s) and address(es) of the appointed guardians)

respectively make oath and say as follows:

1. That .... *(full name of deceased)*
    of .... *(full address of deceased)* deceased, who was born on the .... day of .... 19 .. and died on the .... day of .... 20 ..
    aged ....

(see note to Form A1.1, para 5, page 341)

> domiciled in England and Wales intestate a [widow] [widower] leaving .... *(insert full names of surviving minor child(ren))* [his] [her] child[ren] and the only persons now entitled to [share in] [his] [her] estate who [is] [are] [a] minor[s] of the age[s] of .... [and .... respectively].

2. That there is no person or body with or deemed to have parental responsibility or guardian appointed or deemed to be appointed guardian of the said minor[s] *(delete the foregoing words in this paragraph if there is a person or local authority with parental responsibility who has been passed over by the order referred to below)* and that we [are the .... *(state relationship (if any) of the applicant(s) to the minor(s))* of the said minor[s] and] have been appointed by order of Mr [District Judge] [Registrar] .... dated the .... day of .... 20 .. for the purpose of taking letters of administration of the estate of the said deceased for [his] [her] [their] use and benefit until [he] [she] [one of them] shall attain the age of eighteen years.

3. That a minority [and a] [but no] life interest arises under the intestacy.

4. That there was no land vested in the said deceased which was settled previously to [his] [her] death and which remained settled land notwithstanding [his] [her] death.

5.   That we will (a) collect, get in and administer according to law the real and personal estate of the said deceased for the use and benefit of the said minor[s] until [he] [she] [one of them] shall attain the age of eighteen years; (b) when required to do so by the Court, exhibit in the Court a full inventory of the said estate and render an account thereof to the Court; and (c) when required to do so by the High Court, deliver up to that Court the grant of letters of administration.

6.   That to the best of our knowledge, information and belief the gross value of the estate passing under the grant [amounts to] [does not exceed] £ ...... and the net value [amounts to] [does not exceed] £ ...... [and that this is not a case in which an Inland Revenue Account is required to be delivered].

See note to Form A1.1, para 10, page 342.

Sworn etc.

A1.39 Oath for administrator(s) pursuant to order under s 116 Supreme Court Act 1981

IN THE HIGH COURT OF JUSTICE
FAMILY DIVISION
[Principal] [.. District Probate] Registry
In the Estate of .... deceased

1.   I/We, ...

Full and correct name(s) of applicant(s) for the grant.

2.   of ....

Full, permanent, postal address of the [first] applicant

      [and .... of ....]

Full, permanent, postal address of the [second] applicant (if any)
[respectively] make oath and say as follows:

3.   That ....

Full and correct name of the deceased.

      of ....

Full, permanent, postal address including postcode.

[formerly of ....]
deceased, who was born on the .... day of .... 19 .. and
who died on the .... day of .... 20 .. aged .... *(See*

note to Form A1.1, para 5, page 341) domiciled in England and Wales [intestate].

(Delete the word 'intestate' where the deceased left a valid will.)

[4.   That no minority or life interest arises under the intestacy.]

See note to Form A1.9, para 6, page 355.

5.   That to the best of my/our knowledge, information and belief there was no land vested in the deceased which was settled previously to his death (and not by his will, *if appropriate*) and which remained settled land notwithstanding his death.

6.   That on the .... day of .... 20 .. it was ordered by Mr [District Judge] [Registrar] .... that letters of administration of the estate of the deceased be granted to me /us under and by virtue of Section 116 of the Supreme Court Act 1981.

Insert any limitation imposed by the District Judge's or Registrar's order.

[7.   That the paper writing now produced to and marked by me/us contains the true and original last will and testament of the said deceased] *(Delete if intestate)*

8.   That I/we will (a) collect, get in and administer according to law the real and personal estate of the said deceased limited as aforesaid *(if appropriate)*; (b) when required to do so by the Court, exhibit in the Court a full inventory of the said estate and render an account thereof to the Court; and (c) when required to do so by the High Court, deliver up to that Court the grant of letters of administration.

9.   That to the best of my/our knowledge, information and belief the gross value of the estate passing under the grant [amounts to] [does not exceed] £ ...... and the net value [amounts to] [does not exceed] £ ...... [and that this is not a case in which an Inland Revenue Account is required to be delivered].

See note to Form A1.1, para 10, page 342.

Sworn etc.

A1.40 Oath for administrator(s) *ad colligenda bona*

IN THE HIGH COURT OF JUSTICE
FAMILY DIVISION
[Principal] [....................................... District Probate] Registry
In the Estate of .... deceased

1.   I/We, ...

Full and correct name(s) of applicant(s).

2.   of ....

Full, permanent, postal address of the first applicant

   [and .... of ....]

Full, permanent, postal address of the second applicant (if any)
[respectively] make oath and say as follows:

3.   That ....

Full and correct name of the deceased.

   of ....

Full, permanent, postal address including postcode.

[formerly of ....]
deceased, who was born on the .... day of .... 19 .. and
who died on the .... day of .... 20 .. aged .... *(See
note to Form A1.1, para 5, page 341)* domiciled in England and Wales
(or as the case may be).

4.   That [no] [a] life interest or [but no] [a] minority interest arises in
   the estate.

*This statement is required as the grant is always of administration;
whether the deceased died testate or intestate need not be included.*

5.   That   by   order   of   Mr   [District   Judge]   [Registrar]
   .... dated the .... day of .... 20 .. it
   was ordered that letters of administration of the estate of the said
   deceased be granted to [me] [us] limited to

*(state the limitation imposed by the District Judge's or Registrar's order
and see para 6 below or add, as hereinafter stated).*

6.   That I/we will (a) collect, get in and administer according to law the
   real and personal estate of the said deceased limited to collecting,
   getting in and receiving the estate and doing such acts as may be
   necessary for the preservation of the same and until further representation be granted but no further or otherwise *(this is the normal
   limitation imposed, but where the District Judge's or Registrar's
   order provides for a more specific limitation the wording of the order
   should be followed)*; (b) when required to do so by the Court, exhibit
   in the Court a full inventory of the said estate and render an account
   thereof to the Court; and (c) when required to do so by the High
   Court, deliver up to that Court the grant of letters of administration.

7.   That to the best of my/our knowledge, information and belief the
   gross value of the estate passing under the grant [amounts to] [does

not exceed] £ ...... and the net value [amounts to] [does not exceed]
£ ...... [and that this is not a case in which an Inland Revenue
Account is required to be delivered].

See note to Form A1.1, para 10, page 342.

Sworn etc.

A1.41 Oath for grant of administration *de bonis non*: deceased testate or intestate

IN THE HIGH COURT OF JUSTICE
FAMILY DIVISION
[Principal] [.. District Probate] Registry
In the Estate of .... deceased

1.   I/We, ...

*The full and correct names of each of the applicants must be given (see
notes to Form A1.1, para 1, page 340).*

2.   of ....

*The full, permanent, postal address and occupation or description of each
of the applicants must be given (see notes to Form A1.1, para 2, page
340).*
make oath and say:

3.   That .... *(insert full name of the deceased and any
      aliases or former names)* of ....
      .... *(full postal address of the deceased
      including postcode)* deceased, who was born on the .... day
      of .... 19 ... and died on the .... day of ....
      20 ... aged ....

(See notes to Form A1.1, para 5, page 341)

      domiciled in [England and Wales *or as the case may be*] having
      made and duly executed his last Will and Testament [and .....
      codicil[s]].

*Where the deceased died intestate, the words from 'having' to 'Testament'
should be excluded and the word 'intestate' substituted.*

4.   [Wherein he did not name any executor.] *or*
      [Wherein he named .... *(insert name of execu-
      tor)* the sole executor who died on the .... day of ....
      20 ..] *or*
      [That on the .... day of .... 20 .., letters of adminis-

tration (with will annexed) of the estate of the said deceased were granted out of the [Principal] [.. District Probate] Registry to .... *(insert name of grantee)* the residuary legatee and devisee in trust *(or as the case may be)* named therein and that the said .... *(insert name of grantee)* died on the .... day of .... 20 .. leaving part of the estate of the deceased unadministered.]

Full details of the previous grant, the grantee(s) and his/their title must be given, together with the reason (e.g. death as in this example, or incapacity) why the original grant can no longer be used to continue the administration of the estate.

All persons with a prior right to that of the grantee, or any other person entitled in priority to share in the estate by virtue of any enactment, must be cleared off and the manner in which they have been cleared off must be stated; e.g. that the deceased died a widow without issue or was a bachelor without issue or parents.

Where application is made to the Principal Registry, or to a Registry other than the one from which the original grant issued, the original grant, or an office copy thereof, should be lodged with this oath. Where the original grant was a grant of probate, explanation must be given in the oath of why the executor of the last surviving proving executor cannot act (e.g. that the last surviving proving executor died intestate) to break any chain of representation.

5. That no minority or life interest arises in the estate.

See note to Form A1.9, para 6, page 355.

6. That to the best of my/our knowledge, information and belief there was no land vested in the said deceased immediately before his death which was settled previously to his death (and not by his Will *(delete on intestacy)*) and which remained settled land notwithstanding his death.

See notes to Form A1.1, para 6, page 341.

7. *(Where the deceased died testate)* That I/we believe the paper writing now produced to and marked by me/us to be [the true and original last Will and Testament] [an office copy of the last Will and Testament] of the said deceased.

8. That I am/we are the [residuary legatee[s]] [residuary devisee[s]] *(or as the case may be)* named in the said will.

The title of the applicant to the grant and, where necessary, any other clearings off of persons with prior entitlements to the grant not included in paragraph 4 above must be set out.

9. That I/we will (a) collect, get in and administer according to law the real and personal unadministered estate of the said deceased; (b) when required to do so by the Court, exhibit in the Court a full inventory of the said estate left unadministered and render an account thereof to the Court; and (c) when required to do so by the High Court, deliver up to that Court the grant of letters of administration.

See note to Form A1.1, para 9, page 342.

10. That to the best of my/our knowledge, information and belief the gross value of the unadministered estate passing under the grant [amounts to] [does not exceed] £ ......

An Inland Revenue Account (Form A5C) is required to be delivered to the Registry (not IR Capital Taxes) in all applications for second or subsequent grants unless the criteria to constitute the case an 'excepted estate' were met on the first application. Where the case is an excepted estate the value the unadministered estate does not exceed (usually the gross value appearing in the original grant) should be inserted; see note to Form A1.3, para 10, page 346.

Sworn etc.

A1.42 Oath for *cessate* grant of administration: deceased testate or intestate

IN THE HIGH COURT OF JUSTICE
FAMILY DIVISION
[Principal] [.. District Probate] Registry
In the Estate of .... deceased

1. I, ... of ....

Full name and address of the applicant (see notes to Form A1.1, para 1, page 340).

2. make oath and say:
    That .... of ....
    formerly of ....

Full name and address of deceased; see notes to Form A1.1, para 4, page 341.

3. deceased, who was born on the .... day of .... 19 .. and died on the .... day of .... 20 .., having made and duly executed his last Will and Testament [and codicil[s]].

Where the deceased died intestate omit the words from 'having' to 'Testament' and insert the word 'intestate'.

4.   [Wherein he did not name any executor.] *or*
[Wherein he named .... *(full name of executor)*
the sole executor [who predeceased the said deceased] [who survived
the deceased but died without proving the said Will] [who has
renounced probate of the said Will].]

5.   and wherein he named me ...., [the lawful
widow, the residuary legatee and devisee, *or as the case may be.*]

*The relationship of the applicant to the deceased and the capacity in which
the grant is applied for must be given, clearing off all persons with a prior
right.*

6.   That on the .... day of .... 20 .. letters of administration (with will annexed) *(or as the case may be)* of the estate
of the said deceased were granted out of the [Principal] [District
Probate] Registry to .... *(insert name of
previous grantee and relationship to applicant)* for my use and
benefit until [I should regain my mental capacity, *or as the case
may be*].

*Where the grant was originally obtained for the use and benefit of a minor
the words 'attain the age of eighteen years' should be substituted for the
words 'regain my mental capacity'. Where the grant was taken by the
attorney of the person entitled and the attorney dies, the oath should recite
this fact and that the new applicant is the (or one of the) person(s) entitled.*

7.   [That I have now regained my mental capacity] *or* [On the ....
day of .... 20 .. I attained the age of eighteen years] by
reason of which the said grant has ceased and expired.

8.   That no minority or life interest now arises in the estate of the said
deceased.

*Omit the word 'now' if there was no life or minority interest in the estate
passing under the previous grant.*

9.   That to the best of my knowledge, information and belief there was
no land vested in the said deceased immediately before his death
which was settled previously to his death (and not by his Will) and
which remained settled land notwithstanding his death.

Omit the words 'and not by his Will' where the deceased died intestate.

10. *(Where the deceased died testate)* That I believe the paper writing
now produced to and marked by me to be [the true and original last
Will and Testament] [an office copy of the last Will and Testament]
of the said deceased.

11. That I am [the lawful widow], the residuary legatee and devisee, *or
as the case may be; see para 5 above* [named in the said Will].

12. That I will (a) collect, get in and administer according to law the real and personal estate of the said deceased; (b) when required to do so by the Court, exhibit in the Court a full inventory of the said estate; and (c) when required to do so by the High Court, deliver up to that Court the grant of letters of administration (with Will annexed) *(or as the case may be)*.

13. That to the best of my knowledge, information and belief the gross value of the estate now unadministered passing under the grant [amounts to] [does not exceed] £ ...... [and that this is not a case in which an Inland Revenue Account is required to be delivered].

See note to Form A1.3, para 10, page 346.

Sworn etc.

A1.43 Oath for grant of administration to a trust corporation (with or without will annexed)

IN THE HIGH COURT OF JUSTICE
FAMILY DIVISION
[Principal] [..................................... District Probate] Registry
In the Estate of .... deceased

1. I/We, ... of ....

Full name(s) and address(es), which may be the business address(es) of the trust corporation's nominee(s), and their occupation(s) or description(s).

2. in the employ of ....
   (full title of trust corporation) whose registered office is situate at
   .... *(full address of registered office)*

3. make oath and say:
   That .... of . ...
   (full name and address of deceased including postcode), formerly of
   ...., deceased, who was born on the ....
   day of .... 19 .. and died on the .... day of
   .... 20 .. aged .... *(see note to Form A1.1, para 5, page 341)* domiciled in England and Wales having made and duly executed his last Will and Testament [and codicil[s]]

Where the deceased died intestate omit the words from 'having' to 'Testament' and insert 'intestate'.

4. [wherein he did not name any executor, *or as the case may be*]

Omit this paragraph if the deceased died intestate.

5. leaving .... *(full name)* [his lawful widow the only person now entitled to his estate] [a widower without issue or parent or any other person entitled to share in his estate by virtue of any enactment, *or as the case may be.*]

6. *After setting out the clearances the names and capacities of entitlement (e.g. residuary legatees and devisees) should be set out* .... who have consented to a grant of letters of administration [(with will annexed) *(Delete if deceased died intestate)*] to .... *(insert name of trust corporation).*

7. That the said .... *(name of trust corporation)* is a Trust Corporation as defined by Rule 2(1) of the Non-Contentious Probate Rules 1987 and has power to accept the grant now applied for and that the said .... *(name of trust corporation)* by a resolution dated the .... day of .... 20 .. (a certified copy of which is annexed hereto) *or* (which has been lodged with the Senior District Judge of the Family Division in which [I am] *or* [we are] identified by the position(s) I/we hold and which resolution is still in force) appointed me/us for the purpose of applying for letters of administration [(with will annexed) *(delete if deceased died intestate)*] of the said deceased's estate

(see also note to Form A1.4, para 7, page 348).

8. That no minority or life interest arises in the estate of the said deceased.

See note to Form A1.9, para 6, page 355.

9. That to the best of my/our knowledge, information and belief there was no land vested in the deceased immediately before his death which was settled previously to his death (and not by the Will [and codicil[s]] of the deceased) and which remained settled land notwithstanding such death.

See note to Form A1.1, para 6, page 341.

10. *(Where the deceased died testate)* That I/we believe the paper writing now produced to and marked by me/us to contain the true and original last Will and Testament [and ...... codicil[s]] *(see note to Form A1.1, para 3, page 340)* of the said deceased.

11. That the said *(name of trust corporation)* will (a) collect, get in and administer according to law the real and personal estate of the said deceased; (b) when required to do so by the Court, exhibit in the Court a full inventory of the said estate and render an account thereof to the Court; and (c) when required to do so by the High

Court, deliver up to that Court the grant of letters of administration [(with will annexed)] *(Delete if deceased died intestate)*

See note to Form A1.1, para 9, page 342.

12. That to the best of my/our knowledge, information and belief the gross value of the estate passing under the grant [amounts to] [does not exceed] £ ...... and the net value [amounts to] [does not exceed] £ ...... [and that this is not a case in which an Inland Revenue Account is required to be delivered].

See note to Form A1.1, para 10, page 342.

Sworn etc.

A1.44 Oath for administrators limited to settled land

IN THE HIGH COURT OF JUSTICE
FAMILY DIVISION
[Principal] [.. District Probate] Registry
In the Estate of .... deceased

1. We, ... of ....

Full names, addresses and occupations or descriptions of the applicants (the special executors in regard to settled land or the trustees of the settlement at the time of this application or the personal representatives of the deceased).

See notes to Form A1.1, para 1, page 340 (see also 10.22 et seq).

2. make oath and say:
   That...................... of ....

(full name and address including postcode of the deceased; see note to Form A1.1, para 4, page 341)

deceased, who was born on the .... day of .... 19 .. and died on the .... day of .... 20 .. domiciled in .... aged ....

(see note to Form A1.1, para 5, page 341).

3. That on the .... day of .... 20 .. [probate] [letters of administration] (save and except settled land) [was] [were] granted at the [Principal] [.............. District Probate] Registry to .... *(insert name(s) of grantee(s) and their relationship, if any, to the deceased, e.g. 'the lawful widow and the son')* and the [only] person[s] entitled to the estate of the deceased.

Delete para 3 where no previous grant has issued.

4. That there was land vested in the said deceased which was settled previously to his death and which remained settled land notwithstanding his death [under the Will of .... deceased which was proved in the [Principal] [.............. District Probate] Registry on the .... day of .... 20 ..] *or* [under a deed of settlement dated the .... day of .... 20 ..].

5. That we are the [special executors in regard to the said settled land] *or* [the trustees of the settlement] *or* [the personal representatives of the said deceased] *(the order of entitlement is prescribed by Rule 29 in force with effect from 14 October 1991).*

6. That we will (a) collect, get in and administer according to law the estate of the said deceased limited to the said settled land; (b) when required to do so by the Court, exhibit in the Court a full inventory of the said estate (limited as aforesaid) and when required to do so render an account thereof to the Court; and (c) when required to do so by the High Court, deliver up to that Court the grant of letters of administration.

7. That to the best of our knowledge, information and belief the gross value of the estate, limited to the said settled land, passing under the grant amounts to £ ...... and the net value amounts to £ .... *As the settled land does not pass under the deceased's will or intestacy the excepted estate provisions do not apply: an Account must be delivered.*

See note to Form A1.1, para 10, page 342.

Sworn etc.

A1.45 Oath for administrator after order: content or tenor of will unknown

IN THE HIGH COURT OF JUSTICE
FAMILY DIVISION
[Principal] [.. District Probate] Registry
In the Estate of .... deceased

1. I, ...

Full and correct names of applicant.

2. of ....

Full, permanent, postal address of applicant.

3. make oath and say:
    That ....

Full and correct name of the deceased.

of ....

Full, permanent, postal address including postcode.

4.   was born on the .... day of .... 19 .. and died on
     the .... day of .... 20 .. aged .... domiciled in
     England and Wales.

See note to Form A1.1, para 5, page 341.

5.

   (a)   That the said deceased was known to have made a will but
         neither the original nor any copy can be produced nor can the
         content or tenor of the will be substantiated.

   (b)   That by order of Mr [District Judge] [Registrar] .... dated
         the .... day of .... 20 .. it was ordered that letters of
         administration be granted to me limited until the original will
         or an authentic copy be proved.

6.   That no minority or life interest arises in the estate.

7.   That there was [no] settled land vested in the deceased immediately
     before the death of the deceased which remained settled land
     notwithstanding [his] [her] death.

8.   That I am the lawful [widow] [husband] of the deceased and the only
     person now entitled to [his] [her] estate.

9.   I will (a) collect, get in and administer according to law the real and
     personal estate of the said deceased; (b) when required to do so by
     the Court, exhibit in the Court a full inventory of the said estate and
     render an account thereof to the Court; and (c) when required to do
     so by the High Court, deliver up to that Court the grant of letters of
     administration.

10. That to the best of my knowledge, information and belief the gross
     value of the estate passing under the grant [amounts to] [does not
     exceed] £ .... and the net value [amounts to] [does not exceed] £ ....
     [and that this is not a case in which an Inland Revenue Account is
     required to be delivered].

See note to Form A1.1, para 10, page 342.

Sworn etc.

Note: Application for the order is made to a District Judge or Registrar
on affidavit. The oath and the grant will be silent as to the deceased being
testate or intestate because of the uncertainty.

A1.46 Oath for administrator (with or without will annexed) (foreign domicile)

IN THE HIGH COURT OF JUSTICE
FAMILY DIVISION
[Principal] [..................................... District Probate] Registry
In the Estate of .... deceased

1. I .... of ....

(name, address and occupation or description of proposed grantee)

2. make oath and say as follows:
    That .... of ....
    .... *(full name, address
    and postcode)* deceased, who was born on the .... day of
    .... 19 .. and died on the .... day of .... 20 ..
    at .... aged ....

*(see note to Form A1.1, para 5, page 341). Include the date of birth (if
known) or if the death was registered in the United Kingdom.*

domiciled in .... *(insert country, state or province)*
[intestate] [having made and duly executed his last Will and
Testament [and codicil[s]] and that I believe the paper writing now
produced to and marked by me to contain [an official copy] [notar-
ially certified copy] of, *(or as the case may be)* the true and
original last Will and Testament [and codicil[s]] of the said
deceased.]

3. That .... *(name of person entrusted or bene-
    ficially entitled)* is [the person] [one of the persons *(if more than one
    person is entitled to benefit and not all of them are applying)*]
    [entrusted with the administration of the estate of the said deceased
    by the Court having jurisdiction at the place where the deceased died
    domiciled] *or*
    [beneficially entitled to [share] the estate of the deceased by the law
    of the place where the deceased died domiciled] *or*
    [that by order of Mr [District Judge] [Registrar]
    .... dated the .... day of .... 20 .., it
    was ordered that [letters of administration (with will annexed)]
    [letters of administration] of the estate of the said deceased be
    granted to me under and by virtue of Rule 30(1)(a), (b) or (c) *as
    appropriate* of the Non-Contentious Probate Rules 1987.

4. That no life or minority interest arises in the estate.

*Should such an interest arise the grant must be made to at least two
grantees, unless a District Judge or Registrar directs otherwise or the
applicant is a trust corporation.*

5. That there was no land vested in the said deceased which was settled previously to his death [and not by his Will *(delete if intestate)*] and which remained settled land notwithstanding his death.

6. That I will (a) collect, get in and administer according to law the real and personal estate of the said deceased; (b) when required to do so by the Court, exhibit in the Court a full inventory of the said estate and render an account thereof to the Court; and (c) when required to do so by the High Court, deliver up to that Court the grant of letters of administration [(with will annexed)].

7. That to the best of my knowledge, information and belief the gross value of the estate in England and Wales passing under the grant amounts to £ ...... and the net value of the estate amounts to £ ......

Where the deceased died after 6 April 2002, had never been domiciled in the United Kingdom for tax purposes and the gross value of the estate in England and Wales does not exceed £100,000, the excepted estate provisions apply and no Inland Revenue Account need be delivered. The oath must recite these facts. Where the above criteria do not apply, an Account in Form IHT 200 must be controlled before a grant may issue; Form D18, stamped to show the Account has been delivered and any tax due paid, must be lodged with the grant application; the gross and net values must be stated as they appear in the Account.

Sworn etc.

Notes: (1) Where the grant is applied for by the attorney of the person entrusted with administration or entitled to benefit, a statement to this effect should be included in the oath in para 3; para 6(a), after the word 'deceased', should include the words 'for the use and benefit of the said .... and until further representation be granted'.

(2) This precedent assumes, where appropriate, an order under Rule 30(1)(a) or (b) has been made. Where such an order has not been made, it may be requested in this oath by adding in para 3 'that I am [the person entrusted with administration by the court of the place having jurisdiction where the deceased died domiciled] [the person [one of the persons] beneficially entitled to [share in] the estate] as evidenced by the [affidavit] [notarial statement] [certificate of inheritance] *(or as the case may be)* [made] [granted] by .... and I hereby apply for an order under Rule 30(1) [(a)] [(b)]'.

See CHAPTER 14, and in particular paras 14.26–14.28 and 14.41–14.44.

Affidavits

A1.47 Affidavit of [plight and condition of] [alteration to] will

IN THE HIGH COURT OF JUSTICE
FAMILY DIVISION
[Principal] [... District Probate] Registry
In the Estate of .... deceased

I, ... of ....

(full name and address of deponent and his occupation or description)

make oath and say:

1. That I am [the executor] [the surviving executor] [one of the execu-
    tors] *(if the deponent is not an executor, the title under which he
    claims to prove the will should be given)* named in the last Will and
    Testament of .... *(full name
    and address of the deceased)* deceased, the said Will bearing date
    the .... day of .... 20 .., being now produced to me and
    marked ' .... ' and having perused the said Will and in particular
    observed ....

*Set out the alterations, interlineations, erasures or obliterations which are
present in the text; additionally any other aspect of the will's condition,
for example a tear, must be set out. An explanation of the finding of the
will in its present condition together with, where possible, details of its
whereabouts between execution and finding, should also be included.
Where the evidence is of alterations to the will, the affidavit should be
made, if possible, by a witness present at execution. If no witness is available or cannot speak to the alterations, then the deponent may be any
person who can speak to the facts. If the alteration or damage was caused
after the will was found, set out details.*

2. [That the said Will is now, in all respects, in the same condition as
    when found by me as aforesaid] *or* [That the said damage to the Will
    was caused by ....] *or* [That .... amended/altered the Will
    after the testator's death because .... (e.g. the executor did
    not know the will should not be altered but he changed the address
    of the beneficiary ....)].

*If there was any other document attached which was removed by the depo-
nent, the explanation should be set out in 1 above. Should this be the case,
the words 'save and except as set out above' should be added to this paragraph.*

Sworn by the above-named deponent ....

at ....

on the ....

Before me, ...

A Commissioner for Oaths/Solicitor

A1.48 Affidavit of search for will

IN THE HIGH COURT OF JUSTICE
FAMILY DIVISION
[Principal] [...................................... District Probate] Registry
In the Estate of .... deceased

I, ... of ....

(full name and address of deponent and his occupation or description)

make oath and say:

1. That I am [the sole executor] [one of the executors] named in the last Will and Testament of .... *(full name and address)* deceased, the said Will [bearing date the .... day of .... 20 ..] [being undated] [being incompletely dated] *(or as the case may be)* being now produced to me and marked '....'.

2. That I have made all possible searches and enquiries for any other Will including a search of the home of the deceased and of all places where it is likely that he kept his important papers or valuable personal belongings.

3. That I have been unable to discover any testamentary document other than the said Will.

4. That I have made enquiries of *(set out details of persons of whom enquiries have been made, e.g. the deceased's solicitor, bank manager, or close friend or relation with whom a further testamentary document might have been left for safe keeping)* in an effort to trace any other testamentary document without success.

5. That I believe the deceased died without having left any Will or testamentary document other than the said Will referred to above.

Sworn etc.

A1.49 Affidavit of handwriting

IN THE HIGH COURT OF JUSTICE
FAMILY DIVISION
[Principal] [.. District Probate] Registry
In the Estate of .... deceased

I, ... of ....

(full name and address of deponent and his occupation or description)

make oath and say:

1. [I am [the brother, *or as may be, stating the relationship, if any*] of
    .... *(full name and address)*, deceased] *or*
    [I have known the deceased for many years] *or*
    [I have worked with the deceased for many years] *(or as the case may be)*
    and have frequently, during the period I have known him, received correspondence from him and have seen him sign his name to documents so that I am well acquainted with his handwriting and signature.

2. I have examined the paper writing now produced to me and marked
    '......' which purports to contain the last Will and Testament of the said deceased bearing date the .... day of .... 20 .. and being subscribed thus .... *(insert details of the deceased's signature, e.g. J. Doe or John Doe)*

3. That I believe [the whole of the said Will together with] the signature of .... *(name of deceased)* to be in the true and proper handwriting of the deceased.

Sworn etc.

A1.50 Affidavit of due execution

IN THE HIGH COURT OF JUSTICE
FAMILY DIVISION
[Principal] [.. District Probate] Registry
In the Estate of .... deceased

I, ... of ....

(full name and address of deponent and his occupation or description)

make oath and say:

1. That I am one of the subscribing witnesses to the last Will and Testament of .... of ....

Full name and address. Where the address is different from that appearing in the Will, add 'formerly of' and state the previous address. Any variations or differences in the deceased's actual names and the names appearing in the Will must be explained. Where the deponent is not a subscribing witness this paragraph should state 'I was present at the execution of ....' or whatever the situation is enabling the deponent to give evidence as to execution. An explanation of why a subscribing witness is not making the affidavit (e.g. his death) must be included.

2. [The] [A copy of the] said Will being now produced to me and marked ' ......' and bearing date the .... day of .... 20 .., that the said deceased executed the said Will [on the date stated therein] [*(or, if the will was dated in error)* on the .... day of .... 20 ..] by [signing his name] [making his mark] at the foot or end thereof as the same now appears thereon [in the presence of me .... *(if the deponent is a subscribing witness)* and .... *(name of other subscribing witness)* the other subscribing witness thereto] both of us being present at the same time and that we then both attested the said Will in the presence of the said deceased] *or*
    [in the presence of .... *(names of subscribing witnesses)* who are both now dead] *or*
    [in the presence of .... *(names of subscribing witnesses)* whose whereabouts, despite enquiries, cannot be traced.]

3. *(Where appropriate)* That before the execution of the said Will by the deceased the same was read over to him by .... and at the time he seemed perfectly to understand the same and its contents.
    (or, where appropriate) That the said .... *(name of deceased)* died a .... *(insert status, e.g. widower without issue, parent, brother, sister of the whole blood or any other person entitled in priority to share in the estate by virtue of any enactment)* and that I am .... *(insert relationship to deceased)* being one of the persons entitled to the deceased's estate if he had died intestate and that .... *(insert names of other persons entitled to share)* are all *sui juris* and have consented to the admission of the said Will to proof without further proof of execution as appears from the consents now produced to and marked by me ' ...... '.
    (or, where appropriate) That the said deceased executed the said Will on the date stated thereon by signing his name at the foot or end thereof as the same now appears in the presence of me and .... *(insert name(s) of other subscribing witness(es))* both of us being present at the same time and that after the deceased had signed we attested and subscribed the said Will in the presence of the said deceased but that .... *(insert name(s) of other subscribing witness(es))* signed our names above that of the deceased because there was insufficient space for us to sign below the deceased's signature.

(or, where appropriate) That the said deceased executed his last Will on the date stated thereon by acknowledging his signature as the same now appears thereon to be his signature in the presence of me and .... *(insert name(s) of other subscribing witness(es))* both of us being present at the same time by indicating his signature on the said Will and asking us to witness his signature and we then attested and subscribed the said Will in the presence of the said deceased.

Or as the case may be.

Sworn etc.

A1.51 Affidavit as to executor's identity

IN THE HIGH COURT OF JUSTICE
FAMILY DIVISION
[Principal] [... District Probate] Registry
In the Estate of .... deceased

I, ... of ....

(full name, address and occupation or description of the executor)

make oath and say:

1. .... *(full name and address)* deceased, died on the .... day of .... 20 .. , having made and duly executed his last Will and Testament bearing date the .... day of .... 20 .., wherein he appointed .... *(insert name of executor as it appears in the Will)* of .... as [his sole executor] [one of his executors].

2. That I was at the date of the execution of the said Will living at the address .... *(insert address)* [and was the only person of that name living there at that time *(or as the case may be)*].

3. That the deceased told me he had appointed me as his executor and that [the deceased always referred to me as .... *(insert name appearing in the Will)*] or [I am sometimes known as .... *(insert name appearing in the Will)*], *or as the case may be.*

Sworn etc.

A1.52 Affidavit as to alias

IN THE HIGH COURT OF JUSTICE
FAMILY DIVISION
[Principal] [... District Probate] Registry
In the Estate of .... deceased

I, ... of ....

(full name and address of deponent and his occupation or description)

make oath and say:

That .... otherwise ....

of .... *(true name, alias and address of deceased)*

died on the .... day of .... 20 .. [having made and duly executed his last Will and Testament bearing date the .... day of .... 20 .. and thereof appointed me ....
(full name of executor) one of the executors *(or as the case may be)*.

or [That I am the lawful son *(or as the case may be)* of ....
otherwise .... of .... *(true name, alias and address of deceased)* deceased who died on the .... day of .... 20 .. intestate].

That the true name of the deceased was .... *(insert true name of the deceased)*.

or [That the said deceased made and executed his said Will in the name of .... *(alias of deceased)*].

[That the said deceased held *(identify a specific asset held by the deceased in the alias name)* in the name of ....].

In the circumstances it is desired that the grant of [probate of the Will] [letters of administration [(with Will annexed)]] should issue in the name of .... otherwise ....

Sworn etc.

A1.53 Affidavit for leave to swear death

IN THE HIGH COURT OF JUSTICE
FAMILY DIVISION
[Principal] [... District Probate] Registry
In the Estate of .... presumed deceased

I, ... of ....

(full name and address and occupation or description of the person making the application for the grant)

make oath and say:

1. .... of ....

(full name and address, occupation or description, and age or date of birth of the person presumed dead)

2. That .... *(full name of the presumed deceased)* was last seen alive on the .... day of .... 20 ..

Insert details of the circumstances in which the presumed deceased was last seen, i.e. where and by whom and the reason for his being in that place and what his intentions were. Details of inquiries by the police, coastguard or other official body, including advertisements inserted in newspapers, made to find him and the results obtained must be set out and relevant letters, reports and newspapers exhibited. Details of any letters/telephone calls received from the presumed deceased since his disappearance must be given, and any letters exhibited.

3. That the presumed deceased died [testate] [intestate].

Where the presumed deceased died testate his will should be lodged with this affidavit. If the presumed deceased died intestate or the residue of his estate is not fully disposed of by his will the names of persons entitled to share in the estate, or in the undisposed of residue, must be given, together with their relationship to the presumed deceased and whether they are sui juris.

4. That the presumed deceased had ....

Give details of all life assurance policies assuring the presumed deceased against death and whether the assurance companies have accepted the presumed deceased as dead, or the position taken by them as regards this application. All correspondence received from any assurance company should be exhibited.

5. That the presumed deceased had accounts with .... Bank plc and/or .... Building Society and that these accounts have not been used since the disappearance of the presumed deceased.

Details of the value of these accounts must be given, together with details of all assets which comprise the estate.

6. That I believe the presumed deceased is dead. *(Set out any other reason(s) for the deceased being presumed dead).*

7. That the gross value of the estate is £.... and the net value is £.....

Sworn etc.

Notes: (1) Where the death is alleged to have occurred as a result of a ship foundering or an aircraft crashing, details of the presumed deceased's being aboard and the view taken by the ship's or aircraft's insurers should be included; reports of rescue services (if any) may be exhibited. Any supporting evidence by other persons should be put in separate affidavits and lodged with the applicant's affidavit.

(2) It is invariably advisable to submit the evidence to lead the order to the District Judge/Registrar for approval prior to having the affidavit(s) sworn.

(3) Generally see Chapter 5 at 5.2 *et seq.*

A1.54 Affidavit in support of a privileged will

IN THE HIGH COURT OF JUSTICE
FAMILY DIVISION
[Principal] [..................................... District Probate] Registry
In the Estate of .... deceased

I/We am/are .... of ....

(full name(s) and address(es) and occupation(s) or description(s) of executor(s))

make oath and say:

1. That I/we am/are [the sole executor] [two of the executors] [the surviving executor] [residuary beneficiary] named in [a reconstruction of] the last Will and Testament of .... *(full name and address)*, deceased, who died on the .... day of .... 20 .. , the said Will of the deceased bearing date the .... day of .... 20 .. , being now produced to and marked by me/us ' ...... '

2. That the said deceased made the said Will while he was [a soldier on active military service] [a seaman at sea] [an airman in actual military service] and at the date of making the said Will was domiciled in England and Wales.

3. That the said deceased was at the date of making the said Will ....

Set out details of his rank and unit and the military operation in which he was involved when he made his will. Where the deceased was not killed as a result of enemy action but died later, his will may still be allowed as a privilege. All the circumstances should be set out in full. See CHAPTER *2, para 2.49 et seq.*

Sworn etc.

A1.55 Affidavit to lead order under s 116 Supreme Court Act 1981

IN THE HIGH COURT OF JUSTICE
FAMILY DIVISION
[Principal] [.. District Probate] Registry
In the Estate of .... deceased

I, ... of ....

(full name and address of applicant(s) and his/their occupation(s) or description(s))

make oath and say:

1.   .... of .... *(name and last permanent address of deceased)* died on the .... day of .... 20 .. [having made and duly executed his last Will and Testament bearing date the .... day of .... 20 .. and thereof appointed .... *(name of executor)* his sole executor] *or* [intestate] a bachelor without issue or parent leaving .... *(name)* his brother of the whole blood] *(or as appropriate).*

2.   The said *(name of executor or person entitled under intestacy, or as the case may be)* cannot now be traced. Despite intensive enquiries, the results of which are exhibited hereto and marked ' .....' the whereabouts of the said .... cannot be ascertained.

(or insert whatever is the reason requiring the right of the person entitled to the grant to be passed over; see CHAPTER 5, para 5.27 et seq).

3.   I am the *(here set out the relationship to the deceased, if any, and all other facts to assist the court in determining that the applicant is a proper person to whom to grant administration).*

4.   The gross value of the estate amounts to £.......................

5.   No life or minority interest arises in the estate.

6.   Notice of this application has been given to .... *(name(s) of person(s) to be passed over) (Delete this paragraph if no notice has been given).*

7.   That in the circumstances I apply for an order under section 116 of the Supreme Court Act 1981 directing that letters of administration be granted to me.

Sworn etc.

Note: Application may be made by any person to pass over a prior entitlement. It is usually preferable for a draft of the affidavit to be submitted to the court for approval or directions as to further evidence before it is sworn.

A1.56 Affidavit to lead order appointing persons to take administration for the use and benefit of a person mentally incapable of managing his affairs

IN THE HIGH COURT OF JUSTICE
FAMILY DIVISION
[Principal] [... District Probate] Registry
In the Estate of .... deceased

We .... of ....

(full name(s) and address(es) of administrator(s) and their occupation(s) or description(s))

make oath and say:

1.   .... of .... *(name and last permanent address of deceased)* died on the .... day of .... 20 .. domiciled in England and Wales [having made and duly executed her last Will and Testament bearing date the .... day of .... 20 .. and thereof appointed .... *(name of executor)* her sole executor and residuary legatee and devisee] *or* [intestate leaving .... *(name)* her lawful husband, the only person entitled to her estate] who is now by reason of mental incapacity incapable of managing his affairs *(or as the case may be)*.

2.   We exhibit hereto *(here specify the medical evidence to support the claim of mental incapacity)* marked ' .....'.

3.   No one has been authorised by the Court of Protection to apply for letters of administration ([with will]) of the estate of the said deceased and there is no one acting under a registered enduring power of attorney.

4.   We are the *(set out the relationship, if any, to the deceased)*.

5.   We have given notice of the proposed application to the Court of Protection pursuant to Rule 35(5) of the Non-Contentious Probate Rules 1987 [and exhibit hereto its acknowledgement]. *(If the acknowledgement has been received, it may be exhibited. In any event, it must be filed with or before application for the grant)*.

6.   We apply to this Honourable Court for an order directing that letters of administration [(with will annexed)] be granted to us under and pursuant to Rule 35(4) of the Non-Contentious Probate Rules 1987 for the use and benefit of the said .... *(name of incapable person)* and until further representation be granted.

Sworn etc.

Note: See CHAPTER 5, para 5.62 *et seq* for the practice for applying for the order referred to in this affidavit. Application may, since the amendment to Rule 35(4) by the 1998 amending rules, be made by a sole applicant.

A1.57 Affidavit to lead order appointing persons to take administration for the use and benefit of a minor

IN THE HIGH COURT OF JUSTICE
FAMILY DIVISION
[Principal] [.. District Probate] Registry
In the Estate of .... deceased

We .... of ....

(full name(s) and address(es) of applicant(s) and their occupation(s) or description(s))

make oath and say:

1. .... of .... *(name and last permanent address of deceased)* died on the .... day of .... 20 .. domiciled in England and Wales intestate a single [man] [woman] leaving .... *(name)* her son, the only person entitled to her estate who is now a minor aged .... years.

2. The marriage of the said deceased with .... *(name of former spouse)* was dissolved by final decree of the .... court in England and Wales and the said deceased did not thereafter remarry. *If the marriage was dissolved by a decree or order of a court outside England and Wales, the decree or pronouncement of the foreign court must be recognisable as valid under s 46 Family Law Act 1986, and details of evidence to establish validity must be recited.*

3. ...., the former husband of the said deceased and the person with parental responsibility for the said minor has [renounced administration for the use and benefit of the said minor] *or* [refuses or neglects to apply for letters of administration for the use and benefit of the said minor] *or (whatever the reason is for the person with parental responsibility, assuming the parent survives, not applying or for the passing over of his title).*

4. There is no one [other than ....] *(if a parent survives)* having or deemed to have parental responsibility for the said minor under section 2(1), 2(2) or 4 or paragraph 4 or 6 of Schedule 14 to the Children Act 1989 or by virtue of an adoption order made under the Adoption Act 1976 and there is no person appointed or deemed to be appointed guardian of the said minor under section 5 or paragraph 12, 13 or 14 of Schedule 14 to the Children Act 1989.

[There is no one with parental responsibility by virtue of a residence order made under section 8 of the Children Act 1989] *or*
[There has been no care order made under section 31 of the Children Act 1989 committing the said minor to the care of a local authority].

5.   The said minor has not been made a ward of court and there are no proceedings pending to make the said minor a ward of court nor have there been or are there pending any proceedings in any court to which the Children Act 1989 applies. *(If there have been proceedings under the Act, details of these and of any order(s) made must be recited – see para 4 above).*

6.   We are the *(set out the relationship, if any, to the minor child and the deceased).*

7.   The said minor resides at .... *(here set out where the child lives, and for how long, and in whose de facto care he is).*

8.   *(Here set out any other relevant facts in support of the application.)*

9.   The gross value of the estate is £ .... and the net value £ ....

10.   We hereby apply for an order under Rule 32(2) of the Non-Contentious Probate Rules 1987 directing that letters of administration be granted to us for the use and benefit of the said minor and until he shall attain the age of eighteen years.

Sworn etc.

Note: Although Rule 32(2) provides for a District Judge or Registrar to appoint a person to apply for the grant and that person to nominate his co-administrator under paragraph (3) of the Rule, it is the usual practice for the court to appoint two persons to apply to avoid the additional requirement to nominate, there having to be two administrators as there is a minority interest. See CHAPTER 5, paras 5.57–5.61.

A1.58 Affidavit in support of application to prove a copy will or reconstructed will

IN THE HIGH COURT OF JUSTICE
FAMILY DIVISION
[Principal] [...................................... District Probate] Registry
In the Estate of .... deceased

I, ... of ....

(full name and address of person seeking to prove the copy will and his/her occupation or description

make oath and say:

1.   .... of .... *(name and last permanent address of deceased)* died on the .... day of .... 20 .. domiciled in England and Wales having made and duly executed his last will and testament dated the .... day of .... 20 .. [with .... codicil[s] thereto].

2.   Following execution of the will the same was [deposited with ....
      (here set out the place of deposit, e.g. the deceased's bank, his solicitors) or [handed to the deceased].

3.   Following the death of the deceased the original of the said will cannot be found *or* that the said will was in the possession of .... at the date of death but cannot now be found.

4.   *(Set out the circumstances of the case and, where the will was or had been in the deceased's possession, rebutting the presumption that the will was revoked during the deceased's lifetime and any other facts relevant to proof of the copy will.)*

5.   I produce herewith marked '......' a [photocopy] [copy draft] [carbon copy] *(or as the case may be with details of the provenance of the copy)*

[6.   *(Where application is to admit a reconstruction)* Following execution of the said will neither the original nor any copy can be found. The reconstruction exhibited hereto marked '......' contains the content of the original will because .... *(here set out the evidence to support the content of the reconstruction, i.e. that the deceased and his spouse executed 'mirror image' wills at the same time: the reconstruction being made up from that will).*]

7.   I request the Court to make an order under and pursuant to Rule 54 of the Non-Contentious Probate Rules 1987 to admit the said copy will to proof; the grant to be limited until the original will or a more authentic copy be proved.

Sworn etc.

Notes: (1) It is usual for the affidavit to be made by the proposed applicant for the grant but, subject to the court's leave, the affidavit may be made by any other person with knowledge of all the facts.

(2) This affidavit may be adapted for use where an original codicil has been lost.

(3). It is preferable for a draft affidavit to be submitted to the Registry for approval/directions as to further evidence before it is sworn. The court may also require an affidavit of due execution (see Form A1.50, page 416).

A1.59 Affidavit in support of application to rectify will (s 20 Administration of Justice Act 1982)

IN THE HIGH COURT OF JUSTICE
FAMILY DIVISION
[Principal] [...................................... District Probate] Registry
In the Estate of .... deceased

I, ... of ....

(full name and address of deponent and his/her occupation or description

make oath and say that .... of ....

died on the .... day of .... 20 .. having made and
duly executed his last Will and Testament dated the .... day of
.... 20 .. [with a codicil thereto dated the .... day of
.... 20 ..] a copy of which is exhibited hereto marked 'A' [and
therein named me the sole executor] [and that I am one of the partners in
the firm of ...., Solicitors] [which firm drew
up the said Will [and codicil] [and that I am the draftsman of the said Will
[and codicil]] *(or as the case may be)*

That in the said Will [the appointment of executors has been omitted] [the
appointment of executors is defective because .... *(insert
reason why the appointment is defective)*].

[The following clause has been omitted from the said [Will] [codicil]
.........................]

[Clause .... *(identify appropriate clause)* was not intended by the
testator to be revoked by the said codicil.]

[That since the sealing of the grant of probate on the .... day of
.... 20 .. it has been discovered that the original last Will and
Testament of the deceased dated the .... day of .... 20 .. is
defective in that .... *(set out the rectification required; this
paragraph to be completed where rectification sought after the Will has
been proved)*].

That it is clear from the [draft] [Will] [codicil] [exhibited hereto and
marked 'B'] [instructions taken from the said deceased] that the words
.... *(insert required addition or otherwise)* should be [included]
[excluded] [amended so as to read ....] and I hereby
request an order to be made to rectify the said [Will] [codicil] accordingly
pursuant to Section 20 of the Administration of Justice Act 1982.

[That no one is prejudiced by the rectification sought] *or* [That notice of
the application has been given to ...., being the persons
prejudiced by the rectification, [and their responses, *if any*] are exhibited
hereto and marked 'C'].

Sworn etc.

Note: The Family Division's jurisdiction is limited to unopposed applications. See CHAPTER 5, para 5.20.

A1.60 Affidavit to lead interpretation of a will (s 21 Administration of Justice Act 1982)

IN THE HIGH COURT OF JUSTICE
FAMILY DIVISION
[Principal] [...................................... District Probate] Registry
In the Estate of .... deceased

I, ... of ....

(full name and address of deponent and his/her occupation or description

make oath and say that .... of ....

died on the .... day of .... 20.. having made and duly executed his last Will and Testament dated the .... day of .... 20.. [with a codicil thereto dated the .... day of .... 20..] [and therein named me the sole executor] [and that I am one of the partners in the firm of ...., Solicitors] [which firm drew up the said Will [and codicil]] [and that I am the draftsman of the said Will [and codicil]] *(or as the case may be)*.

[That in the said Will the appointment of executors is defective because .... *(insert reason why the appointment is defective)*].

[That the gift of residue *(or as the case may be)* is meaningless or ambiguous because *(here set out the facts)*].

In the circumstances I request the Honourable Court to interpret the Will so as to *(here set out the interpretation requested)* under Section 21 of the Administration of Justice Act 1982.

Sworn etc.

Note: Generally the Probate Registry may only exercise its jurisdiction to interpret a will where the interpretation affects title to the grant. Where there is conflict over the meaning of or effect of a gift, this would be a matter of construction falling within the Chancery Division's jurisdiction.

A1.61 Affidavit of foreign law

IN THE HIGH COURT OF JUSTICE
FAMILY DIVISION
[Principal] [...................................... District Probate] Registry
In the Estate of .... deceased

I, ... [an advocate, *or as the case may be*] of *(full name and address of deponent and his/her occupation or description* make oath and say:

1. I am fully conversant with the laws and constitutions of
   ....
   (insert country, state or province concerned) and [practise] [have practised] as an [advocate] in that [country] [state] [province] for ...... years.

2. I am informed and verily believe that ....
   (full names of deceased) of .... *(full address of deceased)* deceased died on the .... day of ....
   20 .. domiciled in .... *(country, state or province)* [having made his last Will and Testament bearing date the .... day of .... 20 ..] *or* [intestate].

[3. I have referred to the [official] [notarial] copy of the last Will and Testament of the deceased, which is now produced to and marked by me '......' and I say that the said Will was made in conformity with and is valid by the said laws and constitutions.]

Where the provisions of the Wills Act 1963 are relied on, details of the law which validated the will in the place where the deceased died domiciled must be set out.

Omit this paragraph if the deceased died intestate.

[4. In accordance with the said laws and constitutions the original of the said Will is deposited [at] [with] .... and cannot be removed from such custody. The said copy produced to and marked '......' by me is acceptable as evidence of the contents of the original Will in the Courts of .... *(country, state or province).*]

Omit this paragraph if the deceased died intestate.

[5. In the circumstances I say that .... *(full names of proposed administrator(s))* is/are beneficially entitled to [share in] the said estate by the said laws and constitutions of ....
(country, state or province).]

Omit this paragraph if only evidence to validate the will is required.

Sworn etc.

A1.62 Affidavit of facts (where validity of will to be established under the Wills Act 1963)

IN THE HIGH COURT OF JUSTICE
FAMILY DIVISION
[Principal] [.. District Probate] Registry
In the Estate of .... deceased

I, ... of ....

(full name and address of deponent and his/her occupation or description

make oath and say:

1. I am a [Judge] [solicitor] [lawyer practising in .... *(name of country)*] *(or as the case may be)* [and my qualifications for making this affidavit are ....].
    I refer to the [last Will and Testament] [Codicil] bearing date the .... day of .... 20 .. of ....
    of
    .... *(full name and address)* who died on the .... day of .... 20 .. the said [Will] [codicil] being now produced to and marked by me ' ...... '.

2. [That the said [Will] [codicil] was executed at ....
    in .... *(insert country, state or province)*] *or*
    [That at the time of execution of the said [Will] [codicil] the deceased was domiciled in or had his habitual residence in .... *(insert country, state or province)*] *or*
    [That at the date of his death the deceased was domiciled in or had his habitual place of residence in ....
    (insert country, state or province)] *or*
    [That at [the time of execution of the said [Will] [codicil]] [the date of his death] the deceased was a National of .... *(insert country, state or province)*]

3. *(include if necessary)* Of the systems of internal law in force in .... *(insert country, state or province)* relating to the formal validity of Wills at the time of execution of the said [Will] [codicil] or at the date of the deceased's death the said .... *(insert name of deceased)* was most closely connected with the .... internal system of law by reason of his .... *(insert grounds for the connection, e.g. residence, religion, place of birth, ownership of property; where the deceased was a British national, to validate the will in England and Wales it must be shown that he was most closely connected with the system of law in England and Wales – Scotland having its own system of law).*

Sworn etc.

A1.63 Affidavit to lead to issue of a subpoena to bring in a testamentary document

IN THE HIGH COURT OF JUSTICE
FAMILY DIVISION
[Principal] [... District Probate] Registry
In the Estate of .... deceased

I, ... of ....

(full name and address of deponent and his/her occupation or description

make oath and say:

1. .... of ....*(full name and last permanent address of deceased)* died on the .... day of .... 20 .. domiciled in England and Wales having made and duly executed his last will and testament bearing date the .... day of .... 20 .. and therein appointed .... *(name of executor)* his [executor] [executors] and me [one of] the residuary legatees and devisees *(or as the case may be)*.

2. That the said will is now in the possession, custody or power of the said .... *(name of executor)* and .... *(name of other executor, if any)* (or one of them) and that [he] [they] have neglected or declined to prove the said will or renounce probate thereof.

3. I request that the said will should be brought in to the [Principal] [............... District Probate] Registry in order that I may prove the same or otherwise act as I am advised.

4. That the said .... *(name(s) of executor(s))* reside at .... [and at .... respectively].

Sworn etc.

Note: This form, suitably adapted, may be used where persons other than executors are holding the will. For a form of subpoena, see Form A1.73.

A1.64 Affidavit of service of warning

IN THE HIGH COURT OF JUSTICE
FAMILY DIVISION
[Principal] [... District Probate] Registry
In the Estate of .... deceased

I, ... of ....

(full name and address of deponent and his/her occupation or description make oath and say:

1. That on the .... day of .... 20 .. I duly served .... *(full name of caveator or the solicitor acting on his behalf)* with a true copy of the warning now produced to and marked by me ' ...... ' [by delivering to and leaving the same with .... *(name of person served)* [before the hour of 4 in the afternoon] [before the hour of 12 noon on Saturday]] [by sending the same by prepaid [registered] [first class] post to their office at ....].

2. That no summons for directions under Rule 44(6) of the Non-Contentious Probate Rules 1987 has been received by [me] [my firm].

Sworn etc.

A1.65 Affidavit to lead amendment of grant

IN THE HIGH COURT OF JUSTICE
FAMILY DIVISION
[Principal] [....................................... District Probate] Registry
In the Estate of .... deceased

I, ... of ....

(full name and address of deponent and his occupation or description) make oath and say that on the .... day of .... 20 .. *(insert date of grant)* a grant of [probate] [letters of administration [(with will annexed)]] of the estate of .... of .... *(insert full name and address of deceased)* deceased [was] [were] granted at the [Principal] [........................ District Probate] Registry to me this deponent [the sole executor named in the Will of the said deceased] [the residuary legatee and devisee named in the Will of the said deceased] [the lawful widow and relict and the only person entitled to share in the estate of the said deceased] *(or as the case may be)*

That in the said grant of [probate] [letters of administration [(with will annexed)]] .... *(insert error or omission contained in the grant)* whereas .... *(insert correct details which should have appeared in the grant)*.

That the error arose .... *(insert the reason for the error or omission)*

I apply for an order that the said grant of [probate] [letters of administration [(with will annexed)]] be amended by .... *(insert correction required)*

Sworn etc.

Note: This affidavit may be adapted where the deponent is (a member of the firm of) the extracting solicitor. Where the error was occasioned by the solicitor, he is best able to depose to the facts.

A1.66 Affidavit to lead revocation of the grant

IN THE HIGH COURT OF JUSTICE
FAMILY DIVISION
[Principal] [...................................... District Probate] Registry
In the Estate of .... deceased

I, ... of ....

(full name and address of deponent and his occupation or description)
make oath and say that on the .... day of .... 20.. *(insert date of grant)* a grant of [probate] [letters of administration [(with Will annexed)]] of the estate of .... of .... *(insert full name and address of deceased)* deceased [was] [were] granted at the [Principal] [.............. District Probate] Registry to me this deponent [the sole executor named in the Will of the said deceased] [the residuary legatee and devisee named in the Will of the said deceased] [the lawful widow and the only person entitled to share the estate of the said deceased] *(or as the case may be)*.

That the said grant of [probate] [letters of administration] [(with Will annexed)]] issued on the basis *(here set out the basis)* [that the Will dated .... was the last Will of the said deceased] [that the said deceased died intestate a bachelor without issue] *(or as the case may be)* whereas [the said deceased *(here set out the reason why revocation is necessary)* [had in fact made a later Will dated ......] [was married to .... who remained his lawful wife]] [the grantee died before the grant of .... issued] *(or as the case may be)*.

I hereby apply for an order that the said grant issued on the ...... day of .... 20.. be revoked and declared null and void.

Sworn etc.

Note: See Chapter 18, at para 18.9 *et seq.*

Forms

A1.67 Consent to Will being admitted

IN THE HIGH COURT OF JUSTICE
FAMILY DIVISION
[Principal] [... District Probate] Registry
In the Estate of .... deceased

1. Whereas .... of ....
   (full name and address of deceased) deceased, died on the .... day
   of .... 20 .. having made and duly executed his
   last Will and Testament bearing date the .... day of
   .... 20 .. and in the said Will appointed
   .... *(names of executors)* [the sole executor]
   [the executors] [the residuary legatee and devisee *(state capacity,
   e.g. 'in trust')*] thereof.

2. And whereas the following [alterations, *or as the case may be*]
   appear in the said Will, namely: ....

*Set out alterations, or as the case may be, or whatever defect(s) there
is/are in the will of which no satisfactory explanation can be given, which
require(s) the consent of persons who may be prejudiced.*

3. And whereas [........................... and ....
   (insert names of subscribing witnesses to the will) are dead] *or* [the
   whereabouts of .... and
   .... *(insert names of subscribing witnesses to
   the will)* is unknown].

4. And whereas the said deceased died a .... *(insert status
   of deceased at the date of death, e.g. 'a widow', 'a spinster')*
   without issue or parent .... *(insert appropriate clearings)*,
   or any other person entitled in priority to share in her estate by
   virtue of any enactment leaving ....

*Set out the names of all persons, and their respective interests, who would
be prejudiced if the will should be proved in its present form, including
the alterations, or as the case may be.*

5. I, ... *(name of person consenting)* do hereby
   give my consent to [probate of the Will] [letters of administration
   (with Will annexed)] being granted to .... *(name of
   person applying for the grant)* without proof of due execution.

Signed by the said ....
in the presence of ....
of ....
this .... day of .... 20 ..

Appendix 1: Forms – Forms

(The consent should be signed in the presence of a disinterested person who should then sign his own name)

Note: Rule 12(3) provides that a District Judge or Registrar may accept for proof any will (where there is doubt as to due execution) without evidence of execution provided he is satisfied that the distribution of the estate is not affected by allowing the will to proof (i.e. where the person(s) who receive(s) benefit under the will receive(s) the same benefit under an intestacy or an earlier will).

A1.68 Power of attorney to take letters of administration (with or without will annexed)

IN THE HIGH COURT OF JUSTICE
FAMILY DIVISION
[Principal] [..................................... District Probate] Registry
In the Estate of .... deceased

1. Whereas .... of ....
   (full name, address and occupation or description of deceased)
   deceased, died on the .... day of .... 20 .. domiciled in [England and Wales, *or as the case may be*] [having made and duly executed his last Will and Testament bearing date the .... day of .... 20 .. and in the said Will appointed .... *(full name of executor donating his power)* [the sole executor] [one of the executors] [the sole surviving executor] thereof] [residuary legatee and devisee] *or as the case may be, or* [*(in the case of intestacy)* intestate a [widower, bachelor, *or as the case may be*] leaving .... *(name and entitlement of person donating power)*].

2. I, the said .... *(name of person donating power)* presently residing at .... *(address)* do hereby nominate, constitute and appoint .... *(full name, address and occupation or description of attorney)* to be my lawful attorney for the purpose of obtaining [letters of administration (with Will annexed)] [letters of administration] of the estate of the said deceased to be granted to him for my use and benefit until [I shall apply for and obtain [probate of the said Will] [letters of administration (with Will Annexed)] [letters of administration]] *or, as is more common,* [until further representation be granted] and I hereby promise to ratify and confirm whatever my said attorney shall lawfully do or cause to be done in the premises.

In witness whereof I have hereunto set my hand and seal this .... day of .... 20 ..

Signed, sealed and delivered by the said
....
in the presence of ....

435

A1.69 Enduring power of attorney

ENDURING POWER OF ATTORNEY

Part A: About using this form

1. **You may choose one attorney or more than one.** If you choose one attorney then you must delete everything between the square brackets on the first page of the form. If you choose more than one, you must decide whether they are able to act:
   • Jointly (that if, they must all act together and cannot act separately) or
   • Jointly and severally (that is, they can all act together but they can also act separately if they wish).
   On the first page of the form, show what you have decided by crossing out one of the alternatives.

2. **If you give your attorney(s) general power** in relation to all your property and affairs, it means that they will be able to deal with your money or property and may be able to sell your house.

3. **If you don't want your attorney(s) to have such wide powers,** you can include any restrictions you like. For example, you can include a restriction that your attorney(s) must not act on your behalf until they have reason to believe that you are becoming mentally incapable; or a restriction as to what your attorney(s) may do. Any restrictions you choose must be written or typed where indicated on the second page of the form.

4. **If you are a trustee** (and please remember that co-ownership of a home involves trusteeship), you should seek legal advice if you want your attorney(s) to act as a trustee on your behalf.

5. **Unless you put in a restriction preventing it** Your attorney(s) will be able to use any of your money or property to make any provision which you yourself might be expected to make for their own needs or the needs of other people. Your attorney(s) will also be able to use your money to make gifts, but only for reasonable amounts in relation to the value of your money and property.

6. **Your attorney(s) can recover the out-of-pocket expenses** of acting as your attorney(s). If your attorney(s) are professional people, for example solicitors or accountants, they may be able to charge for their professional services as well. You may wish to provide expressly for remuneration of your attorney(s) (although if they are trustees they may not be allowed to accept it).

7. **If your attorney(s) have reason to believe** that you have become or are becoming mentally incapable of managing your affairs, your attorney(s) will have to apply to the Court of Protection for registration of this power.

8. **Before applying to the Court of Protection for registration** of this power, your attorney(s) must give written notice that that is what they are going to do, to you and your nearest relatives as defined in the Enduring Powers of Attorney Act 1985. You or your relatives will be able to object if you or they disagree with registration.

9. **This is a simplified explanation** of what the Enduring Powers of Attorney Act 1985 and the Rules and Regulations say. If you need more guidance, you or your advisers will need to look at the Act itself and the Rules and Regulations. The Rules are the Court of Protection (Enduring Powers of Attorney) Rules 1986 (Statutory Instrument 1986 No. 127). The Regulations are the Enduring Powers of Attorney (Prescribed Form) Regulations 1990 (Statutory Instrument 1990 No. 1376).

10. **Note to Attorney(s)**
    After the power has been registered you should notify the Court of Protection if the donor dies or recovers.

11. **Note to Donor**
    Some of these explanatory notes may not apply to the form you are using if it has already been adapted to suit your particular requirements.

YOU CAN CANCEL THIS POWER AT ANY TIME BEFORE IT HAS TO BE REGISTERED

Part B: To be completed by the 'donor' (the person appointing the attorney(s))

Don't sign this form unless you understand what it means

Please read the notes in the margin which follow and which are part of the form itself.	
Donor's name and address.	I _____
	of _____
Donor's date of birth.	born on _____
	appoint _____
See note 1 on the front of this form. If you are appointing only one attorney you should cross out everything between the square brackets. If appointing more than two attorneys please give the additional name(s) on an attached sheet.	of _____ • [and _____ of _____
Cross out the one which does not apply (see note 1 on the front of this form).	• jointly • jointly and severally] to be my attorney(s) for the purpose of the Enduring Powers of Attorney Act 1985
Cross out the one which does not apply (see note 2 on the front of this form). Add any additional powers.	• with general authority to act on my behalf • with authority to do the following on my behalf:
If you56 don't want the attorney(s) to have general power, you must give details here of what authority you are giving the attorney(s).	
	in relation to
Cross out the one which does not apply.	• all my property and affairs: • the following property and affairs:

Part B: continued

Please read the notes in the margin which follow and which are part of the form itself.
If there are restrictions or conditions, insert them here; if not, cross out these words if you wish (see note 3 on the front of this form).

• subject to the following restrictions and conditions:

If this form is being signed at your direction:-
• the person signing must not be an attorney or any witness (to Parts B or C).
• you must add a statement that this form has been signed at your direction.
• a second witness is necessary (please see below).

I intend that this power shall continue even if I become mentally incapable

I have read or have had read to me the notes in Part A which are part of, and explain, this form.

Your signature (or mark).

Signed by me as deed and delivered _____

Date.
Someone must witness your signature.
Signature of witness.

on _____

in the presence of _____

Your attorney(s) cannot be your witness. It is not advisable for your husband or wife to be your witness.

Full name of witness_____

Address of witness_____

_____

_____

A second witness is only necessary if this form is being signed by you personally but at your direction (for example, if a physical disability prevents you from signing).
Signature of second witness.

in the presence of _____

Full name of witness _____

Address of witness_____

_____

_____

Part C: To be completed by the attorney(s)

Note: 1. This form may be adapted to provide for execution by a corporation

2. If there is more than one attorney additional sheets in the form as shown below must be added to this Part C

Please read the notes in the margin which follow and which are part of the form itself.

Don't sign this form before the donor has signed Part B or if, in your opinion, the donor was already mentally incapable at the time of signing Part B.

I understand that I have a duty to apply to the Court for the registration of this form under the Enduring Powers of Attorney Act 1985 when the donor is becoming or has become mentally incapable.

If this form is being signed at your direction:-

I also understand my limited power to use the donor's property to benefit persons other than the donor.

- the person signing must not be an attorney or any witness (to Parts B or C).

I am not a minor

- you must add a statement that this form, has been signed at your direction.
- a second witness is necessary (please see below).

Signature (or mark) of attorney.

Signed by me as a deed and delivered _____

Date.

on _____

Signature of witness.

in the presence of _____

The attorney must sign the form and his signature must be witnessed. The donor may not be the witness and one attorney may not witness the signature of the other.

Full name of witness _____

Address of witness _____

_____

_____

A second witness is only necessary if this form is not being signed by you personally but at your direction (for example, if a physical disability prevents you from signing). Signature of second witness.

in the presence of _____

Full name of witness _____

Address of witness _____

_____

_____

439

A1.70 Caveat

IN THE HIGH COURT OF JUSTICE
FAMILY DIVISION
[Principal] [.. District Probate] Registry
In the Estate of .... deceased

Let no grant be sealed in the estate of ....
of ....
(full name and address of deceased) deceased, who died on the .... day
of .... 20 .. at ....
without notice to ....

(Name of party entering or on whose behalf the caveat is entered)

Dated this .... day of .... 20 ..

Signed ....
[Solicitor [Probate Practitioner]
for the said ....]
[*Or, if the caveator is
acting in person,* .... in person]
whose address for service is ....

A1.71 Warning to caveator

IN THE HIGH COURT OF JUSTICE
FAMILY DIVISION
LEEDS DISTRICT PROBATE REGISTRY

In the Estate of .... deceased

To .... of .... *(name and address
of caveator)* a party who has entered a caveat in the estate of
.... *(full name of deceased)*, deceased.

You have eight days (starting with the day on which the warning was
served on you):

(i) to enter an appearance either in person or by your solicitor or
probate practitioner at the Leeds District Probate Registry *(the nominated Registry)* setting out what interest you have in the estate of the
above-named .... *(full name and address of the
deceased)* deceased, contrary to that of the party at whose instance
this warning is issued; or

(ii) if you have no contrary interest but wish to show cause against the
sealing of a grant to such party, to issue and serve a summons for
directions by a District Judge of the Principal Registry or a Registrar
of a District Probate Registry.

If you fail to do either of these the court may proceed to issue a grant of probate or administration in the said estate notwithstanding your caveat.

Dated this .... day of .... 20 ..

Issued at the instance of .... *(insert name and interest including the date of the will, if any, under which the interest of the party warning arises, the name of his solicitor or probate practitioner and the address for service. If the party warning is acting in person, this must be stated.)*

A1.72 Appearance to warning

IN THE HIGH COURT OF JUSTICE
FAMILY DIVISION
LEEDS DISTRICT PROBATE REGISTRY
In the Estate of .... deceased
Caveat no .... dated the .... day of .... 20 ..
Full name and address of deceased: ....
....
Full name and address of person warning: ....
....

(Insert the interest in the estate of the person warning)

Full name and address of caveator: ....
....

(Insert the interest in the estate of the caveator and the date of the will, if any, under which the interest arises)

Enter an appearance for the above-named caveator in this matter

Dated this .... day of .... 20 ..

Signed ....
[Solicitor [Probate Practitioner]
for ....] .... in person]
whose address for service is ....
....

A1.73 Subpoena to bring in testamentary document

IN THE HIGH COURT OF JUSTICE
FAMILY DIVISION
[Principal] [.. District Probate] Registry
In the Estate of .... deceased

Elizabeth the Second, by the grace of God, of the United Kingdom of Great Britain and Northern Ireland and of our other realms and territories Queen, Head of the Commonwealth, Defender of the Faith.

To:... of ....

(insert name and address of person being subpoena'd)

It appears by an affidavit of ....
sworn on the .... day of .... 20 .. and filed in the [Principal Registry of the Family Division of our High Court of Justice] [............. District Probate Registry] that a certain document, being or purporting to be testamentary, namely .... *(here describe the document)*, bearing date the .... day of .... 20 .. of .... *(insert name of deceased)* deceased, late of .... who died on the .... day of .... 20 .., is now in your possession, custody or power:

We command you that, within eight days after service hereof on you inclusive the day of such service, you do bring into and leave with the proper officer of the [Principal Registry of the Family Division] [.................. District Probate Registry] aforesaid the said document now in the possession, custody or power of you the said .... Witness, the Right Honourable .... Lord High Chancellor of Great Britain, the .... day of .... 20 ..

(Signed)
[District Judge] [District Probate Registrar]

Subpoena issued by .... of ....

[solicitor] [probate practitioner] for ....

To be endorsed prominently on the front of the copy to be served: You the within-named .... are warned that disobedience to this subpoena by the time therein limited would be a contempt of court punishable by imprisonment.

NB – the Principal Registry of the Family Division of the High Court of Justice is at First Avenue House, 42–49 High Holborn, London WC1 6NP and the proper officer referred to is the Probate Manager *or* [The .... District Probate Registry is at .... and the proper officer referred to is the Probate Manager].

Note: For form of affidavit to lead the issue of the subpoena, see Form A1.63.

A1.74 Citation to accept or refuse grant

IN THE HIGH COURT OF JUSTICE
FAMILY DIVISION
[Principal] [..................... District Probate] Registry In the Estate of
.... deceased

Elizabeth the Second, by the grace of God, of the United Kingdom of
Great Britain and Northern Ireland and of Our other realms and territories, Queen, Head of the Commonwealth, Defender of the Faith,

To .... of ....

(full name(s) and address(es) of each person being cited)

Whereas it appears by the affidavit of .... *(full
names of citor)* sworn on the .... day of
.... 20 .. that ....
of .... *(full name and address of deceased)* died
on the .... day of .... 20 .. having made and duly
executed his last Will and Testament dated the .... day of
.... 20 .. [now remaining in the [Principal Registry
of the Family Division] [................. District Probate Registry]] and
[thereof appointed you the sole executor] [wherein he did not appoint an
executor] [wherein he named you the residuary legatee and devisee] *or as
the case may be or*

[*(if the deceased died intestate)* and that the deceased died intestate a
[widower] [widow] *(insert any further clearings)* or any other person entitled in priority to share in the estate by virtue of any enactment] leaving
.... *(name of citee)* the lawful .... *(relationship of citee to the deceased)* and [one of] *(or as the case may be)* the
person[s] entitled to share in the estate of the said deceased.

Now this is to command you .... *(name of citee)* that
within eight days of service hereof upon you, inclusive of the day of such
service, you do cause an appearance to be entered for you in the Principal
Registry of the Family Division of Our High Court of Justice at First
Avenue House, 42–49 High Holborn, London WC1 6NP *(or, if the citation is issued from a District Probate Registry, the name and address of
that Registry)* and accept or refuse [a grant of probate of the said Will]
[letters of administration (with will annexed)] [letters of administration] of
all the estate which by law devolves to and vests in the personal representative of the said deceased or show cause why a grant should not be
granted to [you] *(name of other person entitled if appropriate)*.

And take notice that in default of your appearing and accepting and extracting [probate of the said Will *(or as the case may be)* as aforesaid our said
Court will proceed to grant [letters of administration (with will annexed)]
[letters of administration] to the said .... *(name of citor or
other person entitled, as appropriate)* notwithstanding your absence.

Dated this .... day of .... 20 ..
Extracted by ....
of ....
Solicitor/Probate Practitioner
Signed ....
District Judge or Registrar

Note: This form, suitably amended, may be used for a citation to propound a testamentary document or citation to take probate against an executor who has intermeddled.

A1.75 Appearance to citation

IN THE HIGH COURT OF JUSTICE
FAMILY DIVISION
[Principal] [... District Probate] Registry
In the Estate of .... deceased
Caveat no .... dated the .... day of .... 20 ..
Citation dated the .... day of .... 20 ..
Full name and address of deceased ....
....
Full name and address of citor ....
....

(insert the interest in the estate of the citor)
Full name and address of person cited ....
....

(insert the interest in the estate of the person cited and the date of the will, if any, under which the interest arises)

Enter an appearance for the above-named person cited in this matter

Signed by the said ....
(name of person appearing)
this .... day of .... 20 ..
[Solicitor/Probate Practitioner for ....]
[.... in person]
whose address for service is ....
....

A1.76 Renunciation (general form)

IN THE HIGH COURT OF JUSTICE
FAMILY DIVISION
[Principal] [...................................... District Probate] Registry
In the Estate of .... deceased
Whereas .... of ....
(full name, address and occupation or description of deceased) deceased,
died on the .... day of .... 20 .. [having made and
duly executed his last Will and Testament bearing date the
.... day of .... 20 ..] *or*

[intestate]

[wherein he appointed .... *(full name of
executor renouncing)* as [sole executor] [and residuary legatee and
devisee] *(if the executor is entitled to apply under a lower entitlement)*]
[one of the executors] [executors] [who [has] [have] since died without
proving the said Will]

[Wherein he did not appoint any executor but named me ....
(full name of person renouncing) [as residuary legatee and devisee *(or as
the case may be)*].]

[Wherein he named me residuary legatee and devisee].

[leaving me .... *(insert name, relationship to the deceased
and capacity in which entitled to the grant)*]

I, the said .... *(full name of person renouncing)* declare that
I have not intermeddled in the said deceased's estate and will not hereinafter intermeddle therein with the intent of defrauding creditors [and do
hereby renounce all my title to probate and execution of the said Will and
to letters of administration (with will annexed)] *or*

[do hereby renounce all my right and title to letters of administration
[(with will annexed)]

of the estate of the said deceased.

Signed by the said ....
(full name of person renouncing)
this .... day of .... 20 ..
in the presence of ....
....
*(name, address and occupation or description of
witness who must be a disinterested party)*.

A1.77 Renunciation of probate by partners in firm on behalf of other partners

IN THE HIGH COURT OF JUSTICE
FAMILY DIVISION
[Principal] [... District Probate] Registry
In the Estate of .... deceased

Whereas .... of ....

(full name, address and occupation or description of deceased) deceased, died on the .... day of .... 20.. having made and duly executed his last Will and Testament bearing date the .... day of .... 20.. wherein he appointed the partners in the firm of .... *(name of firm)* at the date of his death, or the firm which at that date had succeeded to and carried on their practice, to be the executors of his Will.

Now We *(names of renunciants)* being two of the partners in the said firm of .... at the said date of death do hereby on our own behalf and that of all the other partners in the said firm and with their authority renounce all our right and title to probate and execution of the said Will [and to letters of administration with Will annexed as residuary legatees and devisees in trust *(delete if inappropriate)*] and We declare that We and the other partners have not intermeddled in the said deceased's estate and will not hereinafter intermeddle therein with the intent of defrauding creditors.

Signed by the said ....
(names of renunciants)
this .... day of .... 20..
in the presence of ....
(name, address and occupation or description of witness who must be a disinterested party).

A1.78 Retraction of renunciation

IN THE HIGH COURT OF JUSTICE
FAMILY DIVISION
[Principal] [... District Probate] Registry
In the Estate of .... deceased

Whereas .... of ....

(full name, address and occupation or description of deceased) deceased, died on the .... day of .... 20 .. having made and duly executed his last Will and Testament bearing date the .... day of .... 20 .. and therein appointed me .... *(name of executor who has renounced)* [his sole executor, *or as the case may be*] *or*

leaving me .... *(name of executor who has renounced)* [the residuary legatee and devisee in trust, *or as the case may be*] or

[intestate leaving me .... *(name of renunciant, his relationship to the deceased and his capacity in entitlement)*], and whereas I renounced [probate and execution] [letters of administration (with will annexed)] [letters of administration] of the estate of the said deceased and whereas a grant of [probate] [letters of administration (with will annexed)] [letters of administration] was made at the .... Registry to .... *(name of grantee)* and whereas the said .... *(name of grantee)* died on the .... day of .... 20 .. leaving part of the said estate unadministered.

Now I the said .... of ....

(name and address of renunciant) do hereby declare that I retract my said renunciation of [probate] [letters of administration (with will annexed)] [letters of administration] of the estate of the said deceased.

Signed by the said ....
in the presence of ....
(signature of renunciant to be witnessed by a disinterested party)
Dated the .... day of .... 20 ..

Note: A renunciation may only be retracted by leave of the court (see CHAPTER 6).

A1.79 Notice under s 47A Administration of Estates Act 1925 of election to redeem life interest

IN THE HIGH COURT OF JUSTICE
FAMILY DIVISION
[Principal] [.. District Probate] Registry
In the Estate of .... deceased

Whereas .... of ....

(full name, address and occupation or description of deceased) deceased, died on the .... day of .... 20 .. [wholly] [partially] intestate leaving his/her lawful wife/husband and .... *(names of children)* lawful issue of the said deceased. And whereas [probate] [letters of administration] of the estate of the said deceased was/were granted to me .... *(name of surviving spouse)* and to .... *(name of second grantee)* at the .... Probate Registry on the .... day of .... 20 ..

And whereas the said .... *(name of second grantee)* has ceased to be a personal representative because .... *(set out the reason(s))* and I am [now] the sole personal representative.

Now I, the said .... *(name of grantee)* hereby give notice in accordance with Section 47A of the Administration of Estates Act 1925 that I elect to redeem the life interest to which I am entitled in the estate of the late .... *(name of deceased)* by retaining £ ...., its capital value, and £ ...... the costs of the transaction.

Dated the .... day of .... 20 ..
Signed ....
To the Senior District Judge of the Family Division

A1.80 Notice to non-proving executor (Rule 27(1))

IN THE HIGH COURT OF JUSTICE
FAMILY DIVISION
[Principal] [.. District Probate] Registry
In the Estate of .... deceased

Notice is hereby given to you ....
(name of executor having power reserved)

that .... *(name of deceased)* died on the .... day of .... 20 .. having made and executed his last Will and Testament dated .... 20 .. and therein appointed you and .... executors. .... *(name of proving executor)* intends to apply for probate as [one of] [the other] *(or as the case may be)* executor and that power is to be reserved to you to apply for double probate (if you should ever so wish).

Dated the .... day of .... 20 ..
Signed ....
(name of solicitors) solicitors for ....
(name of proving executor)

A1.81 Application for a standing search

IN THE HIGH COURT OF JUSTICE
FAMILY DIVISION
[Principal] [.. District Probate] Registry
In the Estate of .... deceased

I/We apply for the entry of a standing search so that there shall be sent to me/us an office copy of every grant of representation in England and Wales in the estate of:

Full name of deceased: ....

Full address: ....

Alternative or alias name: ....

Exact date of death: ....

which either has issued not more than twelve months before the entry of this application or issues within six months thereafter.

Signed: ....

Name in block letters: ....

Address: ....

....

Reference (if any): ....

Note: An application for a standing search may be lodged at any Registry or sub-Registry (Rule 43).

A1.82 Certificate to be attached to an international will

Certificate

(Convention of 26 October 1973)

1. I, ... of ....

(Full name, address and occupation or description)
a person authorised to act in connection with international Wills

2. Certify that on the .... day of .... 20 .. at

....

(Insert place of execution)

3 ....

(Insert testator's full name, address, date and place of birth)

in my presence and that of the witnesses

4.

    (a) ....

(Insert name, address, date and place of birth of first witness)

    (b) ....

(Insert name, address, date and place of birth of second witness)

    has declared that the attached document is his Will and that he knows the contents thereof.

5.   I furthermore certify that:

(a)   in my presence and that of the witnesses:

(1)   the testator has signed the Will or has acknowledged his signature previously affixed;

*(2)   following a declaration of the testator stating that he was unable to sign his Will for the following reasons

(i) ....

I have mentioned this declaration on the Will

*The signature has been affixed by ....
(name and address)

(b)   the witness and I have signed the Will;

*(c)   each page of the Will has been signed by .... and numbered;

(d)   I have satisfied myself as to the identity of the testator and of the witnesses as designated above;

(e)   the witnesses met the conditions requisite to act as such according to the law under which I am acting;

*(f)   the testator has requested me to include the following statement concerning the safekeeping of his Will: ....

Place

Date

Signature *(and, if necessary)* Seal

* *To be completed if appropriate*

A1.83 Nomination of second administrator: minority interest

IN THE HIGH COURT OF JUSTICE
FAMILY DIVISION
[Principal] [.. District Probate] Registry
In the Estate of .... deceased

Whereas .... of ....

(full name, address and occupation or description of deceased) deceased,
died on the .... day of .... 20 .. domiciled in England
and Wales intestate, a .... *(insert status of deceased, e.g. 'married
man')* leaving .... *(insert name of person first entitled
(applicant) to share in the estate, e.g. his lawful widow)* and
.... *(insert names of other persons entitled to*

share in the estate) [his] [her] .... *(state relationship of these other person(s) to the deceased, e.g. son and daughter)* the only person[s] entitled to [share in] [his] [her] estate.]

And whereas the said .... [is a] [are] minor[s] aged ....[and .... respectively].

And whereas I, the said .... *(name of applicant)* am the .... *(state relationship)* and .... *(state capacity, e.g. parent with parental responsibility) (guardian)* of the said minor[s].

And whereas there is no other person with parental responsibility/guardian of the said minor[s].

Now I, the said .... *(name of applicant)* do hereby nominate and appoint .... *(name of nominee, address and occupation)* to be my co-administrator in the estate of the said intestate, [he] [she] being a fit and proper person to act in that capacity.

Dated this .... day of .... 20 ..

Signed by the said *(name of applicant)*
....
in the presence of ....
(signature (name) and address of disinterested witness).

Appendix 2

Fees payable in probate matters

A2.1   These fees are extracted from the Non-Contentious Probate Fees Order 1999 (as amended) and are accurate at the time of going to press (April 2003).

Nature of Matter	*Fee payable*

1. On an application for a grant (or for resealing a grant) where the assessed value is:

   (a)   not more than £5,000   No fee

   (b)   more than £5,000   £50.00

2. On an application for a grant by a personal applicant (or for resealing such a grant) where the assessed value is:

In addition to fee 1(b) above

not more than £5,000   No fee

more than £5,000   £80.00

Note: 'Assessed value' for the purposes of Fees No 1 and 2 is defined as the value of the net real and personal estate (excluding settled land if any) passing under the grant as shown:

  (i)   Where the death occurred on or before 12 March 1975 in the Inland Revenue Affidavit; or

 (ii)   Where the death occurred on or after 13 March 1975 in the Inland Revenue Account; or

(iii)   In a case in which in accordance with the arrangements made between the President of the Family Division and the Commissioners of Inland Revenue, or Regulations made under s 94(1)(a) of the Finance Act 1980 and from time to time in force, no such affidavit or account is required to be delivered, in the oath which is sworn to lead the grant;

and in the case of an application to reseal a grant under the Colonial Probates Act 1892 means the said value, as so shown, passing under the grant upon its being resealed.

3.	On an application for a duplicate grant or any second or subsequent grant (including one following a revoked grant) in respect of the same deceased person, other than a grant preceded only by a grant limited to settled land, trust property or to a part of the estate	£15.00
4.	For the entry or extension of a caveat	£15.00
5.	On an application for a standing search to be carried out in an estate for a period of six months	£15.00

(This fee is also payable on an application to extend the search for a further six-month period.)

6.	On the deposit of a Will for safe custody in the Principal Registry or a District Probate Registry	£15.00
7.	For the inspection of an original or copy Will or any other document	£15.00
8.	On a request for a copy of any document, whether or not provided as a certified copy:	
	(i) for the first copy	£5.00
	(ii) for every copy of the same document if supplied at the same time	£1.00
	(iii) where copies of any document are made available on a computer disk or in other electronic form, for each copy	£3.00
	(iv) where a search of the index is required, in addition to fees (i), (ii) and (iii) above as appropriate, for each period of 4 years searched after the first 4 years	£3.00

Note: In respect of Fee No 8(i) above, it is the practice in the Probate Registries to charge only £1.00 for the first copy at the time of application for the grant.

9.	(i) For administering an oath, for each deponent to each affidavit	£5.00
	(ii) For marking each exhibit	£2.00

Note: These fees are not payable where a personal application for a grant is made.

10.	(i) On the filing of a request for a detailed assessment where the party filing the request is legally aided and no other party is ordered to pay the costs of the proceedings	£120.00

Appendix 2: Fees payable in probate matters

(ii)	On the filing of a request for a detailed assessment hearing where fee 10(i) does not apply	£250.00
(iii)	On an application for a default costs certificate	£40.00
(iv)	On an appeal against a decision made in detailed assessment proceedings	£100.00
(v)	On applying for the court's approval of a Legal Aid Assessment Certificate	£30.00
(vi)	On a request to set aside a default costs certificate	£60.00

Note: This fee is payable at the time of applying for the court's approval and is recoverable only against the Legal Aid Fund.

11.   For perusing and settling citations, advertisements, oaths, affidavits, or other documents, for each document settled   £10.00

General notes:

(1)   Fees for grants are charged on the *net* estate;

(2)

- Joint property passing by survivorship;
- Nominated property;
- Civil Service gratuities; and
- Assets held outside the United Kingdom, do not attract any fee on application for the grant.

(3)   All cheques for fees should be made payable to Her Majesty's Paymaster General (HMPG). The cheque should be endorsed, on the reverse, with the deceased's name.

Appendix 3

A3.1 District probate registries and sub-registries – contact details

Registries	Sub-registries	Addresses, telephone numbers, fax numbers and document exchange (DX) numbers
Birmingham		The Priory Courts, 33 Bull Street, Birmingham B4 6DU Tel: 0121 681 3400 Fax: 0121 236 2465 DX 701990 Birmingham 7
	Stoke on Trent	Combined Court Centre, Bethesda Street, Hanley, Stoke on Trent ST1 3BP Tel: 01782 854065 Fax: 01782 274916 DX 20736 Hanley
Brighton		William Street, Brighton BN2 2LG Tel: 01273 684071 Fax: 01273 625845 DX 98073 Brighton 3
	Maidstone	The Law Courts, Barker Road, Maidstone ME18 8EW Tel: 01622 202048/7 Fax: 01622 754384 DX 130066 Maidstone 7
Bristol		Ground Floor, The Crescent Centre, Temple Back, Bristol BS1 6EP Tel 1: 0117 927 3915 Tel 2: 0117 926 4619 Fax: 0117 925 3549 DX 94400 Bristol 5
	Bodmin	Market Street, Bodmin, Cornwall PL31 2JW Tel: 01208 72279 Fax: 01208 269004 DX 81858 Bodmin

	Exeter	Finance House, Barnfield Road, Exeter EX1 1QR Tel: 01392 274515 Fax: 01392 493468 DX 8380 Exeter
Cardiff – **Probate Registry of Wales**		PO Box 474, 2 Park Street, Cardiff CF1 1ET Tel: 029 2037 6479 Fax: 029 2037 6466 DX 122782 Cardiff 13
	Bangor	Council Offices, Ffordd Gwynedd, Bangor LL57 1DT Tel: 01248 362410 Fax: 01248 364423 DX 23186 Bangor 2
	Carmarthen	14 King Street, Carmarthen SA31 1BL Tel: 01267 236238 Fax: 01267 229067 DX 51420 Carmarthen
Ipswich		8 Arcade Street, Ipswich IP1 1EJ Tel: 01473 284260 Fax: 01473 231951 DX 3729 Ipswich
	Norwich	Combined Court Building, The Law Courts, Bishopsgate, Norwich NR3 1UR Tel: 01603 728267 Fax: 01603 627469 DX 5202 Norwich
	Peterborough	1st Floor, Crown Buildings, Rivergate, Peterborough PE1 1EJ Tel: 01733 562802 DX 112327 Peterborough 1
Leeds		3rd Floor, Coronet House, Queen Street, Leeds LS1 2BA Tel: 0113 243 1505 Fax: 0113 247 1893 DX 26451 Leeds (Park Square)
	Lincoln	360 High Street, Lincoln LN5 7PS Tel: 01522 523648 Fax: 01522 539903 DX 703233 Lincoln 6

	Sheffield	PO Box 832, The Law Courts, 50 West Bar, Sheffield S3 8YR Tel: 0114 281 2596 Fax: 0114 281 2598 DX 26054 Sheffield 2
	Liverpool	Queen Elizabeth II Law Courts, Derby Square, Liverpool L2 1XA Tel: 0151 236 8264 Fax: 0151 227 4634 DX 14246 Liverpool 1
	Chester	5th Floor, Hamilton House, Hamilton Place, Chester CH1 2DA Tel: 01244 345082 Fax: 01244 346243 DX 22162 Northgate
	Lancaster	Mitre House, Church Street, Lancaster LA1 1HE Tel: 01524 36625 Fax: 01524 35561 DX 63509 Lancaster
Manchester		9th Floor, Astley House, 23 Quay Street, Manchester M3 4AT Tel: 0161 834 4319 Fax: 0161 832 2690 DX 14387 Manchester 1
	Nottingham	Butt Dyke House, Park Row, Nottingham NG1 6GR Tel: 0115 941 4288 Fax: 0115 950 3383 DX 10055 Nottingham
Newcastle upon Tyne		2nd Floor, Plummer House, Croft Street, Newcastle upon Tyne NE1 6NP Tel: 0191 261 8383 Fax: 0191 230 4868 DX 61081 Newcastle upon Tyne 14
	Carlisle	Courts of Justice, Earl Street, Carlisle CA1 1DJ Tel: 01228 521751 DX 63034 Carlisle
	Middlesbrough	Teesside Combined Court Centre, Russell Street, Middlesbrough TS1 2AE Tel: 01642 340001 DX 60536 Middlesbrough

	York	1st Floor, Castle Chambers, Clifford Street, York YO1 9RG Tel: 01904 666777 Fax: 01904 666776 DX 720629 York 21
Oxford		Combined Court Building, St Aldates, Oxford OX1 1LY Tel 1: 01865 793050 Tel 2: 01865 793055 Fax: 01865 793090 DX 96454 Oxford
	Gloucester	2nd Floor, Combined Court Building, Kimbrose Way, Gloucester GL1 2DG Tel: 01452 522585 Fax: 01452 421849 DX 98663 Gloucester
	Leicester	90 Wellington Street, Leicester LE1 6HG Tel: 0116 285 3380 Fax: 0116 285 3382 DX 17403 Leicester 3
Winchester		4th Floor, Cromwell House, Andover Road, Winchester SO23 7EW Tel 1: 01962 853046 Tel 2: 01962 863771 Fax: 01962 840796 DX 96900 Winchester 2

District probate registries and sub-registries are open every weekday, from 9.30 am until 4.00 pm.

The probate department of the Principal Registry of the Family Division is at:

First Avenue House
42–49 High Holborn
London WC1V 6NP
   Tel: 020 7947 7431
   Fax: 020 7947 6946/7454
   DX 941 London/Chancery Lane

The department is open every weekday from 10.00 am until 4.30 pm.

Appendix 4

Checklist of steps before lodging an application for a grant

A4.1   The following 'checks', to be made before lodging the documents to lead the grant, cover the areas where mistakes are commonly found by examiners in Probate Registries; these errors and omissions account for some 30% to 35% of grant applications being 'stopped' and invariably delay the issue of the grant. The requirements for these matters to be observed is provided by statute, rule or practice direction.

A. OATH FORM

A4.2

1. All forms of grant

Extracting solicitors:	Full name, address and postcode, and DX no; reference if required.
Name of deceased:	Insert the deceased's full, true name. Where the deceased was known by another name and such name is required to appear in the grant, confirm the true name and state the reason for the alias, if necessary in a separate paragraph at the end.
Addresses:	Ensure the permanent residential addresses of the deceased (including postcode) and applicant(s) are shown (with no discrepancies between the oath (and will and Form D18)). Business addresses of applicants applying in a professional capacity may be shown where appropriate.
Dates of birth and death:	Check the dates of birth and death are the same as those given in the death certificate. Where the certificate states 'on or about', the oath should specify when the deceased was last seen or known to be alive, and when the body was found.

Survival clause:	Where the appointment of an executor, or the benefit derived (giving title to the applicant to apply), is subject to a survival clause, check that the relevant period has expired.
Age of deceased:	Age of deceased at death to be inserted *especially* in 'excepted estate' cases, i.e. where no Inland Revenue Account is to be delivered.
Domicile:	Ensure domicile inserted: where the domicile is outside England and Wales and where different systems of law operate in different parts of the country ensure that the state, territory or province of domicile is inserted, e.g. in the State of Texas, United States of America; the province of Ontario, Canada.
Settled land:	Ensure the clause relating to settled land has been completed.
Attorney applications:	Ensure the fact that the attorney of the person entitled is recited and that the limitation for the use and benefit of .... and until further representation is granted is included after the words 'I will collect, get in and administer the real and personal estate of the said deceased.' If there is an enduring power of attorney—

(1) where application is made under Rule 31 (see CHAPTER 10) the oath must also state that 'no application has been made to register the power of attorney with the Court of Protection and that the donor is mentally capable of managing his affairs';

(2) where application is made under Rule 35 (see CHAPTER 5) the oath must show that the power has been registered and the donor is incapable.

The original (registered) power of attorney must be lodged with a copy for the Registry. Alternatively a copy of a power of attorney (other than a registered power) may be lodged certified to be a *true and complete* copy.

Estate value:

- Inland Revenue

  Account delivered: Ensure the figures for the estate values appearing in the oath are the same as those appearing in Form D18.

- Excepted estates: Ensure the gross value appropriate to the date of death and net value of the estate are inserted *and* that the clause stating the case is an excepted estate is inserted. The net estate should be the actual value rounded up to the nearest £1,000.

Jurat: Ensure the jurat is completed and dated and has been signed by the deponent(s) *and* the commissioner(s).

2. Testacy

Name(s) of executor(s):   Check the names correspond with those in the will; check signatures to oaths to make sure the deponent's full name is recited, i.e. check for medial initials; if any difference, explain in oath (or by filing separate affidavit of identity) e.g. William Bailey commonly known as and referred to in the will as Bill Bailey.

Clearing executors: Where not all the executors are applying, ensure the oath clears those not proving by reciting their previous death, renunciation, or having power reserved.

Ensure the oath states that, where appropriate, notice has been given to the non-proving executors. If the giving of notice has been dispensed with, this fact must be recited.

Codicil(s):   Ensure that any codicil(s) are referred to, e.g. 'the last will and testament with two codicils'.

3. Intestacy   The oath must establish the applicant's title by 'clearing off' all classes with prior entitlement and state his/her own relationship to the deceased, e.g. the deceased died a widow without issue or parent or brother or sister of the whole or half blood or their issue, grandparent or uncle or aunt of the whole blood or any other person entitled in priority to share the

461

estate by virtue of any enactment ..... I am a cousin german of the whole blood and (one of) the (only) person(s) entitled to the estate. If the deceased was divorced, recite details of the decree absolute, the court which made it and the date, and that the deceased did not remarry.

Life or minority interests: Where application is made for a grant of administration(which includes administration with will) check the clause relating to any life or minority interests has been completed. Generally, two applicants will be required when such interests arise.

B. WILL

A4.3

1. Check the will (and any codicils) are properly signed by the testator and witnesses, dated, and the attestation clause was properly completed. Check the codicils refer to the correct will. If there is a defect or unauthenticated alteration, evidence of due execution on affidavit by a witness will be required unless the provision of Rule 12(3) (see CHAPTER 2 para 2.29) applies.

2. Check the will has been marked by the signature of the deponent(s) and commissioner(s).

3. If a will or codicil is exhibited to an affidavit, a proper exhibit notation (dated and signed by the commissioner) must be endorsed on the will or codicil.

Survival clause in will: Where the will contains a survival clause, e.g. 'I appoint .... provided he survives me by 28 days' ensure the survival period has elapsed before the oath is sworn. If it has not elapsed confirm in covering letter when lodging papers that survival period has now elapsed and applicant still alive.

The clause also applies to residuary beneficiaries applying for letters of administration (with will annexed), where executors do not apply, but there is a survival clause relating to those receiving their beneficial interest, e.g. 'I give the rest and residue of my estate to .... provided he survives me by 28 days.'

C. INLAND REVENUE ACCOUNT

A4.4

1. Check the correct form of Account appropriate to the case has been completed.

2. Check the Account has been signed and dated by the applicants.

3. Check the Account against the oath to ensure that all names and addresses recited are the same.

4. If the estate attracts inheritance tax, the tax has been paid and Form D18 receipted.

5. If the deceased was domiciled abroad, the Account has been controlled by IR Capital Taxes. See also Chapter 12.

6. If the death occurred before 13 March 1975 the Account is sworn.

Index